Travels Into the Inland Parts of Africa

TRAVELS

INTO THE

Inland Parts of *AFRICA:*

CONTAINING A

DESCRIPTION

OF THE

Several Nations for the fpace of Six Hundred Miles up the River GAMBIA , their Trade, Habits, Cuftoms, Language, Manners, Religion and Government, the Power, Difpofition and Characters of fome NEGRO Princes, with a particular Account of JOB BEN SOLOMON, a *Pholey* who was in *England* in the Year 1733, and known by the Name of the *African*

To which is added,

Capt. STIBBS's Voyage up the GAMBIA in the Year 1723, to make Difcoveries;

WITH

An Accurate MAP of that River taken on the Spot: And many other Copper Plates

ALSO

EXTRACTS from the *Nubian*'s Geography, LEO the *African;* and other Authors antient and modern, concerning the NIGER, NILE, or GAMBIA, and Obfervations thereon

By FRANCIS MOORE, *Factor feveral Years to the Royal* African *Company of* England.

LONDON:

Printed by EDWARD CAVE, at *St John's Gate,* for the AUTHOR, and fold by J STAGG, in *Weftminfter Hall;* and at *St John's Gate* aforefa.d   M.DCC,XXXVIII.

TO HIS
GRACE
THE
Duke of *Montagu*, &c.

My LORD,

BENEVOLENCE is the diftinguifhing Character of your GRACE; and your good Nature is not bound up by any narrow Rules : It is not circumfcribed to a Circle of Friends, Relations or Countrymen, but extends to all Human Kind : Nay, your GRACE (like the Good Man in the Scripture) is well known to be always merciful even to Creatures below the Human Species.

In

DEDICATION.

In the Wilds of *Africa* your Humanity is praiſed, and the grateful *Arabs* pray for you in the Deſarts.

IT is this Character of your GRACE that makes me venture to lay this Book at your Feet, hoping that your Goodneſs will extend to me, and receive it with the ſame Condeſcenſion, as the Great *Perſian* KING accepted Water from the Hands of a Peaſant. I am,

My LORD,

With the profoundeſt Reſpect,

Your GRACE's

Moſt Devoted

and moſt Obedient

Humble Servant,

FRA. MOORE.

PREFACE.

T is the Buſineſs of every one, who gives a Book to the Pub-lick, to make it as agreeable as he can to the Reader. For this Purpoſe Invention, Stile, Learn-ing, and the Ornaments of Elo-quence, are employed by thoſe, who are Ma-ſters of them, for ſetting off their Compoſitions. As I cannot pretend to any of thoſe Accom-pliſhments, and can value my ſelf upon no-thing but Truth, and it is not the Man-ner of writing, but the Subject, that is to ſay, the Deſcription of a Country, much talk'd of, and little known, which muſt pleaſe in the fol-lowing Relation, I therefore, beſides my Jour-nal, thought it my Duty to ſpare no Pains in giving the Reader from the beſt Authors a ge-neral Notion of the Countries from the River Gambia, to the more known ones along the Me-terranean Sea.

I kept the Journal when in Gambia, not with any Deſign of printing it, but to improve my ſelf, and keep in my Mind the Things worth Notice. I was then very young, and had nei-ther Time nor Capacity to make thoſe Obſerva-tions which the Learned World might deſire;

but

but what I have set down is true, and is an exact Account of a wild Country. I have not attempted to embellish the Work, since I am persuaded that Readers will make Allowances for the Age of the Journalist, and will rather chuse to read real Facts told in the plainest way, than beautiful Works of Imagination. Since my coming to England, *I was prevailed upon to publish this Journal, because it gives an Account of the Inland Parts of* Africa, *to know which the World was very curious, and of which few Accounts have been hitherto published, and those either very ancient, or stuff'd with Fables.*

Besides my own, I have added another Journal by Captain Stibbs. *In the Year* 1720, *his Grace the Duke of* Chandos *being concerned in the Royal* African *Company, and having considered of their Affairs with that Greatness of Mind natural to him, soon determined that the carrying on the Trade in the piddling Manner which it had been for some Years past, would never answer the great Capital Stock of the Company; and concluded it would be right to make some noble Attempts for the opening a Trade into the Inland Parts of* Africa; *and for that Purpose, Captain Stibbs was sent to discover how far the River* Gambia *was navigable, and whether there were Gold Mines upon it; but they set out upon that Expedition so late in the dry Season, that they did not accomplish the End intended. And the Difficulties he met with disgusted him so, that*

he

he ufeth *Arguments to prove that the* Gambia
is not the Niger, *nor a River of long Courfe ;*
which Fact if he could eftablifh, would juftify
him in not having pufh'd his Difcovery far-
ther

   Befides this Journal, I have added fome
Paffages out of the antient Geographers and
Hiftorians relating to the Niger Nile, *fuppofed*
to be the Gambia. *Some Part of* Africa *was*
known from the earlieft Ages, frequent men-
tion being made of it in Scripture, *and in the*
Greek *and* Roman *Authors ; but the* Romans *were acquainted only with what lay*
near the Mediterianean *Sea, the Countries to*
the South of Mount Atlas *having been but*
very little, if at all, known to them. The
ancient Perfians, Greeks, *and* Romans, *in vain*
attempted to difcover the Head of the Nile,
and generally believed that all beyond the Tro-
pick of Cancer *was uninhabitable Defarts,*
(tho' Herodotus *from the Priefts of* Egypt *gives*
fome Account of that famous River, and of its
dividing into two Streams, one of which only
paffed through Egypt *into the* Mediterranean
Sea : *I have inferted his Account. Long fince*
that, the Nubian Geographer *fpeaks concerning*
the Negroes, *and the* Niger Nile. *He flou-*
rifhed in the 12th *Century, and wrote in* Arabick *very fully of all the Nations lying on the*
Niger. *His Work firft printed in* Arabick, *at*
Rome, *was afterwards tranflated into* Latin,
and printed at Paris, 1619, *under the Title of*
Geographia Nubienfis.

The

The next we meet with, of any Note, is Leo the African, *by Birth a* Moor, *of noble Parentage, bred up in the* Mahometan *Religion, and Nephew to the Ambaffador fent by the King of* Fez *to the King of* Tombuto, *whom he accompanied in that Journey. This* Leo *was taken by* Italian *Corfairs, near the Ifle of* Gerby, *as he failed between the Towns of* Tripolis *and* Tunis *in* Barbary. *He was a Man of Learning, and had with him feveral* Arabian *Books, befides his own Manufcripts. At that time* Leo *the* Xth *was Pope, whofe Love to Learning was univerfally known: To him therefore the Corfairs prefented the* Moor *and his Books. This was a grateful Prefent, as it gave him a Knowledge of much of the Inland Parts of* Africa, *unknown to the Antients. The Pope encouraged him, and he embraced the* Romifh *Religion, and his* * *Defcription of* Africa *was publifhed in* Italian. *He gives an Account of all the* Negro *Nations in his Time, from the Mouths of the* Niger *Eaftward to the* Red Sea.

As thefe two Authors, who were both Africans, *have given a better Account of the Inland Parts of* Africa *than any other, I have extracted from them fo much as relates to the River* Gambia, *which, with the Kingdoms bordering thereon, feems to have been the utmoft Bounds of the Inland Difcoveries of the* Mahometans *Southward.*

By

* 1ft Vol. of *Ramufo's* Collection of Navigations and Voyages, publifhed at *Venice,* 1554.

By Leo *it appears that Caravans went from* Fez *in the Empire of* Morocco, *through* Segelmaffa, *to* Tombuto, *which was then the Name of a powerful Kingdom,* erected *by one* Soni Heli Ifchia *over the* Negroes *upon the River* Niger. *I have given all thofe Parts of his Book which relate to the Way that the Caravans took in their Journeys from* Fez *to the* Niger, *which is through* Morocco, *crofs the Mountains of* Atlas, *to the Province of* Dara, *which is in* Numidia, *and from thence over the Sandy Defarts of* Libya.

The Portuguefe *for many Years pufhed their Difcoveries, and fettled along the Weftern Coaft of* Africa *as far as* Angola, *they afterwards difcovered the* Cape of Good-Hope, *and going round it, failed to the* Eaft-Indies. *They fettled alfo in many Places on the Eaftern Coaft of* Africa, *up even to the* Red Sea; *and from the Coaft of that Sea, difcovered the Heads of the* Nile, *which rifes in* Abyffinia, *fubject to a Chriftian Prince, called* The Negus. *The Inhabitants have a Patriarch, confecrated by him of* Alexandria.

Ludolphus, *the* German, *hath collected, partly from the Writings of the* Portuguefe *Monks and Jefuits, but chiefly from the Information of a Native of* Abyffinia, *called* Gregory, *the Hiftory of that Country. A Chapter of his, relating to the Origin and Springs of the* Nile, *I have thought proper to infert, fince it contains his Reafons for believing that the River* Nile *divides, and that the Weftern Branch*

of

of it traverses all Africa, *and falls into the* Atlantick Ocean *near* Cape Verd, *and is call-ed* The Niger Nile.

Since the declining of the Portuguese *Power, the* English, Dutch, *and* French *have possessed themselves of this Coast, the* French *having a Fort in the River* Senegal, *and another at* Goree, *the* English *several Forts in the River* Gambia, *and on the Gold and Slave Coasts, and the* Dutch *having taken from the* Portuguese St. George Del Mina *on the Gold Coast; and several other Settlements depending thereon.*

I mention in my Journal, *that I would in-sert a Letter from* Governor Rogers, *concern-ing the Natives Account of the Lakes, from which the* Gambia *comes, but that Letter being either lost or mislaid, I have not been able to procure it from the Company, though they have been pleased to allow me to publish several Extracts of Letters relating to the Discovery of the Gum-Trade, a thing which, if followed, would be of very great Advantage to* England, *for there is a great deal of that Commodity used in all Silk Manufactures, and could it be had in the River* Gambia, *it might be brought to* England *without Inter-ruption from the* French, *because the* English *Company possess the Forts in the River* Gambia. *But the* French *have of late Years endeavour-ed to monopolize the Trade of Gum upon the Coast of* Senegal, *under pretence of an exclu-sive Right, because they stand possessed of two Forts on that Coast; and they sup-*

port

port their Claim by haraffing the Natives on Shore, who attempt to trade with any Ships at Sea, and by Squadrons of Men of War, who chafe off all the Ships who attempt to trade there with them ; and if they could purchafe all the English Forts upon the Coast of Africa, they would then claim an exclufive Trade to all Africa.

As I mentioned above, I have given Extracts out of various Authors; to thofe Extracts I have added Notes, and attempted to difcover the modern Names of the Places mentioned by thofe early Authors, always producing the Reafons on which I ground my Belief.

I thought my collecting from various Authors what is known of that Part of Africa, which lies on the Niger, would be pleafing to the Reader, who might be defirous to fee the whole at one View, and fave the Trouble of turning to many Books. He may from thefe Collections form his Judgment of what is true, by comparing one Account with the other, and fee whether there is a Probability that the Niger and the Nile flow from the fame Fountains, or that the Niger and the Gambia are the fame. Perhaps it may give fuch Infight to others, who fhall be hereafter employed in that Country, as to make them pufh their Difcoveries farther. If I had had the Conveniency of thofe Books in Africa, they would have taught me to have made fuch Enquiries as would have enabled me to give a much better Account than I can now poffibly do

LET-

LETTER

TO THE

PUBLISHER.

S I R,

Urfuant to your Defire, I have perufed the Journal, and other Pieces, in the following Book . They will give great Light into what the curious World has long defired to know, *The Infide of* Africa ; for tho' that Country is famous in Hiftory from the antienteft Times, yet the Inland Parts of it are to this Hour unknown to the People of *Europe* The Bounds of it have been often changed , the Antients reckoning *Ægypt* no Part of *Africa* The prefent Geographers divide the World into Four Parts: They account *Africa,* including *Ægypt,* as One It is a vaft Peninfula, joyned to *Afia* by an Ifthmus, or Neck of Land, which feparates the *Red Sea* from the *Mediterranean,* and borders upon *Judea* and *Arabia* It is in Figure almoft Triangular , 4980 Miles from North to South, and 4575 Miles from Eaft to Weft. The Northern Coaft, bounded by the *Mediterranean* Sea, was known to the *Græcians* and *Romans* Upon it the *Græcians* fettled *Cyrene,* and other Colonies , and the *Phœnicians* the Great City of *Carthage.* The *Romans* having fubdued *Carthage,* conquer'd the Kingdoms of *Numida* and *Mauritania,* and all that Part of *Africa* which bordered upon the *Mediterranean* Sea, now call'd *Barbary,* and the Empire of *Morocco .* But the *Ro-*

m n,

mans never difcover'd far beyond Mount *Atlas* · They knew nothing of *Guinea*, and very little of the Heads of the *Nile*. Upon the Declenfion of the *Romans*, their Provinces in *Africa* follow'd the Fate of the reft of the Empire, were fubdued by the Northern Nations, and the *(a) Vandals* erected a Kingdom there, which was again conquer'd by the *Græcian* Emperor's Forces under *Belifarius*. The Eaftern Empire continuing to decline, the *Arabians*, under *Mahomet*, and his Succeffors the Caliphs, (in whom the Powers of Priefts, Prophets, and Kings were united) made furprizing Conquefts by the Affiftance of their new Religion. In their Wars, amongft other Actions, they invaded and conquer'd *Africa*, a Climate pleafing to the *Arabs (b)*, being like their own, and a Soil mix'd with Defarts, which is natural to them. They ftrove to deftroy the *Punick*, the *Roman*, and the old *Numidian* Language, and introduced the *Arabick* ; yet is there ftill left among the Natives one of the antient Languages, call'd *(c) Aquel Amarig*, but whether *Punick* or *Numidian* is not certain. There is alfo in the Mountains of *Atlas* a Nation ftill remaining, who retain the *(d) Roman* Cuftoms. The *Mahometan* Religion prevail'd univerfally. Their firft Conquefts were in the Time of *Otman*, Third Caliph ; but on the Diffolution of the Empire of the *Saracens*, in *Africa*, as elfewhere, the feveral Governors became Kings in their different Provinces

(e) Ægypt was governed by a Republick of Soldiers, call'd *Mamluks*, or *Mamaliks*, which afterwards was fubdued by the *Turkifh* Emperor. About two Ages fince, three Republicks of Soldiers, under the Protection of the *Turkifh* Emperor, grew up on the Coaft of *Barbary*, viz. *Tripoly*, *Tunis*, and *Algiers*. That Part of *Africa*, which is now the Empire of *Morocco*, was formerly divided into many Governments under different Princes or Republicks · It is very fertile, and was very rich · The two moft confiderable Kingdoms were thofe of *Fez* and *Morocco*, each of which had a noble Town for its Capital, and flourifh'd in Arts and Arms, and grew very rich, by reafon of the Commerce for Gold with the *Negroes*, which was then brought over Land from *Tombuto*. The Natives of the Country, who were of the *Numidian* and *Mauritanian* Race, which are
divided

(a) Vide *Procopium*   (b) Vide *Leo*'s Extracts, p 28
(c) Ibidem   (d) Ibid p 40   (e) *Knowles*'s Hift.
of the *Turks*

divided into Five Tribes, being driven out upon the *Arabian* Conqueſt, retired Southward, and they divided all the Coun- try of the *Negroes* which lies upon the *Niger* into Fifteen Parts, which they call'd Kingdoms, and each Tribe was to take and conquer Three of them · Which they did, and theſe were the Fifteen Kingaoms of the *Negroes*, in which the Race of the Kings and Lords were *Libyans*, with high Noſes, and thin Lips, and *Mahometans* by Religion, and the conquer'd People were *Negroes*

Before the *Moors* mix'd amongſt them, the *Negroes* were entirely ignorant of Arts and Letters, and of the Uſe of Iron · They lived in common, having no Property in Lands nor Goods, no Tyrants, nor ſuperior Lords, but ſupported themſelves in an equal State upon the natural Produce of the Country, which afforded plenty of Roots and Game, and Honey made by Bees in hollow Trees . Ambition or Avarice never drove them into Foreign Countries, to ſubdue or cheat their Neighbours. Thus they lived without Toil or Superfluities *(a)*. And this the *Greeks* and *Romans* be- lieved to be the Firſt State of Mankind, which they deſcribe in the *Golden Age:* And as there is no Winter between the Tropicks, perhaps they mean that Climate, by the perpetual *Spring*, they attributed to the *Golden Age*; and very likely this innocent State of theirs is the Reaſon that *Homer* ſaid Gods converſed with them, and made them every Year a Viſit for 12 Days.

Ζεὺς γὸ ἐπ ωκεανὸν μετ' ἀμύμονας Αἰθιοπῆας
Χθιζὸς ἔβη μῇ δαῖτα (θεοὶ δ' ἅμα πάντες ἕποντο)
Δωδεκάτη δέ τι αὖθις ἐλεύσετ') οὔλυμπόνδε. (b)

And thus *Ovid*,

Aurea prima ſata eſt Ætas, quæ Vindice nullo,
Sponte ſua fine Lege Fidem, Rectumque colebat.
Pœna Metuſque aberant; nec Verba minacia fixo
Ære legebantur; nec ſupplex turba timebant

Judicis

(a) Vide *Leo's* Extracts, p. 65
(b) *The Sire of Gods, and all th' Ethereal Train,*
On tre warm Limits of the fartheſt Main,
Now mix with Mortals, nor diſdain to grace
The Feaſt of Æthiopia's blameleſs Race
Twelve Days the Pow'rs indulge the genial Rite,
Returning with the Twelfth revolving Light POPE.

Judicis Ora *fui, fed erant fine Vindice tuti.*
Nondum cæfa fuis, peregrinum ut viferet Orbem,
Montibus, in liquidas Pinus defcenderat Undas,
Nullaque Mortales, præter fua, Littora norant;
Nondum præcipites cingebant Oppida Foffæ:
Non Tuba directi, non Æris Cornua flexi,
Non Galeæ, non Enfis, erant. Sine Militis ufu,
Mollia fecuræ peragebant Otia Gentes.
Ipfa quoque immunis Raftroque intacta, nec ullis
Saucia Vomeribus, per fe dabat omnia Tellus:
Contentique Cibis nullo cogente creatis,
Arbuteos Fœtus, montanaque Fraga legebant,
Cornaque, & in duris hærentia Mora Rubetis,
Et quæ deciderant patula Jovis Arbore Glandes.
Ver erat æternum, *placidique tepentibus Auris*
Mulcebant Zephyri natos fine Semine Flores.
Mox etiam Fruges Tellus inarata ferebat:
Nec renovatus Ager gravidis canebat Ariftis.
Flumina jam Lactis, jam Flumina Nectaris ibant;
Flavaque de viridi ftillabant Ilice Mella (a)

The

(a) *The Golden Age was firft, when Man yet new*
No Rule but uncorrupted Reafon knew,
And with a native Bent did Good purfue.
Unforc'd by Punifhment, unaw'd by Fear,
His Words were fimple, and his Soul fincere
Needlefs was written Law where none opprefs'd,
The Law of Man was written in his Breaft
No fuppliant Crowds before the Judge appear'd,
No Court erected yet, nor Caufe was heard;
But all was fafe, for Confcience was their Guard.
The Mountain-Trees in diftant Profpect pleafe,
Ere yet the Pine defcended to the Seas
Ere Sails were fpread, new Oceans to explore,
And happy Mortals, unconcern'd for more,
Confin'd their Wifhes to their native Shore.
No Walls were yet, nor Fence, nor Mote, nor Mound,
Nor Drum was heard, nor Trumpet's angry Sound.
Nor Swords were forg'd, but void of Care and Crime,
The foft Creation flept away their Time
The teeming Earth, yet guiltlefs of the Plough,
And unprovok'd, did fruitful Stores allow
Content with Food which Nature freely bred,
On Wildings, and on Strawberries, they fed;

Cornels

The *Libyan* Tribe of *Sanhagia* (who wore Coats of Mail, were Horsemen, and used Spears headed with Iron, Scymitars and Arrows) coming amongst these harmless and naked People, made as rapid Conquests as the *Spaniards* did in *America*, and contemned the Natives as much, looking upon them as Brutes, becauſe they were not *Mahometans*, nor inſtructed in Avarice, nor ruled by Tyrants, for which the *Moors* upbraided them, as wanting the Knowledge of Religion, Property and Government

The *Nubian* Geographer, and *Leo* the *African*, give an Account of these Fifteen Kingdoms, in which the *Moors* propagated the *Mahometan* Religion, and all the Countries lying on the *Niger*, from *Æthiopia* to the *Atlantick* Ocean, were ſubdued by them.

About the 14th Century, a Native *Negroe*, call'd *Soni Heli Ischia*, expell'd the *Moorish* Conquerors But tho' the *Negroes* threw off the Yoke of a Foreign Nation, yet they return'd not to their firſt Simplicity of Manners, Tyranny, Luxury and Avarice, which the *Negroes* had learnt from the politer *Moors*, continued to tyrannize over the *Negroes*, after they were freed from the Men who had introduced them They only ſhifted their Chains. and changed a *Libyan* for a *Negroe* Maſter *Soni Heli Ischia* continued the Regal Government, and himſelf became King, and led the *Negroes* on to Foreign Wars, filling all *Africa* with Blood and Slaughter He conquer'd moſt of the Fifteen Kingdoms upon the *Niger*, expelling the Kings and *Moorish* Tribes from their Dominion over the *Negroes* He generally put the Kings to death, but when he invaded the *Folloffs*, being apprehenſive by their Neighbourhood to the Deſarts, that they would be ſupported by all the Race of *Sanhaga*, he agreed to leave the Family of *Sanhaga* in Poſſeſſion of the Kingdom of *Gualata*, they remaining Tributary to him And the Family of *N'jay* to this Hour continue Kings of the *Folloffs*. They ſeem by their Name

to

Cornels and Bramble Berries gave the reſt,
And falling Acorns furniſh'd out a Feaſt
The Flowers unſown, in Fields and Meadows reign'd,
And Weſtern Winds immortal Spring maintain'd
In following Years the bearded Corn enſu'd,
From Earth unaſk'd, nor was that Earth renew'd;
From Veins of Vallies Milk and Nectar broke,
And Hony ſweating thro' the Pores of Oak GARTH

to be of the Tribe of *Sanhaga*, who, having escaped the Storm of *Ischia*'s Arms, still maintain the *Moorish* Power in that Country: Whereas all the rest of the *Moorish* Kingdoms are destroyed, and *Ischia* upon the ruins erected a mighty Empire, having conquer'd all from *Tombuto* Westward to the Sea, and Eastward to the Frontiers of the *Abyssines*, making above 3000 Miles in Length.

Since *Leo*, the *Europeans* have had very little Knowledge of these Parts of *Africa*, nor do they know what is become of so mighty an Empire It is highly probable that it broke to pieces, and that the Natives again resumed their Customs, and indeed, in *Gambia*, as far as the Author of the Journal has been, we find a mixture of the *Moorish* and *Mahometan* Customs with the original Simplicity of the *Negroes*

In the Kingdom of *Gualata*, or the *Jolloiffs*, (now *Barsally*,) Government, or Tyranny, is extended to its utmost Lines by the Family of the *N'jay*'s In other Parts, particularly amongst the *Mundingoes*, the Authorities of the Kings are much less, and amongst the *Floops* and *Fuleys* they have no Kings at all, the Lands in general are common, every one taking as much as they want, and no one desiring more than they use, but the Crops are the Properties of those who have tilled the Ground And this and the Valuing of Gold, the *Negroes* have kept from the *Moorish* Customs, as also a great Veneration for the *Mahometan* Religion

The present *Morocco* Embassador, Admiral *Perez*, says, that the Town of *Tombuto* is still in being, and that it is subject to the Emperor of *Morocco*, and govern'd by a Bassa or Governor appointed by him, who is generally of the Race of the antient King And that the chief Part of the Army of *Blacks*, which has made so considerable a Figure of late in the Empire of *Morocco*, and hath made and unmade Emperors, was raised and is recruited from *Tombuto*.

As the Knowledge and Conquests of the *Romans* extended not much beyond Mount *Atlas*, so the utmost Discoveries of the *Arabians*, *Moors* and *Mahometans*, extended not much to the South of the River *Niger* On the Western Coast of *Africa*, the *Portuguese*, in the Year 1498, urged on by Thirst of Gold, and a Fondness of propagating by Arms the *Romish* Religion, (Enthusiasm in

A   Re-

Religion and Knight-Errantry in Arms being then the Faſhion) diſcover'd *Africa* to be a Peninſula, and ſailed round the Cape of *Good Hope* to the *Eaſt Indies* They harraſſed extremely the *Mooriſh* Governments of *Morocco* and *Fez*, came by the Sea into the Rivers *Senegal* and *Gambia*, and furniſhing the Natives with thoſe Things which they before bought from the *Moors*, turned the Trade of Gold and Elephants Teeth from *Morocco* to *Portugal* Having paſs'd the Cape of *Good Hope*, they diſcover'd the Eaſtern Part of *Africa*, and made very conſiderable ſettlements at *Mozambique*, upon that Part of *Africa*, which is bounded by the *Eaſt Indian* Sea, then entering the *Red Sea*, and landing on the *African* Side, they diſcover'd the *Chriſtian* Kingdom of *Abyſſinia*, and the ſecret Heads of the *Nile*, a Diſcovery which had baffled the Enquiries of all the antient World, which had been in vain attempted by the *Perſians*, *Greeks* and *Romans*, and which was eſteem'd ſo great an Enterprize, that *Lucan* makes *Cæſar* ſay,

> Sed cum tanta meo vivat ſub Pectore Virtus,
> Tantus Amor Veri, nihil eſt quod noſcere malim
> Quam Fluvii Cauſas per ſecula tanta latentes,
> Ignotumque Caput, Spes ſit mihi certa videndi
> Nihacos Fontes, Bellum civile relinquam *.

And in another Place the wiſe *Achoreus* ſays,

> Quæ tibi noſcendi Nilum, Romane, Cupido eſt,
> Et Phariis, Perſiſque fuit, Macetumque Tyrannis;
> Nullaque non Ætas voluit conferre futuris
> Notitiam, ſed vincit adhuc Natura latendi
> Summus Alexander, Regum quos Memphis adorat

Invi-

---

* Long has my curious Soul, from Early Youth,
Toil'd in the noble Search of ſacred Truth.
Yet ſtill no Views have urg'd my Ardour more,
Than *Nile*'s remoteſt Fountain to explore,
Then ſay what Source the famous Stream ſupplies,
And bids it at revolving Periods riſe,
Shew me that Head from whence, ſince Time begun,
The long ſucceſſion of his Waves has run
This let me know, and all my Toils ſhall ceaſe,
The Sword be ſheath'd, and Earth be bleſs'd with Peace.

Invidit Nilo, *miſitque per ultima Terræ*
Æthiopum Lectos , illos rubicunda peruſti
Zona Poli tenuit Nilum *videre calentem.*
Venit ad Occaſum, Mundique extrema Seſoſtris,
Et Pharios *Currus Regum Cervicibus egit .*
Ante tamen veſtros Amnes, Rhodanumque Padumq;
Quam Nilum *de Fonte bibit. Veſanus in Ortus*
Cambyſes *longi Populos pervenit ad Ævi,*
Defectuſque Epulis, & paſtus Cæde ſuorum,
Ignoto te, Nile, *redit* *.

A Deſcription of the Fountains and Courſe of the *Nile*
cannot but be agreeable to the Curious, and therefore the
Chapter on that Subject from the Learned *Ludolphus* is
very proper , but whether the *Nile* divides, flowing part
into the *Mediterranen,* and part into the *Atlantic* Sea, and
                                                        whe-

---

* Nor, *Cæſar,* is thy Search of Knowlegde ſtrange ,
  Well may thy boundleſs Soul deſire to range,
  Well may ſhe ſtrive *Nile*'s Fountain to explore,
  Since mighty Kings have ſought the ſame before :
  Each for the firſt Diſcov'rer would be known,
  And hand, to future Times, the Secret down : |
  But ſtill their Pow'rs were exercis'd in vain,
  While latent Nature mock'd their fruitleſs Pain.
  Philip's Great Son, whom *Memphis* ſtill records
  The Chief of her illuſtrious ſcepter'd Lords,
  Sent, of his own a choſen Number forth,
  To trace the wond'rous Stream's myſterious Birth.
  Thro' *Æthiopia*'s Plains they journey'd on,
  'Till the hot Sun oppos'd the burning Zone ;
  There, by the God's reſiſtleſs Beams repell'd,
  An unbeginning Stream they ſtill beheld
  Fierce came *Seſoſtris* from the Eaſtern Dawn,
  On his proud Car by captive Monarchs drawn ;
  His lawleſs Will, impatient of a Bound,
  Commanded *Nile*'s hid Fountain to be found
  But ſooner much the Tyrant might have known
  Thy fam'd *Heſperian Po,* or *Gallick Rhone*
  Cambyſes too, his daring *Perſians* led,
  Where hoary Age makes white the *Æthiop*'s Head;
  'Till ſore diſtreſs'd, and deſtitute of Food,
  He ſtain'd his hungry Jaws with human Blood,
  'Till haif his Hoſt the other half devour'd,
  And left the *Nile* behind 'em unexplor d

whether the *Gambia* be one of the Branches of the *Nile*
the Author pretends not to decide, but hath laid all the
Discoveries that have yet been made before the Reader.

There remains still unknown the Inland Parts of *Africa*;
and of part of those, the *Journal* hereto annex'd gives an
Account, that is to say, of what lies upon the River *Gambia*, and very probably this is the Country described by *Leo*
under the Names of *Glana*, *Ghinea* and *Gualata*

Perhaps it may not be difagreeable to the Reader, to give
some general Notion of the Country from the *Gambia*
to the *Mediterranean* Sea. At a confiderable Diftance to
the South of the *Streights* of *Gibraltar* is *Atlas*, a Ridge of
Mountains, which run parallel to the *Mediterranean* Sea,
fo extremely high, and fo little known, that the Antients
faid they fupported the Sky.

> *Oceani finem juxta Solemque cadentem*
> *Ultimus Æthiopum Locus eft, ubi maximus Atlas*
> *Axem Humero torquet Stellis ardentibus aptum*
>
> VIRG.

The Land between thofe Mountains and the Sea is extremely fertile, yielding Wheat, Olives, Cattle, &c. The
Tops of the Mountains are cover'd with perpetual Snow.
The fides are cloathed with Woods, and in their Valleys
rife thofe clear cool Streams that render *Mauritania*, now
call'd the Kingdom of *Morocco*, fertile. To the South of
Mount *Atlas*, extending from the Ocean to the *Nile*, parallel to the *Mediterranean* Sea, is the *Land of Dates*.
This is a fteril Country, full of fandy Defarts, producing
no Corn, yet not quite fo barren, but that in many Places the Palm-Trees grow, and the Fruits which they yeild,
call'd Dates, fupply the Natives inftead of Bread *, and
ferve their Cttle for Forage ‡, fo that Providence hath
wifely given Food to the Inhabitants of the Defarts. This
remarkable Difference of Food, viz. eating Dates inftead
of Corn, could not efcape the piercing Eye of *Homer*,
he call'd them *Lotus*; and defcribes the Wine drawn from
the Palm-Tree, as well as the fweet Dates.

——— αὐτὰρ

---

* *Leo's Extracts*, p 31.   ‡ Ibid. p 63.

—————— αυτὰρ δεκάτη ἐπέβημεν
Γαίης Λωτοφάγων, οἵ τ' ἄνθινον εἶδαρ ἔδουσιν
Ἔνθα δ' ἐπ' ἠπείρου βῆμεν, κỳ ἀφυσσάμεθ ὕδωρ.
Αἶψα δὲ δεῖπνον ἕλοντο θοῆς παρὰ νηυσὶν ἑταῖροι.
Αὐτὰρ ἐπεὶ σίτοιό τ' ἐπασσάμεθ ἠδὲ ποτῆτος,
Δὴ τότ' ἐγὼν ἑτάρους προΐην πεύθεσθαι ἰόντας
(Ἄνδρε δύω κρίνας, τρίτατον κήρυχ' ἅμ' ὀπάσσας)
Οἵτινες ἀνέρες εἶεν ἐπὶ χθονὶ σῖτον ἔδοντες
Οἳ δ' αἶψ' οἰχόμενοι μίγεν ἀνδράσι Λωτοφάγοισι
Οὐδ' ἄρα Λωτοφάγοι μήδεν θ ἑτάροισιν ὄλεθρον
Ἡμετέροις, ἀλλά σφι δόσαν λωτοῖο πάσασθαι
Τῶν δ' ὅς τις λωτοῖο φάγοι μελιηδέα καρπόν,
Οὐκ ἔτ' ἀπαγγεῖλαι πάλιν ἤθελεν, οὐδὲ νέεσθαι
Ἀλλ' αὐτῇ βούλοντο μετ' ἀνδράσι Λωτοφάγοισι
Λωτὸν ἐρεπτόμενοι μενέμεν, νόστε τε λαθέσθαι *

To the South of the Land of Palms lye the *Libyan* Defarts, one wide extended waſte of Sand, boundleſs and level to the Eye, as the Sea, and when the Wind blows,
agitated by it, which is finely deſcribed in *Cato.*

So, where our wide Numidian *Waſtes extend,*
Sudden th' impetuous Hurricanes deſcend,
Wheel thro' the Air, in circling Eddies play,
Tear up the Sands, and ſweep whole Plains away

The

* The Tenth we touch'd, by various Errors toſt,
The Land of *Lotos* and the flow'ry Coaſt
We climb'd the Beach, and Springs of Water found,
Then ſpread our haſty Banquet on the Ground.
Three Men were ſent deputed from the Crew,
(An Herald one) the dubious Coaſt to view,
And learn what Habitants poſſeſs'd the Place
They went, and found an hoſpitable Race
Not prone to ill, nor ſtrange to foreign Gueſt,
They eat, they drink, and Nature gives the Feaſt;
The Trees around them all their Food produce,
Lotos, the Name, divine, nectareous Juice!
(Thence call'd *Lotophagi*) which whoſo taſtes,
Inſatiate riots in the ſweet Repaſts,
Nor other Home, nor other Care intends,
But quits his houſe, his Country, and his Friends.

Pope

The he'pleſs Travellꝛ w th wild Surprize,
Sees the dry Deſart all around in n riſe,
And, ſmother'd in the duſty Whirlwind, dies

                        CAIO.

Even thoſe miſeraole Countries are inhabited The
Arabians dwell with pleaſure amongſt the Sands, for *Leo*
ſays, an *Arabian* without a Deſart, is like a Fiſh out of
Water Providence hath made man to be capable of in-
habiting all Parts of t is Earthly Globe, and hath given
him ſuch kind of Organs as form themſelves to the Heat
or Cold, Moiſture or Drowth of the Climate he is bred
in The *Laplanders* live with Comfort near the Pole, and
the *Lbyars* are happy in theſe Deſarts The ſame Wiſdom
that has contrived Mens Organs capable of becoming
ſuitable to the Climate, has given other Animals, and
Food for thoſe Animals ſuitable to it likewiſe Amongſt
theſe Sands there are ſome Places leſs barren, where
Thorns, Briars and the poorest of Herbage grows, yet
ſuch as the Camels can feed upon The Oſtrich alſo, and
ſome other kinds of Creatures found by Nature to ſubſiſt
amorgſt theſe Sanus, live here, and the rambling Tribes
of *Arabs* feed upon their Fleſh, but their chief Dependance
is upon the Camel, which is their Wealth They keep
them as we do Sheep, they make Cloathing of their Hair
for themſelves, and their Horſes feed upon their Milk, and
they alſo eat their Fleſh The *Arabs* Manner of Life is
ſo different from thoſe Nations who live upon Corn, and
the Produce of Agriculure, that the Extraorimarineſs of
it cannot but make the 30th and 31ſt Pages of the Extracts, from *Leo,* agrreeable To the South of theſe Deſarts lve the Rivers *Senega* and *Gambia,* which run parallel to the *Mediterra & Sea* All the Lands that theſe
Rivers water or o erflow are fertile, or all that is not cultivated bears Wood, and what is cultivated produces ſuch
Corn as grows in warm Countries, and plenty of Paſture
for Cattle. This is inhabited by the *Negroes,* a Race of
People who appear to be different from the reſt of Mankind, their Hair being wooly, and their Colour black,
their Noſes flat, and their Lips large, but whether theſe
are an original Race, or whether the Difference ariſes from
the Climate, the Vapours of that particular Soil, the
Manner of breeding their Children, and from the Mothers

                                      forming

forming of their Features, is not here determined, tho'
there are some curious Facts relating to it mention'd in the
Journal

The Book consists of several Pieces, which are necessary
to give the Reader a true Notion of *Africa* The Author
who hath compiled it, hath not alter'd the Tracts which
he hath quoted, but given them as they were wrote, tho'
they sometimes contradict each other By which means
the Reader may form a better Judgement of the Truth,
than if he was to rely upon a single Traveller.

The 1*st* is, Travels into the Inland Parts of *Africa*, being a Journal kept by Mr *Francis Moore*, Factor for the
Royal *African* Company, who lived five Years in the Country of *Gambia*, travelled by Land as well as by Water, and
went up, 500 Miles from the Sea This Journal contains
a Map of the River *Gambia*, from an Actual Survey taken
upon the Place by Mr *John Leach*, and several Draughts
of Birds, Insects, and Buildings

To illustrate his own Journal, and to shew the Truth
of it, (a Thing most valuable, as all Rarities are in Travels) he hath added all the other Pieces

1*st*, A Journal of Capt *Stibbs* up the same River

2*dly*, Some Remarks of Capt *Stibbs*, together with the
Author's Observations upon them

3*dly*, Extracts from the *Nubian* Geographer, and from
Leo the *African*, a very valuable Book

4*thly*, A Chapter from *Ludolphus*'s History of *Æthiopia*,
a laborious and learned Man, who has spared no Pains to
enquire into the Heads and Course of the *Nile*

5*thly*, The Passage quoted from *Herodotus* by *Ludolphus*
set down at length

6*thly*, Some Words of the *Mandingoe*, which is the
most extensive of the native *Negroe* Languages

7*thly*, Some Letters and Papers relating to the Company and the Gum-Trade

8*thly*, The Journal of a Person who went up the River
in K *Charles* the IId's Time Which Journal is frequently mention'd by Capt *Stibbs*, and their Accounts differ

And *Lastly*, The Royal *African*'s Company's Establishment at *James* Fort in the Year 1730

Upon the whole, There can hardly be a more curious
Subject than this, The * Factor, in a plain honest Way,

gives

* Travels into the Inland Part of *Africa*, from p 1 to 234

gives an Account of the River *Gambia* , where there is a great Trade drove by the *Engliſh* A River, which is wonderful in many Things which he mentions The Tide flows up it many hundred Miles The Climate ſo different from ours that there is no Winter, which occaſions a Difference in the whole Vegetable and Animal World To ſhew you whereabouts this River lies, he has collected from various Authors, Accounts of thoſe Countries which reach from thence to the *Mediterranean* Sea over againſt *Gibraltar*, in which there is a Scene of natural Wonders, or rather Nature varying from the ordinary Method in which, with us, ſhe works WholeNations with their Herds living in Deſarts almoſt without Water *, others upon Fruits of Trees without Grain, † The Heads of the *Nile* are here plainly revealed ‡, and the Tops of Mount *Atlas* made known Nations, ſafe in the inacceſſible Faſtneſſes of thoſe Mountains, have preſerved the *Roman* Garb ‖, and the *Roman* Courage And here in a few Days Travel they mount up from the exceſſive Heats of the Deſarts of *Libya*, to the perpetual Winter on the Tops of *Atlas* Here is deſcribed the Manner and Reaſon of the ‡ Decay of the *Saracen* Empire, from the Height of Politeneſs in the Time of *Manſor*, to the loweſt Degree of *Barbariſm*

I am, &c

* *Leo's* Ext p, 29   † Ibidem   ‡ Ludolph.
‖ *Leo's* Ext, p 40   ‡ Ibid p 45.

E R R A T A

PAGE 87 Line 23 for *not* read *hardly*
     P 108 Bottom Line, for *beſſted* read *being*
P 114 L 1 for 1724, read 1734.
P 159 L 3. for *Boots*, read *Roots*
P 160 L 15 for *Pare* read *Pau*
P 205 L 21 for *ſo* read *to,*
Part of P 210,211, and 212, ſhould be turn-comma'd, i e Extracts, mark'd thus "
     P 15 Title Page, for *foregoing Journal* read *The Niger-Nile or Gambia*
     P 17 for *Fracaſtora* read *Fracaſtore*

T R A-

TRAVELS

Into the INLAND PARTS of

AFRICA, &c.

 N the Month of *July*, 1730, I was examined and found qualified by the Accomprant-General belonging to the Royal *African* Company of *England*, and by him reprefented to the Directors as fuch . Upon which they were pleafed to appoint me a Writer in their Service, at their Settlement at *James* Fort, in the River *Gambia*, on the Coaft of *Guinea*, in *Africa*   In Confequence thereof, I contracted with them , and on the 23d fign'd Articles for the Term of three Years.   A Copy of which, for the Information of thofe concern'd this Way, is given in the Appendix, No. I.

1730.
July.

The Author appointed Writer to the R A-frican Comp

Appendix, No I.

1730
September

Difpatch
Sloop
bound
for Gam-
ba

On the 2d of *September* I fet out from *London* for *Gravefend*, in order to go to *Gambia*, in the Royal *African* Company's Sloop the *Difpatch*, *Robert Hall* Mafter : But when I arriv'd at *Gravefend*, the Sloop had been gone about two Hours . Upon which I agreed with the Mafter of a Sloop call'd the *Thomas* and *Samuel*, (bound for *Malaga*, and juft then under Sail) to carry me to the *Downs* We had not gone above three Leagues before fhe fprung a Leak, infomuch that fhe was obliged to come back again to *Gravefend*, but a *Feverfham* Hoy coming by at that Time, I agreed with the Mafter to carry me to *Feverfham*, where we arrived in the Night The next Day I hired Horfes, and fet out for *Canterbury*. I got frefh Horfes there, and proceeded to *Deal*, where the Sloop lay waiting for a fair Wind, and for fear of the worft, I went on

Goes on
Board her
in the
Downs

Board immediately During the Time we lay there, feveral homeward-bound Ships came in, many of them with their Topmafts and Mizenmafts loft We had generally thick hazy Weather, with bluftring Winds, and a great deal of Rain.

Sets fail.

On the 10th in the Evening, the Wind being fair, we weigh'd Anchor, and fet fail in Company with a great many other outbound Ships. We failed pleafantly on till the next Morning at 8 o'Clock, at which Time the Wind turn'd againft us, and blow'd prodigious hard, the Seas ran Mountains high, and the Sloop labour'd very much Our Rigging was out of Order, and we could not get down our Topfail, but were obliged

ged to cut it away. We could not fee Land
for Mift and Rain. The Water ran over
our Decks, and the Sloop lay along fo much,
that all our Guns on one Side were under
Water for a confiderable Time, by reafon
of our not being able to get down our Topfail. We made fhift to get back to the Forced to
Downs by about 8 at Night, where we an- put back
chored and moored, as feveral other Veffels by ftormy
had done before us. Weather.

On the 16th the *Falmouth* Man of War
came into the *Downs*, having loft her Main-
topmaft. On the 18th in the Evening, being
fair Weather, we fet out again for Sea On Sets fail a-
the 20th early in the Morning we made the gain.
Ifland of *Alderney*, at about five Leagues
diftance The next Morning we faw the high
Land near *Plymouth*, at about fix or feven
Leagues diftance.

On the 2d of *October*, the Wind, which *October*
had been fair for us all the Way from the
Downs, turned againft us, and blew exceffive
hard, infomuch that in the middle of the A Storm
Night it fplit our Mainfail from Top to Bottom, but having a new one on Board, we
got it bent as foon as poffible, and then lay
to, with the Head of the Sloop to the Wind,
driving towards the Coaft of *Barbary* at the
Rate of about two Miles an Hour, our Lives
depending on the Mainfail, which we expected, by the Wind coming in fuch terrible
Squalls, to fplit every Minute.

On the 4th, the Seas continuing ftill to
increafe, and the Wind very boifterous, the
Cap-

1730   Captain perſuaded us to bear away to the

Bear away for the Coaſt of Spa r
neareſt Port, which was *Cadiz*, in *Spain*, about 130 Leagues from which we then were; ſo about Noon we lowered our Mainſail, and hoiſted our Squareſail, and ſcudded away before the Wind, at the Rate of ten Miles an Hour   The ſame Evening we ran by a Brigantine, which was lying to, as we had done

Diſcover the Town of Caaz
On the 7th, the Storm began to be pretty well over, and the next Morning early we made the Town of *Cadiz*, whoſe Churches at a Diſtance look like a Fleet of Ships, about Noon we came into the Harbour, ſoon after a Boat, with the King of *Spain*'s Colours and an Officer, came a-board us, to

Health-Officers come on board
demand whence we came, and whither bound, as alſo to know our State of Health; this is not only cuſtomary, but very reaſonable, in order to prevent Veſſels from bringing any Infection among them, which if they have any Suſpicion of, they will make them perform a Quarantine of forty Days   The Boat ſtayed on board us about an Hour, and then went away, the Officer at his going took ſeveral of the Captain's Papers with him to the *Engliſh* Conſul, and told us not to offer to come a ſhore till we had got a Licence, for if we did, we ſhould certainly be put to Death   The next Morning the Captain ſent our Chief Mate to the Conſul,

The Author, to obtain a Bill of Health, and land.
to make Oath, if required, that we were all well, upon which he immediately procured us a Licence, and then we Paſſengers landed. The firſt Thing I heard in Town, was, that the late Storm had forced ſome of the Veſſels
a-ſhore,

a-fhore, as they lay at Anchor in the Harbour, and the Captain of one of them told me, that he and his Men with much Difficulty faved their Lives Four Days we ftay'd at *Cadiz*, during which Time I made the following Obfervations

CADIZ, or *CALIS MALIS*, was anciently called *Gades* It ftands upon an Ifland feparated from the Main of *Andaluzia*, a Province of *Spain*, by a narrow Arm of the Sea, over which there is a Bridge. It lies not above ten or twelve *Spanifh* Leagues by Land from *Gibraltar*, and about twenty from *Seville*. This Town was firft built by the *Phœnicians*, and made a great Figure in the ancient Hiftory. It is the Port from whence all the King of *Spain*'s Ships are fitted out for *America*, and the Channel through which the Riches of *Peru* and *Mexico* are conveyed to *Europe*. It hath been feveral Times attacked by the *Englifh*, and was taken by the Earl of *Effex* and Sir *Walter Raleigh*, in the Reign of Queen *Elizabeth* The Town is, as I guefs'd by walking round the Walls of it, about three Miles in Circumference, there are fome magnificent Houfes in it, but the Generality are badly built, though all of Stone, and very ftrong, the Streets ftink, by reafon of their throwing all the Naftinefs into them It lies very low, and is ftrongly fortified both by Workmanfhip and Nature All the Part towards the Harbour is furrounded with Rocks, that ftretch out above a Mile from the Town, except only at the Place where the Boats land, called the *Mole-head*, upon which there are two lofty Pillars of white Marble erected, and

Situation of Cadiz,

built by the Phœnicians,

Defcription of it.

B 3 on

1730 on each are the King of *Spain*'s Arms finely
carved   That Part of the Town which does
not face the Water, is ftrongly fortified with
Baftions and Outworks   About a Quarter of
a Mile from the *Mole-head* is a Gate, and a
conftant Guard, which fearch all Perfons that
pafs, when you are through that Gate, you
come into the *Herb-Market*, where is a fine
Stone Bafon with Steps round it, erected in
the Middle of the Market-Place   On the
Right-hand of this Market is a Street with
Shops on both Sides of it, and Stalls in the
Middle, like unto thofe in *Covent-Garden* at
London

Spanifh
Womens
Habit
THE Women generally go with their Hair
tied up without any Caps, they feem to be
very agreeable, and have fine black Eyes,
but wear Veils, and fometimes cover their
Faces with the Tails of their Gowns, which
they generally wear loofe, but thofe Ladies
who go abroad in Coaches, wear no Veils
at all

Churches
THE Churches are very numerous, and
finely adorned with gilded Altars, carved
wooden Images drefs'd in rich Cloaths, others
of Wax-work, and a vaft Number of Candlefticks, in which are Candles always burn-
Manner of
Burying
ing.   Here I faw two Burials, different from
any I ever faw before· One of the Perfons
deceafed, after having had Mafs fung over
him in a Church, was carried in a Coffin
(covered with Fifh-fkin) to a burying Vault
a great Way under the Church, where was
neither Bones nor Coffins to be feen, only a
Heap of about 300 Skulls, piled upon one
ano-

another like Cannon-Balls in a Fortification.
Here the Corps was brought by four Men,
who threw it off their Shoulders out of the
Coffin, and there left it, carrying the Coffin
back with them. The other Perſon had
Maſs ſung over him by about an hundred
Prieſts, all drefs'd in White, with long Wax
Candles burning in their Hands, which they
carried before the Corps, along the Streets,
to the Church. As ſoon as Maſs was over,
the Perſon was taken out of his Coffin with
his Shroud on, in the Middle of the Church,
and was put into a Hole about two Foot
ſquare, with his Feet firſt, and as ſoon as
the Corps was in, the Hole was ſtop'd up,
under which, I ſuppoſe, there was a Vault.

THE Coaches are not drawn by Horſes, Coaches
but by Mules, and inſtead of ſitting on the
Coach-Box, the Coachman rides upon one of
the Mules, this is ſaid to owe its Original
to a Nobleman's loſing his Life by the Evidence of his Coachman, who overheard what
he ſaid in the Coach, as he ſat upon his
Box.

AN Inhabitant of the Town told me, that Garriſon
there were then in this Town ten Regiments
of Soldiers, but ſuch poor Creatures I never
ſaw, moſt of them being ſuperannuated, and
ſcarce able to carry their Arms. Their Fruit,
ſuch as Apples, Grapes, and Pomegranates Proviſions
are very plenty, delicious, and cheap. The
Wine is very ſtrong and good, and ſold by
Retail at about four Shillings *per* Gallon.
The Bread is nothing near ſo good as our
B 4   *Engliſh,*

Englifh, it is four, occafioned by its being raifed with Leaven inftead of Yeft

AT about two Leagues Diftance I faw the *Spanifh Flotilla* lying in the Harbour, near which is a Caftle built in the Sea, in it, I am told, are 100 Pieces of Cannon.

ABOUT five Miles Weft, and directly acrofs the Harbour from *Cadiz*, is a Town Port St called *Port St Mary's*, which was, in the Marys Time of Queen *Anne*, taken by the *Englifh* Forces under the Command of his Grace the Duke of *Ormond*, where the King of *Spain* has a fine Palace, that at a Diftance looks fomething like the Royal Hofpital at *Green-wich*.

Murders IT is very dangerous to be abroad in this frequent Town after it is dark, for during the fhort Time I was here, two Perfons were murder'd paffing the Street by Night, one of them was laid on a Bier all Day in the open Market-Place, to fee if any Body would own him, as well as to gather Money to bury him, when I faw him, his Brains were running out, the Spada having went in at his left Eye. and out at the back Part of his Skull This was an *Englifhman*, but the other was a *Spaniard*, whom I did not fee, but a Perfon that faw him, told me that the Wound was given him in at his Back, and went quite through his Body

Anchor ON the 13th, having taken in frefh Water, from and mended our Rigging, Sails, &c and the Cadiz Wind being fair, we weighed Anchor for

Sea ,

Sea, as foon as we were got out of Sight of
Land we met with Calms, fo that we moved
but flowly.

On the 19th, we had a great Deal of
Thunder, Lightning, and Rain, and in the
Evening we caught a Hawk, altho' we were
a great Way out of Sight of Land.

On the 20th, we had a very hard Gale of
Wind right againft us, we were obliged to
lye to, with the Head of the Sloop to the
Wind, as we had before done, during which
we had a great many very hard Squalls of
Wind, accompanied with dreadful Thunder,
Lightning, and Rain

On the 21ft, the Sloop fprung a Leak
under the Captain's Cabbin, we were afraid
we fhould have been obliged to run back to
fome Port or other to have it ftop'd, but by
the Diligence of the Boatfwain and Carpenter
they found it out, and ftop'd it.

On the 25th, about 4 o' Clock in the
Evening, we made *Palma*, one of the *Canary*
Iflands, and tho' we judged ourfelves to be
fix Leagues from it, the Top feemed to be
above the Clouds.

These *Canary* Iflands are in Number
twelve. " They were difcovered about the
" Year 1420, for King *Henry* III. of *Spain*,
" by *John de Betancour*, a *Frenchman*. In
" them he left *Mafiot de Betancour*, his Ne-
" phew, who conquered *Gomera*, and ex-
" changing them with Prince *Henry* for fome
" Lan:'

Canary Iflands

1730. " Land in *Madera*, he went and lived there
" And whereas the Iflands were twelve in
" Number, and there remained eight not con-
" quered, *viz Grand Canaria, Palma, Gra-*
" *ciofa, Infierno, Alegranca, Santa Clara,*
" *Roche,* and *Lobos,* the Prince fent a Fleet,
" in which were 2500 Foot, and 120
" Lances, commanded by Don *Ferdinand de*
" *Caftro,* who landing there converted many
" Infidels. But upon Complaints made
" from *Spain,* to whom that Conqueft apper-
" tained, it was given over.   Afterwards
" King *Henry* IV of *Portugal* gave them to
" Don *Martin de Ataide,* Count of *Atonguia.*
" And laftly, in the Treaty between *Alphonfo*
" of *Portugal,* and *Ferdinand* of *Caftile,* it
" was agreed that they belonged to *Caftile.*
" The Inhabitants of thefe Iflands were go-
" verned by a certain Number of Perfons,
" they varied in their Worfhip, they ufed
" no Weapons but Sticks and Stones, their
" Cloathing, upwards, was Skins, the lower
" Part, a Covering made of Palm-Leaves
" of divers Colours, they took off their
" Beards with fharp Stones, their Governors
" had the Maidenheads of all **W**omen that
" married, they feafted their Guefts with
" them at their Vifits, their Children fucked
" Goats, and their common Food was
" Wheat and Barley, Milk, Herbs, Mice,
" Lizards, and Snakes * "

THESE Iflands now belong to the King
of *Spain,* and are entirely inhabited by the *Spa-*

---

* *Vid* Difcovery and Conqueft of the *Indies* by the
Portuguefe.

niards,

niards, the whole Race of the Natives being   1730.
by them extirpated. The *Englifh* had formerly a great Trade for Wine here, but now
it is much leffened   In one of thefe Iflands
is the *Pike of Teneriff,* formerly believed to
be the higheft Land in the World, but that
Opinion is now much difputed.

On the 26th, very early in the Morning,   *Ferro*
we had the Glimpfe of another of the *Canary*
Iflands called *Ferro,* it being veiy hazy Weather, we were got within a League of it before we faw it. At Day-light we plainly
faw the Breakers which furround it, and
a great Number of Rocks, particularly one
at the Weft End of it, which, at about two
Leagues Diftance, refembles St *Paul's* Church
at *London*   About Noon we had a ftirk
Calm (which I find are very frequent about
thofe Iflands) and having a very great North-
Weft Swell we were all Hands obliged to tug
at an Oar, and it was no fmall Fatigue to us
to prevent the Sloop's being hove upon the
Rocks   In the Evening there was a pretty
frefh Gale fprung up fair for us, upon which
we made what Hafte we could towards *Gam-*
bia, having for three Days together a grcit
deal of Thunder, Lightning, and Rain.

On the 2d, we crofs'd the *Tropick of Cancer,*   *November.*
and this Morning fpied the Land off *Cape Blan-*   *Cape Blan-*
co, at about fix Leagues diftant. Saw feveral   *co,* on the
Tropick Birds, which are very remarkable, by   Continent
a fingle Feather in their Tails about a Foot   of *Africa*
long. We faw alfo great Numbers of Flying   Tropick
Fifh, fome are as large as fmall Herrings, their   Birds
Fins are in Length and Breadth proportion-   Flying
                                  able   Fifh.

able to Wings, and so long as these Fins continue wet, so long they can fly; I believe
some of them flew half a Mile on a Stretch.

Dolphins, The Dolphin is a great Enemy to these
Fish, and to his chasing them we owe the
Pleasure of seeing them fly, which is in
order to avoid his Jaws. The Dolphin is
reckon'd to swim swifter than any other Fish,
and altho' they fly from him, yet does he
often catch them after they have fled even a
long Way The Dolphins are generally
painted with twisted Tails, but I never saw
how ta- so strait a Fish , we caught several of them,
ken by making an artificial Flying Fish, and
skipping it to and fro very fast, on the Surface of the Water, at the Stern of the
Vessel.

Senega On the 6th, we spied the Land near *Sene-*
River *gal* River, " Which was first discovered about
" the Year 1420, by *Lancelot,* Servant to
" Prince *Henry,* the fifth Son of King *John*
‘ I of *Portugal·* It was by the Natives
" call'd *Ovedee,* but received from *Lancelot*
" the Name of *Sanaga,* because a Black of
‘· that Name was released there. It was then
" believed to be one of the Branches of the
" *Nile,* because they were informed that it
" rose far to the Eastward *."

Cape de The next Day we made *Cape de Verde,*
Verde. particularly the two Paps " This Cape
" was discovered about the Year 1419. by
‘· D*on* *Ferrandez* a *Portugueze,* who valued
" himself upon it not a little, and returned

* *V d* Disc and Conq of *Ind* by the *Portuguese*

                                       " to

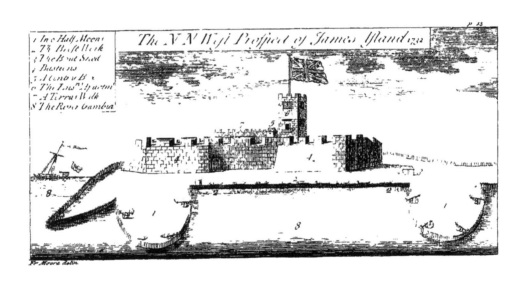

p. 33

The N N West Prospect of James Island 1732

1 In e Half Moon
2 The Baselleek
3 The Bout Shed
4 Bastions
5 A Centry B
6 The Inst Quarter
7 A Terras Walk
8 The Riv Gambia

Fr. Moore delin.

" to *Portugal* highly pleafed with his Dif- 1730.
" covery *."

ON the 9th, we made *Cape St Mary's*, and *Cape St*
the fame Evening came to an Anchor at the *Mary's*
Mouth of the River *Gambia*, at fuch a Dif- *The River*
ance as not to diftinguifh well the Shore, *Gambia.*
but the next Day, as we failed up the River
near the Shore, the Country look'd beautiful,
being for the moft Part woody, but between
the Woods pleafant green Rice Grounds,
which after the Rice is cut are ftocked with
Cattle　About Four in the Afternoon we
paffed by *Charles Ifland*, which lies on the
North Side of the River, very clofe to the
Shore of the Kingdom of *Barrah*.　About
Eight at Night, being within a Mile of
James Fort, we had from thence a Shot fir'd
over us, to bring the Sloop to, we came to
an Anchor, and the Captain went afhore
with his Letters, and returned about Midnight.

ON the 11th, at Sunrifing, we faluted the
Fort with feven Guns, and had five returned
After which, we Paffengers went a-fhore, *The Paf-*
viz. Meff. *Charles Houghton* and *John Hamil-* *fengers*
'on, Factors, *Philip Galand* and myfelf, *land*
Writers.　When we landed, the Soldiers
were drawn up before the Gate, a File of
which conducted us to the Governor　In the
Evening, one of the Soldiers died, by Name
John Skinner, having been ill a long while;
he had been about three Years in the River
Gambia, but before he came over thither had

* *Ibidem*

ruin'd

1730　ruin'd his Conſtitution in the *Eaſt* and *Weſt*
Indies.

James Iſland JAMES ISLAND lies almoſt in the
Middle of the River *Gambia*, which is here
at leaſt, ſeven Miles wide　It belongs to the
Royal African Company of *England*, who pay
a ſmall annual Tribute to the King of *Barrah* for the ſame　It lies three Miles from
the neareſt Shore, and about ten Leagues
from the River's Mouth　At low Water it
is about three Quarters of a Mile in Circumference, upon which there is a ſquare Fort of
The Fort Stone regularly built, with four Baſtions,
upon each are ſeven Cannons well mounted,
which command the River all round　Under
the Walls of the Fort, facing towards the
Sea, are two round Batteries, on each of
them are four large Cannons, well mounted,
which carry Shot of 24 Pounds weight, and
between thoſe are nine ſmall Guns mounted
for Salutes

In the Fort are ſome very good Apartments, in which the Governor, chief Merchants, Factors, Writers, and Enſign lye,
and under ſome of theſe Apartments are very
good Storehouſes.

The Garriſon ONE Officer, one Serjeant, two Corporals, one Gunner and Gunner's Mate, and
thirty Soldiers, are by the Eſtabliſhment the
Sickneſs Garriſon of this Fort　But Sickneſs, occaoccaſion'd ſion'd chiefly by the exceſſive drinking of diby Drinking ſtilled Liquors, often reduces it to a very
weak Condition, till ſuch Time as Recruits
can be raiſed in *England,* and by the Company
ny

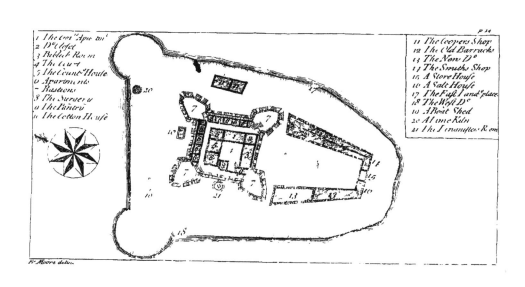

1 The Gov.ᵗ Apa.ᵗᵐ
2 Dᵗᵒ Closet
3 Publick Room
4 The Court
5 The Council House
6 Apartments
7 Bastions
8 The Nursery
9 The Pantry
11 The Cotton House

11 The Coopers Shop
12 The Old Barracks
13 The New Dᵒ
14 The Smiths Shop
15 A Store House
16 A Sale House
17 The Fish Landing place
18 The West Dᵒ
19 A Boat Shed
20 A Lime Kiln
21 The Launisters Room

Fᵗ Moore delin.

ny fent over hither. The Soldiers and Tradefmen, and other Servants, lye out of the Fort,
in Barracks built, as the Fort is, with Stone
and Mortar The Whole is fortified with
Palifades, and furrounded with the River, that
makes an excellent Ditch, being (as I faid
before) three Miles wide in the narroweft
Part There are alfo other Barracks built
oppofite to thofe of the Soldiers, for the Ufe
of the Company's Caftle Slaves and Black
Servants · Under them there are Storehoufes,
and under thofe of the Soldiers are Slave-
houfes.

In the Day-time there are three Sentries,
one at the Gate of the Fort, one at the Door
of the Publick Room, and another walking
round the Fort, to fee what Boats come and
go to and from the Ifland, and to report the
fame to the Governour Thefe are duly re-
lieved every two Hours Towards the Evening there is a Sentinel pofted on the Baftions
within the Walls of the Fort, whofe Bufinefs
it is to challenge all Boats or Canoes that
come near the Ifland , and if they refufe to
anfwer at three times challenging, he fires
his Mufquet at them, and by that means a-
larms the Fort At Night when the Gates
are lock'd (which is whenever the Governour
pleafes to order it) two Sentinels patroll
without the Fort to take care that the Slaves
do not rife or mutiny, and that no Boats
come or go from the Ifland without Permif-
fion Every now and then they cry, *All is
well*, if they find it fo , but if they find it
otherwife, they fire their Mufquets to alarm
the Fort.

1730
James
Fort

Keeps the
Right of
Trading
for *Eng-*
land

French ex-
clufive
Trade

T H E Fort is called *James* Fort, and is the chief Settlement that the Royal *African* Company have in this River. This Fort keeps the Right of Trading to the River *Gambia* for the Company, and confequently for the Subjects of *England*. Were this once in the Hands of the *French*, who, I am very well inform'd, in the Year 1719 would have purchas'd it for the *Mississippi* Company, could they have obtained Leave for the fo doing, they would then exclude not only the Company, but all other Nations, from Trading hither, as they already have from the Coaft of *Senegal*, where they maintain an exclusive Trade by Force, and take all Ships This they juftify by two Forts, which they poffefs on the Coaft of *Senegal* The Royal *African* Company of *England* had formerly an exclufive Trade here, but for the Encouragement of the Plantations in *America*, the Parliament thinking fit that all his Majefty's People fhould enjoy the Liberty of Trade to *Africa*, for the Company's Right, and in Equity to them, who are at the Charge of maintaining the Forts for the Benefit of others, did firft grant them Ten *per Cent.* upon all feparate Ships that fhould Trade to the Coaft, and fince that ceafed, have for fome Years paft granted to the Company 10,000 *l* each Year for the Maintenance of their Forts. This is a very advantageous Bargain to the Nation, for as thefe Forts are neceffary to be kept up as Marks of the *British* Poffeffions in *Africa*, if the Company did not maintain them, the Crown would be obliged to do it, or let them fall into the Hands of Foreigners, and

The North Prospect of James Island 1732

it would coft the King to maintain them with
the Garrifons and Governors under his Majefty's Commiffions, three or four times as
much as it does now. By this Agreement,
befides a free Trade, the feparate Traders
have had their Ships often affifted, their Cargoes taken off at good Prices, and have
reaped feveral other Advantages, as well as
the Publick · And the Increafe of Duties,
which arifes from the Increafe that thefe
Advantages have made in the *American*, as
well as the *African* Trade, more than makes
up to the Publick, the Money that is given
by them for this Purpofe

Advantages reap'd by feparate Traders.

1730

BESIDES the Fort, there are feveral Factories
up the River fettl'd for the Conveniency of Trade.
They are all under the Direction of the Governor
and chief Merchants at this Fort, to whom
the Factors remit all their Trade For this
Purpofe the Company have here three or four
Sloops of about thirty Tons each, and about
the fame Number of Long Boats, fome of
them are conftantly employed in fetching
Provifions and Water from the Main for the
Ule of the Garrifon, and the reft are employed in carrying Goods up to the Factories,
and bringing from them Slaves, Elephants
Teeth, Wax, or whatever Trade they have
by them, down to *James* Fort, from whence
moft of it, except Slaves, is fent home by
the Governor and chief Merchants to the
Company in *England* Thefe Factories are
fupplied with Factors fent over by the Company, or, for want of them, the moft able
Writers, who have given Security to the
Company for their Honefty, which is gene-

C   rally

rally done by two Bondfmen for the Sum oi 1000*l* befides the Perfon's own Bond for the like Sum   Notwithftanding this giving Secu rity, feveral of the Company's Factors have been fo bafe as to embezzle their Goods, an. fquander them away to the Amount of very large Sums , yet have they met with fuci Indulgence from the Court of *Chancery*, tha I have not known one Inftance of their eve being able to oblige the Bondfmen to pay the Penalties of their Bonds   For the Factor and Chiefs, when the Company has begui to call them to Account on their Bonds a Common Law, have thrown the Difpute into *Chancery* , and if the Perfons with whom they tranfacted are not *Chriftians*, Oaths canno be adminiftred, nor Evidence given by them for want of which the Company has bee defrauded with Impunity , and, unlefs the had more Power over their Servants, the will run great Rifque of their ftill fufferin confiderably   The Governors and Chief always take care to fupply their Factories u the River with Goods in the dry Seafon, fo it is impoffible to do it after the Rains ar fet in, by reafon of the River running cor tinually down with a rapid Stream for fom Months together.

    I shall give a fhort Defcription of th River, and begin from the Point of *Barral* which forms the Mouth, and fo up the Nor thern fide to *Fatatenda*, the fartheft Plac that I have been, and which is 500 Mile from the Sea , then I fhall begin at *Ca* *St Mary's*, and defcribe the South-fide of th River to over-againft *Fatatenda*

Defcription of the North Side of the 1730.
River GAMBIA, *from the Mouth*
to FATATENDA, *being* 220 *Leagues.*

THE Mouth of the River *Gambia* lies
in 13' 20° North Latitude, and in 15'
20° Weft Longitude   It is form'd on the
North Side by *Barrah* Point, and on the South
by *Banyon* Point, about four Miles over But
fome think that it reaches lower, and that
it is form'd by the Broken iflands on the
North, and *Cape St Mary's* on the South ,
and I am apt to think, that the latter Opinion is the trueft   *Barrah* Point is in the
Kingdom of *Barrah,* the King is by Race a
Mundingo, and Tributary to him of *Barfally.* *Barfally.*
In this Country the Royal *African* Company
of *England* have two Factories, one at *Gillyfree*
over-againft *James* Fort, the other at *Colar,*
which is up a River of the fame Name, that
empties itfelf through one Mouth into the
Gambia, about eight Leagues above *James*
Ifland   In this Kingdom, about fix Leagues
from the Sea, is *Charles Ifland,* lying within *Charles*
a Mufquet-Shot of *Barrah* Shore, on which *Ifland.*
Ifland there formerly was a Fort, but now it
is gone to ruin   There are alfo two Shoals
of Sand and Rocks in the River, on the Coaft
of this Kingdom , that is to fay, one at *Le-*
main Point, the other at *Seaca* Point ; the
former lying about fix Miles below *James*
Fort, the latter the fame Diftance above
it   *James Ifland* lies oppofite to *Gillyfree,*
from which a Sfut of Sand and Rocks

runs out a good Way to the N N. W vulgarly call'd the Company's *Spit*. Several Ships, particularly fome from *Liverpool*, have run aground upon it, but by the Company's Affiftance have got off again without any Damage or Charge, and tho' fome muft inevitably have been loft, if not affifted by the Fort, yet have the Mafters refufed figning an Acknowledgment of their having been fo affifted, giving no other Reafon for it, than that their Owners had not order'd them to fign any fuch thing Since they were to do nothing without Orders, we defired to know whether their Owners order'd them to run aground upon the *Spit?*

Cuftoms paid in *Barrah*   T o this King the Separate Traders generally pay Cuftom, which amounts to about One hundred and twenty Barrs, it being a Country of good Trade, efpecially when the Merchants come down with their Slaves, which happens according to the Numbers they bring, which are fometimes fo large, that the Company's Factories up the River are not able to purchafe them all , and very often when they can

Reafons for the Merchants coming fo low down the River fell them all up the River, yet if they hear that there are a good many Ships in *Barrah*, they will bring their Slaves down to them, having found by Experience that by White Mens outbidding one another, they have fometimes had very large Prices for their Slaves, whereas had they not been fo eager to buy from, and out bid one another, they might have bought the Slaves for half the Money they paid for them.—Unlefs the feparate Traders pay their Cuftom here, the King will not allow them to have either Wood or Water in his Country,

try , for which Reafon only a pretty many　1730.
Mafters of Ships chufe to pay the King's Cuftom, and yet do not ftay to trade here, but
proceed directly up the River　This Country
reaches about 20 Leagues along the River,　*Barrah,*20
and then begins the Kingdom of *Badibu*　In　Leagues
it, and over-againft *Tancrow*, all in *Caen*, which
lies on the South-fide of the River, is an
Ifland, parted only by a fmall Gut of Water
from the Main Land of *Badibu*　This Ifland
formerly ufed to fupply the Fort with Stones;
but in the Year 1733, Mr *Richard Hull*, the
Royal *African* Company's chief Merchant at
James Fort, found Plenty of Stones much
nearer the Fort on another fmall Ifland, till
then not perceived to be an Ifland.　The King
of *Badibu* is a *Mundingo*, and his Country ex-　*Badibu,*20
tends about 20 Leagues.　Leagues

THE next is called *Sanjally*, a petty Kingdom, but not tributary to any other　This
King is likewife a *Mundingo*, whofe Dominions extend about fourteen Leagues along　*Sanjally,*
the River Side , and then begins *Barfally*,　14 Leag
which is a very noted Country,　governed by
a King of the *Jolloiff* Nation, of whom
more will be faid.　In this Country is the
Company's chief Factory of *Joar*,　clofe to
the Town of that Name,　and about two
Miles from the River, the Road to which
lies one Mile over a fine pleafant Savannah,
the other Mile along a narrow Creek.　The
Separate Traders generally come up hither
to trade at *Rumbo*'s Port,　which is about
three Miles from *Joar*, and the fame Diftance
from *Cower*, where is the greateft Refort of
People, and the moft Trade of any Town in
　the

1730   the whole River , for it is to this Place that
the Merchants always bring their Slaves, pro
vided that they are not in great Haste to return
home, or cannot meet with a very good Mar
ket for them before they come down so low
At *Jou* the Water of the River is always
fresh

Barsally   THE Country of *Barsally* extends itself
about fifteen Leagues along the River, and
then begins the Kingdom of *Yany*, by the
Nubian Geographer called *Ghana*, which is
large and wide, and divided into two Parts,
one called the Upper, and the other the
Lower *Yany*, each governed by a distinct
King, one a *Jelloiff*, the other a *Mundingo*
In the Lower *Yany* the Company have a small
Factory at *Yanmerew*, kept by a *Portuguese*,
whose only Business is to buy Corn and Rice
for the Use of *James* Fort. Upon the Shore
of this Kingdom lies *Bird Island*, about
twelve Leagues above *Joar*, upon which
there is scarce a Tree, but it seems to be
marshy Ground About thirty Leagues
above this Island, near the same Shore, are
several other Islands, called *Sappo*, which are
very numerous, and some of them very
large, but not inhabited , there is one above
them called *Lemain Island*, about four Leagues
in Length, on which are great Numbers of
wild Beasts and Palm Trees, which induces
the Natives to go often to them, to hunt,
and draw Palm Wine About six or seven
Tides above *Yanmerew*, is the River *Sami*,
which rises a vast Way in land, it abounds
in Crocodiles, and is said to part Lower
from Upper *Yany*, it enters the *Gambia* be
tween

tween *Brucoe* and *Yamyamacunda*   Thefe two   1730.
Kingdoms reach about eighty Leagues along *Yany,* 80
the River, and the next to them is *Woolly,*   Leagues
through which Country the Merchants are
obliged to pafs on their Way down to *Cower.*
Woolly extends itfelf a long Way up the *Woolly,* 7
River, but at about feven Leagues from *Yany* Leagues.
is the Company's Factory of *Fatatenda,*
where the River is as wide as the *Thames* at
London Bridge, and to which Sloops of forty
Tons come up with Cargoes, and the Tides
rife three or four Foot high, This is about
500 Miles on the North Side the River
Gambia. I fhall not pretend to give an
Account of Places higher up, on this Side
of the River, becaufe I never was above *Fa-*
tatenda, therefore I fhall return to the Sea,
and briefly run over the Countries on the
South Side

Defcription of the South Side of the River
GAMBIA, *from the Sea, to over-*
againft FATATENDA, *being* 500 *Miles.*

THE Kingdom of *Cumbo* extends itfelf *Cumbo,* 11
about eleven Leagues from *Cape St Ma-* Leagues.
ry's, which is at the Entrance of the River
Gambia, to a Place called *Cabata River,* noted
for Plenty of Goats, Fowls, and Cattle.
There's a common Word in the *Mundingo*
Language, fignifying an Ox, Bull, or Cow,
which they call *Neefa,* and they diftinguifh
Cows from Bulls by the Addition of the
Male or Female Gender, as *Neefa Moofa,* a
C 4   Cow,

1730 Cow, *Neesa Kea*, a Bull, the *English* translating this Word with the Female Gender, call
all Cattle Cows, tho' there is sometimes but
one Cow in ten Head. In this Country the
Company have a small Factory, to purchase
Provisions for the Support of the Garrison
at *James* Fort.

*Fonia, 7
Leag-* THE next Country is *Fonia*, it begins
where *Cabata* River falls into the *Gamb i*,
and reaches to the River *Vintain*, being about
seven Leagues along the River Side, but inland it is very large, and governed two
Emperors, who are of a *Banyoon R...* n
is a Sort of *Floops*, and have each their distinct Districts. And now I speak of Emperors, I must observe that when these Countries
were first discovered, they were then large,
and worthy of that Title, but tho' they are
now much lessened, not only in Territories,
but by having sold into Slavery infinite Num
bers of their Subjects, yet do they still retain their ancient Grandeur of Titles, in being called Kings and Emperors.

*Vintain
River* BETWEEN *Fonia* and *Caen*, lies the River
Vintain, whose Mouth is about a Mile over,
this River is navigable a great many Leagues
About three Leagues from the Mouth of it is
the Town of *Vintain*, situate in *Fonia*, and
above that, on the same Side the River, is
Geregia, at each of which Places the Com-
pany have a Factory, chiefly for Elephants
Teeth, Bees-wax, and other dry Goods.

OVER-AGAINST *James* Fort, near the
Main, on the South Side the River is an
Island,

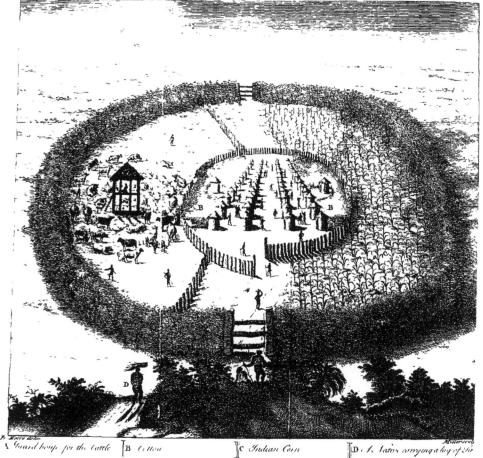

A Guard house for the Cattle   B Cotton   C Indian Corn   D A Native carrying a log of Fir

Iſland, lately diſcovered to be ſuch, called *1730*
Cabuſheer Iſland, ſeparated from the Main *Cabuſheer*
only by a large Brook　This Iſland produces *Iſand*
great Quantities of Iron-Stone, with which
it now ſupplies the Fort, whereas before the
Year 1734 we were obliged to ſend for Stones
from an Iſland beforementioned over againſt
Tancrowall.

THE next Country to *Fonta* is *Caen*, go-*Caen*, 23
erned both by an Emperor and a King, Leagues
both *Mundingoes*, who have their different
Revenues ariſing from the Cuſtoms and other
Things.　In this Country the Company have
a Factory ſettled at *Tancrowall*, which is a
large Town cloſe to the Water-ſide.　Above
that Town, about three Leagues, are a Parcel of Rocks, at a Place called *Tendctas*, lying a good Way out from the Shore, which
are dry at Low-Water.　This Country extends about twenty three Leagues along the
River-Side.

THE next above *Caen*, is *Jagra*, famous *Jagra*, 12
for laborious People, by which Means it Leagues.
abounds with Corn and Rice　In this Country is *Elephants Iſland*, which is four or five
Miles long, full of Trees, and withal marſhy
This Kingdom extends itſelf about twelve
Leagues, and then begins the Country of
Yamina, which abounds chiefly in Corn and *Yamina*, 14
Fowls　In it is a large Iſland, which is very League
pleaſant, likewiſe a ſmall Iſland, almoſt in
the Middle of the *Gambia*, called *Sea-Horſe
Iſland*, full of Trees, and marſhy Ground, a-
bounding in Sea-Horſes, from whence I believe it takes its Name　This Country ex-
tends

1730.
Eropina,
14 Leag.
Jemarrow,
32 Leag.

tends about fourteen Leagues; and then is *Eropina*, a petty Kingdom, extending about 14 Leagues along the River Side. After which begins *Jemarrow*, governed by an Emperor, who is a *Mundingo*; here the Company have a Settlement near a large Town called *Brucoe*, which is inhabited by People of the *Mundingo* Race, but strict Followers of *Mahomet*. About half a Mile below this Town is a Ledge of Rocks dry at Low-Water, which reaches from the Northern Shore $\frac{5}{6}$ of the Way over the River, and leaves so narrow a Channel under the South Shore, that it is very dangerous for large Ships to pass it, and our Sloops are obliged to take the Opportunity of slack Water to go through this Place, which is called *Pholey's Pass*. In the same

Pholey's Pass.

Empire, about nine Miles above *Pholey's Pass*, are a great many Rocks, near a Town called *Dubocunda*, which reach from the South Side $\frac{2}{3}$ a-cross the River; and about three Miles above this, is another Ledge of Rocks, dry at low Water, but there is a deep Channel on the North Side. This Country runs about thirty two Leagues along the River; and then begins *Tomany*, which is a very large Country, consisting of more

Tomany, 26 Leagues

Towns than any other which I know on the whole River. The Company have a Factory at a small Town called *Yamyamacunda*, which makes a considerable Trade in dry Goods, provided it is well supplied: A little below the Town, in the Middle of the River, are some Rocks, but never dry; and over-against the Factory, on the North Side the River, about half a Mile from it, is a standing Lake, about two Miles long, which

abound

abounds in Fiſh This Country extends up 1730.
the River Side about twenty ſix Leagues,
and is governed by a *Mundingo*, by Name
Hume Badgy, of whom more will be ſaid
hereafter.

ABOVE *Tomany* begins *Cantore*, in which,
on the South Side of the River, and about
ſix Miles below *Fatatenda*, is a Town called
Colar, ſix Miles beyond which is the fartheſt
I have been; and it being little known to
white People, I ſhall conclude with ſaying
that *Colar* in *Cantore* (for there is another *Colar* in *Barrah*) is, I believe, about 500
Miles from *Cape St Mary*'s, the South Part
of the Entrance into *Gambia* River.

HAVING given an Account of the River
as far as I can, by my own Knowledge, the
Curious, I believe, will be deſirous to know
the Heads of the River, and the more inland
Parts of *Africa* I therefore ſhall, for their
Satisfaction, give what I could learn of it
from the Accounts of the Natives, which I
cannot affirm as certain, but ſhall add the
Authority on which I found my Relations

THE Company have been very deſirous to
know how far the *Gambia* was navigable, and
to open new Trades up that River. They
ſent over ſmall Sloops in Frames for Diſcoveries, and Mr *Thomas Harriſon*, one of our
chief Merchants, went up the River, in a
Sloop, for that Purpoſe; and his Return
from that Voyage is herein mentioned, on
the 10th Day of *June*. 1732. Upon Examination

mination of this Matter, I found that Mr *Harryon* himself did not go far above *Patenda*, but remained in the Sloop, and sent up a Boat on Discovery, with Mr *Jo Leith*, who went about twenty Leagues, and then beginning to want Provisions, and undergoing several Hardships, and also discovering some Rocks that seemed to cross the River, had not Time or Conveniency to search whether there was any Passage among the Rocks But by the Tradition of the Country People, the River is passable a great Way farther up, to some large Lakes Others believe that the *Senegal*, which falls into the Sea on the North, and the *Cassamansa*, which falls into the Sea on the South, rise both out of the same Lakes as the *Gambia* doth, and that those Lakes are supplied by a Branch which separates from the *Nile*, after it leaves the Mountains, and the Kingdom of the Abissines *Herodotus*, and long since him, the Nubian Geographer, both say, that a Branch of the Nile runs westward, and after a very long Course falls into the *Atlantick* Ocean. What makes this seem improbable, is, the great Distance from *Æthiopia* to the Mouth of the *Gambia*, but if we consider that the Mountains of *Atlas* run from *Nubia*, East and West, to Cape *Blanco*, which hinders any River, rising in the South of *Africa*, from falling into the *Mediterranean* Sea, it will be less difficult to believe that if a Branch of the *Nile* does divide to the Westward, it must fall into the Ocean by the *Gambia*, *Senegal*, and *Sierra Leone*, being augmented it its Passage by all the Waters which fall to the South of Mount *Atlas*. This is certain, that the Sea-Horse, the

the Crocodile, and other Animals for which 1730.
the *Nile* is famous, abound in the *Gambia*
It also overflows at a certain stated Seafon.
But thefe being Matters of Curiofity, we
muft leave to the Learned to difpute, and to
fome future Difcoverers, by Experience, to
clear up

THESE different Kingdoms upon the Banks Inhabi-
of the *Gambia* are inhabited by feveral Races tants of
of People, *Mundingoes*, *Jolloiffs*, *Pholeys*, *Floops* *Gambia*
and *Portuguefe* The moft numerous are call'd *Mundin-*
Mundingoes, as is likewife the Country where *goes.*
they inhabit They are generally of a black
Colour, and well fet. When this Country
was conquer'd by the *Portuguefe*, which was
about the Year 1420, fome of that Nation
fettled in it, who have cohabited with the
Mundingoes, till they are now very near as
Black as they are , but as they ftill retain a Their
fort of a baftard *Portugi efe* Language call'd Language.
Creole, and as they chriften and marry by the
Help of a Prieft fent yearly over hither from
S *Jago*, one of the *Cape de Verd* Iflands,
they reckon themfelves ftill as well as if they
were actually White, and nothing angers them
more than to call them *Negroes*, that being a
Term they ufe only for Slaves, and their not
underftanding the true Meaning of the Word
is the Reafon of their being fo very much
affronted at it.

ON the North Side of the River *Gambia*, *Jolloiffs*
and from thence in-land, are a People call'd
Jolloiffs, whofe Country is vaftly large, and
extends even to the River *Seregal* Thefe
People are much blacker, and much hand-
fomer

1730 fomer than the *Mundingoes*, for they have not
the broad Nofes and thick Lips peculiar to
the *Mundingoes* and *Iloes* In fhort, all the
Countries hereabout and I have feen vaft
Numbers of People from each) cannot com.

Exceeding
Black up to the *Jr* for Blacknefs of Ski
and Beauty of Features

Pholeys In every Kingdom and Country on each
Side of the River there are fome People of
a tawny Colour, call'd *Pholeys*, much like the
Arabs, which Language they moft of them
fpeak, being to them as the *Latin* is in Eu
rope, for it is taught in Schools, and their
Law, the *Alcoran* is in that Language They
are more generally learned in the *A* ,
than the People of *Europe* are in *Latin*, for
they can moft of them fpeak it, tho' they
have a vulgar Tongue befides, call'd *Pra*
They live in Hoards or Clans, build Towns,
and are not fubject to any Kings of the Coun
try, tho' they live in their Terr tories ; for
if they are ill-treated in one Nation, they
break up their Towns, and remove to another.
They have Chiefs of their own, who rule
with fo much Moderation, that every Act of
Government feems rather an Act of the Peo
ple than of one Man This Form of Go
vernment goes on eafily, becaufe the People
are of a good and quiet Difpofition, and fo
well inftructed in what is juft and right, that
a Man who does ill, is the Abomination of
all, and none will fupport him againft the
Chief

In thefe Countries the Natives are not ava
ricious of Lands , they defire no more than
what

what they ufe, and as they do not plough 1730
with Horfes or Cattle, they can ufe but very
little, therefore the Kings are willing to give
the *Pholeys* Leave to cultivate Lands, and live
in their Countries   They plant near their
Houfes Tobacco, and all round their Towns
they open for Cotton, which they fence in
together, beyond that are their Corn-Fields,
of which they raife the four Kinds ufual all
over this Country ; that is to fay, *Indian*
Corn, or Maife, which grows in great Pods,
and is the Food of the Natives of *America*,
as well as *Africa*, therefore is fo well known
as not to need being defcribed   Befides which
they have Rice, and the larger and the leffer
Guinea Corn   In *Gambia* is no Wheat, Barley,
Rye, Oats, nor any other *European* Grain , but
there is a kind of Pulfe between the Kidney-Bean
and Pea, and Potatoes and Yams   The *Indian* *Indian*
Corn they fet in Holes, three or four together, Corn.
about four Foot diftant from each other, fo that
it grows like Hops. This fhoots to about eight
or ten Foot high, being a large Cane, with
the Ears growing out of the Sides   The Rice, Rice
which is the fecond Kind, and efteem'd their
choiceft Food, they fet in Rills, as we do
Peafe, it grows in wet Grounds, the Ears Larger
like Oats The larger *Guinea* Corn is round, and *Guinea*
about the Size of the fmalleft Peafe   They Corn
fow it by Hand, as we do Wheat and Barley ;
it grows to nine or ten Foot high, upon a
fmall Reed, the Grain is at the Top in a large
Tuft   The leffer *Guinea* Corn is call'd by the
Portuguefe Manfaroke   This likewife is fowed Manfa-
by Hand, and fhoots to the fame Height, roke
upon a large Reed, on the Top of which the
Corn grows, on a Head like a Bulrufh   The
Grain

1730 Grain itfelf is very fmall, and like Canary-Seed in Shape, only larger ——Thefe are all the Bread-Kind that are ufed in *Gambia* , and indeed the Natives make no Bread, but eat the Flower of the various Grains, as Thickners to Liquids. The *Indian* Corn they moftly ufe when green, parching it in the Ear upon

The Rice Coals, and then it eats like green Peafe They boil their Rice chiefly as the *Turks* do. They always by beating in wooden Mortars make Flower of the *Guinea* Corn and Manfaroke, as they do fometimes of the two former Species The Natives never bake Cakes or Bread for themfelves (as I faid before) but thofe of their Women accuftomed to *Europeans* have learnt to do both

I HAVE chofe to mention their various Kinds of Grain, now that I am fpeaking of the *Pholeys*, becaufe they are the greateft Planters in the Country, tho' they are Strangers

Manners of the *Pholeys* in it They are very induftrious and frugal, and raife much more Corn and Cotton than they confume, which they fell at reafonable Rates, and are very hofpitable and kind to all , fo that to have a *Pholey* Town in the Neighbourhood, is by the Natives reckon'd a Bleffing And their Behaviour has gain'd them fuch general Reputation, that it is u-niverfally look'd upon as infamous to violate the Laws of Hofpitality towards them As

Humani-ty their Humanity extends to all, they are doubly kind to People of their own Race, infomuch that if they know of one of them being made a Slave, all the *Pholeys* will redeem him And as they have plenty of Food, they never fuffer any of their own Nation to want, but

but fupport the Old, the Blind, and Lame,
equally with the others, and, as far as their
Ability goes, affift the Wants of the *Mundin-*
goes, great Numbers of whom they have maintain'd in Famines. They are very rarely
angry, and I never heard them abufe each Temper.
other, yet this Mildnefs does not proceed
from want of Courage, for they are as brave
as any People of *Africa*, and the *Jolloiffs*,
nay even the King of *Barfally* does not dare
to meddle with them. They ufe their Arms
very dexteroufly, which are the Lance, a Sagay,
Bows and Arrows, fhort Cutlaffes, which
tney call Fongs, and Guns upon Occafion.
They fettle commonly near fome *Mundingo*
Town, there being fcarce one of any Note
or Bignefs (efpecially up the River) but what
there is another of thefe *Pholeys* not far from
it They are ftrict *Mahometans*; none of them Religion
(unlefs here and there one) will drink Brandy, or any thing ftronger than Water and
Sugar.

THEY breed Cattle, and are very dexte- Cattle.
rous at managing them, fo that the *Mundin-*
goe leave theirs to their Care, the whole Herd
belonging to Towns feed all the Day in the
Savannahs, and after the Crop is off, in the
Rice Grounds They are watched by fome
Herdfmen, who prevent their going into the
Corn, or running into the Woods They
have a Place near each Town for the Cattle,
in the Middle of which they raife a Stage
about eight Foot high from the Ground,
and eight or ten Foot wide To this is a
Ladder, and over it a Roof of Thatch, with
the Sides all open They drive great Numbers

1730 bers of Stakes in Rings round the Stage and every Night they duly bring up the Cattle, who are so tame, and well accustom'd to it, that they come up with Ease, each Beast is tied separate to a Stake, with a strong Rope, which they make of the Barks of Trees

Milk After the Cattle are tied, they milk the Cow, and four or five Men stay upon the Stage all Night, with their Arms, to guard them from the Lyons, and other wild Beasts. The Calves they wean from the Cows, and keep in a com

Breed mon Penn, which is made with so strong and high a Fence round it, that no wild Beast can pass it In the Morning they again milk the Cows, and then let them go into the Savan nahs, as usual

THEY are great Huntsmen They kill Lyons, Tygers, and other wild Beasts, and

Manner of often go twenty or thirty in a Company to Hunting hunt Elephants, whose Teeth they sell, and whose Flesh they smoak, dry and eat, keeping it several Months together. The Elephants

Elephants (as they say) generally go an hundred or two mischiev- hundred in a Drove, and do great Mischief, ous not only to the small Trees, which they pull up by the Roots with their Trunks, but likewise to the Corn To prevent which, the Na tives, on Notice or Suspicion of their coming, make Fires all round their Corn to keep them out, for if they get once in, they will with their broad Feet trample it down for perhaps half a Mile together.

WERE it not for these *Pholeys*, I believe, many of the *Mundingoes* would want Sustenance, they selling them a great deal of Corn

They

They are almoſt the only People who make
Butter, which they barter up the River for
Salt They are very particular in their Dreſs,
and never wear any other than white Cotton
Clothes, which they make themſelves. They
are always very clean, eſpecially the Women,
who keep their Houſes very ſweet, and which
are built in a very regular Method, a good
Way diſtant from each other, to avoid Fire,
forming very good Streets and Paſſages, a
thing which the *Mundingoes* do not regard.
[I have given a Draught of a *Pholey* Town,
with their Cotton and Cattle Ground, moſt
of their Towns are upon the ſame Model]
They are great Admirers of large white, and
large yellow Beads, which laſt are call'd by
their own Name, *viz Pholey Beads.*

THESE are almoſt the only People high
up the River, of whom Beaſts can be purcha-
ſed We uſed to purchaſe a Cow for an Iron
Barr, but of late ſome of the Maſters of the
Sloops in this River have raiſed the Prices, ſo
that now we are obliged to give ſometimes
two Iron Barrs for one Beaſt, it being a very
hard Matter to make them lower the Prices
again, when once they have had an Opportunity of raiſing them They are very Super-
ſtitious in ſome Things, one of which is, that
if they know any Body boils the ſweet Milk
which they buy of them, they will not for
any Conſideration ſell that Perſon any more,
becauſe they ſay, that boiling the Milk makes
the Cows dry

ON the South-ſide of this River, over-
againſt *James* Fort, in the Empire of *Fonia,*

D 2   and

1730

Their
Dreſs.

Buildings

Odd Noti-
ons

Fonia

Foops

and but a little Way inland are a Sort of People call'd *Foops*, who are in a manner wild. They border close to the *Mundingoes*, and are bitter Enemies to each other. Their Country is of a vast Extent, but they have

Have no King

no King among them, each of their Towns being fortified with Sticks drove all round, and filled up with Clay. They are independant of each other, and under the Government of no one Chief, notwithstanding which, they unite so firmly, that all the Force of the

Strict Union

Mandingoes (tho' so very numerous) cannot get the better of them. In the Year 1721, the Governour of *James* Fort sent a Sloop and a Shallop on a trading Voyage to *Cacheo*, a Settlement belonging to the *Portugueze*, lying about twenty Leagues to the Southward of the Mouth of this River, and in their Way thither in going up a River the Shallop ran aground on a Place belonging to the *Foos*

A Skirmish

who came down in great Numbers to the Water-side, and attack'd the Shallop with Bows and Arrows, which being well-mann'd with about five white armed Men, and seven Castle-Slaves, who on Occasion serve as Soldiers, they fought bravely, and kill'd a great many of the *Floops* In about half an Hour's time the Water rising, and the Shallop being afloat, it gave the *Floops* the slip, and left them to bury their Dead. When the Sloop return'd to *James* Fort, the Governor gave each of the black People a new Suit of Clothes. These *Floops* have the Character never to forgive, or let the least Injury go unrevenged,

Their Gratitude

but then, to make amends, the least good Office done them is always repaid by them with a grateful Acknowledgment.

GAMBIA River is navigable for Sloops
above 200 Leagues, the Tides reaching so
far from the Mouth of it The Sides of the
River are for the most part flat and woody,
for about a quarter of a Mile inland, in some
Places not so much, and within that are pleasant open Grounds, which they use for their
Rice, and in the dry Season it serves the Cattle for Pasture Inland it is generally very
woody, but near the Towns there is always a
good large Space of clear'd Ground for Corn.
The Soil is mostly Sand, with some Clay, Soil on the
and a great deal of rocky Ground.   Near the Banks of
Sea, and the lower part of the River, are no the River
Hills to be seen , but high up the River are *Gambia*
some lofty Mountains, from the Tops of
which are pleasant Prospects   The Hills are
of Iron-Stone , and tho' they are sometimes
little else but a continued hard Rock, yet are
they full of Trees   In every Kingdom there Lords of
are several Lords of Soils, commonly call'd the Soil
Kings of the Towns where they dwell   It is
their Property to have all the Palm-Trees
and Ciboa-Trees, insomuch that no one durst
cut any Leaves, or draw any Wine from them,
without their previous Knowledge and Consent.
The Men who have the Liberty of drawing
Wine, give two Days Produce in a Week to
the Lord of the Soil, as an Acknowledgment;
and White Men are obliged to make a small
Present to them, before they can have liberty
to cut Ciboa Leaves or Grass to cover a
House   And here perhaps it will not be improper to mention the Palm-Tree, a fine strait Palm-
Tree, that grows to a prodigious Height, Tree
out of it the Natives extract a sort of white
Liquor like Whey, call'd Palm-Wine, by

1730
Palm-
Wine

How
made

making an Incifion at the Top of the Trunk
of the Tree, to which they apply Gourd
Bottles , into them runs the Liquor by the
means of a Pipe, which they make of Leave.
This Wine is very pleafant to drink as foon as
drawn, being extraordinary fweet, but 's ap
to purge very much In a Day or two it fer
ments, grows hard and ftrong, like *Rh*
Wine, at which time the Natives drink it in
abundance, it being then no way prejudicial
to the Health It is very furprizing to fee
how nimbly the Natives will go up the
Trees, (which are fometimes fixty, feventy,
or an hundred Foot high, and the Bark
fmooth) They have nothing to help them

Method of
climbing
Trees

to climb, but a Piece of the Bark of a Tree,
made round like a Hoop, with which they
enclofe themfelves and the Tree, and fo fet
ting their Feet againft the Tree, and their
Backs againft the Hoop, (upon which their
Lives depend) they go up very faft Some
times they mifs their Footing, and fall down
and lofe their Lives.

Ciboa-
Tree

THE Ciboa Tree is very much like a P
Tree, and grows to a great Height The
Leaves which grow on the Top are very uf
ful for covering of Houfes, and the Native
extract Wine out of it juft the fame W
out of the Palm-Tree It is not quite f
fweet as the Palm-Wine, but taftes not un
like it The Trunk of this Tree, when young,
is, as well as the Palm, very fappy, b
when old, is very tough

Language

THE moft general Language is M
by which Name the Country and Peop

call'd . If you can fpeak that Language, you may travel from the River's Mouth up to the Country ot *Jonrous* (alias Merchants ,) fo call'd from their buying every Year a vaft Numbei of Slaves there, and bringing them down to the lower Parts of this River to fell to the White People . Which Country, I believe, cannot by all Reports be lefs than fix Weeks Journey from *James* Fort.

THE next Language moftly us'd here is call'd *Creole Portuguefe*, a baftard Sort of *Portuguefe*, fcarce underftood in *Lisbon* , but it is fooner learnt by *Englifhmen* than any other Language in this River, and is always fpoken by the Linguifts, which ferve both the feparate Traders and the Company   The two foregoing Languages I learnt whilft in the River.

Author learns it.

THE *Arabuk* is fpoken by the *Pholeys*, and by moft of the *Mahometans* in the River, tho' they are *Mundingoes* , but thofe who can write *Arabick*, are very ftrict at their Devotions three or four Times a Day, and are very fober and abftemious in their Way of Living, chufing rather to dye than drink ftrong Liquors, and rather faft than eat any thing which is not kill'd by one of their own Way of Thinking They have a great Veneration paid them by all the *Mundingoes*, infomuch that if any of them are ill, they apply to a *Mahometan* for Cure, but not by inward Potions, as any one would reafonably imagine, but they put fo much Faith in them, that they defire them only to write a fort of a Note on a fmall Piece of Paper, for them to wear about them,

Sobriety

Superfti. tion

D 4   ima-

1730.   imagining that as they have a Paper about
them written by a Holy Man, no Ill can
happen to them, or continue long with them
But the worst of it is, that they pay a great
Price for these Papers, by which means the
Busheri   *Mahometans*, commonly call'd *Bushreens*, are
generally richer, and have greater Plenty of
Things about them, than the Generality of
the *Mundingoe*

AMONGST the *Mundingoes* there is a Cur
Language, entirely unknown to the Women,
being only spoken by the Men, and is seldom
us'd by them in any other Discourse than
concerning a dreadful Bugbear to the Women,
Mumbo-   call'd *Mumbo-Jumbo*, which is what keep to
Jumbo   Women in awe And tho' they should
to understand this Language, yet were
Men to know it they would certainly order them

BESIDES the foregoing Languages,
are also others which every Kingdom
culiar to itself, as is that of the *Phul*
joams. Jolosfs and *Bumbrongs*, the last
which are very distant from the River,
Merchants Country

Trade   THE chief Trade of this Country is Gold,
Slaves, Elephants Teeth, and Bees-Wax The
Gold is of a very good Quality, and finer
than the Sterling Gold They bring it in
small Barrs, big in the middle, and turned
round into Rings, from 10 to 20
The Merchants who bring this and the other
Inland Commodities, are Blacks of the
Race and are call'd in *Mundingo*

coes They are very unwilling to tell much 1730
of the Inland Countries; all that I could gather from them concerning the Gold was, that
it is not wafh'd out of the Sand, but dug out Gold,
of Mines in the Mountains, the neareft 20 how got
Days Journey from *Cower*. In the Country
where the Mines are, they fay there are Houfes
built with Stone, and cover'd with Terrafs,
and that the fhort Cutlaffes with wooden
Handles, and Knives, which they bring down
with them, are made there, the Steel of which
is very good

THE fame Merchants bring down Ele-
phants Teeth, and in fome Years Slaves to Slaves.
the Amount of 2000, moft of which they
fay are Prifoners taken in War   They buy
them from the different Princes who take
them, many of them are *Bumbrongs* and *Pet-
charies*, Nations who each of them have different Languages, and are brought from a vaft
Way inland. Their Way of bringing them
is, tying them by the Neck with Leather-
Thongs, at about a Yard diftance from each
other, 30 or 40 in a String, having generally
a Bundle of Corn, or an Elephant's Tooth
upon each of their Heads. In their Way
from the Mountains they travel thro' very
great Woods, where they cannot for fome Carry
Days get Water, fo they carry in Skin-Bags their
enough to fupport them for that Time   I Water
cannot be certain of the Number of Merchants who follow this Trade, but there may
perhaps be about an Hundred, who go up
into the Inland Country with the Goods,
which they buy from the White Men, and
with them purchafing in various Countries
                              Gold,

1730. Gold, Slaves and Elephants Teeth They ufe Affes as well as Slaves in carrying their Goods, but no Camels nor Horfes

BESIDES the Slaves which the Merchants bring down, there are many bought along the River Thefe are either taken in War, as the former are, or elfe Men condemn'd to Crimes, or elfe People ftolen, which is very frequent The Company's Servants never buy any of the laft, if they fufpect it, without fending for the Alcade, or chief Men of the Place, and confulting with them about the Matter. Since this Slave-Trade has been us'd, all Punifhments are chang'd into Slavery there being an Advantage on fuch Condemnations, they ftrain for Crimes very hard, in order to get the Benefit of felling the Criminal. Not only Murder, Theft and Adultery, are punifh'd by felling the Criminal for a Slave, but every trifling Crime is punifh'd in the fame manner

Punifh-ment

THERE was a Man brought to me in Tomar, to be fold for having ftolen a Tobacco-pipe. I fent for the Alcade, and with much ado perfuaded the Party grieved to accept of a Compofition, and leave the Man free

Hard Sen-tence

IN Cantore, a Man feeing a Tyger eating Deer, which he had kill'd and hung up near his Houfe, fir'd at the Tyger, and the Bullet kill'd a Man The King not only condemn'd him, but alfo his Mother, three Brothers and three Sifters, to be fold They were brought down to me at Tamsamacunda, it made my Heart ake to fee them, and I did not buy them,

Long Sen-tence

them ; upon which they were sent farther down the River, and sold to some separate Traders Ships at *Joar*, and the King had the Benefit of the Goods for which they were sold.

SEVERAL of the Natives have many Slaves born in their Families . There is a whole Village near *Brucoe* of 200 People, who are all the Wives, Slaves, or Children of one Man And tho' in some Parts of *Africa* they sell their Slaves born in the Family, yet in the River *Gambia* they think it a very wicked thing , and I never heard of but one that ever sold a Family-Slave, except for such Crimes as would have made them to be sold had they been free If there are many Family Slaves, and one of them commits a Crime, the Master cannot sell him without the joint Consent of the rest , for if he does, they will all run away, and be protected by the next Kingdom, to which they fly The Slaves sold in the River, besides those brought by the Merchants, may amount in a Year to about 1000, more or less, according to the Wars upon the River.

Family-Slaves

THE third great Merchandise of the River is Ivory, or Elephants Teeth, got either by hunting or killing the Beasts, or pick'd up in the Woods. It is a Trade us'd by all Nations hereabouts, for whoever kills an Elephant has liberty to sell him and his Teeth ; but those traded for in this River are generally brought from a good Way inland, and a great many of them by the Merchants I never saw a full-grown Elephant, so shall not

Ivory

speak

1730 speak concerning them, but the Teeth I have had some Experience in Some are found in the Woods, but whether they are of Ele phants long dead, or whether the Ele phants shed their Teeth, I have not been able to learn But I have known Men bring in Teeth which they have found in the Woods, without any Skull or Bones fix'd to them The big

Large Tooth

gest Tooth I ever saw, weigh'd 130*l* The larger they are, the more valuable by the Pound One Tooth which weighs 100 Pound, is worth more than three Teeth which weigh 140 Pounds Many of them are broken-point ed, these are considerable less in their Value, some are white, others are yellow, but the Difference of Colour makes no Difference of Price.

Bee Wax

THE 4th Branch of Trade is Bees Wax which may be much increas'd. The Man gro's make Bee-Hives of Straw, in Shape like ours, and fix a Bottom-Board into the Hive thro' which there is a Hole for the Bees to go in at, they then fling them by Wyths to Boughs of Trees When they take the Combs they smother the Bees, and pressing off the Honey (of which they make Hon Wine) they boil up the Wax with Wat strain it, and press it through Hair-Clothes into Holes made into the Ground for the purpose They make and sell Quantities of it in this River That which is cleare't from Dirt is the best, we try it by boring through the Cakes, which are from 20 Pounds to 120 Pounds Weight.

1730

A BARR is a Denomination given to a certain Quantity of Goods of any Kind, which Quantity was of equal Value among the Natives to a Barr of Iron, when this River was first traded to. Thus, a Pound of Fringe is a Barr, two Pounds of Gunpowder is a Barr, an Ounce of Silver is but a Barr, and 100 Gun Flints is a Barr, and each Species of trading Goods has a Quantity in it called a Barr, therefore their Way of reckoning is by Barrs, or Crowns, one of which does not sometimes amount to above one Shilling Sterling, but that happens according to the Goods which they are in Want of, sometimes cheap, sometimes dear. These five Articles, *viz.* Spread-Eagle Dollars, Cryftal Beads, Iron Barrs, Brafs Pans, and Arrangoes, are called the Heads of the Goods, becaufe they are deareft. When you agree with the Merchants for Slaves, you always agree how many of the Heads of the Goods you fhall give him upon each Slave, which is three or four, if Slaves are worth forty or fifty, but when Slaves are dearer, as they oftentimes are, at eighty Barrs *per* Head, then you muft give five, and fometimes fix of the Heads upon every Slave, and there is an Affortment made of the Goods, by Barrs of different Species, which come out to the Price of the Slaves. The Men and Women ufed to be much dearer than Boys and Girls, but there have been fo many Veffels in the River of late Years, for young Slaves, to carry to *Cadiz* and *Lifbon,* that there is fcarce any Difference between the Prices of young Slaves and grown ones.

A Barr.

Heads of Goods

Price of Slaves.

I

1730   I ARRIVED (as I mention'd before) on the tenth of *November*, and I had to myself a good Apartment, near the Compting-House I dieted with the reſt of the Writers, at what was the ſecond Table, we had freſh Proviſions in Plenty, there being a Beaſt killed every other Day, we had Fowls brought daily by the Natives, to ſell to the Governor, and he allowed any Perſon, who did not care for Beef, to

Proviſion   have them at a very eaſy Rate Our Table, as well as the Governor's, was almoſt every Day ſupplied with Greens out of the Company's Garden at *Gillyſree*, and for which we paid nothing Flower we were well ſupplied with by the Company, and having a Baker on the Iſland, and an Oven, we had very good Bread made us every Day. Oyſters we had when we pleaſed, for at Low-water we could get them at the N N. W. Point of the Iſland We had Wine and Brandy at a moderate Price, and when there was any Quantity of Beer on the Iſland, we were allowed a pretty good Share of it. In ſhort, we wanted for nothing that was neceſſary in regard to Diet, but then it is right for every one who comes over here, to bring Bedding, Cheſts, and Cloathing It is uſual, as ſoon

Waſhing   as a Perſon arrives here, to agree with ſome Woman at *Gillyfree* to waſh their Linnen, which they do by the Month, and with Soap of their own making, reckon'd exceeding good, ſo that it is unneceſſary to bring Soap out of *England* When any one wants to go a-ſhore, it is but aſking Leave of the Governor, who ſeldom denies it.

ON the 12th of *November*, our third chief Merchant, Mr *Thomas Harriſon*, went up
             the

the River, on board the Company's Sloop,   1730
Adventure, to fettle a Factory at *Tancrowall*,
which lies on the South Side of the River,
about twelve Leagues above *James* Fort.

On the 13th, came up to the Fort the Sloop ar-
Company's Sloop *Fame*, *John Boys* Com-rives from
St Jago.
mander, having been on a trading Voyage to
St Jago, one of the *Cape de Verde* Iflands,
from whence fhe brought fome *Portu-*
guefe Mafons, to repair the Fort   I never
was at thefe Iflands, but *Dampier* gives the
following Account, which agrees with what
I have generally heard.

" *SAINT JAGO* is a Town lying on the Account of
" South-Weft Part of one of the *Cape de* that Ifland
" *Verde* Iflands, of the fame Name , which
' is the Seat of the General Governor, and
" of the Bifhop of all the *Cape de Verde*
" Iflands   This Town ftands fcattering
" againft the Sides of two Mountains, be-
" tween which there is a deep Valley, which
" is about 200 Yards wide, againft the Sea.
" In the Valley, by the Sea, there is a ftrag-
" gling Street, Houfes on each Side, and a
" Brook of Water in the Bottom, which
" empties itfelf into a fine fmall fandy Bay,
" where the Sea is commonly very fmooth ,
" fo that here is good Watering and Landing
" at any Time, tho' the Road is rocky,
" and bad for Ships   Juft by the Landing-
" Place there is a fmall Fort, almoft level
" with the Sea, where is always a Court of
" Guard kept   On the Top of the Hill,
" above the Town, there is another Fort,
" which, by the Wall that is to be feen from
" the

1730
"	the Road, feems to be a large Place
"	They have Cannon mounted there, but I
"	don't know what Ufe that Fort can be of,
"	unlefs it be for Salutes. The Town may
"	confift of 200 or 300 Houfes, all built of
"	rough Stone, having alfo one Convent,
"	and one Church

Its Inha-
b ants

"	The People, in general, are black, or
"	at leaft of a mix'd Colour, except only
"	fome few of the better Sort, *viz* the Go
"	vernor, the Bifhop, fome Gentlemen, and
"	fome Padres, or Priefts, for fome of thefe
"	alfo are black The People about *Praia*
"	are thievifh, but thofe of *St Jago* Town,
"	living under the Governor's Eye, are
"	more orderly, tho' generally poor, having
"	little Trade.

Bad Road
for Ships

"	*SAINT JAGO* Road is one of the
"	worft that I have feen There is not clean
"	Ground enough for above three Ships,
"	and thofe alfo muft lye very near each
"	other, one even of thefe muft lye clofe
"	to the Shore, with a Land-faft there, and
"	that is the beft for a fmall Ship The
"	Ifland *Fuogo* fhews itfelf, from this Road,
"	very plain, at about feven or eight
"	Leagues Diftance, and in the Night are
"	feen the Flames of Fire iffuing from its
"	Top* "

THE Governor and chief Merchants of
James Fort do fometimes fend Veffels to thefe
Iflands for Salt, which is one of the beft

* *Dampier's Voyages.*

Com

Commodities for *Gambia* River In the Year 1730.
1733 they fent a Scooner thither, at which
Time the People of *St Jago* were in fuch
Want of Corn, by Reafon of their having
had no Rain, that they were almoft ftarved,
and contracted with the Company's Supercar-
go, for a Lading of Corn, in Barter for
Skins, which is a great Trade at thefe
Iflands

On the 14th, failed the Company's Snow, Ship fails
Gunea Pacquet, Capt *William Martin*, on a down for
trading Voyage down the Gold Coaft, and fo the Gold
to *Cape Coaft* Caftle, the head Settlement the Coaft
Company have in all *Africa*, with her went
Mr *Philip Galand*, my Ship-Mate, in order
to learn the *Coaft* Trade. About Midnight
our Enfign was called down by the Centinels, Slaves at-
who were then on Duty, in order to pre- tempt an
vent the Slaves from making their Efcape, Efcape
they having got an Iron Bar out of the Slave-
Houfe Window, but it was then too fmall
for a Man to get out at, fo that they were
taken and fecured in another Place for that
Night, and on the next Day the Ringleader
of them being found out, and proving to be
an old Offender, he was ordered one hundred
Lafhes

On the 16th, Mr *John Hamilton*, my Ship- Factory
Mate, was ordered up to manage the Factory at *Tancro-*
at *Tancrowall*, now fettling there by Mr *Har-* *wall*
rion, chiefly for Bees-Wax, for which they
muft pay a dear Rate, there being a Compe- A *Portu-*
titor, called Seignior *Antonio Vols*, a noted *guefe Black*
Black *Portuguefe*, who lives near the Factory, drives a
and trades very largely with moft of our great Trade
F   *Englifh* there

English separate Traders who use this River, and very often trades with the Company He is reckon'd to be worth 10,000*l* Sterling, has got a vast Number of House-Slaves, (*viz* Slaves which live with him as Servants, a Grandeur much used both by the *Portugue* and *Spaniards*) which he keeps for Service and Breed, and are esteemed by him almost as much as his own Children. And as he has got a great many Canoas, he sends his own Men Slaves with them to all Ports of Trade up the River, and by that Means engrosses a great deal of Trade, insomuch that he has commonly a great many Slaves, and good Quantities of Elephants Teeth and Bees Wax by him, with which he turns a Penny with the separate Shipping, and is well skilled in his Way of bartering, he being thoroughly Master of the prime Cost, in *England*, of all sorts of Goods, taking always care to keep his Warehouse well stocked with Goods, and has the upperhand vastly of some of his Neighbours, who are sometimes obliged to stand still half a Year together for want of Goods to trade with

TANCROWALL is divided into two Parts, one for the *Portuguese*, and the other for the *Mundingoes*, the former living always in square large Houses, the latter in round Huts, made of a good, fat, binding Clay, which soon hardens, about twenty Feet Diameter, and about eight Feet high, over them there is a Covering like a Beehive, made either of Straw or *Palmetto* Leaves, so well fitted that the Rain cannot penetrate them, nor the Heat of the Sun strike through them

They

They very much refemble fome Ice houfes I have feen in *England*

THIS Town of *Tancrowall* is the Refidence of a Prieft, who is yearly fent over from *St Jago*. Here is alfo a Church, where, during the Prieft's Stay, is Mafs almoft every Day. Here are a great many other *Portuguefe*, who have among them feveral Canoas, which they fend up the River to trade once or twice a Year, by which means they have made this Town a Place of great Refort, and the richeft in the whole River. It is pleafantly Situated by the Water-Side, about half a Mile in Length, with a woody Hill behind, that runs fome Miles along the River-Side about half a Mile from it, between is pleafant Walking in the Dry-Seafon.

ON the 17th, early in the Morning, the Fr ih Factory it *Albreda*, four Miles diftant, *Albreda* was on Fire. It made a dreadful Figure. The *on Fire* Governor, with twelve Soldiers, went over to their Affiftance, notwithftanding which, the Houfe was much damaged, a great deal of Flower and Bread fpoiled, and one Slave burnt to Death.

ON the 22d, the Governor went up in the *Difpatch* Sloop to *Geregia*, a Place up Inland River about fourteen Leagues from *Geregia,* the Fort, where the Company have a Factory *a Factory* for dry Goods chiefly, under the Direction of Mr *William Roberts*. The Factory-Houfe being very bad, and ready to fall, and the King of the Country not willing that a new one fhould be built nearer the River Side than the

old

1730 old one was, is the Reafon of the Governor's going up, in order to have it built in a Place moſt commodious for the Company's landing Goods, and on occafion to withdraw them At the fame time went up the *Adventure* Sloop to the fame Place, with our Enfign, a Corporal, Drummer, and fixteen or twenty Soldiers

Defcribed *GEREGIA* is a fmall Town lying on the South-Side of *Vintoin* River, and about eleven Leagues from the Mouth of it, which enters the *Gambia* about three Leagues above *James* Fort It is inhabited by *Portugueſe* and *Banyoons*, the former are, as in other Parts of the Country, very civil, but the latter are fcarcely civilized. The Factor here buys a great deal of Bees-Wax Towards the Water-Side the Land is pretty well clear'd, and affords excellent Shooting

O the 29th, the *Diſpatch* and *Adventure* came down from *Geregia* with the Governor and Soldiers, having made the King of *Geregia* condefcend to let the Factory-Houfe be built in whatever Place the Governor pleafes The Sailors of the *Diſpatch* told me, that in their Way to *Geregia* one of their Crew dropt Sailor dog overboard in the Night and was drown'd Out of his The next Day after they found the Body float-Grave by ing, and buried it near the River-Side, but Wolves the next Day they found him again a great Way higher, taken out of the Ground by Wolves, who had eaten his Head, one of his Arms, and part of his Breaft. Upon which they took him and buried him very deep in the Ground, to prevent the Wolves from coming at him again O

On the 5th of *December*, Mr *Robert Banks*, 1730
a Writer, went up to *Vintain* in the *Fame* *December*
Sloop, *John Boys* Master, to settle a Factory *Vintain*
there, for which Purpose he carried with him
a small Cargo of Goods

On the 12th, we perceived a Ship coming *Three*
up the River · When she was over-against *French*
Albreda, the Governor order'd a Shot to be *Ships put*
fired to bring her to ; upon which she saluted *in at Al-*
our Fort with nine Guns, which return'd the *breda*
same Number, and soon after she came to
Anchor at *Albreda*. The same Night about
nine of the Clock, being Moon-light, I perceiv'd two Vessels coming up the River , the
Governor hearing of it, came directly upon
the Bastion, and order'd a Shot to be fired
to bring them to, upon which they came to
Anchor , but not sending their Boats to tell
us who they were, the Governor order'd another Shot to be fired over them   Then the
Captain of one of them came to the Fort,
and told the Governor, that they were two
French Sloops from *Senegal* to *Albreda* to water , that the Kings about the River *Senegal*
being at War, made it dangerous watering
thereabouts. I could not forbear smiling to
see how the *Frenchman* was frightned, when *Timorou-*
the File of Musqueteers met him at the Wa- *ness of a*
ter Side to conduct him to the Governor , he *Captain.*
looked so very simple, and quaked so very
much, that he could hardly speak a plain
Word

On the 18th, the *Fame* Sloop, *John Boys*
Master, sailed up the River for *Yamyama-* *Yamyama*
cunda, with Mr *Conner*, Factor for that Place, *cunda*
E 3   in

1750 in joint Commiſſion with Mr *John Brown*, whoſe Colleague Mr *Matthew Wilſon* is order'd down to this Fort by the Return of this Sloop

Oyſters growing upon Trees

THIS Evening I ſupped upon Oyſters which grew upon Trees This being ſomewhat remarkable, and moſt People in *L*[...] unacquainted with, I ſhall give them a Notion of it Down the River where the Water is ſalt, and near the Sea, the [...] is bounded with Trees called *Mangroves* whoſe Leaves being long and heavy, weigh the Boughs into the Water, to theſe Leaves the young Oyſters fſten in great Quantities, where they grow till they are very large, and then you cannot ſeparate them from the Tree, but are obliged to cut off the Boughs, the Oyſters hanging on them reſemble a Rope of Onions

D[...]

ON the 20th, I went to *St Domingo* on the Main Continent of *Africa*, over againſt *Jane* Fort, being the firſt Time of my going aſhore I walked from *St Domingo* to *G*[...], about a Mile and half, all the Way through Graſs eight or nine Foot high, and the Way ſaw a great Number of Lizards, ſome of which have Heads as yellow as Gold Not being able to get a Boat to carry me to the Fort, I was obliged to ſtay all Night

St Domingo deſcribed

St Domingo lies on the North Side of the River, directly oppoſite to *James Iſland*, about three Miles from it It conſiſts only of a few round Houſes belonging to the Company, in which ſome of their Caſtle-Slaves live, who are there to cut Wood for the Uſe of the Fort, and to take care of a Well which the Company

pany have there to fupply the Garrifon, and
to help fill the Casks which are daily brought
over from the Fort for that purpofe Having
lain at *Gillyfree* all Night, the next Morning
I went and hired a Canoa to carry me to the
Ifland . The Canoa was very fmall, and juft
wide enough for a Man to fit down in When
we were got a little Way from the Shore, the
Sea-Breeze blowing very frefh, we had like to
have overfet the Canoa, and it was with much
ado that I perfuaded the Black Fellows to
carry me to Shore again , where, after being
about two Hours, the Governor's Boat came
over for me, with which I went to the Ifland

O n the 24th, one of the Shallops, brought Shallops
over in Frames in the *Difpatch* Sloop, was brought
launched by the Name of the *James Ifland*, over in
and *Thomas Gilmore* our Serjeant was made Frames
Mafter of her

After we had dined, we went afhore to *Sea a*
St Domingo, and from thence to *Seaca*, about
two Miles above it, on the fame Side the
River, a very fmall Town, inhabited by *Po-*
rtuguefe, who have a Church, feldom made ufe
of, the Prieft being there but twice in a Year
This, and *Tancrowall*, and *Geregia*, being the
only Places he frequents whilft in this Country, unlefs it be a Vifit now and then to the
Governor of our Fort At *Seaca* is a large Large
Cotton-Tree about thirty Yards in Circum- Cotton
ference , it grows out in Spurs, and that makes Tree
it feem fo very large, being meafured in and
out all round its Spurs to make thirty Yards,
'or if the outfide Circumference of the Tree
vere meafured it would not be above fifteen

ON the 31ſt, early in the Morning, we ſaw a Veſſel coming up the River When ſhe was over-againſt *Albreda*, the Governor ordered a Shot to be fired to bring her to. Upon which ſhe immediately lowered her Sails, but did not think fit to come to an Anchor, till ſhe had run upon the Company's Spit of Sand and Rocks, which runs out from the Iſland, where ſhe ſtruck Upon which the Governor ordered our Enſign to go on Board her, and bring her into the right Channel, during which Time ſhe ſent her Boat with one of the Mates to tell the Governor, that ſhe was the Brigantine *John* and *Anne*, Capt. Thomas Stoneham, a ſeparate Trader from London In the Evening ſhe came to anchor on the North Side of the Iſland, and ſaluted the Fort, and in about three Days time the Captain

went aſhore to *Gillyfree*, and was there ſeized by the Natives, for anchoring at the Port of *Gillyfree*, and not paying his Cuſtoms to the King of *Barrah*, he immediately ſent over Word of his being confined, upon which the Governor ſent our Enſign over to his Aſſiſtance, and upon Promiſe of his paying the King's Cuſtom of One hundred and twenty Bars Country-Money, next Day he was permitted to go on board his Veſſel, and on the Day following he paid the ſaid Sum

ON the 3d, early in the Morning, we had a Tornado of Wind and Lightning After which, our third Chief, Mr *Thomas Harriſon*, came down in the *Diſpatch* Sloop from Toncrowall. After Dinner Mr *Kerr* our Enſign, and myſelf, with two or three Soldiers, went to try the *James Iſland* Sloop, which was

was launched about ten Days go We went
about nine Miles above the Island, and meeting with a very fresh Sea Breeze, and our
Rigging out of Order, and the Man at the
Helm none of the experteft, we had like to
have loft both Veffel and Selves, fhe having A great
no Deck, and the Gunnel lying under Water, Danger.
occafioned our Ballaft, which was fix Barrels
of Water, to rowl all to Leeward, and fright-
en us very much, expecting fhe would have
filled before fhe righted, but (thank God)
we got her upright, and got fafe back to the
Fort by eight of the Clock at Night This
Day there was a young Elephant brought a-
live as a Prefent to the Governor, and Advice brought from *Joar* of the Death of Mr *Forbes*
Robert Forbes, Writer, after a fhort Illnefs dies
contracted by hard Drinking

On the 10th, Capt *Stoneham*, with the Ship fails
John and *Anne* Brigantine, failed for the *Cape* for *Cape*
de Verde Iflands, for Salt to trade with in this *de Verde*
River After Dinner the Governor and myfelf Iflands
went on Board a large *French* Ship at *Albreda*,
call'd *Le St Michael*, Capt *Tredilha* Commander, where having ftay'd about two Hours
we went afhore, and fupped at *Albreda*, and
about Midnight we returned to *James* Fort

ALBREDA is a pretty large Town near Tb a
the River-Side on the North, about a Mile defcribed
or two below *James* Fort, near which the
French Eaft-India Company have a Settlement
confifting of a Factor, two Writers, and four *French*
or five other White Men They have two Factory
or three very handfome Houfes built of Clay, there
like unto the *Portuguefe* Houfes, with Walls
about

about ten Feet high, covered with Thatch, being supported by strong Forkillas, and a Space left between the Walls and the Roof to let in the Air. They are very neat and well furnifh'd, and drive a confiderable Trade, but are much hinder'd by the *Englifh* not allowing them to give above forty Barrs *per* Head for Slaves. But in the Year 1735, there being great Demand for Slaves at the *Miffifippi*, where the *French* Gentlemen themfelves informed me they fend their Slaves, they broke thro' that Agreement, and gave fifty Barrs *per* Head for Slaves, with feven of each of the Heads

R**val the** of the Goods, which amounted to more than
Fr— in Ten Pounds Sterling, their Goods being bet-
the Slave ter in their kind than our *Englifh* gene-
Trade are, was the reafon of their purchafing a great many Slaves in that Year, notwithftanding there were no lefs than three *Liverpool* Veffels trading about a Mile above the *French*, at the Port of *Gillyfree*, who gave Seventy or Eighty Barrs *per* Head, and yet were not able to purchafe near the Number of Slaves which

C—rac the *French* did. In the Year 1724 there was
between a Contract made between the *French* Agent
them. at *Gree* and the *Englifh* at *James* Fort, that the *French* fhould fettle a Factory in the River *Gambia* below *James* Fort, in order to make what Trade they could; and altho' the *Englifh* Company's Stock was then at the loweft Ebb, and not that only, but it is very probable that the *French* were refolved to fettle there, either with or without Leave; yet is it to be obferved, that the Royal *African* Company, in lieu of the *French* having a fingle Settlement in *Gambia*, obtained Leave to to fend Veffels when they pleas'd, to trade

bo

both at *Joally* and *Portodally*, two Places near　1731
Goree, which produce great Trade, and which
the *French* are at a great deal of Pains, as
well as Cost, to engross to themselves　By
which means, notwithstanding the Articles, our
Voyages there often miscarry

This Factory of theirs at *Albreda* is not *French*
within reach of our Cannon　Whenever they contro'd
want to go up the River above *James* Fort for by the
Wood, or any thing else which they cannot so *English*
well be provided with below, they are obliged
to ask Leave of our Governor, who seldom
or never denies them, but puts a Man on
Board to see that they do not make any
Trade, neither are they allowed to go above
Elephants Island, which is about thirty Leagues
above *James* Fort

On the 11th, in the Evening, we saw two TwoShips
large Vessels coming up from Sea, about Se- arrive, one
ven at Night one of them fired two Guns, with Sol
being a Signal known by the Governor only, diers
who order'd the Gunner to return one　About
an Hour after came up the Ship *Elizebeth*,
Captain *John Carruthers*, a separate Trader,
and anchor'd near the Island, having brought
over ten Soldiers from the Company for this
Garrison　Early the next Morning came up
the Ship *Herbert*, Captain *Plater Onley*, who
anchored at *Gulyfree*　And the next Day
came up a Vessel and anchored at the Fort,
but could not salute it by reason of her being
loaded with Horses from *Cape de Verde Islands*
She was the *Ruby* Brigantine, Captains *Creague*
and *Colwell*

O 4

Separate
Trader
runs on
the S

Got off

O n the 25th, came up a Ship call'd the *William* and *Betty*, Captain *Whitloe* from Liverpool, a separate Trader, who, not being us'd to the River, ran upon the Company's *Spit* of Sand Upon which, the Governor sent three Boats full of Hands to her Assistance, but it being Tide of Ebb, they cou'd not get her off till the next Morning, at which time they got her afloat, the Ship receiv'd no Damage, the Company's Hands staying on Board her all Night. The *Elizabeth*, Captain *Carruthers*, sail'd up the River to. *Joar* to trade

Bonetta
arrive

O n the 31st, the *Ruby* Brigantine sail'd up the River At Noon we saw a Vessel coming up the River, which proved to be the Company's Ship *Bonetta*, Captain *John Livingstone*, with a large Cargo, which we had a long while expected By this Ship came over several Persons in the Company's Service.

Fame
Sloop from
Tamyamacunda

Proceed
goes up
Factories

O n the 3d of *February* the *Fame* Sloop came down from *Tamyamacunda*, with Mr *Matthew Wilson*, a Writer, on Board from thence And in three Days after that, our third Chief Mr *Thomas Harrison*, and Mr *John Nind* Factor, embarked on Board the *Dutch* Sloop, *Robert Hall* Commander, on a Trading Voyage to *Fatatenda*, almost two hundred Leagues above *James* Fort, where the Company intend shortly to settle Factory

On the 10th, came up to anchor at the 1731
Fort, the Company's Snow *Succeſs, Robert* Succeſs
Cummins Commander She was conſign'd to Snow
Cape Coaſt Caſtle, but ſpringing a Leak at
Sea ſhe thought proper to put in here to ſtop
it The next Morning we ſaw a Veſſel coming up the River, about Noon, being but a
little below the Fort, ſhe ſent her Boat to acquaint us that ſhe was a ſeparate Trader, the
Arabella, Capt *Pyke,* from *London,* after *Arabella*
which he came to Anchor over-againſt *Gilly-* *from Lond.*
free, and the next Evening ſailed up the River for *Joar.*

On the 15th, about One in the Morning,
died Mr *William Ruſling,* a Writer, having Mr *Will*
been ill about two Months Some few Days *Ruſ'g*
before he died, he deſir'd, that whenever he dies.
ſhould die, I would ſee that his Grave was
dug ſix Foot deep, for Fear of the Wolves
eating him In the Morning the Flag was
hoiſted half-maſt up, and in the Evening he
was buried at *Gillyfree,* in a Grave according
as he deſired. He loſt his Life by not being Cauſe of
ruled by the Doctor, who adviſed him to his Death
ſtay more at home, and keep himſelf warm
The next Day the Governor, Capt *Living-*
ſtone, Capt *Jenkins,* and myſelf, went on board
the *Succeſs,* Capt *Cummins,* to accompany
him down to the River's Mouth, the *Adven-*
ture Sloop going down with us, to bring us
back again Before we weighed Anchor, the
John and *Anne,* Capt *Stoneham,* arriv'd from *John* and
the *Cape de Verde* Iſlands, whither he went the *Anne* from
tenth of *January* laſt He ſaluted our Flag *Cape de*
at Maintopmaſt Head, with five Guns, and *Verd*
the Fort returned the ſame Number We
came

1731. came to Anchor about Eight at Night, a
little below *Charles Island*, and the next
Morning we went afhore at *Barrow Point*
in the Kingdom of *Combo*, to buy fome Cattle and Fowls for Capt *Cummins*, after which
we dined on board him, and then paired
About Sunfet we ran upon the Rocks a-
breaft of *Charles Ifland*, being one Moment
in four Fathom and half, and the next Mo-

A Mif-
fortune.
ment fail upon the Rocks   We carried off
our Anchors, and in an Hour's Time hove
her off, but foon after ran upon another and
worfe Place, fo that all Hands were obliged
to work, nor was the Governor himfelf ex-
cepted, for he help'd me in taking up the
Floor of the Cabbin, and throwing overboard about a Ton of Ballaft   At Midnight

Remedied
we got her afloat, and free from the Rock,
and went to Anchor farther off the Ifland,
till next Morning, when we went a fhooting
Wild-Fowl upon the Ifland, where I found a
Cherry-Tree, fcarce in this Country, the Fruit

Cherry-
Tree
found
whereof was not ripe , the Tree and Leaves
much refemble ours, and is about the fame
Bignefs   At Noon we weighed Anchor, and
as we paffed by *Albreda* the *French* Chief faluted the Flag at our Topmaft-head with
nine Chambers, to which we returned feven
Guns, being all we had on board , foon after
we came to *James* Fort

On the 19th, in the Morning, came up to
Albreda, a Brigantine with a white Flag at
the Topmaft-head having on board the Fa-
General of *Seree* , Monfieur *Levens* , he
faluted our Fort with feven Guns, which I returned the fame Number   The fame Day

ing the Ship *Kent*, Capt *Francis Wheeler*, 1731
from the *Gold Coast*, arrived, and anchored at
James Fort, in order to take in some Boys
and Girls, which he had contracted for of our
chief Merchants   Another Shallop, which
was brought over in Frames, by the *Dispatch*
Sloop, from *England*, was launched this
Evening, by the Name of the *Gambia* , and
our Corporal, *William Child*, was made
Master of her.   The next Morning the *French*
General, and several other *French* Gentlemen,
came and dined with our Governor, who saluted them with a great many Guns, and
treated them with a very handsome Dinner.
The same Evening the *John* and *Anne* Brigantine, Capt *Stoneham*, sailed up the River.
And the next Day the Governor, several others,
and myself, went to visit the *French* General,
at *Albreda*, where we were very merry, and
stayed till Midnight.

Gambia Shallop launched

O n the 22d, the *Ruby*, Capts *Creague* and
Colwell, came down to the Fort, having sold
all their Horses, which, as I said before, they
brought from the *Cape de Verde* Islands   The
Generality of Horses in this River, are brought
from the Borders of *Barbary*, but as the
Grand *Jolloiffs* are nearest them, they buy
them up, and reap an Advantage, by selling
them to the *Mundingoes* and *Mahometans*.
They never sell Mares, so that all the Time
I was in *Gambia* I saw no more than one
Mare, and she was brought in this Vessel, by
Capts *Creague* and *Colwell*, from *Cape de
Verde* Islands   The same Day one of the
Emperors of *Fonia* came to the Fort, being
saluted with five Guns, on his Landing   His
Name

Horses.

Emperor of Fonia visits the Governor

1731 Name is *Taffel*, and came to fee the Governor, or rather to afk for fome Powder and Ball, in order to defend himfelf againft fome People with whom he is at War, he is a young Man, very black, tall, and well fet, he was His Drefs drefs'd in a Pair of fhort yellow Cotton Cloth Breeches, which came down to his Knees, and a Garment on his Back, of the fame Cloth, made like a Surplice, he had no Shoes nor Stockings, but a very large Cap, with Part of a white Goat's Tail faften'd in it, being a great Fafhion among the Great Men of this River. He and his Retinue came in a large Canoa, holding about fixteen People, all armed with Guns and Cutlaffes, with him came two or three Women, and the Mandingo fame Number of *Mandingo* Drums, which are Drum about a Yard long, and a Foot, or twenty Inches diameter at the Top, but lefs at the Bottom, made out of a folid Piece of Wood, and covered, only at the wideft End, with Manner of the Skin of a Kid. They beat upon them beating with only one Stick, and their left Hand, to which the Women will dance very brifkly, they ftayed here all Night, and then went home, having nine Guns fir'd at their going off.

On the 28th, the *Ruby* Brigantine, Capts *Creague* and *Colwell*, failed for the *Gold* Coaft, intending to be here again next *Auguft*. But, poor Men, they had the Misfortune to be cut off by the Natives down the Coaft. *Col-* Capt C *well* and moft of the Sailors were killed, but *Creague* faved himfelf in his Boat, with the Help of his black Boy, out of the Cabbin

Who

Window, being fo ill, it is faid, that he 1731
could not get out himfelf

On the 8th of *March*, two Porcupines were *March*
brought alive to the Governor   Soon after,
Mr *Henry Johnfon*, a Writer, was fent up to
Cu'ar, to fettle a Factory, chiefly for dry
Goods, *viz*. Elephants Teeth, Bees-wax, and
Gum, but the Company having the Misfor-
tune to have Perfons there who traded more *Colar* Fac-
for themfelves than their Mafters, they were tory fettled
a great Charge to no Purpofe, and fo in
the Year 1733, they thought proper to break and with-
it up, fince which they have had no Settle- drawn
ment there

On the 17th, the Company's Sloop, *Fame*,
John Boys Mafter, failed for *Cohone*, in Bar- *Cohone.*
fally, on a trading Voyage, which lies in the
fame Kingdom as the Company's chief Factory at *Joar*, about a hundred Miles from it,
and near the Sea   There the King commonly
refides, and as there is good Profit to be TheKing's
made for the Company by thefe Voyages, Place of
provided their Supercargoes are honeft, they Refidence
generally fend two or three Times in a
Year   Whenever the King of *Barfally* wants
Goods or Brandy, he fends a Meffenger to
our Governor, at *James* Fort, to defire he
would fend a Sloop there with a Cargo, this
News being not at all unwelcome, the Governor fends accordingly.   Againft the Arrival of the faid Sloop, the King goes and ran- Short Ac-
facks fome of his Enemies Towns, feizing count of
the People, and felling them for fuch Com- him
modities as he is in want of, which commonly is Brandy or Rum, Gunpowder, Ball,

F   Guns,

1731

H s Way of Traffick

and get-t ngSlaves

Guns, Piftols, and Cutlaffes, for his Atten, dants and Soldiers, and Coral and Silver for his Wives and Concubines In cafe he is no at War with any neighbouring King, he then falls upon one of his own Towns, which are numerous, and ufes them in the very fre Manner After the *Fame* Sloop had been gone about five Days, fhe came back to the Fort, having loft three Anchors, and narrowly efcaped being loft herfelf, in trying to go over the Bar which is at the Mouth of the River *Joally*, on her Way to *Cohone*, the Smith immediately fet to work and re fitted her, and on the Morrow fhe fet ou again on her Voyage

Fam S oop camaged

The Baret-ta goes dowr to Cepe Ccaf te trade

ON the 29th, the Company's Ship *Ben* failed on a trading Voyage down to *Sier. Leone*, and *Cape Coaft* Caftle, &c with whom went Mr *Thomas Burfey*, a Writer, in joint Commiffion with Capt. *Livingftone*, who commanded the faid Ship

ON the 4th came up the Company's Sloop *Adventure* from *Cutcheo*, with about eight Tons and half of Bees-Wax. *Cutcheo* is a Settlement belonging to the King of *Portugal*, lying about 20 Leagues to the Southward of the Mouth of this River, and about three Days Travel over Land from *Geregia*, where we have a Factory, who trade much for Wax brought from thence · We alfo make often Voyages by Water, but the former I take to be the moft profitable to the Company, and yet even by that they are no great Gainers, the Wax being fo very foul, that fometimes there will be Twenty or Thirty *per Cent* Lofs upon

upon it. The Ship *Kent,* Captain *Francis*
Wheeler, sailed for *Lisbon,* with a Cargo of
young Slaves, In the Afternoon I went over to   Descripti-
Gilyfree in the Kingdom of *Barrah,* a little   on of *Gil-*
below *James* Fort, a large Town near the   *lyfree*
River, inhabited by *Portuguese, Mundingoes,*
and some *Mahometans,* who have here a pretty
little Mosque to pray in. This Town is used
to supply all private Shipping with Linguisters,
but the King of *Barrah,* in the Year 1733,
made it no less than Slavery for any of his
Subjects to serve as Linguisters on Board of
any Vessels, but what pay his Customs, and
trade in his Country The Company have a
Factory here pleasantly situated, facing the
Fort, and likewise some Gardens, which supply the Fort About the Town is fine Shoot-   Fine
ing, and were it not somewhat too Sandy,   Shooting.
it would be pleasant walking Here are great
Numbers of Plantain and Banana Trees, the   Banana
latter of which is a long Fruit, six or seven   Tree
Inches in Length, cover'd with a yellow and
tender Skin, when ripe The Pulp of it is
soft as a Marmalade, and of a very good
Taste It grows on a Stalk about six Yards
high, and the Leaves are two Yards long,
and about a Foot wide. One Stalk bears only one single Cluster or Bunch, which perhaps may consist of forty or fifty Bananas,
and when the Bunch is gather'd, they cut off
the Stalk, otherwise it could not bring forth
any more Fruit. The Plantain is not much   Plantain
unlike the Banana, but somewhat longer, and   Tree
very much of the same Taste There are also
Guavas, which resemble our Peaches, only   Guavas
the Outside is much rougher, and there is no
Stone in the Inside, but Kernels less than those

Oranges
and
Limes

of Apples This is reckon'd an excellent Medicine against the Flux Here are a great many Orange-Trees and Lime-Trees, with the Produce of which the Fort is supplied to make Punch, &c

Physical
Nuts and
Tabacombas Fruits

HERE are also other Fruits, such as Physical Nuts and Tabacombas, the first are Nuts, which contain three or four small kernels, one or two of which is a Purging-Dose, but they are apt to vomit as well as purge, these are frequently used by the Natives The Tabacomba is almost like a Bon-Chretien Pear, the Rind not unlike that of a Pomegranate when it is ripe it opens of itself, and contains four or five Fruits, small, and of a reddish Colour, with large Stones, and very insipid

Pelican

HERE I saw a Number of Pelicans, which is a Bird as large as a Goose, and much the same Colour, its Bill is very long, under the lower Part of it is a Bag, some of which will contain two Gallons of Water, when well stretch'd. They live upon Fish, and therefore are commonly near the Rivers

Poison'd
Arrow.

A NATIVE carried me to his House, and shewed me a vast Number of Arrows, which were daubed over with a black Mixture, said to be of such rank Poison, that if the Arrow did but draw Blood it would be mortal, unless the Person who made the Mixture had a mind to cure it, in whose Power it only was to do it, for he said there were no poisonous Herbs, but what there are others which would expell them

ON the 11th, in the Evening, seeing a Vessel coming up the River, we fired a Shot to bring her to, upon which she sent her Bo-

to acquaint the Governor that she was a separate Trader, call'd the Snow *Mary*, Captain
Gordon, from *Glasgow*, but last from *Barba-*
does with Rum and Sugars Sure never was
a Vessel's Arrival more welcome than this was
to our common Gentry, who were afraid they
would have been obliged to be without Liquor ^{Rum and}
all the Rains, but now their Fears were over
Soon after came down the *Arabella*, Captain
Pyke, a separate Trader, from *Joar*, loaded
with Slaves , and having stay'd a Day or two
at *James* Fort, sail'd for *Maryland*, having
among his Compliment of Slaves one Man
call'd *Job Ben Solomon*, of the *Pholey* Race,
and Son to the High-Priest of *Bundo* in *Foota*,
a Place about ten Days Journey from *Gillyfree*,
who was travelling on the South Side of this
River, with a Servant, and about twenty or
thirty Head of Cattle, which induced a King
of a Country a little Way inland, between
Tincrowall and *Yamina*, not only to seize his
Cattle, but also his Person and Man, and sold
them both to Captain *Pyke*, as he was trading
at *Joar* He would have been redeemed by
the *Pholeys*, but was carried out of the River
before they had Notice of his being a Slave.
The same Day the *Elizabeth*, Capt *Carruthers*,
came down from *Joar* with his Compliment
of Slaves

The marginal notes read:
- Rum and Sugar arrive opportunely.
- Job Ben Solomon taken and sold

On the 18th, in the Morning, the *John* and
Anne Brigantine, Captain *Stoneham*, a separate
Trader, came down the River with most of
his Men sick The same Morning the Governor, Mr *Younger Nelme*, and my self, went on
Board the *Mary*, and breakfasted with Captain *Gordon* , from thence we went, according

F 3   to

1731
French
General's
grand En-
tertain-
ment

to Appointment, and dined at *Albreda*, with
the *French* General, having for Dinner no less
than Seventy three Dishes, and at Supper more
than half that Number, during which time
the Factory and Shipping fired above two
hundred Guns. The next Day the *M y*,
Captain *Gordon*, sailed for the Coast, as did
likewise the *Sierra Leone*, Captain *fe   , of
South Carolina*, which last arrived here before
I came, and delivered his Cargo to the Governor and Chief Merchants, for which we
paid One hundred and eighty Slaves. In the
Evening the Wife of our Serieant Mr *G w*
was brought to Bed of a Girl, they both are
well, notwithstanding the Opinion of a great
many People in *England*, who think it mo-
rally impossible for a White Woman to lie
in this Country, and bear Children

French Ge-
neral goes
to *St Jago*

On the 20th, the General came to the
Fort to take his Leave of the Governor. On
his Landing, the Governor saluted him with
thirteen Guns, a great Number whilst here,
and thirteen more at Midnight when he went
away. The next Day after he embarked on
Board the Duke *de Bourbon* for *St Jago*, and
saluted the Fort with thirteen Guns, which
returned the same Number

*D   a   b
Sloop
cc   rom
F   aa*

On the 24th, the Company's Sloop *D
frith* came down from *Fatatenda*, with Mr
Harr   on Chief Merchant, and Mr *7o   N*
Factor, who went up from hence the other
February last

X

On the 2d of *May*, the *John* and *A*
Captain *Storeham* sailed for *Sierra Leone* the
Co

Crew being in very indifferent Health About 1731
two Days afterwards the *Herbert*, Captain
Onley, failed for *Virginia* or *Maryland*, as did
also the Day after the *William* and *Betty*,
Captain *Whitloe*, for the *West-Indies*.

On the 15th, the *Adventure* Sloop fail'd Rain, the
up for *Yamyamacunda*, from whence she took first I had
Mr *James Conner* on Board her as Super- *Africa*
Cargo to *Fatatenda* on a Trading-Voyage
About Day-light we had a very smart Shower
of Rain, the first I had seen since my
Arrival in this Country. In the Evening
came up a Long-Boat belonging to his Maje- Man of
sty's Ship the *Pearl*, Captain *Lee* Commander, War's
who lay at the River's Mouth, and, accord- Long Boat
ing to form, sent to our Governor to know comes to
if there were any Pyrates in the River, or *James* Fort
thereabouts The next Day the Company's *Guinea*
Snow, *Guinea* Pacquet, Captain *Martin*, came Pacquet
up to *James* Fort, from a Trading Voyage returns
down the Coast We had expected her two Coast
Months past, but the reason of her Stay was
occasion'd by her being obliged to turn to
Windward all the Way back from the Coast
The *Greyhound* Galley, Captain *Ramsay*, from
England, a separate Trader, came up in the
Evening, and anchor'd near the Fort

On the 19th, we had for the first Time a Tornado
Tornado of Thunder and Lightning, Wind
and Rain.

On the 22d, the *Elizabeth*, Captain *Car-* A separate
ruthers, a separate Trader, loaded with Slaves, Trader
failed for *South Carolina*. The *Fame* Sloop *Fame* Sloop
returned from the King of *Barsally*'s Town from *Cohone*
    F 4   Cohone, in *Barsaly*

1731. *Cohone*, having made a tolerable Voyage; she directly unloaded, and putting on Board a Cargo for *Joar* Factory, she proceeded immediately up thither, and from thence to *Yamyamacunda*, in order to bring down all the Dry Goods from each Factory, to send Home by the *Guinea* Pacquet, which will go very soon for *England*. The next Evening

Our Smith attempts to shoot the Enfign. our Smith, *James Collins*, being drunk, fired a Musquet at our Ensign's Head, which very narrowly miss'd two others, and the Ball was very near going into the Publick Room Window, where the Governor was sitting with a great many Gentlemen: He was well secured in Irons, and put into the Slave-House

June. On the 4th of *June*, the *Sea-Nymph* Sloop came down from *Geregia*, with Mr *William Roberts*, the Company's Factor there, and a good Quantity of Cotton and Bees-Wax The

Sea Nymph Sloop loses her Topmast, and is set on Fire by Lightning Captain said, that whilst the Sloop lay at anchor at *Geregia*, she had her Topmast split to pieces by the Lightning, and ten Fowls kill'd in the Coop upon Deck, and her Forecastle set on fire, but very soon extinguish'd As it happen'd no Body was upon Deck, being just before drove off by a smart Shower of Rain · But, what was most remarkable, tho' the Bones of the Fowls which were kill'd by the Lightning were broke all to pieces, yet their Skins were neither torn nor crack'd

This Day two *Jolloiff* People came to the Island with some Cloths to fell. The *Jolloiffs* make the finest Kind of Cotton-Cloths, and that in large Quantities Their Pieces are generally twenty seven Yards long, and

and never above 9 Inches wide; they cut them
to what Length they pleaſe, and ſew them
together very neatly, to make them ſerve the
Uſe of broader Cloths. They clean the Cotton from the Seed by Hand, and ſpin it by
Hand with Spindle and Diſtaff, they weave
them with a Shuttle and a Loom of very
plain, coarſe Workmanſhip. They make
them up into Pairs, one about three Yards
long, and one and half wide, to cover their
Shoulders and Body; the other almoſt of the
ſame Width, and but two Yards long, to
cover from their Waiſt, and downwards. Such
a Pair is the Clothing either for a Man, or a
Woman; they only differing in their Manner
of Wearing. I have ſeen a Pair of Cloths
ſo fine, and ſo bright dyed, as to be worth
Thirty Shillings Sterling. Their Colours are
either Blue or Yellow, ſome very lively, the
firſt is dyed with Indico, the latter with Barks
of Trees. I never ſaw any of them Red.

*1731.
Jolloiffs
ingenious
in manu-
facturing
Cotton*

On the 16th, our Smith *James Collins,*
who had fired at our Enſign as before mention'd, was drummed out of the Company's
Service, with an Halter round his Neck, and
afterwards ſent on Board the *Guinea* Pacquet,
in which he took his Paſſage for *England*; ſhe
having this Evening broke ground, and fallen
a little Way down the River   The next Day
the Governor and Mrs *Davis* went in her to
accompany our Second Chief, Capt. *Stibbs,*
as far as the River's Mouth: He went home
on account of his ill State of Health. The
Fame Sloop came down the River, and proceeded along with the *Guinea* Pacquet, in order
to bring back the Governor and Mrs *Davis.*

*Our Smith
ſent to
England.*

O n

1731   On the 26th, Mr *William* Rober, ,re
Factor at *Geregii*, set out for *Joar*, and w,
him took Mr *John Harrison* as his Assistan,
Mr *Thomas Saxby*, the present Factor there,
being order'd down to the Fort, on account
of several Extravagancies by him there com
mitted

Author
goes to
Vintain
A Descri-
ption of
that Place

On the 29th, about Noon, the Governor
and I set out for *Vintain*, where we arrived in
three Hours. It lies about six Leagues from
James Fort; some Part of the Way is up a
River of the same Name. This Town belongs
to one of the Emperors of *Foma*, and is very
pleasantly situated on the Side of a Hill,
close to the River. It is inhabited both by
Portuguese and *Mahometans*, the latter having
for their Devotions a handsome Mosque, with
an *Ostrich*'s Egg at the Top on the Outside
It is noted for Plenty of Provisions, a great
many of which are brought by the *Foys*,
who border on it It also produces good Quantities of Bees-Wax, to buy which the Com
pany have here a small Factory Above the
Town is fine green Grass, and some Trees
which make it very pleasant.

As soon as we came to Town, the Alcade
and all the chief People, came to welcome us,
and soon after the Emperor arrived (in whose
Dominions this Town lies) The common

Dress of
the People

People were dress'd with a Cloth round their
Middles, which came down about their Knees,
and another Cloth over their right Shoulder,
(the Men having generally one Arm bare,
which the Women have not) and the Womens
Cloths come generally down as low as the

fmall of their Legs They are very proud
of their Hair, fome wear it in Tufts and
Bunches, and others cut it in Croffes quite
over their Heads The Men commonly wear
Caps made of Cotton-Cloth, fome plain, and
fome with Feathers and Goats Tails The
Women gererally wear Handkerchiefs tied
round their Heads, leaving their Crowns bare,
and for want of Handkerchiefs they ufe Slips
of blue or white Cotton-Cloth. Others will
let their Hair hang down on each Side of
their Heads, plaited like Horfes Manes, on
which they ftring Coral, and for want of it
Pipe beads A great many of them (efpecially up the River) wear on the Crowns of
their Heads a good Number of fmall Horfe-
Bells, which, when their Hair is plaited, and
they are in all their Finery, makes 'em look
not unlike the Fore-Horfe of a Country Far-
mer's Team.

T H E Y are not very proud in the Furniture of their Houfes, for the moft that any
of them have is a fmall Cheft for Clothes, a
Mat raifed upon Sticks from the Ground to
lye on, a Jarr to hold Water, a fmall Calabafh to drink it with, two or three wooden
Mortars in which they pound their Corn and
Rice, a Basket or two to fift it in when beat,
and two or three large Calabifhes, out of
which they eat it with their Hands. They
are not very careful of laying up a Store a-
gainft a Time of Scarcity, but chufe rather
to fell what they can, and in the Time of
Famine they can faft two or three Days without eating, (which I myfelf know to be true,
there being a very great Famine in the Year

*The Na-
tives Hou-
fhold Fur-
niture*

*Oecono-
my*

1732,

1732, efpecially high up the River, where I then was) but then they are always fmoaking Tobacco, which ferves to amufe 'em   This Tobacco they raife themfelves   They fow it as foon as they have cut their Corn   That which grows near the River is very ftrong, but a little Way from it, it is much weaker. Their Pipes are made of Clay, very neat, and of a reddifh Colour, the Stems are only a Piece of Reed, or fmall Stick bored through with an hot Iron Wyre, fome of which are fix Foot long   After they are bored they polifh them with rough Leaves till they are very fmooth, white and handfome, and withal very ftrong, they faften the Bowl and Stem together with a Piece of red Leather, fometimes with a fine Leather Taffel hanging o it about the middle of the Stem, and tho' the End of the Reed goes into the Bowl of the Pipe, it fits almoft as well as Pipes that are made all in one, they clean the Reeds, when foul, by drawing long Straws thro' them, and the earthen Bowls by fcraping them with a fmall Knife   The Merchants which travel much, carry with them Pipes of a great Size, fome of them holding no lefs than half a Pint   Thefe are their Travelling Pipes

THEIR Towns are Numbers of Houfes built promifcuoufly together, the Huts are generally fourteen or fifteen Yards in Circumference, built with Mud and binding Clay and cover'd with long Grafs or Ciboa Leaves, commonly call'd *Palmetto*   Their Doors are very fmall, and don't go upon Hinges, but are let into the Houfe-Wall.   They generally keep

Marginal notes: 1731.   Tobacco   Pipes   Huts

keep their Houses very clean, but I cannot say sweet, by reason of their stinking Fish, and other things which they keep in them

On the 2d of *July*, in the Afternoon, we set out from *Vintain* for *Geregia*, when we went to take Water, we were accompanied to the Boat by the Emperor, and almost all the Men in the whole Town. In the Evening we reach'd *Geregia*, where, during the Time we stay'd, I shot a wild Goose, which weigh'd twenty Pounds, and likewise a long green Snake about five Foot long, as he was wrapt round a poor Lizard, endeavouring to kill him *July* Author goes to *Geregia*

On the 5th, being disappointed of Horses to carry us over Land to *Tancrowall*, we set out in the Governor's Cutter About Midnight we reach'd *Vintain*, where we stopt till Day-light, and then we set out from it, and I observ'd that at about two Miles Distance the Town look'd just like a Parcel of Bee-Hives When we came to *Vintain* River's Mouth, we met with the Tide of Flood, which carry'd us up to *Tancrowall*, where we staid about four Days, and the Governor having done his Business, we then set out for *James* Fort, about Two a-Clock in the Afternoon By the Time we came to *Seaca* Point (which is within six Miles of the Island) it was quite dark, but having continual Flashes of Lightning, we could see the Fort very plain We steer'd by the Lightning till we were within two Miles of the Fort, and then it ceased We could see no Land, it was excessive dark, a Tornado came upon us, and the Wind Goes from *Geregia* to *Tancrowall* Returns to *James Fort*

blew

1731 blew so very hard, that we were obliged to take down our Awning for fear of Oversetting, we would have come to a Grapling, but had not Rope enough   The Thunder rattled dismally, and the Rain wetted us soon to the Skin   In this Condition we tumbled and tossed at the Mercy of the Waves for about an Hour and half, the Tornado still continuing, and the Sea running very high   At last the Lightning began again, and we saw some Land, to which we rowed directly, and it proved to be a Point, upon that we were to the Port, and got ashore, and in going from the River Side to the Town on a narrow Path between the Rice-Grounds, we got several Slips, and it was seldom that we were both upon our Legs at once, however we got safe to the Governor's House, and having a good Fire made, we shifted ourselves, drank large Drams of Cordial Waters, went to Bed, slept three or four Hours, and then went over to the Island   I was soon after taken ill of a Fever

ON the 19th, Mr *Ierman*, a Merchant of *Carticos*, came over Land to *Georgia*, and from thence by Water to the Port, to visit the Governor

ON the 13th of *August*, a little Girl Slave belonging to our Governor, as she was washing herself up to her Knees in the River, was taken away by a Shark

ON the 15th, being Sunday, I was able to read Prayers to those few People, who could come into the Publick Room, there being

[margin notes:] No to be neglected at certain co

Author is ill

August

A Girl carried away by a Shark

The Author recovers

being a great many very ill in their Beds, as   1731.
I had been for this Month paft, but was then
pretty well recover'd.

On the 24th, the Governor and Mr *Har-
r on* fent for me, and told me, that as they
were in Expectation of my being appointed
a Factor by the next Advice from the Company, they had thought it proper to fend me
up to *Joar* in the mean Time, to learn the
Nature of the Trade, and the Temper of the
Natives, and order'd me to prepare myfelf
for the Voyage.

On the 28th, about Ten at Night, I em- Author
bark'd on Board the *Fame* Sloop, *John Boys* goes up
Mafter, and proceeded up the River towards the River
Joar, having receiv'd from the Governor and to *Joar*
Chief Merchants the following Orders.

Mr F R A N C I S M O O R E.

James Fort, Aug 28, 1731.

S I R,

Y*OU are, on Receipt hereof, to embark on* His O.-
Board the Company's Sloop Fame, *Capt.* ders
Jonn Boys, *and proceed to* Joar *Factory under
the Direction of Mr* William Roberts, *Factor,
whom we have order'd to give you the beft Light
into the Nature of the Trade, and every thing
elfe neceffary to qualify you to take upon you the
Management of the Company's Affairs, where
and whenever it fhall be required of you*

*You are therefore, upon your Arrival there,
to apply yourfelf to him , and, fo long as you
fhall continue there, to aid and affift him in
every*

1731. *every thing that relates to the Trade, and the Company's Affairs, and especially to be on all Occasions obedient to his Commands, in order to enable you to be the sooner qualified as aforesaid.*

You are to advise us, from Time to Time, of the Progress you make, and give us a particular Account of your Remarks of the Trade, and above all, the Methods you shall think best to be used to please the Traders, and to encourage them to trade with the Company with the least Expence. We wish you Health, and are

Your Loving Friends,

ANTHONY ROGERS.

THO. HARRISON

September.   ON the Passage we met with a great many hard Tornados, which by their being very formidable, obliged us to come often to Anchor   About thirty Leagues from the Fort we met the *Greyhound* Galley, Capt. *Ramsay,* a separate Trader, who had been lying at *Joar* all the Rains, and not purchased above seventy five Slaves, and some of them he was obliged to take by Force, they being free People, crossing the River in a Canoa, whom he took on Account of old *Serin Donso,* a noted Broker at *Cower,* near *Joar,* who having had a great deal of Money from Capt. *Ramsay,* on Promise of bringing him a great deal of Trade, and not being so good as his Word, he very justly seized these People, and the Natives hearing of it, obliged the old
Broker

Broker to redeem them, which he accordingly did.

THIS Ship having loft her Voyage, for want Obfervati-
of being able to flave foon, and being obliged ons on the
to lie, at great Expence and Hazards of Slave
Men's Lives, all the wet Seafon, made me Trade
think what great Advantage it might be both
to the feparate Traders, and the Company, if
the great Mart of Exchange was to be at
James Fort: That is to fay, if the Company Advantage
kept a Stock of Slaves at the Fort, suffici- of *James*
ent to furnifh any Ship immediately, with a Fort for a
whole Cargo, which as foon as difpofed of, Mart
they might be again fupplied from their Out-
Factories. The feparate Trader would afford to give a larger Price at *James* Fort, than
he can up the River, for there is the Charges of
going up, the Uncertainty of getting the Cargo,
and when he has fometimes got half a Cargo, he
may lie fome Months before he can be able to
compleat it; all the Time he lies there he runs
the Hazard of the Sicknefs and Rebellion of
thofe Slaves he already has, they being apter
to rife in a Harbour than when out at Sea;
fince if they once get Mafters of a Ship, in
the River, their Efcape to Shore is almoft
certain, by running the Ship aground; but
at Sea it is otherwife, for if they fhould fur-
prize a Ship there, as they cannot navigate
her, they muft have the Affiftance of the
White Men, or perifh Befides, whilft the
Ships lie in the River, the Crews are apt to
be fick, and confequently not able to guard
their Slaves; of which feveral Inftances have
been, and Ships loft thereby. They are alfo
liable to Palavers, which often turn out very

G ex-

expensive, and they are obliged to pay Cuſtoms, and make exceſſive large Preſents to
the Kings and Brokers, as thoſe who have
been trading to *Joar* muſt know by Experience. All this would be avoided by buying
a Cargo at once. The Company would have
a Conveniency alſo by it, ſince they cannot,
without Diſadvantage, buy dry Goods, without buying Slaves with them. If therefore
they ſold the Slaves to the ſeparate Traders,
they might aſſort their Warehouſe with the
European Goods from them, and thereby
command all the dry Goods in the River, in
ſpite both of the *Portugueze* and *French*, and
with good Care of the Factors, there might
be dry Goods enough procured for to load
home the Company's Ships with Speed, ſo as
they might not be upon Charges, and loſe
Time by going on trading Voyages down
the Coaſt, none of which, in my Time, ever
turned out to the Company's Advantage.

O N E Night we anchored off *Elephant's
Iſland*; from whence we had a vaſt Number
of Muſquetoes and Sand Flies, who diverted
us ſo prettily that we could not get any Sleep
all Night On the 4th of *Sept* we reached

Author
arrives at
Joar.
Joar, but I was ſo miſerably mauled, on the
Way, by the Muſquetoes, that I could hardly
walk from the Boat up to the Factory. In
the Evening, the *Adventure* Sloop, *John Leach*
Maſter, came to *Joar*, having been on a
trading Voyage to *Fatatenda*, where, by the
Violence of the Freſhes, ſhe loſt all her Anchors, and was obliged to uſe her Guns inſtead of them. She got an Anchor and Cable
from

from the *Fame*, and the fame Night failed for
James Fort.

ON the 9th, the King of *Barfally* came to   *King of*
Town, attended by three of his Brothers,   *Barfally*
viz. *Boomey Haman Seaca*, who was formerly   *arrives at*
King, and elder than the King, *Boomey Ha-*   *Joar.*
man Benda, younger than the King, and *Boo-*
my Loyi Eminga, younger than him, befides
which there were above 100 Horfemen, and
above the fame Number of Men on Foot.
Notwithftanding he has a very good Houfe of
his own in this Town, yet would he come and
lie at the Factory.   In the firft Place he took
Poffeffion of Mr *Roberts*'s own Bed, and then   *His Beha-*
having drank Brandy till he was drunk, at   *viour.*
the Perfuafion of fome of his People, order'd
Mr *Roberts* to be held, whilft himfelf took
out of his Pocket the Key of his Storehoufe,
into which he and feveral of his People went,
and took what they pleafed, his chief Hank
was Brandy, of which there happen'd to be
but one Anchor, he took that out, drank a
good deal of it, made himfelf drunk, and
then was put to bed.   This Anchor lafted
him three Days, and then he went all over
the Houfe to feek for more ; at laft he came
into a Rome where Mr *John Harrifon* lay
fick, and feeing there a Cafe in which was fix
Gallons and half of Brandy belonging to
him and me, he ordered *Jack Harrifon* to
get out of Bed and open it, but he told him
very ferioufly that there was nothing in it
but fome of the Company's authentick Papers, which muft not be opened   The
King was too well acquainted with Liquor-
Cafes to be put off fo, and therefore ordered
fome

1731   some of his Men to hold him in his Bed, whilst he took the Key out of his Breeches Pocket, he then open'd it, and took all the Liquor out of it, and was not sober so long as it lasted, but I must do the King this Justice, by saying that he very often sent for Mr *Harruin* and myself to drink with him As soon as this Brandy was drank up, he talked of going home, upon which, his People, even his chief Ministers, who are the General, and the Keeper of his Majesty's Stores, amused themselves in taking what they thought best, which, with one Thing or another, amounted to twenty Pound Sterling, and they had the Assurance to open even Chests and Boxes What Resistance could three Men make against 300? Sometimes the King would ride abroad, and take most of his Attendance with him, but then, when he was gone abroad, we were plagued with the Company of *Bemey Human Benda*, and his Brother, who were, if possible, worse than his Majesty.

Behaviour of one of the King's People   ONE Day it happen'd that he took a Mug of Water, and pretending to drink, took his Mouth full, and then putting the Mug on the Table, he spurted the Water out of his Mouth into my Face, upon which, considering that if I suffer'd such Insolence from Black Men, it would make them the more bold and insulting. and that it was better to venture dying once, than to be continually abused, and the Occasion of other *English* being contemn'd. so I took the Remainder of the Water, and threw it into his Breeches, upon that, he had Recourse to his Knife, and

endeavour'd

endeavoured to ftab me, but was prevented by his favourite Attendant, who, feeing what had pafs'd, held his Arm, and reprefented to him the unhandfom Ufage he had given me, and the Provocations I had received to wet him Upon which he was fo much afhamed, that he came and lay down upon the Floor, with his Garment off, and took my Foot and placed it upon his Neck, and there lay till I defired him to rife After which, no Man was a greater Friend to me, nor more willing to oblige me in any refpect than he was.

ANOTHER time he came at Night, after our Gate was fhut, and broke it down, and coming into the Houfe, with a Piftol in his Hand, demanded Entrance into the King's Chamber, but the King's Attendants ftopt him, and tried to awake the King, but found it impracticable The next Morning he being acquainted with it, fent his General to charge him not to come in his Prefence any more till he fhould fend for him, and that for his Attempt to kill him the Evening before, he fined him three Slaves

THE King and all his Attendance profefs the Mahometan Religion, notwithftanding they drank fo much Strong Liquors, and when he is fober, or not quite fuddled, he prays Some of that Perfwafion are fo ftrict, that they will fooner die than drink Strong Liquors, but the King is of quite another Opinion, for he will fooner die than drink Small when he can get Strong He dreffes the fame as moft of the Kings in this Country do, with a Garment like a Surplice, which comes no lower than

than the Knees, a Pair of Breeches of the same Sort of Cloth, about seven Yards wide, gather'd round the middle, he wears no Stockings, but always a Pair of Slippers, (except when he ri es) a small white Cotton Cap, and commonly a Pair of Gold Ear-rings His People, as well as himfelf, wear always white Cloths and white Caps, and as they are exceeding black, it makes them look very well He is a tall Man, very paffionate, and sometimes when any of his Men affront him, he does not fcruple to fhoot them, at which, I am told, he is very dexterous And sometimes when he goes aboard a Company's Sloop at *Cotore*, (his own Town and Place of Dwelling) he is for fhooting at all the Canoes

which pafs by him, killing perhaps one Man or two frequently in a Day He has got a great many Wives but never brings above two or three abroad with him He has feveral Brothers, to whom he feldom fpeaks, or permits into his Company, and when they do come, they pull off their Caps and Garments, and throw Duft upon their Foreheads, as every one does which come into the King's Prefence (except White Men) As foon as the King dies, his Brothers or Sons go to fighting for the Crown, and whoever is the ftrongeft, is made King

THIS King is potent, and very bold His Dominions are large, and divided into feveral Parts, over which he appoints Governors, call'd *Boone*, who come every Year to pay Homage to him Thefe *Boones* are very powerful, and do juft what they pleafe

with the People , and altho' they are feared,   1731
yet are they beloved

OTHER Kings generally advise with their   He is ab-
Head People, and scarcely do any thing of   solute
great Consequence, without consulting with
them first , but the King of *Barsally* is so
absolute, that he will not allow any of his
People to advise with him, unless it be his
Head Man (and chief Slave) call'd *Ferbro*, viz
Master of the Horse) who carries the King's
Sword in a large Silver-Case of a great Weight,
and who gives Orders for what things the
king wants to have, or to be done, and in
Battle he is the Leader of his Men

THE King's usual Way of Living is to   His odd
sleep all Day till towards Sun-set, then he gets   Way of
up to drink, and goes to sleep again till Mid-   Living
night , then he rises and eats, and if he has
any strong Liquors, will sit and drink till Day-
light, and then eat, and go to sleep again.
When he is well stock'd with Liquor, he will
sit and drink for five or six Days together,
and not eat one Morsel of any thing in all
that time   It is to that insatiable Thirst of
his after Brandy, that his Subjects Freedoms
and Families are in so precarious a Situation;
for he very often goes with some of his Troops
by a Town in the Day-time, and returns in
the Night and sets fire to three Parts of it,
and sets Guards at the fourth to seize the   His Way
People as they run out from the Fire , he ties   of getting
their Arms behind them, and marches them   Slaves
to the Place where he sells them, which is
either *Joar* or *Colone*

1731
He leaves Joar

On the 16th, the King and his Guards went away for *Cohore*, having amongst them stript Mr *Roberts's* Chamber, and carried away his Clothes and Books, which last they took to *Cower*, and offer'd to sell to the *Mahometan* Priest, who looking over the Books, and not understanding any of them, and being a Friend to Mr *Roberts*, told them, That he believed they were Books wherein he kept the Account of his Goods, and that to take them away would inevitably ruin him Upon which they left them with him, to give back to the Person they belonged to

October

On the 17th Day of *October*, Mr *[illegible] Harr[illegible]*, my Fellow-Writer, went down to *James* Fort in the *Fame* Sloop, in order to be cured of a Flux, with which he was very much afflicted, but I believed he would be never free from it, unless he left off the strong Liquors, which are usually drunk in that Country All this Month was excessive hot, and it began to be very foggy Mornings

November
Cold Mornings and Evenings

On the 1st of *November* I found the Mornings and Evenings begin to be exceeding cold, but in the middle of the Day the Sun very hot.

Author detects a Thief

On the [illegible]th, at Midnight, being not very well, I happen'd to awake, and seeing a Light in the Storehouse, I immediately rose, and taking a loaded Pistol in my Hand, went towards the Light, where I found one of our Black Servants very busy in robbing the Store, I seiz'd him, and had him put in Irons, without Mr *Roberts* knowing any thing of the

Mr

Matter, altho' he lay in the next Room, with the Key of the Stores always under his Pillow: The Fellow got it from under his Head without awaking him, and thinking that I was afleep too, was the reafon of his lighting the Candle, in order to pick and chufe what fort or Goods he liked beft , and had he not lighted a Candle, it is probable I fhould not have detected him

On the 12th, I faw an *Oftrich*, with a Man riding upon the Back of it, who was going down to the Fort, it being a Prefent to our Governor, from Mr *James Connei*, who bought it when he was trading at *Iato'enda* in *Auguft* laft   The Evenings and Mornings were very cold   I was very ill with Pains in my Bones, and Boils breaking out all over me, fo that for four Days I was fcarce able to crawl

A large Oftrich

On the 22d of *December*, Captain *Robert Cole*, a feparate Trader, who was late in the Company's Service, and went home laft Year, came to anchor at *Rumbo's* Port in the Snow *Tryall*, in order to purchafe young Slaves for *Lisbon*

December.

On the 3d of *January* came up a *New-England* Scooner call'd the *Gambia*, *John Wise* Mafter, loaded with Salt and Rum, he ftay'd here but a fhort while, and then proceeded up the River to *Caffan*, about four Tides above this Place   We bought fome Wild Hog and Venifon, and found it very good Eating, but very lean   I alfo faw an Alligator about fix Foot long, kill'd by a Native

January.

Native with a Spear, as he was fwimming in the River.

A Camel.   O n the 18th, I faw a large Camel belonging to the King of *Barfally*, which was prefented to him by the King of *Demel*, a Country near the River *Senegal*. A Meffenger which Mr *Roberts* fent down to the Fort, return'd this Day with Letters from *England* for us both, wherein I found that Mr *Oglethorpe* had been fo indulgent as to have 2000*l*. Security given for me, and upon his Recommendation the Company was pleafed to appoint me Factor. I receiv'd likewife Letters from the Governor, and other Gentlemen at *James* Fort; which, among other Things, inform'd me of the Death of one of my intimate Friends and Acquaintance, Mr *Charles Houghton*, Factor, with whom I came over. On *New Years*-Day he and one Mr *Sergeant* lying in a Room, and not being well, went to Bed before Night. About Midnight Mr *Houghton* awaked, and not being able to go to fleep again, and ill withal, defir'd *Sergeant* to give him a few Drops of *Laudanum* (of which there was a fmall Vial in the Window) in a Glafs of Water. That carelefs Fellow *Sergeant*, being in the Dark, pours the *Laudanum* into the Water by guefs, and gives it to Mr *Houghton*, who drank it up, went to fleep, and never waked after. He was a very worthy Man, and would have been of great Service to the Company, had he lived.

Author made Factor.

Account of the Death of Mr Cha. Houghton.

K of Barfally comes again to Joar.   O n the 21ft of this Month of *January*, arrived the King of *Barfally*, who yefterday
                                        fell

fell upon one of his own Towns, and having taken a good many Prifoners, brought them along with him, with Intent (I believe) to fell them to Captain *Clarke,* a feparate Trader, now at anchor at *Rambo's* Port. On his Arrival he took Poffeffion of Mr *Roberts's* Bed and Room for himfelf, and the Slavehoufe for his Slaves and People who look after them. He foon inquired after that Fellow which I found robbing the Stores, whom Mr *Roberts* fome time fince fent down to the Fort, he being an intimate Acquaintance of the King's. The King's Behaviour this Time was not much unlike the laft, which obliged me to write the following Letter to the Governor.

To ANTH. ROGERS, *Efq; Governor of*
JAMES FORT.

Joar *Factory,* Jan 22, 1731-2.
SIR,

ON the 18th *Inftant I received your agree-* Author's
able Letter, as alfo fome from Mr Ogle- Letter to
thorpe *and Mr* Hayes. *I muft now acquaint* the Go-
you, that the Day after, the King of Barfally vernor.
arrived with a fmall Retinue of about a hun-
dred Men, and forty or fifty Slaves, moft of
which are unmerchantable He came directly to
the Factory, and took Poffeffion of Mr Roberts's
Room for himfelf, and the Slavehoufe for his
People and Captives. He endeavour'd as much
as poffible to get the Key of the Stores, which
Mr Roberts *prevented with much Difficulty by*
rufhing out of the Room. Soon after he fent his
Men to feize me, who when they brought me to
him, laid me along upon the Bed, and fearched
my

my Pockets for the Key of the Store, but found it not. He asks much after that Fellow we sen. down for robbing the Stores, and is very angr, at our sending him away from hence. His being so inquisitive after that Fellow, so eager after the Key of the Stores, and his not suffering Peopl. to carry any thing from the Factory, gives m. reason to believe that he intends to strip th. Warehouse ere he departs, which, I am afraid nothing but a Sloop's Arrival (with Mr Harri son) can prevent. I am obliged to bear the In sults of his People to prevent Outrages, but as . am now in hopes of going soon from hence, I wil bear whatever I possibly can, believing it to b for the Company's Interest. I am

S I R,

Your most obedient and

humble Servant

FRA. MOORE

The King tradeswith Captain *Clarke*, and his People behaved ver
C *Clarke.* infolently to Mr *Roberts* and myfelf, on ac
count of that Fellow which we fent down p
the Fort for robbing the Stores

Fame ON the 27th, in the Afternoon, arrive
Sloop ar- the Company's Sloop *Fame*, with a Cargo a
rives with
a Cargo mounting to about five thoufand Barrs, an
a long Letter from the Governor and M
Harrifon, which came away before it was pol
fible for our Letters to be arrived there A
it is concerning the Trade, I am of Opin'o

It will not be thought improper to enter the whole Letter, of which there is an exact Copy, *Appendix*, No. II.

T H E Occasion of this Letter was upon new Instructions coming from *England* ; for the Direction, into which Mr *Oglethorpe* had been lately chosen, and in which Mr *Hayes*, who was perfectly well acquainted with the Trade of *Africa*, had a great Weight, were resolved to leave no means unattempted to re establish that, and the Affairs of the Company ; not by distressing the separate Traders, but by bringing the Company's Servants to do their Duty, and to act with Zeal and Honesty towards the Company. To encourage them in it, the Prices of Provisions at *James* Fort were lower'd, Mr *Hayes* also was thoroughly satisfied that the Trade might be made very advantageous, by enlarging up the River, and encouraging Dry Goods, and by striking out new Trades with the Inland People of *Africa*, who are almost innumerable, and who would demand and consume a great many Manufactures, had they wherewithal to pay for them. To enable them to do which, Mr *Hayes* proposed taking off all Kinds of Goods which that Country produces, and encouraging the Natives with giving them Goods, for what they before thought useless, *viz*. Gums, Dying Barks, Woods, Hides, &c. And to induce the Company's Servants to be vigilant in opening new Trades, they gave Twenty *per Cent*. Encouragement to those who should discover any new Goods, out of the Gains that should arise from them; but this last is not mention'd in the Letter.

T H E

1732
The King
not to be
trusted.

THE King and his Guards not being gone, and their Behaviour extraordinary bad, we did not think it proper to land the Goods, or take a Survey of those in the Store, till such Time as the Coast was clear, being apprehensive that they had a Design of seizing them. During the Time the King had been trading with Captain *Clarke*, he had obliged us to lend him our Storehouse to put his Goods into, where he and his Attendance frequently sat an Hour together drinking and smoaking.

Unfortu
nate Acci
dent

This Evening, as they were carousing there the King took up a Musquet of ours in his Hand, and not imagining it to be loaded, fired it off, and shot a Brace of Balls into the Thigh of *Tomba Mendez*, Son to the late King of *Bar*, by a *Portuguese* Woman, and Cousin to the King. This Man was the Promoter of all the Mischief that was done; or the King himself is a good-natur'd Man, and when sober, is unwilling to use any White Man ill, especially those belonging to the Company. Had the King happen'd to have been sitting on the other Side of the Room, the Ball would have went into the very middle of our Powder-Room, and the Fire perhaps have blowed us all up. However, it was, the King was very angry at Mr *R*— and me for keeping loaded Arms by us, and at the same time ask'd us, If we thought that either he or his People would do us any Harm. Which shews, that he thought we ought to be as obedient to him as his own Subjects, whom he daily makes Slaves of, and that he was so exceedingly mistaken as to think that his Behaviour was very agreeable to us, when nothing can come up to it for Vexa-

a

and Uneafinefs. However, on the third of *February*, very early in the Morning, the king and his Attendance went away, fome of them having broke open my Buroe, and taken Things out to a confiderable Value, the fame Fate attended Mr *Roberts*, and poor Mr *Huryon*, who leaving his Scrutore behind him, had it broke all to Pieces, and fome Things taken away. They alfo took near 200 Barrs of the Company's Goods out of the Storehoufe, exclufive of the Prefents made them by Mr *Roberts*, which were very confiderable. As foon as they were gone, Mr *Roberts*, Boys, and I confulted in what Manner it was beft for us to proceed. I was unwilling to take Charge of this Factory, where we were liable to fo many Infults from the King's People, whenever he came here, which had been twice within five Months, and yet for five Years before *September* laft, he was not near the Factory once. At laft, I agreed to take a Survey of the Goods in Store, and take the Cargo a fhore which the *Fame* had brought up, and that being done, to take my Paffage in the *Fame*, down to the Fort, to acquaint the Gentlemen thoroughly of the King's Manner of behaving towards us, when at the Factory, and withal to have him prevented from coming any more, or elfe it would be impoffible for any one to live there. Three Days we fpent in taking an Inventory, and bringing our Cargo into the Storehoufe, which being done, I immediately fet out for the Fort, as I propofed, carrying with me the following Letter, from my Colleague, Mr *Roberts*, viz.

1732.

February

King, &c depart like Robbers

Confultation had

Refolution

T 2

To the GOVERNOR, *and chief Mer-*
chants of JAMES FORT.

JOAR Factory, *Feb.* 8, 1732.

GENTLEMEN,

Roberts's
Letter.

YOURS, per *the* Fame *Sloop, came safe*
to hand, with the Goods, agreeable to In-
voice. I have perused the several Paragraphs of
your Letter, and shall endeavour, on my Part,
carefully to observe the same, and hope shall not
fail therein. What merchantable Slaves the King
of Barsally *brought, he sold to Capt.* Clarke, *be-*
fore the Sloop arrived, altho' he gave me fair
Promises every Day. As to his Behaviour here,
Mr Moore, *and Capt.* Boys *will inform you*
more than I can express in Writing. We endea-
vour'd to keep him out of the Stores, but to no
Purpose, he would not be resisted, but go in, and
with him ten or twelve of his People, intent upon
nothing but Thieving, which we could in no man-
ner prevent. His own Key-keeper has a Key,
with which they open'd the Stores in the Night-
time, and stole considerable Quantities of Goods,
an exact Account of which you have herein in-
closed. Had not the Sloop come up, nothing could
have prevented their taking the whole Store
They have stole almost all I had, broke my Chest,
and Messieurs Harrison's *and* Moore's *Scrutores,*
and taken most of the Things out of them　All
our Servants ran away, being afraid of being
seized and sold. Unless the King can be pre-
vented from coming here, and acting in this Man-
ner, no Person can pretend to live here; being
not only in Danger of losing what Things we
have,

have, but even our Lives. I hope, Gentlemen, you'll confider, and give Redrefs, our Cafe being quite defperate. I have no more to add, but remain,

> GENTLEMEN,
>
> Your moft humble Servant,
>
> WILLIAM ROBERTS.

ON our Way down we met a large Ship from *Briftol*, called the *Gregory*, Capt. *Robert Smith*, a feparate Trader, going up the River to flave at *Joar*. We alfo met the *Adventure* Sloop going up to *Samy*, with Mr *Lemaigre*, a Company's Factor, who lives there, and trades for the Company, to whom he remits Slaves all the Year round, at forty Barrs *per* Head.

ON the 11th, we arrived at *James* Fort, having had a brifk fair Gale all the Way down. The Governor was gone down in the *Guinea* Packet, Capt. *Martin* (who arrived here from *England* the 15th Inftant) to *Barringding*, one of the King of *Barrah*'s Towns, where he yet ftaid, in order to adjuft fome Difputes between him and the Company, concerning the Governor's affifting fome feparate Traders, who refufe to pay the King's Cuftoms.

ON the 14th, the *Guinea* Packet returned with the Governor; there likewife came up in Company with her a large Ship from *Lifbon*, called the *Andaluzia*, Capt. *Pearfon*, to purchafe Slaves for the *Brazil*. The next Day the *Adventure* Sloop carried up the Al-cade

H

1732 cade of *Vintain*, and his Attendants, to their
own Town, they having been down with the
Governor at the King of *Barrah's* Town

ON the 22d, the Governor and I went on
board the *Guinea Packet*, who was then going
on a trading Voyage to *Cutcheo*, after which
we went on board the *Dispatch* Sloop, to take
Leave of the Captain, being now bound for
England After we had failed a little Way
down with them we came up in the *Cutter*
And the next Day we went over to *Gillyfree*,
with Mr *John Harrison*, to take Charge of
that Factory, in the room of Mr *Hugh Hamilton*, who was going to settle a Factory at
Fattatenda

*Dispatch
Sloop goes
for England*

Soon after, the *Braadwater*, Capt *Pearce*,
failed up the River, and the *Tryal*, Cap
Clarke, came down from *Joar*, having about
feventy young Slaves, by him we received
Advice that the Company's Factory at *Yam-
amacunda* was burnt down

*Factory of
Yamama-
cunda
burnt*

ON the 1ft of *March*, having thoroughly
acquainted the Gentlemen of the Manner we
were uſed in at *Joar*, by the King of *Barrah*, and his Attendants, and having several
Times expreſſed my Uneaſineſs at ſtaying ſo
long from my Factory, and being as often
aſſured by the Governor, that whatever Deficiencies ſhould be made, during my Abſence,
ſhould be placed to my Colleague's particular Account, I ſet out for *Joar*, in the *Diſpatch* Sloop, *John Cooper* Maſter, but having ſtrong Land Breezes againſt us, we could
not arrive there in leſs than five Days,

March

*Authors
Reprefen-
tation*

*Sets out
again for
Joar*

Jn 5

having by the Way Occafion to drink fome
of the River Water, occafioned by Neglect
of not filling Cafks below, we found the fame
to be brackifh forty Leagues above the Fort
On my Arrival at *Joar*, I delivered Mr *Ro-*
berts the following Letter

JAMES FORT, *Feb* 28, 1731

Meff. { WM ROBERTS
and
FR MOORE,

*T*HIS *will be delivered to you by Mr*   Letter in
Moore, and ferves to anfwer Mr Ro-   Anfwer to
berts's Letter, of the 8th Inftant   Mr Roberts's

We have in the moft mature Manner confi-
der'd the Goods, which you, Mr Roberts, fay
were ftolen by the King of Barfally, *but when*
we compared the fame with the Inventory you
fent down, and the Goods difburfed by you, with
that Inventory taken the 31ft of December laft,
we find that what is reprefented by you to be
ftolen by the King, are all the Goods that appear
to be deficient by cafting up your own Books only,
without giving any Proof to us that they were
actually ftolen by him or People, no otherwife,
than that whatever Goods fhall to you appear to
be deficient at the King's coming to Joar, *tho'*
from any Neglect of yours whatever, muft, in
Courfe, be ftolen by him. Thefe Proceedings of
yours, now, Mr Roberts, when compared with
what has appeared againft you formerly, con-
cerning Deficiencies, tho' out of mier Neglect
only, without any fuch or other Caufe whatever,
you muft believe, cannot influence us to pafs fuch

H 2   *Account,*

1732

Accounts, without absolute Prejudice to the Company's Interest. You are therefore to take Notice, that unless we are better satisfied concerning the Affair, than what is made to appear by Mr Moore *and Capt* Boys, *we cannot, on any Account, admit of allowing such a Loss to the Company. For it is apparent by what you, Mr* Moore, *have acquainted us, that Mr* Roberts *might have taken an Inventory of the Company's Goods in Store, from the Time he first received the News of the King's coming, to his Arrival at* Joar. *Your Deficiencies, upon a second Survey, at his Departure, might justly then be supposed to be made away with by the King and People, (as they did forcibly enter into the Company's Warehouse.) And what leaves you no Excuse for not doing this when you first heard of his coming, was your frequent Declarations, long before, that you expected no otherwise, whenever he came to* Joar. *This, and many other Proceedings, which do not cohere with the Company's Interest, obliges us to acquaint you, and you are hereby directed, that Mr* Moore, *your* Colleague, *have the* Charge *of keeping the Warehouse, and you the* Books; *and for the more effectual preventing any Abuses being offered to either Party, it is expected, upon Receipt of this, that a Survey be taken, in order that you, Mr* Moore, *have no Pretence from being accountable, in case of any Deficiencies happening hereafter, and which is to be done in the Presence of Capt* Cooper *to avoid Disputes.*

THERE goes by this Sloop a small Cargo, which Mr Moore *has sign'd Receipts for. We have not to add, but wish you Health, and remain*

Your Friends and humble Servants,
ANT. ROGERS, THO. HARRISON.

We

We set directly about taking an Inventory of the Company's Effects, on my being appointed to look to the Stores, at which Mr *Roberts* was exceeding angry, and let fall a great many Expressions, which relish'd of nothing but ruin to myself and the Company's Affairs. Soon after, the *Sea-Nymph* sail'd for *James* Fort, with a Parcel of fine Slaves which Mr *Roberts* had purchased during my Absence.

1732 Misunderstanding with Mr Roberts.

Sea-Nymph with Slaves for James Fort.

On the 8th, came up the *Fame* Sloop, with Mr *Hugh Hamilton*, and *Edward Peeters* his Assistant, now going to settle a Factory at *Fatatenda* The *James Island* Shallop came up also, with Mess. *Philip Galand* and *Henry Johnson* Writers, who were going to settle another Factory at *Brucoe*, about seventy Leagues above this Place They stay'd here but one Night, and then proceeded on their Voyages.

Fame Sloop, &c for Fatatenda and Brucoe

On the next Day my Colleague, Mr *Roberts*, quitted the Factory, on account of my being in Charge of the Store All the Servants belonging to the Factory he took along with him, except our Girl-Cook, and she would not be perswaded to go away on any Account He dressed himself in Clothes like the Natives, and went and lived at *Cower*, which lies about three Miles from *Joar*, across a fine large Savannah, on which there are no Trees, but fine low Grass, which makes it pleasant for Walking, Riding and Shooting. This Town is so large, that it is divided into three Parts, *Cower*, *Jonacunda* and *Touracunda*, the first and last of which are inhabited mostly

Roberts quits the Factory

And goes and lives at Cower

H 3 by

by *Matometans*, the other by *Jolloffs* e ch of these are about a Mile round, situated at the Bottom of Hills on the West, and a fine Plain of open Pasture-Ground on the East The make exceeding good Cotton-Clothes here, very dear to purchase, and much valued by all the Women on the River. Here lives the old Man, so well known to all White Men call'd *Seen Don'o*, who exacts upon every Body very much, and his such great Power over all the Merchants who bring their Slaves here, that unless you fee him, it is in vain to expect Trade This is the chief Town on the whole River, and as I hinted before, the best Place for Trade

On the 12th, the *Ardaluzia*, Capt P, so, came up to anchor at *Rumbo*'s Port, in order to purchase Slaves, she had not a forceable Cargo, and therefore bought but to, those which he did buy, lying him in about Ten Pounds Sterling *per* Head

On the 22d I receiv'd Advice, that Cap Myer of the *New-England* Scooner was some few Days since cut off by the People of Cy, a little Way up the River, at the Port no of *Ciavo* I, a *Portuguese*, who lives there

On the 23d, I receiv'd Advice from Capt P, that he had heard some of the Natives talking in broken *Portuguese* about beating me, by the Perswasion of my Collegue *Robert*, and therefore desired I would take care of myself I chose rather to be ill us'd by them, than leave the Factory and Storehouse to be plunder'd by them, and therefore stay'd at home Soon after about thirteen

To

Jolloiffs came, who tore my Clothes, and beat   1732
me, and drew their Swords, and told me they
would kill me if I would not give them Brandy. With much ado I rufh'd out of the
Houfe, and call'd an old Man of the Town,
whom they fear and reverence, who reproved
them, and threatned to fend Word of it to
the King, which made them go away afhamed *Still at*
of what they had done, and promife not to *Variance*
go near Mr *Roberts* any more, he having put *with Ro-*
them on to do fo   *bert*

FOR feveral Days we lived in this manner,
he at *Cower* with all the Company's Servants,
and I at the Factory by myfelf, having much
ado to prevent People ftealing the Goods,
fometimes they would be fent fingly by *Ro-*
berts in the Night-time to rob me, but I   *April*
very often met with them, and ufed them accordingly, which made *Roberts* take occafion
to fend Word to the Gentlemen that I ufed
the Natives very ill At length, on the 5th
of *April*, the *Adventure* Sloop arrived with
Mr *Harrifon* and Mr *James Davis*, by which
Conveyance we receiv'd the following Letter.

To Meff. WM ROBERTS *and*
FRA. MOORE.

Letter to
themb.th.

James Fort, *Mar.* 29, 1732

Gentlemen,

*T*HIS *goes by the* Adventure *Sloop, and*
ferves to acquaint you, that in Confidera-
tion of the fundry Complaints made by you a-
gainft each other, and the Dangers that threaten
the Company's Affairs under fuch irregular and
diftracted Management, we have appointed Mr

H   *James*

James Davis *to take upon him the Direction of the Royal* African *Company's Affairs at* Joar Factory *You are therefore hereby directed and required, upon Receipt hereof, to deliver up to him all the Company's Effects in your Possession*

YOU, Mr Roberts, *are to continue at* Joar Factory, *and assist* Mr Davis *in repairing the Factory, till such Time as* Mr John Brown *comes to* Joar *to* Mr Davis's *Assistance, then you are to come down to the Fort with our Books of Accounts settled by both you and* Mr Moore, *who is also to observe, that he is to proceed along with* Mr Thomas Harrison *to* Yamyamacunda *Factory, and there join with* Mr James Conner *in directing the Company's Affairs there till further Orders, we being the more willing to give him an Opportunity of making amends for his past ill Conduct, but must recommend to him to use milder and more affable Treatment to the Natives there, than he has used at* Joar

AS for you, Mr Roberts, *we look upon you as a lost Man, and one (whilst you continue your insatiable Thirst after Liquor) incapable of rendring the Company any Service. Such are the Representations we have had, which we should not be fond of giving Belief to, did not the Irregularity and Distraction that appeared in your Management of late, but too plainly confirm it We are*

Your Friends and Servants,

Anth Rogers,
Tho Harrison

I ALSO received Advice, that the Boat belonging to the Company was return'd to *James* Fort, from whence she sail'd a Twelve-month

month ago, and was thought to be loft In
the Evening Mr *Harrifon* fent to *Cozer* for
Mr *Roberts*, who being afhamed to come, de- *Roberts*
fired the Meffenger to fay that he could not fent for
find him , but the Fellow being Mr *Harrifon's*
Servant, refufed to impofe a Lye upon him,
and therefore told him the Truth

THE next Morning we took a Survey of *Davis*
all the Company's Effects here, and deliver'd made Di-
them up to Mr *Davis*, taking from him pro- rector at
per Receipts Mr *Harrifon* fent another Mef- *Joar*
fenger for Mr *Roberts*, who finding it impracticable to abfcond, condefcended to come a-
long with the Meffenger , when he came he
acknowledged his Fault in abfenting the Factory, and own'd that he fent People to infult
me After which, Mr *Harrifon* told him, that
when Mr *Brown* came hither from *Yamyama-*
cunda, he muft go down to the Fort by the *Roberts*
firft Conveyance, in order to go to *England* order'd for
with the *Guinea* Pacquet, which would fet out *England*
in about two Months time.

ON the 9th, in the Evening, Mr *Harrifon*
and I fupp'd on Board the *Andaluzia*, to take
leave of Capt *Pearfon* Afterwards we embark'd on Board the *Adventure* Sloop, in order to proceed up the River.

JOAR lies in the Kingdom of *Barfally*, *Joar* de-
about three Miles from *Cower*, acrofs a fine fcribed.
Savannah, furrounded with Woods, which
harbour wild Beafts, which you may hear
howling and roaring every Night It is a
bout two Miles from the River *Gambia*, fome
part of which is up a narrow Creek, fcarce
wide

enough for a Boat, the other part is very pleasant Walking in the dry Time, but in the rainy Season it is generally cover'd with Water. This Town is inhabited by *Portugues*, but is much lessen'd of late Years. At present it consists of not above ten Houses, besides the King's and the Company's, which two contain as much Ground as all the other. About a Mile from it, there is a Ledge of Hills, high and rocky, but nevertheless full of Trees, which the Natives tell me runs a hundred Leagues up the River. In the Summer it is very pleasant Walking upon and about those Hills, but in the rainy Season it is dangerous, by reason of the vast Number of wild Beasts, who are obliged to keep to the Mountains by reason of the low Lands being almost cover'd with Water. In the Creek is very good Fishing, and on the Savannas good Game. The Ships that come up to trade here, always take in their Stock of Water out of the River, which is reckon'd to be very good.

Description on of the Cameleon   DURING the Time I was at *Joar* I saw several Cameleons, which some People think live upon the Air only, and that the Object before them makes them change their Colour, which is a vulgar Error, for they live upon Flies, and I have seen one catch thirty or forty on a Day with his Tongue, which is near as long as the Cameleon itself, he darts it out about seven, or eight, or ten Inches, and has as I believe a sort of glutinous Substance in the Tongue, for if it but touches the Fly he catches it, and then coils his Tongue under his Jaws in his Throat.

Some

Sometimes they will change their Colours
twenty times a Day, juft as they pleafe;
fometimes they will be of the Colour of the
Object neareft them, but that is as they pleafe
too. In the Space of two Days I have feen
one of all forts of Colours, but I have obferv'd that generally when they fleep they are
of a bright light Yellow. Some of them are
as large as the largeft-fized Lizards, very
ugly, but have fmall beautiful Eyes, which
are made and placed in fuch a manner, as to
look bickward with one, and forward with
the other. I thought that the Tongue and
Eyes of this Creature had been obferv'd only
by myfelf, but after I return'd to *England*,
going to fee the Collection made by that
Learned Gentleman Sir *Hans Sloane*, I found
nothing had efcaped his Curiofity, and that
the Tongue of a Cameleon had been by him
preferv'd in Spirits, and diffected in fuch a manner as plainly fhows, that Nature has wifely
provided the Cameleon with a Weapon with
which he can nourifh himfelf, and that this
little Creature has a Tongue which he ufes to
feed himfelf with Flies, in the fame manner as
the great Elephant ufes his Trunk.

HERE are a fort of Screech-Owls, which in
the Night make a very difmal Noife, and are
taken by the Natives for Witches. If one of
thefe Birds happens to come into a Town at
Night, the People are all up firing at it, and
as I do not find that they ever had the good
Fortune to fhoot any of them, the poor
Creatures ftill continue in the Opinion of
their being Witches. Thefe Screech Owls
were a Terror to the *Egyptians*, and frequent upon the *Nile*.   ABOUT

Owls ta-
ken for
Witches

ABOUT the Savannah are plenty of Deer, wild Hogs, Buffaloes, Geese, Ducks, Partridges, Doves and Quails, all which are very good Eating, and admired by the Natives themselves, and what is worth remarking, the Partridges here have sometimes two large Spurs on each Leg. I had reason to remark it, because one Day as I had just shot one, fearing he would get away, I snatch'd him up, and tore my Hands with his Spurs.

Partridge with Spurs

ABOUT *Joar*, and in no other place on the River, I have seen a remarkable Bird, which comes abroad at Dusk, with four Wings, and about the Bigness of a Pigeon, but tho' this is called a Bird by the Natives, yet whether it is a Bird, or of the Bat-Kind, I am not certain, having never seen one of them dead, tho I have frequently shot at them.

Bird with four Wings

IN the beginning of the rainy Season Purslain grows wild of itself, very good, and not unlike what we have in *England*. We have also another Herb call'd Colliloo, much like Spinage, and eats almost as well.

Wild Purslain

Colliloo

HERE are also Nuts, which are tolerable good Eating, and produce two Kernels in each Shell, they do not look like our Nut but rather like a dry'd Acorn.

Nuts with two Kernels

HERE are also plenty of Crocodiles which the Natives are great Admirers of as likewise their Eggs, which I have frequently seen them eat when there have been young ones in them as long as my Finger which makes them (they say) the nicer.

Crocodiles, their Eggs with young a nice Dish

THIS is one of their nicest Dishes, but their common Food is call'd Coofcoolh, being fifteen

An Unknown Bird taken in the River Gambia in Africa.

Fr Moore delin.   Miller sculp

ing Corn beaten in a Wooden Mortar, and
sifted thro' a fine Basket till it is about as
fine as coarse Flower, then they put it into
an earthen Pot full of Holes like a Cullinder,
which is luted to the Top of an earthen Pot,
in which is boiling Water, and sometimes
Broth in it, the Steam of which cures and
hardens the Flower, and when it is done, they
mix them together, and eat it with their
Hands Fish dried in the Sun, or smoaked,
is a great Favourite of theirs, but the more
it stinks, the more they like it   There is
scarce any thing which they do not eat, large
Snakes, Guanas, Monkeys, Pelicans, Bald-
Eagles, Allegators, and Sea-Horses are excellent Food.   And their Liquor is Palm-Wine,
Ciboa-Wine, Honey-Wine, (which is not
unlike our Mead) Brandy and Rum, but
when they can get the two last, they drink
but a small Quantity of the others   The only Liquor to please a *Mahometan* is Sugar
and Water

The *Mundingoes* have a Custom of building
their Houses close together, which is the Occasion of so many Conflagrations that happen every Year, and if you ask them why they build
not their Houses farther from one another,
they tell you that their Ancestors did not,
that they endeavour'd to imitate them, for
they were wiser than they are now

In every Town, almost, they have a large
Thing like a Drum, called a *Tantong*, which
they beat only on the Approach of an Enemy, or some very extraordinary Occasion, to
call the neighbouring Towns to their Assistance

1732 ance. This fame *Tantong* can, in the Night Time, be heard fix or feven Miles.

Natives given to Mirth and Dancing. THEY are naturally very jocofe and merry, and will dance to a Drum or a Balafeu fometimes four and twenty Hours together dancing now and then very regular, and at other Times in very odd Geftures, ftriving always to outdo one another in Nimblenefs and Activity.

Yet apt to quarrel THEY are very fubject to fcold with one another, which they call fighting, for if two Perfons abufe each other very heartily, they call it a great Fight, and are generally a good while before they come to Blows, which however does fometimes happen; and then they do fight in Earneft, either with Knives, Sagays, or Cutlaffes, whichfoever they are provided with, and they very often kill one another; but when that happens, the Murderer flies to another Kingdom, and that King always protects him, and looks upon him kindly, and treats him as one of his own Subjects.

Eafy Condition of Slaves. SOME People have a good many Houfe-Slaves, which is their greateft Glory, and they live fo well and eafy, that it is fometimes a very hard Matter to know the Slaves from their Mafters or Miftreffes; they very often being better cloathed, efpecially the Females, who have fometimes Coral, Amber, and Silver about their Hands and Wrifts, to the Value of twenty or thirty Pounds Sterling.

Frogs large and loud IN the rainy Seafon, at Night, the Frogs, of which there are vaft Numbers, and much larger

larger than thofe in *England*, make as much   1732.
Noife as a Pack of Hounds, and at a good
Diftance is not much unlike it.

BOTH Men and Women, efpecially the lat- Fancy of
ter, take a great Delight in carrying a Bun- carrying
dle of fmall Keys about them, tied round Keys.
their Middles, only for the Sake of being
thought rich.

ON the 10th, we arriv'd at *Yanimarew*,
which is the pleafanteft Port in the whole River, being delightfully fhaded by Palm and
Ciboa Trees, the Leaves of which are made *Yanima-*
ufe of for covering Houfes, and are called *rew* a de-
Palmetto. Here the Company have a fmall lightful
Houfe, with a Black Factor, to purchafe Port.
Corn for the Ufe of the Fort. In 1734 feveral feparate Traders coming to *Joar*, and finding themfelves ill ufed by *Serin Donfo*, the chief
Broker, they one and all came up to this
Place, and made the Merchants bring up
their Slaves from *Joar* after them, which had
like to have occafioned a Quarrel between the
King of *Yany* and the King of *Barfally*, the
latter thinking that the former had fent Meffengers to decoy the Ships from his Port
of *Joar*.

ON the 15th, we left *Yanimarew*, and
proceeded up to *Caffan*, a little above it,
where, about three Weeks before, the *New
England* Scooner was cut off by the Natives
As foon as we arrived there, Mr *Harrifon* *Caffan.*
and I went afhore, where, when the whole
Town was come about us, Mr *Harrifon*
demanded the Slattee to give him an Account

1732   count how he dared to kill Capt *Mayor*, o
the *New England* Scooner To which he an
fwer'd, as near as I could tranflate it, in th
following Manner

Relation of   " So m e Years ago this Place was a Por
the Murder " of great Trade, which made a great man·
o Capt " Ships refort hither , who often ufed u
Mayer " very ill, by carrying away feveral of ou
  ·· Friends and Relations by Force, withou
  ·· any Provocation Even laft Year Cap
  " *Storeham* carried away one of my own Ne
  " phews, becaufe Seignior *Chequo Vofs*, a *Por*
  " *tuguefe*, who lives in this Town, was no· ·
  " good as his Promife, in bringing h·r
  ·· Trade by the Time limited. Now lately
  ' this *New England* Scooner began alfo t·
  ·· impofe upon me in the following Manner
  " Soon after it arrived at my Port, the King
  " o· Lower *Tany*, in whofe Dominion th
  " Town is, fent a Slave to me to fell for him
  " which I carried aboard the Scooner, t·
  " Capt *Mayor* , but he having no very goo·
  " Goods, at leaft not fuch as I liked, mad·
  ·· me defer felling him, till fuch Time as ·
  " could acquaint the King what Sort o
  " Goods he had, upon which the Captain de
  " fir'd I would leave the Slave aboard till th·
  " King's Anfwer came, which I accordingl·
  " did At length I receiv d Orders from th·
  ·· King not to fell the Slave, for he did no·
  " like the Captain's Goods. Upon that, ·
  " went on board, and told the Meffage t·
  ·· the Captain , at which he fell into a grea·
  " Paffion, and would not let me take th·
  " Slave out of the Scooner. I did not f·y
  " much to the Captain, but came home
                                " othe·

" called all my People together, told
" them the Cafe, and then we reckon'd up
" the many Injuries we had received from
" other feparate Traders, and at laft we re-
' folved to take the Scooner, which we did
" the next Morning   In the Action the Cap-
" tain was killed, for which I am very forry ;
' but as for the reft of the Men which were
" on board the Scooner, I gave them the
" Boat and fome Provifions, and let them go
" where they pleafed "

THIS Scooner belonged chiefly to one
Capt *Moore*, of *New England*, who was then
trading in a Sloop at the Port of *Yamyama-*
cunda   The Men, when the Slattee gave
them the Boat, went up to him thither,
where he made a very profitable Voyage

THIS was the Speech of the Slattee, by which
we found the Natives refolved to defend what
they had done ; and we not having Strength
fufficient to reduce them, were glad to go on
board and proceed on our Voyage.

Defcript
of *Caffan*.

CISSAN is a fmall Town on the North
Side of the River *Gambia*, pleafantly fituated
about a Mufquet Shot from the Water-fide,
about three Tides above *Joar*, fortified with
a great Number of Sticks fet in the Ground, Occurren-
and filled with Clay, there being Holes left ce there
for Mufquets, and Watch-Towers at proper
Diftances   This was a noted Town for doing
Mifchief, was always at War with fome of
their Neighbours, and would often feize upon
the Company's Meffengers and Merchants, as
they paffed on the Road to *Goree*, with their

I   the

1732. Slaves. In the Year 1724 moſt of the People of this Town were taken Priſoners, and
the Slattee, whoſe Name was *Mackamarr,*
was obliged to fly, and lives now retired at a
Place called *Medina*; up the River *Samy*; and
ſince that Time People have paſſed peaceably
through the Town, being at this Time one
of the civileſt in the whole River.

Brucoe   ON the 16th, in the Evening, we arriv'd
Factory   at *Brucoe*, which lies on the South Side of the
River, in the Country of *Jemarrow*, about
half a Mile from the Water; between which
the Company are now building a Factory,
under the Direction of Meſſ *Galand* and *Johnſon*

Dubocunda   WE ſtayed at *Brucoe* about three Days, and
then went on our Way up the River, when
we came to *Dubocunda* we went aſhore, and
after having a Conference with the People,
about the Factory now ſettleing at *Brucoe*, it
being under the Care of this Town, by reaſon
the head Men of the Country live here, we
made them Preſents, and then went on board.

Deſcribed   *DUBOCUNDA* lies on the South Side of
the River, about nine Miles from *Brucoe*, it
is divided into two Parts, or, if you pleaſe,
into two diſtinct Towns; one of which is fortified with a vaſt Number of Ciboa Trees,
fix'd in the Ground, and Clay ſtuffed in between, to ſtrengthen it, ſo that it is little inferior to a Brick Wall. The other Town is
only ſurrounded with a Cane Cirk, much like
our *Engliſh* Hurdles, faſtened up with a great
Number of Sticks, as almoſt all the *Gambia*
Towns and Factories too are ſurrounded with.
The

The People live in the open Town till such
Time as they are hotly at War with any
others, and then they fly into that which is
fortified, that being their laft Shift.   Thefe are
a very rebellious Sort of People, and have a
King of their own, whom they call *Suma*,
having driven the lawful Emperor of *Jemar-*
row out of his Town, to the very Borders of
the Country, where he lives retir'd, and
dares not come any Diftance from home.

On the 20th, we arrived at *Cuttejarr*,
about ten Leagues above *Dubocunda*. It lies
on the North Side of the River, the Town
is a Mile from the River Side, between which
the Company had once a Factory ; but being
overflowed in or about the Year 1725, by
which the Company loft a great many Goods,
they moved it to *Samy*, about eight Miles
from *Cuttejarr* by Land, but by Water a
great deal farther.

The next Day we arrived at *Samy* River's
Mouth, which is on the North Side of the
River ; it is famous for great Numbers of
Allegators, infomuch that there is a great deal
of Mifchief done by them every Year   About
twelve Miles up the River is the Town of
Samy, noted for good Trade The Company
had here a Factory under Mr *James Lemaigre*,
a *Frenchman*, who bought a great many Slaves,
and remitted them to *James* Fort, at a fettled
Price He dying in the Year 1733, one *Va-*
lentine Mendez, a Black *Portuguefe*, contracted
with the Company to remit them Slaves at a
certain Price, and now lives at his own Houfe
at *Walha*, about four Miles above *Samy*. I
went

1722 went up with Mr *Harrison* to *Samy* Town, where by the Way we saw vast Numbers of Allegators, especially upon some Islands which are near the Mouth of the River

On the 26th, as we were weighing, we lost our Anchor by a large Tree lying at the Bottom of the River About Noon we arrived at *our imaction*, and went ashore soon after The next Evening Mr *Harrison* proceeded on his Voyage up the River For several Nights we had a great deal of Lightning

On the 6th of *May*, at Night, I was visited by a *Mumbo Jumbo*, an Idol, which is among the *Mandigoes* a kind of a cunning Mystery It is dressed in a long Coat made of the Bark of Trees, with a Tuft of fine Straw on the Top of it, and when the Person wears it, it is about eight or nine Foot high This is a Thing invented by the Men to keep their Wives in awe, who are so ignorant or at least are obliged to pretend to be so as to take it for a Wild Man, and indeed no one but what knows it, would take it to be a Man, by reason of the dismal Noise it makes, and which but few of the Natives can manage It never comes abroad but in the Night time, which makes it have the better Effect Whenever the Men have any Dispute with the Women, this *Mumbo Jumbo* is sent for to determine it, which is, I may say, always in Favour of the Men Whoever is in the Coat can order the others to do what he pleases, either fight, kill, or make Prisoner, but it must be observed, that no one is allowed to come armed into its Presence When the

Margin notes:
Anchor lost

Mumbo Jumbo a mysterious cunning

The Bugbear of the Wives

Management

the Women hear it coming, they run away   1732
and hide themfelves, but if you are acquainted with the Perfon that has the Coat on, he
will fend for them all to come and fit down,
and fing or dance, as he pleafes to order
them, and if any refufe to come, he will fend
the People for them, and then whip them
Whenever any one enters into this Society,   Initiation.
they fwear in the moft folemn manner never
to divulge it to any Woman, or any Perfon   Secrecy
that is not enter'd into it, which they never
allow to Boys under fixteen Years of Age.
This thing the People fwear by, and the Oath
is fo much obferved by them, that they reckon
as irrevocable, as the *Grecians* thought *Jove* did   Reve
of old, when he fwore by the River *Styx*   rence

ABOUT the Year 1727, the King of *Jagra*,   Tragical
having a very inquifitive Woman to his Wife,   Story
was fo weak as to difclofe to her the whole
Secrets of this Myftery, and fhe, being a
Goffip, revealed it to fome other Women of
her Acquaintance, which at laft came to the
Fars of fome who were no Friends to the
King They confulted upon it, and fearing
that if the thing once took Vent, they fhould
not be able to govern their Wives fo well as
they otherwife would, they took the Coat,
put a Man into it, went to the King's Town,
fent for him out, taxed him with it, he not
denving it, they fent for his Wife, and upon
the Spot killed them both So the poor Man
died for obliging his Wife, and the poor Woman for her Curiofity

THERE are very few Towns of any Note   The Idol
but what have got one of thefe Coats, which commo

1732   in the Day time is fixt upon a large Stick
near the Town, where it continues till Night,
the proper Time of using it

On the 10th came down the Frw Sloop
from F... ..., where she was with M... ...
S... a H... ... The next Day one o the Company's Slaves, as he was washing him... ...
the Port, was carried away by a Cr... ...,
and about two Days after the *Fame* Sloop
failed down the River, with Mr *Jua B...*,
to affift Mr *J... ... Davi...*, Factor at *J...*

On the 26th, as I was angling at the Port
I was furprized with feeing a Crocodile c... ...
... and bite a large Fish in two into the
middle

On the 10th of *Jun*, the *Adventure* Sloop,
John Isaac Master, came down hither with
Mr *Hu... ...*, he feem'd to fay, that he had
been about two and twenty Leagues ab... e
Factory, in the Sloop's Boat, to difcover this
River, at which Place he found a Ledge of
Thofe Rocks, which hinder'd him from going
any farther At Night I vifited Mr *L...*
on Board the Sloop, during the Time we had
a very dreadful Tornado, in which a S... ...
large Flies with long Wings came on Board in
fuch prodigious Numbers, that flying into the
Flames of the Candles, the Table was foon
cover'd with thofe that burnt their Wings,
and others which were not burnt, as they
were running on the Table fhed their Wings
and there were nothing but fo many great
large Maggots. We faw fo feveral other
Infects, fome of which I have here reprefented

O...

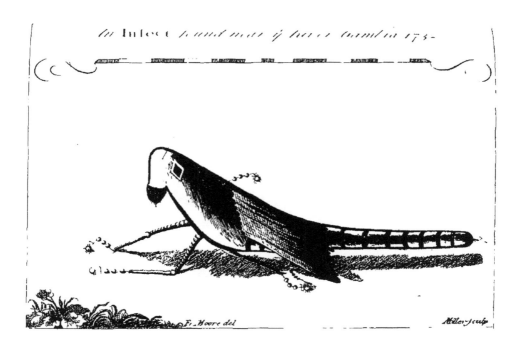

An Insect found near if river Alatamaha 175-

F. Moore del   Miller sculp

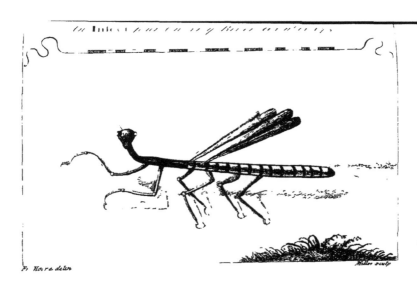

O n the 24th, the River *Gambia* began to   1732.
rise and grow muddy, the Stream always ran
down, and no Tide came up. Soon after I
went on Horseback from *Yamyamacunda* to
Baffy Port, in order to go to *Nackway*,
where Mr *Conner* and I had a *Portuguese* Servant settled to make Trade for the Company;
the reason of my going was to inspect into his
Behaviour, and to examine his Accompts. This
Port of *Baffy* lies in the Kingdom of *Tomany*, *Baffy* Port.
on the South Side of the River *Gambia*, about
a Tide and half above *Yamyamacunda* by Water, and about fifteen Miles by Land; all the
Way to it is very woody, and in the midst
there is a steep Hill full of Rocks and Trees. Way to it.
I lay all Night in one of the Natives Huts,
and the next Morning, leaving my Horse
here, cross'd the River in a small Canoa, and
walked to *Nackway*, being about seven Miles, *Nackway.*
situated in the Kingdom of Upper *Yany*, on
the North Side, and about a Quarter of a Mile
from the River. It has formerly been a Town Described.
of great Trade, but since the separate Traders have been allowed to trade in the River,
it is much decay'd, and now the Merchants
do frequently march thro' this Town towards
Cower with their Slaves. Half the Way from
Baffy Port to *Nackway* is thro' Woods, but
the other half is over a fine large Savannah,
without any Trees, except one or two here
and there, and in the rainy Season it is generally under Water.

O n my Arrival at *Nackway* they wel-
comed me with some Musick called a *Ba-* *Balaseu*
lafeu, which at about an hundred Yards di- Musick
stance sounds something like a small Organ. described.
    I 4   It

1732 It is compofed of about twenty Pipes of very
hard Wood, finely rubbed and polifhed, which
Pipes diminifh by little and little both in
Length and Breadth, and are tied together
with Thongs made of very thin fine Leather
Thefe Thongs are twifted about fmall round
Wands, which are put between every one of
thofe Pipes, in order to leave a fmall Space
Underneath the Pipes are fiftned twelve o
fourteen Calabafhes of different Sizes, which
have the fame Effect as Organ-Pipes In
they play upon with two Sticks, which are
cover'd with a thin Skin out of a Cibou-Tree
Trunk, or with fine Leather, to make the
Sound lefs harfh Both Men and Women
dance to this Mufick, and very much like it,
and they are highly delighted to have a White
Man dance with them, or drink with them,
but if the Liquor belongs to a White Man,
which they are not very well acquainted with,
they are very cautious how they drink, always
making him drink the firft Glafs, for fear of
being poifoned

Character
of the
Natives

THE Natives, really, are not fo difagreeable in their Behaviour as we are apt to imagine, for when I went thro' any of the
Towns, they almoft all came to fhake Hands
with me, except fome of the Women, who
having never feen any White Men, ran
from me as faft as they could, and would by
no Means be perfwaded to come near
Some of them invited me to their Houfe
brought their Wives and Daughters to me,
made them fit down by me, always finding
about me to gape at and admire, fuch Boots,
Spurs, Gloves, Clothes or Wig, each of

being to them Subjects of Difcourfe and Ad-   1732
miration.

THE Girls would have People think they Of the Fe
are very modeft, efpecially when they are in males
Company, but take them by themfelves, and
they are very obliging, for if you will give
them a little Coral, or a Silk Handkerchief,
you may take what Liberty you pleafe with
them But thofe who pretend to be of the
Portuguefe Religion, and therefore call themfelves Chriftians, they indeed are fomewhat
more referved than the *Mundingoes* are But
notwithftanding their Religion and Chriftianity
too, if any White Man has a Fancy to any of
them, and is able to maintain them, they will
make no Scruple of living with him in the
Nature of a Wife, without the Ceremony of
Matrimony.

THE Men commonly wear Swords flung Men dex-
over their Right Shoulders, others carry Sagays trous at
or Spears, about three Yards long, others Arms.
have Bows and Arrows, but all of them wear
knives flung by their Sides, and, indeed, I
have obferved, that they are very dextrous at
uling whatever Sort of Weapon they carry,
which, I am forry to fay, is more than a great
many young Fellows in *England* are, for, I
believe, there are many Hundreds who wear
Swords, that would, upon occafion, be puzzled
which Way to ufe them

THEIR Manner of Salutation is, Shaking Ceremo-
Hands, but generally, when the Men falute nes
the Women, they, inftead of fhaking their
Hands, put it up to their Nofes, and fmell
twice

twice to the Back of it. And nothing can
affront them fo much as to falute them with
your left Hand   When a Man has been a
Day or two from home, the Wife falutes him
on her Knees at his Return, and in the fame
Pofture fhe always brings him Water to drink
This, I believe, is the Effect of, what I before
mention'd, *Mumbo Jumbo.*

THOSE Natives who live high up the
River, have a much better Character than they
had formerly : For it is reported, that they
ufed to lay their Pipes or Calabafhes under
your Feet or Chair (even in your own Houfe)
on purpofe to have them broke, and then to
infift on being paid above twenty times the
Worth of the Commodity , and if you deny
paying it, they infift upon your giving them
the very fame thing which you broke , that
being impoffible to comply with, you muft of
Neceffity acquiefce to whatever Demands they
make, unlefs you have Friends enough among
them to diffwade them from fuch Impofition.

WHEN any Perfon brings you Eggs or
Fowls to buy, it is imprudent to kill or make
ufe of any of them, before the Perfon you buy
them of is actually gone away ; for it feems
it was a Cuftom in this Country (and not yet
thoroughly repealed) that whatever Commodity a Man fells in the Morning, he may, if
he repents his Bargain, go and have the things
return'd to him again, on his paying back the
Money any time before the fetting of the Sun
the fame Day ; and this Cuftom is ftill in force
very high up the River, but here below it is
at prefent pretty well worn out   However I
fhall

fhall here give an Account how a Gentleman, who had the Honour of being at the Head of the Company's Affairs here, was ferved at this very Town of *Nackway*.

NOT above twelve Years ago he went up in a Sloop on a Trading Voyage to *Nackway*, where he got a Hut built, and took his Goods afhore to trade with. It happen'd that one Morning a Man brought a Cow to fell to him, which he bought for an Iron Barr; foon after he bought it, he cut the Cow's Tail off, which being carried to the Ears of the Fellow that fold the Cow, he refolved to make a Handle of it, in order to extort Money from the Governor. Accordingly about Noon the fame Day he came to the Port of *Nackway* in a feeming good Humour, and a great Number of People with him, with a plaufible Story, that as he was going the next Day to marry one of his Daughters to a young Man for whom he had a great Regard, and had nothing to make him a Prefent of, he therefore had thought better of it, and was not willing to fell his Cow, as he intended, and fo defir'd he might have it return'd to him. The Governor not dreaming of the Plot, immediately order'd one of his Servants to bring the Cow, and return it to the Perfon who brought it. Accordingly the Cow was produced, at which the Fellow feem'd furpriz'd, and told the Governor that that was not his Cow. The Governor told him it was. *How can that be*, fays he, *my Cow had a Tail on when I brought her to you this Morning. It is very true*, quoth the Governor, *when I bought it fhe had a Tail, but when I had paid for her, I cut the Tail off. How,*

How, says the Fellow, *durst you have the Afsurance to cut off my Cow's Tail without my Leave? I value the Cow and her Tail at three hundred Barrs, and that Sum you shall pay me before you go from this Place.* The Governor was very much out of Humour (to be sure) and endeavour'd to prove, that after he had paid for the Cow she belong'd to him, but it was all to no purpose, for every one present gave against him (expecting to come in for a Share of the Money) and so he was obliged to go to his Store, and pay the Fellow three hund. Barrs for only docking the Cow's Tail. After he had paid the Money he stay'd at the Por without taking any Notice of the Affront and when he had got his Complement of Slaves he very civilly took his Leave of the People without so much as mentioning the Affront put upon him, and sailed down to *James* Fort.

For a Year, or more, this Affair slept, insomuch that the People of *Nackum* though it was all over and forgot, but at last they found themselves much mistaken, for the Governor fitted out a pretty large Sloop with twelve Guns, and a good many Hands, and gave out she was going on a Trading Voyage up the River, he himself embarked on Board her privately, left the Natives should know of it, and carry the News up the River, which, probably, would have deterr'd them from coming on Board. The Sloop proceeded slowly up the River, trading at every Port, the Governor not showing himself to any, but as soon as he came to anchor at the Port of *Nackum*, the Captain was sent ashore to re the Natives that he had got a fine Cargo of Goods on Board, in order to purchase Slaves, and so desired some to come and take their Custom Accordingly six of the greatest Men in the Town went on Board, when being conducted by the Captain into the Cabbin, they were not a little, nor very agreeably, surprized to see the Governor, one of these six People was the Owner of the Cow's Tail, which the Governor paid so dear for, him and four others the Governor order'd to be put in Irons, and then sent the sixth ashore to tell the People, that he was come up in order to receive Satisfaction for the Money extorted from him for cutting off his own Cow's Tail When the Boat was put off, he order'd thirteen great Guns to be fired, in order to let the People know that he was not without Strength They judging it impracticable to pretend to cope with a Vessel of such Force, sent him ten prime Slaves, which at thirty Barrs *per* Head, amounts to just the Sum which the Governor paid for the Cow. They at the same time acknowledged their Error, and said they were justly served for suffering People to impose upon White Men, especially those who were so Good Friends to them as the Company was The Governor order'd the five Men, but did not much care to go ashore, yet he made a great deal of Trade aboard the Sloop, and carried it so fair and obliging to them, that they never resented this Trick, but have ever since behaved as civil as any other People on the whole River

On the 8th of *July*, in the Morning, Capt P. Master of the *Fame* Sloop, and Mr *Phi-*

lip

Ln G'ind, one of the Company's Chiefs at *Bruroe*, came hither over Land from thence on Horfeback, to acquaint us that the *Bo* had on Board her one hundred Meafures of Salt, and two hundred Gallons of Rum for this Factory, but that the Frefhes were already fo ftrong that he had much ado with his Sloop to reach *Bruroe* We defired Mr G   o have it taken afhore at his Factory, till we had an Opportunity of fending for it MrT *Bow* and *G ind* ftay'd with us about four Days, and then return'd to *Brucoe*, with whom my Colleague Mr *Conner* went, in order to fend up the Rum and Salt by a Canoa, if poffible

On the 16th, in the Night, we had a very violent Tornado, which blowed down an Outhoufe in which my Predeceffors ufed to keep their Cotton, which about a Year or two ago they bought here, for the Compn , in great Quantites, but finding it not to anfwer their Expectations, we had now Order to purchafe none but what is cleaned from the Seeds, which the Natives are too lazy to do

On the 28th, we receiv'd our Rum from *Brucoe*, by a Canoa which we hir'd at *Sir* , with fix young Fellows to row it. Our Reafon for having this Liquor brought here fo foon, was, its being one of the beft Commodities we can have to trade with in the rainy Seafon

On the 2d of *Auguft*, I receiv'd Advice that Mr *Edward Peters*, Affiftant to Mr

Ir J

Hugh Hamilton, the Company's Factor at
Fattenda, died about three Days ago As
soon as he was dead, the Alcade of the next
Town came to the Factory, and demanded
his Bed and Bedding, according to the Custom of the Country, which they were obliged
to comply with

1732

Mr Peters dies

Herriot taken

It is customary, when Factories are set-
led, to put them, and th Persons belonging
to them under the Charge of the People of
the neirest large Town, who are obliged to
t he Care of it, and to let none impose upon
ne White Men, or use them ill, and if any
Body is abused, they must apply to the Alcade the head Man of the Town, and he
will see Justice done you

Observa- ble Custom

This Man is, up the River, called *Tobaubo
Mar*, which is, in *English*, the White Man's
King But in most Parts of the River he is
called Alcade, and hath a great Power For
every Town almost having two common
Lands of cleared Ground, one for their Corn
and the other for their Rice, the Alcade appoints the Labour of all the People, he being
in the Nature of a Governor The Men
work the Corn Ground, and the Women and
Girls the Rice Ground, as they all equally
labour, so the Alcade equally divides the
Crop among them, but, I find, that in case
any are in Want of Corn, the others supply
him, so that unless there is a general Famine,
there is no Fear of their Starving. This Alcade decides all Quarrels, and has the first
Voice in all Conferences, concerning Things
belonging to his Town. If a Person wants
any

Power and Authority of the Al- cade

1732 any Thing to be done by a good Number of People, the beſt Way is to apply to the Alcade, who will agree with you about it, and order People to make Diſpatch with it, but if a Factor does not take Care to keep in with the Alcade, he will ſeldom or never get Things done as they ought to be The Alcade's is a very beneficial Place, for both the Company and ſeparate Traders pay a Cuſtom for every Slave they buy, ſometimes one Barter Head, ſometimes not ſo much, but that is according to the Place you are at This Month we had every Night Wolves and Tygers continually howling near the Factory

Ridiculous Belief of the Natives.

Solemn Vow

Breach of it avenged

ON the 30th, I was invited to the Burial of a Great Man of this Country, who this Morning died ſuddenly And here, I believe it will not be improper to obſerve, that every Body who died in this Country ſince I came, the Natives are ſo ſuperſtitious as to believe them killed by Witches, except only this Man who died this Morning, and he, they do allow, died by the Hands of the Almighty, for breaking his Vow, which, I muſt obſerve, they are very apt to make, and in ſo ſolemn a Manner, that in Remembrance of ſuch Vow, they wear an Iron Manelio on their Wriſt, that they may be put in Mind not to forget it This Man, about a Year ago, had a Preſent made him of a Man Slave, upon which he vowed never to part with him upon any Account, and wore a twiſted Iron Manelio on his right Wriſt About a Week before his Death, not out of any Forgetfulneſs of his Vow, but purely to buy Corn for the Subſiſtence of his numerous Family,

mily, he unadvisedly went and fold the Slave,
which he had vowed never to part with, and
dying suddenly, the Natives allowed that
God Almighty killed him, for breaking his
Vow I went to the Burial, which was thus
They dug a Hole between six and seven Foot   Form of
long, three deep, and two broad, in which   Burial
they very decently laid the Corps, tied up in
a white Cotton Cloth, every body present
pulling off their Caps, then they laid thin
fplit Sticks all acrofs the Grave, even with
the Surface of the Earth, and upon thefe
Sticks they laid Straw, to prevent the Mould
from going into the Grave, and upon the
Straw they laid the Ground which they had
dug out, and trampled it very hard down
with their Feet

WHEN People die, all their Friends and
Acquaintance come and cry over them a Day   Howling
or two, as the *Irifh* do, and bury them in   over the
the Rooms in which they die, or elfe very   Dead
close to it Thofe of their Relations that are
not upon the Spot, do, out of Refpect to the
Deceafed, cry and howl as much at an hundred Miles diftant, as tho' they were actually with the Deceafed at the Time of his
Death

When a King, or any very great Man
dies there a Time fixed for the Cry, which
is fometimes a Fortnight or a Month after the
Deceafe, at which Time vaft Numbers of
people meet at the Houfe of the Deceafed,
and thofe who live near it, feed Cows, vaft
Quantities of Fowls and Rice, or Beef, or
what Provifions they can get, which is

K   given

given to all People that come, fo that for the Time it lafts, there is open Houfe-keeping, which fometimes is for three or four Days together. They begin with Crying, and at Night they go to Singing and Dancing, and continue fo doing till the Time they break up and depart

Their Habit of Body THESE People are naturally pretty healthy, and multiply apace, neverthelefs they have various Diftempers among them, the Fe

Difeafes ver, Small Pox, King's Evil, Worms, Pains in the Head, and Swellings in one of their Legs, infomuch that you will very often fee People with one Leg as big as their Middle, which, I am informed, proceeds from fome Herbs put in their Victuals, by one another, on purpofe to create Affection And what makes it the more likely to be fo, is, that none but grown Perfons are afflicted with this Diftemper.

I KNEW a young Woman up the River, about the Age of Twenty, who, in lefs than

Story of two Months Time had a white Worm come
Worms in out of each Knee, above a Yard in Length,
the lower before the Worm began to appear, it was ex-
Parts ceeding painful to her, and fwelled much, but when the Skin broke, and the Worm peeped out, it was much eafier, the Worm came out about fix or feven Inches in a Day, as faft as it came, they wound it upon a fmall Bit of Stick, and tied it with Thread, or knit a Knot with the Worm itfelf, to prevent it's going in again. Soon afterwards the fame Perfon had another Worm coming out of her Ancle, but with pulling it out too haftily, it broke, and put the young Woman to a vaft deal of

Pain

Pain. The Natives tell me that thefe Worms are bred with drinking thick Water.

W H E N a Child is new born they dip him ∥Way of over Head and Ears, in cold Water, three ∥treating or four Times in a Day, and as foon as they ∥new-born are dry, they rub them over with Palm Oyl, ∥Infants particularly the Back-Bone, Small of the Back, Elbows, Neck, Knees, and Hips. When they are born they are of an Olive Colour, and fometimes do not turn black for a Month or two.

I D O not find that they are born with flat ∥Caufe of Nofes, but if it is the Mother's Fancy to have ∥flat Nofes it fo, fhe will, when fhe wafhes the Child, pinch and prefs down the upper Part of its Nofe.

L A R G E Breafts, thick Lips, and broad ∥Beauties Noftrils are by many reckon'd the Beauties ∥alamode. of the Country. One Breaft is generally larger than the other.

T H E Children go ftark naked till they are ∥Childhood eight or nine Years old, and fome are pink t in their Faces and Breafts for Ornament.

T H E Y give away their Daughters when they are very young, fome as foon as they ∥Females are born, and the Parents can never after- ∥marry'd wards break the Match; but it is in the ∥very young Man's Power never to come and take his Wife, unlefs he pleafes, and unlefs he is fo generous as to give her Leave, fhe cannot, nay dares not, marry any other   They gene- rally take their Wives very young , before

K 2   they

1732

Dowry

FruitCola

they do fo, they are obliged to pay the Parents of the Wife two Cows, two Iron Barrs, and two hundred Cola, a Fruit that comes a vaft Way in-land, unlike in Tafte to any I ever faw, but is an exceeding good Bitter, and much refembles, in Shape, a Horfe-Chefnut when the Skin is off, eating this Fruit relifhes Water

Marriage
Feaft, &c.

W H E N the Man takes home his Wife he makes a Feaft at his Houfe, to which every Body that is willing comes without the Form of an Invitation, for they don't ufe much Ceremony that Way, and there they play and dance for three or four Days fucceffively, the Woman being brought upon Men's Shoulders to her Hufband's Houfe, from her Parents, with a Veil over her Face, which fhe keeps on till fuch Time fhe has been in Bed with her Hufband, during which they dance and fing, beat Drums, and fire Mufquets, and notwithftanding the Woman has, perhaps, had a Child or two before her Hufband took her home, yet is fhe looked upon ftill as a Maid, and the poor Man is fo indulgent as to accept of this Impofition, notwithftanding he himfelf knows it to be fuch, for if he fhould declare to the People that his Wife was not a Maid when he took her home, it would be looked upon as a very great Scandal to him

Abftain 3
Years, till
Weaning
Time

N o marry'd Women, after they are brought to Bed, lie with their Hufbands till three Years are expired, if the Child lives fo long, at which Time they wean their Children, and go to Bed to their Hufbands. They fay that if a Woman lies with

with her Hufband during the Time fhe has a   1732.
Child fucking at her Breaft, it fpoils the
Child's Milk, and makes it liable to a great
many Diftempers   Neverthelefs, I believe,
not one Woman in twenty ftays till they
wean their Children before they lie with a
Man, and indeed I have very often feen Women much cenfur'd, and judged to be falfe
to their Hufbands Bed, upon Account only
of their fucking Child being ill.

Every Man is allowed to take as many *Plurality*
Wives as he pleafes, fome have no lefs than *of Wives.*
a hundred   I know a pretty large Town near
Bracoe, in which are none but one Man, his
Wives, Children, and Slaves.   They are in
great Subjection to their Hufbands, but the
more on Account of *Jumbo Moofa*, before defcribed, and were it not for that Invention,
what would the poor Men do? efpecially
thofe who have fo many Wives   If they are
found lying with any other Men but their *Liberty of*
Hufbands, they are liable to be fold for *Divorce*
Slaves, they are turned off at Pleafure, and
he makes her take all her Children with her,
unlefs he has a Mind to keep any of them
himfelf, if fo, he generally takes Care to
keep fuch as are big enough to affift him in
any Thing which he wants them for   And
even when Man and Wife have been fome
Years parted, he has Liberty to come and
take from her any of the Children which he
had by her   But if a Man has a Mind to part
with his Wife, and fhe is with Child, he cannot oblige her to go till fuch Time as fhe is
deliver'd

K 3   IT

Naming

IT is ufual to fee the Women abroad the fame Day or the Morrow after they are deliver'd About a Month afterwards they name the Child, which is done by fhaving its Head, and rubbing it over with fome Oyl.

Circumcifion

SOME fhort Time before the rainy Seafon begins, they circumcife a great Number of Boys, about twelve or fourteen Years of Age, after which they put on a peculiar Habit, each Kingdom being different in their Drefs, from the Time of their Circumcifion, to the Time of the Rains, they are allowed to commit what Outrages they pleafe, without being called to Account for it, and when the firft Rain falls, then they put on their own proper Habits. .

Rainy Seafon

THE rainy Seafon commonly begins with the Month of *June,* and continues till the latter End of *September,* and fometimes the Beginning of *October;* the firft and latter are the moft violent generally.   The Wind comes firft, and blows exceffive hard, for the Space of half an Hour or more, before any Rain falls, infomuch that a Veffel may be fuddenly furprized and overfet by it, but then a Perfon may fee it a good while before it comes, for it looks difmal and very black, and the Lightnings breaking out of the black Clouds, as they move flowly towards you, makes it appear very awful Both

Terrible Thunder

Thunder and Lightning are very dreadful, the one flafhing fo quick, makes it continually light, and the other fhakes the very Ground under you. Whilft it rains it is generally

nerally pretty cool, but when the Shower is over, the Sun breaks out exceffive hot, which induces fome Perfons to caft off their Cloaths, and lie down to fleep, but before they awake, perhaps, comes another Tornado, and the Cold ftrikes into their Bones, and gives them Fits of Illnefs, which to a great many are very fatal, I mean to White Men, for the Natives are not liable to catch Cold fo eafily. During the rainy Seafon the Sea-Breezes feldom blow, but inftead of them Eafterly Winds, right down the River, which in the Months of *November, December, January,* and *February* do generally blow very frefh, efpecially in the Day-time.

Danger of Colds

Eafterly Winds

Four Months in the Year are unhealthy, and very tedious to thofe who are come out of a colder Climate, but the perpetual Spring, where you commonly fee ripe Fruit and Bloffoms on the fame Tree, makes fome Amends for that Inconvenience. The Air is very pleafant and refrefhing, but it has fomething fo very peculiar in it, that the Keys in your Pockets will ruft.

Nature of the Clime.

As this River lies in the Latitude of 13° 20' N. and in 15° 20' W Longitude, no Wonder that it is very hot, but the moft exceffive Heat is reckon'd to be generally about the latter End of *May,* a Fortnight or three Weeks before the rainy Seafon begins. The Sun is perpendicular twice in a Year, and the Days are never above thirteen Hours long, nor lefs than eleven, I mean from Sunrifing to Sun-fetting, what feemed to me ftrange at firft, was, that as foon as it grows

Longitude and Latitude

light.

1732. light, the Sun rifes, and as foon as it fets,
it grows dark ; and my being us'd to it fo
long in *Africa*, made me think that it was
the fame in *England*, for coming home in
the Month of *July*, and being fometimes,
at Sun-fet, a good Way from home, I have,
for Fear of being benighted, made what
Hafte I could, and have often been there an
Hour before it grew dark.

On the 29th, Mr *Henry Johnfon*, late Chief
at *Brucoe*, arrived here on his Way to *Fatatenda*, he being appointed Writer to Mr *Hugh
Hamilton*, the Company's Factor there, in the
room of Mr *Edward Peters*, who died laft
July. This Day the River began to fall
apace.

October — On the 4th of *October*, early in the Morn
ing, Mr *Johnfon*, and I fet out together on
Horfeback for *Fatatenda*. About Eight o'
Clock we paffed thro' a fmall Town call'd

Canuba. *Canuba*, to which Town belongs a Port two
Miles from it, where *Antonio Vofs* of *Tancro-
wall* every Year fends his Canoas to trade
About Noon we paffed thro' the Town of

Baffy *Baffy*, about ten Miles from *Canuba*, which has
alfo got a fine Port for Trade, to which a
good many Canoas come every Seafon. About
Three in the Afternoon we pafs'd thro' a fmall
Town call'd *Burdab*, where the Ufurper of the
Kingdom of *Tomany* refides. Two Hours after
we pafs'd thro' *Colar*, a Town in the Kingdom
of *Cantore*, after which we continued on the
South Side the *Gambia* fix Miles farther, when
we came overagainft the Factory of *Fatatenda*,
and making a Signal to the Factor, he fent
over

over a Canoa to fetch us: We sent our Horses back to *Colar*, and cross'd the River, which is about as wide there as the *Thames* at *London-Bridge*, it ran then with a rapid Stream, and seem'd very deep. The Tide rises three or four Foot here in the dry Seasons, but in the Time of the Rains it does not reach so high. Both Sides the River is woody, and the Land on the South Side low, but the Factory is situated upon a high steep Rock, close to the River, on the North Side, in the Kingdom of *Woolly*, ten Miles from any Town in *Woolly*. On each Side of the Factory there is a pleasant Prospect of the Course of the River for some Miles, and likewise across it you may see great Part of the Kingdom of *Cantore*, every Night you may hear the Wild Beasts howling and roaring not far from it. On the Road we were obliged to swim our Horses twice. Mr *Hamilton* was not a little glad to see us, having not seen any White Man since *July* last, the Time of his Writer's Death.

River at Fatatenda

AFTER staying here two Days, I intended to return to *Yamyamacunda*, but was prevented by a Message sent to me by *Hume Badgy*, the present Usurper of *Tomany*, who desired I would stay till he came to see me. Accordingly in the Evening he came to the Factory, bringing with him about two hundred Men well-arm'd, which he was then sending to the Assistance of the King of *Woolley*, whose Brother was in Arms against him, and had already taken some of his People and Towns. This *Hume Badgy* is Son of the late King of *Tomany*, who has been dead for some Years, but he,

Hume Badgy

Account of him

he, fearing the People would not make him King, tells them that his Father is not yet dead, and having a great many refolute Fellows in the Town of *Burdab*, whom he takes care to keep well, they protect him, and no Man in the whole Country dares fo much as fay that the old King is dead. This Man himfelf is very old, and very well-beloved by the Town, infomuch that with them and fome other Volunteers he went and conquer'd the whole Kingdom of *Woolly*, and gave it to the prefent King thereof, fo that he does juft what he pleafes in that Country, as abfolutely as he does in *Tomany*, nay, much more, for there are fome People at a Town call'd *Seamore*, within three Miles of *Yamyanacunda*, who do not much fear him, and therefore he goes but feldom to that Factory. As for that at *Fatatenda*, he ufed Mr *Hamilton* very ill, daily begging Goods of him, or taking them by Force, and he has fuch a curfed Thirft after Strong Liquors,

A fad Set that whenever the Factor is fupplied with any for his own Drinking, he will force every Drop from him, unlefs he takes care to bury it in the Woods, (which he told me he had feveral times been obliged to put in Practice) and fo at Night, when the Tyrant and his People are all gone, he ufed to go and vifit his Liquor with as much Secrecy and Caution as a Mifer does his Gold.

I thought to have gone from *Fatatenda* to *Mercany*, along the North Side of the River, but could not, by reafon of the Creeks being fo much out, that it is impoffible to crofs them, fo I crofs'd the *Gambia* at *Fatatenda*

and went on the South Side. Between *Bur-*
dab and *Baſſy* I rode over the ſteepeſt Hill I
ever ſaw in my Life, almoſt a continual Rock
of Iron Stone, and yet full of Trees About
Sun-ſet I got to *Baſſy* Port, and having crof-
ſed the River, walked to *Nackway* by Moon-
light, did my Buſineſs that Night, in the
Morning early walked back to *Baſſy* Port,
and immediately rode home to *Yamyamacunda*,
which I believe to be near forty Miles from
Fatatenda by Land The River being fallen, the Women flock to it in abundance,
and are exceeding buſy in catching ſmall Fiſh Stinking
like Sprats, which they dry and keep by them Fiſh.
as a dainty Diſh, call'd *Stinking Fiſh* As
ſoon as they catch them (which is in a Basket
like a Hamper, by putting a little Ball of
Paſte at the Bottom of it, and holding it under Water a little while, and then raiſing it
gently) they lay them upon a clean Spot of Way of
Ground to dry, after which they pound them Curing
in a wooden Mortar to a Paſte, then they
make them up in Balls of about three Pounds
each, and ſo keep them all the Year round.
A ſmall Quantity of it goes a great Way
They do not dreſs it by itſelf, but mix it with
Rice or Corn, which I have ſeveral times eat
with a good Appetite.

On the 22d I perceiv'd the Tide to ebb
and flow here. For theſe twenty Days it had
been exceſſive hot, but now it began to be
cooler and pleaſant. The Evenings and Mornings were very foggy, and the Women buſy
in cutting their Rice, which, I muſt remark,
is their own Property, for, after they have Houſe-
ſet by a ſufficient Quantity for Family Uſe, wifry
they

they fell the Remainder, and take the Money themfelves, the Husband not interfering. The fame Cuftom they obferve too in regard to the Fowls, wihch they breed up in great Quantities, when they find they can get Markets for them.

Green
Snakes.

I SHOT a green Snake about two Yards long, but in the biggeft Place (I believe) not above three Inches in Circumference. This fort of Snakes is not at all venemous, as the Natives tell me, but they have others fo plenty, which are really venemous, that they never go out hardly without a Medicine in their

Venemous
Snakes

Budget in cafe they fhould be bit. They are very much afraid of the black Snakes, which I have feen three Yards long, and as big as the fmall of my Leg. They tell me there are a great many Sorts of very venemous Snakes,

Strange
Kinds.

particularly fome with a Comb upon their Heads like a Cock, and which they pofitively affirm do crow like a Cock There are alfo Snakes with two Heads, growing out of one Neck, but thofe I never faw.

Guana's

HERE are alfo plenty of Guana's, a very ugly Creature. which refembles a little Allegator The Natives fay, that when a Man comes near them fometimes unawares, they will break his Legs with their Tail ; which one would almoft think impoffible becaufe the whole Guana is commonly not above a Yard long. The Natives, and fome White Men eat this for a dainty Bit , and I am told they eat as well as any Rabbit.

ON the 31ft, in the Morning, I fet out
from

from *Yamyamacunda* over Land on Horfeback
to *Brucoe*, in order to fee the Remainder of
our Salt, which was left there laft *July*, meafur'd and fent up.   About Nine I pafs'd thro'
a Town call'd *Buile*, pleafantly fituated in a
Valley with high Hills on each Side of it.
About Noon I pafs'd thro' *Corah*, a fmall
Town in *Jemarrow*, where the Emperor lives
retir'd, drove away by the People of *Dubocunda*   About fix Miles to the Weftward of
it is a large Town of the fame Name, about
which is a large Tract of Rice-Grounds.   At
Five in the Evening I arrived at *Chaucunda*,
a large Town, with a ftrong Cirk or Fence,
pleafantly fituated near the Foot of a rocky
Hill, on the Skirts of a large Plain, which
reaches to the River *Gambia*, that runs about
four Miles from the Town.

1732.

*Author's
Journey.*

*Buile, a
Town.*

Corah.

*Chaucun-
da.*

H E R E I lay all Night at the Houfe of
the Alcade, (who was when I came for *England* Emperor of *Jemarrow)* in a very large
Room on a Matt raifed with fmall forked
Sticks, and having nothing over me to keep
the Mufquetoes from me, I was miferably bit
by them, and got but very little Reft

Bad Lodg-
ing

T H E S E Mufquetoes are the greateft Plague
to one's Perfon of any other Vermin on the
River.   They are even worfe than fome Flies,
from their being fo little call'd Sand-Flies,
and which are fo fmall that one can fcarce fee
them, but if there is any Wind at all ftirring,
they will not be able to bite   But the Mufquetoes mind neither Wind nor any thing elfe,
but are always plaguing one, efpecially in the
Night.   They are juft the fime as our *Englifh*
Gnats;

Mufque-
toe-Flies

Gnats, when they bite, it itches very much; if you fcratch it till it bleeds, you run the Rifque of having it fore, and when it is healed, it will never be otherwife than of a blackifh Colour.

Novem-
ber
Dubocun-
da, a
Rebellious
Town

THE next Morning early I left *Chaucunda*, and about Noon I arrived at *Dubocunda*, which (as I faid before) is very well fortified, confidering the Country   Every other Town in the Kingdom of *Jemarrow* is fubject to the lawful Emperor, but the People of this Town being of a rebellious Nature, chofe themfelves a King of their own, which they call *Suma*, who has a great deal of Power over all the Towns near his own.   About Three I paffed by a fmall Town call'd *Colycunda*, noted only for pretty Girls, and foon after I arrived at *Brucoe*, which lies I think much about forty Miles from *Tamyamacunda*

Author en-
tertaind
by the
Emperor

HAVING done my Bufinefs, in about two or three Days I fet out at Night, lay at *Chau-cunda*, in the fame Room I did before   The next Morning I arrived pretty early at the Town where the Emperor lives   As foon as I ftopt, he fent me a Difh or Calabafh of Rice and Stinking Meat, being the beft he had, defiring I would come to his Houfe, which I accordingly did   We talked together almoft two Hours, in which Time he told me how the *Dubocunda* People had made him retire to this Place, where he faid he had enjoy'd more Pleafure than ever he did while he was in his Grandeur, and therefore never defired to live in any other manner.   After we had done talking, I took
Horfe

Horſe and went homeward. About Noon I
paſſed thro' the Town of *Fatico*, which lies on
the Frontiers of *Jemarrow*, about ten Years
ago this was a large Town, at which Time a
noted *Pholey* of *Tomany* came, with a great
many others under his Command, in order to
ſettle under the Protection of this Town
of *Fatico*, where they had not been long be-   *Pholeys* a
fore the Towns-People began to uſe them ill, bus'd.
and take away their Cows from them by force.
The poor *Pholeys* endured it a good while,
till at laſt perceiving that they grew worſe
and worſe, they reſolved to bear it no longer,
and ſo taking their Arms, went under the
Conduct of their Head-Man, by Name *Clar-*   Redreſs
gée Solée, and fell upon the Town, kill'd ſeve-   them
ral, and took ſome Priſoners, which they ſold,   ſelves.
in order to repair the Damages ſuſtain'd by
their having their Cows taken from them
Since that time the Town has been neglected,
and very few People care to live in it, becauſe
of the great Scandal it bears for their ill U-
ſage of thoſe *Pholeys*, who were under their
Protection, and want of Hoſpitality   In the
Evening I arrived at *Tamyamacunda*

On the 20th, in the Evening, we had an   Moon e
Eclipſe of the Moon, which was totally dark clips'd
from half an Hour after Eight, till a Quarter paſt Ten, both before and after it ſhone
very bright   This was the firſt Eclipſe I had
ſeen ſince I came into this Part of the World,
and it coming very unexpectedly, ſurprized me
not a little   The *Mundingos* told me, that
the Reaſon of its being dark was, becauſe a   Ridiculous
Cat had put her Paw between the Moon and Opinions.
the Earth,   The *Mahometans* in this Country
were

were finging and dancing the whole Time, on account of their expecting their Prophet *Mahomet* to come in an Eclipfe. About the Month of *January*, thefe *Mahometans* keep a Faft of a whole Month, that is, they eat nothing between the Sun-rifing and its Setting, and are fo ftrict, that before the Sun is quite down, tho' never fo thirfty, they will not drink fo much as a Drop of Water, but pray almoft continually. When this Moon is expired, they make a very great Feaft, at which they kill Abundance of Cows, and are very merry. They always pray at a New Moon, as do likewife the *Mundingoes*, who have fuch Regard to them, that tho' their Quarrels are never fo great, yet will they not, upon any Account, go to fight till the *Mahometans Lent* is expired. When the *Mundin-goes* are going to Battle, they put fo much Faith in thefe *Mahometans*, as to go and buy of them Papers, fo charmed, as they believe, to prevent the Perfon who wears it from being fhot, accordingly they pay for it, and wear it, and if any mifcarry, the old Man pleads for Excufe, that the Perfon was a wicked Liver, and therefore *Mahomet* would have him die. When thefe Papers are wrote, they carry them to a Perfon who makes fine Leather Strings for Pipes, which they call *Crankee*, and he inclofes them in Leather and red Cloth, and being faftned with neat twifted Leather Strings, they wear them acrofs their Shoulders, over their Breafts, and on each Side. Sometimes one may fee a Man with as many of thefe Things as will weigh thirty Pounds

Mahometan and *Mundingoe* Ceremonies.

SOME

S O M E of them when they are going a
Journey will kill a young Fowl, and inspect
the Entrails, and according as they find them,
they will either proceed on their Journey, or
put it off till another Time. They are likewise very superstitious in regard to the Days
of the Week, some of which they say are
bad, and on these Days they never will begin
any Piece of Work.

T H E *Mundingoes* are very ignorant, and
have no manner of Books or Learning among
them, but make shift to count by Tens, and
mark them upon the Ground. The *Maho-*
metans can almost all of them read and write
Arabick, which they take care to teach their
Children, there being Schoolmasters among
them for that purpose.

O N the 18th of *December*, in the Morning
early, Mr *Conner* went overland to *Nackway*.
After he was gone, a Messenger arrived from
the Alcade of *Brucoe*, with Advice that the
Company's Factory was burnt, and the Chief
(Mr *Philip Galand*) run distracted, insomuch
that he had endeavour'd to drown himself;
whereupon the Alcade desired that either Mr
Conner or myself would come there forthwith
to take charge of the Company's Effects. I
immediately sent a Messenger after Mr *Conner*
to acquaint him of this unwelcome News, and
in the Evening he returned; but being very
much fatigued, and fearing that Delay might
prove dangerous to the Company's Interest, I
got myself ready, and about Eight at Night
set out on Horseback for *Brucoe*, where I arrived the next Morning, being above 40 Miles,

L   and

1-32 and found Mr *Galand* very ill at the Alcade's House, and the Alcade in Possession of the Keys of the Warehouse, which was not burnt

On the 21st, at the Persuasion of the Alcade and the People of the Town, as well as by the Resolution of Mr *Galand*, never to take any more the Charge of the Factory upon him, I took an Inventory of the Goods in Store, after which I sent a Messenger away to *James* Fort with the following Letter

BRUCOE, Dec 21, 1732

GENTLEMEN,

IT *is with a great deal of Concern that I am obliged to acquaint you, that on the 18th Instant a Messenger arrived at Yamyamcunda, from the Alcade of this Town, with an Account that the Factory was burnt, and Mr Galand is in mad, and no one being there to take care of the Company's Effects, he desired either Mr* Conner *or myself to come over forthwith When the Messenger arrived Mr* Conner *was gone to* Nackway, *but I sent directly after him, and he return'd the same Night , but, being much fatigued, he said he could not come hither I had no mind to leave my own Factory, but fearing that Delay might prove dangerous, I set out in the Night, and in about twenty Hours I reached this Factory, Mr* Galand *being at the Alcade's House, afflicted not only in Body but in Mind, insomuch that some few Hours before I arrived here, he had endeavour'd to drown himself, which he had done effectually, if a Native had not dived after him, and with much ado saved him He says, he is resolved never to take charge of any thing for the future, but will go down to the Island the first*

O2

portunity I am really afraid he will be never easy till he is there, and the more, because he says it is the utmost of his Wishes to be safe at James Fort *He is downright melancholy, and does not care to talk to any Body, whether his being afraid of the Natives killing him (which he seems to intimate) or whether the Fire was the occasion of this Alteration in him, I cannot tell, but I am sure he is much changed since I saw him last.*

I HAVE this Day, at the Persuasion of the Alcade, taken a true Inventory of all the Company's Effects here, in the Presence of himself and Poolman *the Linguister, which you'll herewith receive signed by us all three. As for what was burnt by the late Conflagration I cannot tell, but I am informed there was but little or nothing of the Company's destroy'd, and but a few Things of Messieurs* Galand *and* Johnson *The Doors of both the Rooms, and the T ck 'las, Ridge-Pole and Braces, were entirely consumed, and the Door of the Hall was very much damaged I beg, Gentlemen, you will send back this Messenger as soon as possible, and let me know whether you approve or disapprove of what I have done already, and to give me your further Orders in what Manner to proceed I am not easy while I am from my own Factory (notwithstanding my Colleague is more careful than he was some Time ago) and it is impossible for me to return before I receive Advice from you In the mean Time I* ' c. n,

Gentlemen,
Your Obedient Humble Servant,

F R A M O O R E

1732.

ON the 31st, in the Evening, a Long-boat, belonging to the *Tryal* Snow, Capt. *Robert Clarke*, a Separate Trader, then at *Joar*, came by this Port, telling the Servant, when they challenged her, that she belonged to Sig. *Antonio Voss*, at *Tancrowall*, and was going up to *Baffy* Port, to bring down some Slaves The Reason of their not being willing to be known, was for Fear of the Natives feizing them, upon Account of the ill Usage they have fometimes received at the Hands of the Separate Traders, by them called Interlopers, and from the Advice, perhaps, of the Accident which happen'd to Capt *Major*, fome few Months fince, at *Caffan*, which I have before mentioned.

Separate Traders abufe the Natives.

ON the 6th of *January*, about Sun-fet, the before-mention'd Long-boat came down from *Yamyamacunda* She called at this Port, and the chief Mate, Mr *Hayes*, came to fee me at the Factory, Mr *Galand* hearing of the Boat's Arrival, came down to the Factory, and defir'd Mr *Hayes* to carry him down with him to Capt *Clarke*, of whom he wanted to purchafe feveral Neceffaries The Alcade and myfelf did what we could to diffuade him from going, but to no Purpofe, fo about Midnight the Boat went away, and Mr *Galand* in it The next Day, about Noon, a Black Fellow, Servant to Mr *Galand*, who went down in the Boat with him, came over Land to the Factory, I was furprized to fee the Fellow come back, and afked him where his Mafter was; he had not, for fome Time, Power to anfwer me for crying, at laft he told me, that his Mafter and Mr *Hayes* were

both

January, 1733

Meff *Galand* and *Hayes* drown'd

both drown'd, and that he himfelf, and the
Sailors which were rowing in the Boat, with
much Difficulty, faved their Lives.

THE next Evening the Sailors and Linguifter, which belong'd to the Boat, came to
the Factory, where they gave me the following Account of the Accident which befel
the Boat.

" ABOUT Four o' Clock Yesterday Particular
" Morning, and about four Hours after we of that
Misfortune
" went from *Brucoe* Port, being abreaft of
" *Sappo* Iflands, we heard a great Noife in
" the Water, juft a-head of the Longboat,
" and being told, by our Black Linguifter,
" that it was a Parcel of Sea-Horfes, our
" Mate, Mr *Hayes*, ordered him to take a
" Gun that was loaded, and fire among
' them, which he accordingly did, but before
' the Light of the flafhing in the Pan was out
" of our Eyes, we rowing very hard, and having
" the Tide with us, were got into the Midft
" of them, and one of them, which we fup-
" pofe was wounded with the foregoing
" Shot, flounc'd and kicked about the Boat
" till fuch Time as he knocked a Piece out
" of the Bottom of her, we finding her be-
" gin to fill, called to Mr *Hayes*, who or-
" der'd us to pull in for Shore directly, we
" did fo, but when we were within about
" twenty Yards of it, the Boat funk right
" down, upon which, every one that could
" fwim, made the beft of their Way to
" Shore, but poor Meff *Galand* and *Hayes*
" not knowing how to fwim, were unfortu-
' nately drown'd. We on Shore ftayed till

L 3   " Ye-

1733   " Yefterday Noon, near the Place where the
" Boat funk, but being almoft ftarved for
" Want of Victuals, and naving no Arms to
" defend ourfelves from the Wild Beafts, we
" thought it beft to come up here, to defire
' you to take Care of us, and affift us till
" fuch Time as Capt. *Clarke* fhall fend for us.
" As the Boit funk right down, we believe
" we fhall be able to fave a good many things
' out of her, provided we had Hooks fit for
" the purpofe "

Attempt to   I GOT a Smith directly, who made them
fth for the Hooks for their purpofe, after which they
Wreck   went down with fix of the Company's Servants,
to fee what they could get out of the Boat
Before they went, I fent a Meffenger over
Land to *James* Fort, with Letters to the Go
vernor and Chief Merchants, to acquaint them
of this melancholy Accident The following
one I fent to Captain *Clarke* by the fame Meffenger

To Captain ROBERT CLARKE.

BRUCCE, Jan 8, 1733

S I R,

Author's   *THIS come to acquaint you, that on the 6th*
Letter to   *In a Night your Long-boat came down*
Capt   *to cut One Hundred and an half of*
B. -Wax, the fame Weg't of Teeth, and one
Gold Slat, as your Mate Mr Hayes told m
He ftaid here till high Water, and then proc
on his Way down, taking with him Mr Philip
Galand, who purpofed to come down to Joar to
fome things of you. Yefterday at Noon an

M*r* Galand's *Servant with the difmal Tidings of the Boat being broke and funk (abreaft of* Sappo Iflands) *by the Sea Horfes, and that Meff* Hayes *and* Galand *were unfortunately drowned , but the other two White Men got fafe to fhore I fent directly my Canoa away with fix Servants with Arms,* &c *to their Affiftance ; but before they arrived there, the People being tired with ftaying, and having nothing to eat, nor defend themfelves from the Wild Beafts, proceeded to this Factory, where they juft now arrived with nothing but a Girl Slave.*

Nathaniel Rogers *and* Thomas Rathbone *our two Sailors tell me, they believe they fhall be able to get a great many of the Goods out of the Boat, which funk right down, fo that it is about five Foot under Water at low Water, and the Maft is ftanding I have got a Smith now making two Hooks for them to get the Things out of the Boat, who will fet out with two Canoas as foon as they are done, and I fhall fend fome of the Company's Servants along with them. This Meffenger will give you a full Account of every thing I beg you'll difpatch him back as foon as poffible. I affure you I'll do all that lies in my Power to ferve you, and remain,*

S I R,

Your moft Humble Servant,

Fra. Moore.

Whilst I was writing the foregoing Letter in my Chamber, I heard a ruffling in the Bufhes near my Window , upon which I took a Piftol in my Hand, and with one Servant

Cow worried by a Wolf

L 4   *went*

went to the Place, and found a Cow with her Guts just torn out by a Wolf

ABOUT two Days afterwards the People return'd back, and brought word, that they could see neither the Boat nor any thing belonging to her, but in their Way up they had found three Cakes of Bees-Wax, an Umbrella, an Oar, and an empty Arm-Cheſt They ſaid that they believed ſome People had been plundering the Boat, for near the Place where they left her they found a Sagay, ſuppoſed to be left there by ſome one who had found better Booty.

Wreck plunder'd

THE next Morning about twenty People belonging to the *Suma* at *Dubocunda* came o the Factory, and ſeized the Bees-Wax which the Sailors had found floating on the Water, and not content with the Wax, they wanted to ſeize the People and ſell them, but the Alcade and myſelf made them let that Diſpute alone till two Days afterward, at which time arrived a Canoa from Capt *Clarke* to retu t People By whom I receiv'd the following Letter.

Protected

RUMBOS Port. Jan. 10, 1 3,

Dear SIR,

I HAVE juſt now receiv'd your new Letter, wherein you acc me of the Lo of my Chief Mate, but return you a t Thanks for your generous Offer in endeavouring to ſave what we can of the Cargo I ſe t a Canoa with my Carpenter, to e if poſ ſible to get my Boat again Dear Moore, his P

C Clarke's Anſwer

Piece of Service done me by your good Nature, will ever put me under an Obligation to sincerely acknowledge your Friendship. I beg you'd dispatch my People with the Canoa down again, and what can be saved, as soon as possible I beg you'd send me the Particulars of what is saved, and not put too much Confidence in my People I beg you'll excuse my short Letter, for I am scarce in my Sens. My best Respects attend you, and I am,

Dear M O O R E,

Your very sincere Friend,

and humble Servant,

ROBERT CLARKE.

T H E same Day the King's People were very resolute to seize Capt. *Clarke*'s Men, declaring that they would make Slaves of them, that they were Interlopers, come up in a Boat to trade without calling to see the King at *Dutrecunda*, that none but the Company should trade in their Country, and therefore unless Capt *Clarke* would give them a hundred Barrs for each of his People, they should be kept Prisoners as long as they lived From Noon till Six o' Clock the Alcade and I endeavour'd to persuade them to let the Men go; at last I told them, that such Usage as this would soon make the Company break up their Factory, and that unless they would release the Men, I would write to the Fort to have no more Goods sent to me, but if they would deliver the Men up to me, I would, as Capt *Clarke* was my Acquaintance, make them a Present of some Brandy and other Goods, which at last they thought proper to agree to, so having given them the things, I sent away the Men in the Cap-

His Men like to be seiz'd by the Natives

Got off with much ado.

Captain's Canoa, and the following Letter along with the Carpenter

BRUCOE, Jan 14, 1733

Dear SIR,

THIS comes by your Carpenter, and serves to acquaint you, that soon after my left, your People with some others went down in order to save what they could out of your Boat, but before they came the Natives had been there, and broke the Boat so that they could not find any where. As they came back they found three Cases of Bees-Wax, an Oar, and some Platters float z on the Water, which they took up and brought here. The King's People came and seiz'd it, and I do assure you it was with a great deal of Difficulty that I and the Alcade of this Town preserved your White Men and Slaves from being taken away. As for your Men, I was obliged to pay six Barrs before I could get the King's Leave to send them down, and as for your Slave I persuaded them it was Mr Saxby's, so that they designed to keep it till such time as he come up, but with much ado I have got Leave to send it down, on Condition that they shall be paid two Barrs for taking care of her, so that I desire you would send by my Messenger a Piece of Silks as to pay them on account of the Slave, and prove tel Saxby to say it is his, or else they will call upon me. As for what I have done, I do assure you had it been for my self I could do no more.

WHEN I wrote to you last I was ignorant of the King's Designs, but I find now, that had your Cargo and Boat been saved, his People would have seiz'd them all, because your Mate is dead

to come to his Port as he went up, tho' there was Trade for him, which had he done, and made the King a Present of but two Bottles of Brandy, would have made him do what he could to serve you, whereas now he is an inveterate Enemy to Interlopers.

THERE was a Box with eight Felt Hats faved, which the King's People did not seize One of them I paid for the Hire of a Canoa, the other seven you'll herewith receive The Alcade of this Town is a very good Man, and has been a great Instrument in saving your People, so that you think proper to send him a small Present, will not be thrown away. Having nought to do, I remain,

Dear S I R,

Your most Humble Servant,

F R A   M O O R E

On the 21st arrived the *James Island* Shallop, Go *Lason* Master, with Forkillas, and all other Posts necessary to rebuild the Factory The Gentlemen order'd me to go over Land to *Jamyamacunda*, to resign the Company's Effects to Mr *Conner*, and to send down poor Cund (who they did not know was dead, by the Return of this Boat

As soon as I had landed the Forkillas and Posts, I set out on Horseback for *Yamyama-cunda*, where having done my Business, I returned to *Brucoe*, where I was now stationed. I saw nothing remarkable in my Journey, only

Shallop with For-killas

1733
Wolves in
Numbers only great Numbers of Wolves running be
fore me as I croffed the Savannahs by Moon
light

On the 31ft the *James Ifland* Shallop fail
ed for the Fort, with whom I fent down M.
Giland's Effects, fome damaged Goods, and
a little Trade   I fent down fome Hides, as
I have feveral times before   As foon as the
Beaft is flea'd, they ftretch the Hide upon the
Ground with Pegs.   It dries in one Day, if
the Weather be fair, and then cutting off the
Peg holes, and doubling it, it is fit for Pack-
age   The next Morning the *Adventur* S'oop,
John Leach Mafter, arrived here on i W
to *Falatenda*, having on Board a Lo d of Sa',
and Mr *Thomas Palmer*, Writer for that Pl c

Bloody
Mutiny
of the
Negroes On the 5th, in the Evening, I receive
Advice, that Capt *Williams*, Mafter o a B
gantine, trading about *Joar*, having boug
a few Slaves, and not looking well to the r,
they mutiny d, rofe, and killed a great Par
of the Ship's Crew, the Captain himfelf had
his Fingers cut by them in a miferable Manner, and it was with great Difficulty he efcaped being killed, which he did in fwimming
afhore, by which means he got fafe to *Joa*
Fort, where he was kindly received by the
Governor, and took his Paffage to *England*
along with Captain *Clarke* in the *Trial* Snow,
as did likewife our third Chief Merchant, Mr
Thomas Harrifon, whofe Brother *John* di the
Tancrou all the very Day that he embarked
from *James* Fort

O

ON the 16th of *March*, at Night, we had a great deal of Thunder and Lightning, and some Rain, which at this Time of the Year is very uncommon The Natives tell me, that this foretells great Wars, and that they are sure, by the Quickness of the Claps of Thunder, and other Things, that it will not be long before it comes to pass

IN less than a Year there were great Wars almost all over the Country, which continued so long, that when I came to *England* they were not over Vast Numbers of Slaves were taken in these Wars, and the chief Trade of the Company's Factories up the River was for Slaves taken

ON the 4th of *April*, in the Evening, the *Bumper* Sloop, from *New England*, Captain *Samuel Moore* Master, who had last Year a Scooner cut off at *Caffan*, came to anchor at *Brucoe* Point, being bound up to *Yamyamacunda*, he had on Board a good Number of Guns, and Hands sufficient, and it was thought he design'd either to make good Trade, or else get Satisfaction of the Natives for the Loss of his Scooner last Year at *Caffan* He stay'd here all Night, and the next Morning pro- ceeded up the River for *Yamyamacunda*.

ON the 27th, at a Town about a Mile from *Brucoe*, I found a monstrous large Scor- pion, being I believe full twelve Inches long These Creatures are reckoned very venemous, and was a Man to be stung by so large a one as this was, I believe it would be present Death. I have known several People stung by small

Scor-

1733 Scorpions, which give an infinite deal of Pain
so violent, that for at least twelve Hours th
Person stung cannot sleep, at the End of whicl
Time the Pain abates, and is soon after qu
over, but what's remarkable is, that notwith
standing the Pain is so violent, yet it swells bu
very little

No, ON the 11th of *May* Mr *Lemaigre* came
down in his own Sloop, with above thirty Slave
on Board, which he was going to sell at *Joa*
to the Separate Shipping. He stay'd here bu
a little while, and then proceeded on his Way
down I having occasion to purchase some
Neceffaries from the Ships below, went with
him in his Sloop, but when we were got with
in twenty Miles of *Joar* we met the *Fame*
Sloop, *Thomas Saby* Master, bound up the
River with a Load of Salt to purchafe Corn
for the Ufe of *James* Fort, and in Company
with him was the *Amerfham* Sloop, Captain
Munday, a Separate Trader, bound to *Ta-*
mincrew to purchafe Slaves, by whom we received Advice that the *Dolphin* Snow, Captain
Lovett, was arrived at *James* Fort from the
Company, with Mr *Richard Hull*, who was
come to relieve Governor *Rogers*, he defigning
to return to *England* by the *Dolphin* Snow
Upon receiving this News, I thought it advife
able to go on Board the *Fame* Sloop, and return to my Factory In the Way we had a
Tornado fmart Tornado, being the firft for this Seafon,
Moon to and the Night we arrived at *Brucoe* we had a
tell, eclip- total Eclipfe of the Moon, which lafted more
fed than an Hour

O

ON the 4th of *June* arrived the *Sea Nymph* 1733
Sloop, *John Brown* Mafter, with Mr *James* *June.*
Boo's, Writer, and a pretty large Cargo, for
this Place   She had likewife Cargoes and
Writers aboard for *Fatatenda* and *Yamyama-*
cunda   By this Conveyance I received the
following Letter ·

Mr FRANCIS MOORE.

James *Fort,* May 27, 1733.

SIR,

'YOU will receive by the *Sea Nymph* Letter to
" Sloop, Capt. *Brown,* a fmall Cargo the Au-
" of Goods proper to affort your Warehoufe thor
' at *Brucoe,* agreeable to your former Indent
' and as our prefent Circumftances will admit
" of, and which we defire you to make the
' beft Ufe of you poffibly can

" As the Company have very confiderably
" advanced your Commiffions on Trade, fo
" we hope all their Servants, and you Mr
' *Moore* in particular, will give the Company
' fuch fincere Inftances of Fidelity and At-
' tachment in all your Tranfactions for them,
" as well as affable Behaviour to the Natives
" and Traders, as will be a fuitable Return
" to them for fuch Favour and Gratuity, vo-
' luntarily, and out of their good Will be-
' ftowed on you, fuch Conduct being agree-
' able to the moft folemn Engagements you
" have voluntarily obliged yourfelf to obferve,
' under fevere Penalties for acting the con-
' trary, in purfuance of which you are ftrict-
' ly to obferve the following Inftructions:
" You

" Y o u are to make a Prefent of five Gal
" lons of Rum to the *Suma*, on account of
" Mr *Hull*'s fucceeding Mr *Rogers* in the Di-
" rection of the Company's Affairs here, with
" the ufual Compliments on the Company's
" Behalf, and to affure him, and other pro-
" per Perfons near you, of the Company's
" Intentions to give very great Encourage-
" ment to trade in thofe Parts, but more e-
" fpecially for Dry Goods, Teeth, Wax, Hides
" or Skins of any Sort, and for Cotton, In-
" dico, Gums, or any thing elfe that may be
" thought proper for a home Market

" THERE is a red Liquor, that bleeds plen-
" tifully from the Bark of a Tree call'd *Pau*
" *de Sangue*, upon Incifion, and in a little
" time hardens to the Confiftence of Gum,
" which is of great Value, and therefore you
" are defired to ufe your utmoft to procure
" large Quantities of it, for which you may
" give half a Barr a Pound, or under   Othe
" Improvements will be attempted, in order
" to enlarge the Demands as well as Return
" from thofe Parts, which you will have time-
" ly Advice and Inftructions how to procee-
" therein

" You are at all times to take fpecial care
" not to diffort your Warehoufe, by being
" very careful to be as fparing of the Heads
" of the Money as poffibly you can, of which
" you are not, without great Neceffity, to iff-
" out, but in Trade only

" You are likewife not to take or pay
· yourfelf, or other Servants, any of the Heads
           " of

" of the Goods, nor any Slaves, Teeth, Wax
' or Gold, or any other Dry Goods, on any
' Account whatſoever , but to remit ſuch as
" you have of each at every Conveyance that
" offers by the Company's Veſſels to the Fort,
" on the Account and Riſque of the Royal
" *African* Company of *England*.

" Y o u are on no account to pay any
" thing to the Account of Wages or any
" Servant belonging to the Company, either
" belonging to the Shipping or others, and
" to take care that ſuch as ſhall be under your
' Care are not permitted to run in Debt to
" the Company , for ſuch Deficiencies and
" Money paid to ſuch as do not belong to
" your Factory, will be placed to your own
" proper Account.

" Y o u are not to confound your Trade
" made with the Natives, *Portugueſe* or Mer-
" chants, as has been, under Pretence to make
" the Merchants and *Portugue* Trade of
" Slaves, Teeth, Wax and Gold, come out
" more reaſonable , and as Slaves are bought
" at much more reaſonable Rates of the Na-
" tives than of the Merchants, ſo likewiſe are
" Teeth, Wax and Gold, bought at under
' or almoſt half the Price as of the *Portugueſe*
" Therefore all Tranſactions for the future are
" expected to be juſtly entred in your Waſte-
' Book, that a fair, clear and true State of
" Trade and other Occurrences may be ſeen,
" and to be a Guide for ſuch new Comers as
" may hereafter happen to ſucceed you

M   " 'T i s

" 'T is on this account that the Company
" have order'd their Accounts to be kept in such
" a Method, as the Profit and Loss of each
" Factory may be easily known   And in pur-
" suance to these Orders you will now, and
" at all Times hereafter, receive Invoice of
" such Goods sent you at prime Cost in Eng-
" land, which you are to charge yourself with,
" in your Books in the same manner   But
" all the particular Species of Goods that are
" paid, sold or issued out by you, are to be
" charged at the real and just Value they are
" rated or sold at in your Parts, in Barrs,
" Shillings and Pence

     " By every Remittance you are to send
" us the real Cost, and the particular Goods
" paid for every particular Species remitted
" of Slaves. Teeth, Gold and Wax , and as it
" has been usual for some of the Company'.
" Servants to be so disingenuous as to act con-
" trary to their Covenants, and their solemn
" Engagements, as to the Particulars paid
" or issued out, so likewise have they in taking
" all Advantages to themselves of what Dry
" Goods they have purchased   But now,
" the Company have settled your Commission
" at Five Shillings per Head for every mer-
" chantable Slave, Five Shillings and Two
" Shillings and Sixpence for every Hundred Wt
" of large and small Teeth, Five Shillings
" for every Ounce of Gold, and Two Shil-
" lings and Sixpence for every Hundred
" Weight of Wax that you shall remit to this
" Fort, we hope it will induce you to dispose
" of their Goods to the best Advantage you
" possibly can, and likewise to account for all
                 " other

" other Advantages, and that not to your own   1733.
" Account, but for the Company Your
" doing otherwife being not only a Breach of
" your folemn Contract or Agreement with
" the Company, but an Injury to their Chief
" Agents, who now draw their Commiffions
" on the clear Profits only that fhall accrue
" thereby

" Y o u are at all Times hereafter to follow
" fuch Inftructions as you fhall farther receive
" from us. In the mean Time, as your ftrict
" Obfervance of thefe will entitle you to our
" Favour, fo will your Neglect oblige us to
" take fuch Meafures as will be to your Pre-
" judice.

" F o r feveral weighty Reafons you are
" not to purchafe any Gold, of the *Portuguefe*
" or others, at above Twelve Barrs *per* Ounce,
" large and fmall Teeth Eight or Sixteen Barrs
" *per* Hundred Weight, and Wax at Twelve
" Barrs *per* Hundred, and as much under as
" you can , for to purchafe Gold or other
" Goods of the *Portuguefe* at above that Rate,
" is only afforting them with Goods and fuch
" Money as they want to make more Trade
" up the River in your Parts, with little or
" no Advantage to the Company when bought
" at a higher Rate

" T h i s will be deliver'd you by Mr *Roots*,
" who is to be your Affiftant, we recommend
" him to your Favour and good Ufage, as he
" fhall merit , and you are carefully to inftruct
" him in the Trade and Cuftoms in your Parts,
' that on your Removal or Promotion to a
' better Poft, he may be capable of tranfact-
M   ing,

1733   " ing the Company's Affairs to their Advan-
     " tage, and you are particularly to let him
     " sign every Day's Trade or Transactions in
     " your Waste-Book, which Book you are to
     " compleat at the End of *June* next, and af-
     " terwards from the End of *June* to the End
     " of *August*, and so on for every two Months
     " afterwards, which Waste-Books you are to
     " remit down by the first Opportunity that
     " shall offer, first taking a true Copy to be
     " kept at your Factory, and perused by your
     " self and others as Occasion shall require '

                 Your Loving Friend,

                 RICHARD HULL

Captain
Moore pro-
tected by
Mr *Conner*

ON the 17th, the Sloop *Bumper*, Captain *Samuel Moore*, came down the River, having been trading up at *Yamyamacunda* these two Months past, and where he had met with a great deal of Success, but chiefly owing to the Company's Factor Mr *James Conner*, who resides there, and protected him against the Insults of the Natives, who several times endeavour'd to take or kill the said Captain *Moore*, for many Injuries they said they had received from him, particularly last Year, at which time they said he made Spread-Eagle Dollars of Pewter, and gave them in Trade for Silver, which so incensed the People, that they are resolved to be revenged on him, if possible, he therefore seldom ventured ashore, and when he did, took care to be well arm'd His Trade was most of it made for him by Mr *Conner*, for which, no doubt, he had very good Commissions

A vile
Cheat pre-
tenced

                                   WITH

WITH this Sloop came alfo the Company's
Sloop *Fame* from buying Corn up the River,
he ftay'd here all Night, but the *Bumper* after
a fhort Stay went away, and in the Night-time
was attack'd by about an hundred Negroes in
the very narroweft Part of the River *Gambia*,
between a large Ifland and the Main Land.
They fought bravely on both Sides, they fay;
and notwithftanding the Sloop run aground in
the midft of the Engagement, yet had they the
good Fortune to get clear of them, but the
Super-Cargo, Mr *Lowther*, had the Misfortune to be fhot in the Belly, and died the next
Day, one Negroe was fhot, and another
wounded in the Leg

Bumper Sloop at-tack'd by the Ne-groes

By the *Fame* Sloop I wrote the following
Letter to the Governor at *James* Fort.

BRUCOE, June 18 1733.

SIR,

THIS comes by the Fame *Sloop, and ferves
to acknowledge the Receipt of yours on the
4th Inflant, and alfo the Cargo you were pleas'd
to fend me by Capt.* Brown   *I fhall take care to
comply with your Orders in regard to the keeping
my Books, and have always endeavour'd to make
it appear that I have a juft Regard for the Company and their Intereft, according to the folemn
Engagement I have made with them*

Author's Letter to the Gov of James Fort

*I AM forry to find you have debarred me
from trading with the* Portuguefe, *becaufe I am
certain it will be a Lofs to the Company, there
being as much Trade to be made with them as with
the* Mundingoes, *and this I can affure you, that
when the Canoas come down the River, and are*

M 3   *or yours*

1733. *defirous to trade with me, they do not want the Money to make more Trade, but only to buy Cloths at* Joar *and* Cower *on their Way down However, as you have given me such pofitive Orders, I am refolved not to trade with them , but fooner than they will fell their Wax and Teeth to me for the Prices you mention'd, they will carry it down to the Separate Traders, and fell it for a greater.*

I AM furprized to find you have debarred me from taking any Iron, or any other of the Heads of the Money to Diet Account, becaufe it is impoffible to buy Provifions without it , and unlefs you will pleafe to allow it, we muft either ftarve or be obli- g-d to leave the Factor

I HAVE by Capt Saxby *fent a Piece of Gum, which I believe was taken from the* Pau de Sangue, *I defire you would pleafe to examine it, and let me know if it is the right Sort , becaufe, if it is, I will do my utmoft to procure large Quan- tities of it, and do not doubt but I fhall get it very reafonably I am forry to acquaint you that the Trade here is very fmall, and I am afraid it will not anfwer the Charges of the Factory, and I dare fay that half the Trade that has been made here has been with the Canoas. Since I received your Orders not to trade with the* Portuguefe, *I have loft the Buying of a good deal of Wax. I have nought to add , but remain,*

S i R,

Your moft humble Servant,

FRA. MOORE.

O n

ON the 19th in the Morning came up a   1733
Long-Boat with Meſſieurs *John Leach* and
John Cooper late Maſters of Sloops in the Com- Meſſieurs
pany's Service , but having got ſomething *Leach* and
wherewithal to purchaſe a few Slaves, they *Cooper* ſet
have now ſet up for themſelves, and are going up for them-
up towards *Cuttejar* or *Samy*, in order to trade ſelves
and ſettle

ABOUT a Week after they were paſſed by
my Factory, I received a Meſſage from the
Gentlemen at *James* Fort, and amongſt others
the following Letter or Order, *viz.*

To Mr M O O R E.

JAMES Fort, June 16. 1733.

SIR,

WHEREAS *Captain* Cooper *and Captain* Letter to
Leach *have ungenerouſly left the Compa-* the Author
ny's Employ, under Pretence of having received from
Letters from their Friends in England *to return* *James*
home, and having not only wrote Letters and Fort
petitioned for their Diſcharge for the ſame by Cap-
tain Naſh, *which was complied with by us , but*
ſince we are informed they only intended to de-
ceive us to ſerve their own private Ends, and
to carry on a Trade deſtructive to the Compa-
ny's Intereſt, and the former Truſt repoſed in
them

THESE *are therefore ſtrictly to enjoin you,*
that on no Account whatſoever you harbour, en-
tertain, exchange, or have any Dealings, Barter
or Converſe, with the abovemention'd Perſons
Your ſtrict Obſervance of theſe Orders will con-
vince us how much you have the Company's Inte-

1733 *rest at Heart, as the contrary will cause a due Resentment, as being a high Breach of Order, the which you must answer at your Peril*

AS to what you write concerning the Portuguese, we don't debar you from making trade with them, but in case you do, we strictly enjoin you not to affort account of the Capitals, nor give any Goods, but what shall be charged at two Barrs for one to them, the common Price up the River And to Necessaries for Defence we do not forbid your taking up of some Iron, but recommend to you to be as frugal of the same as possible

NOTHING more offering at present, as that Mr Rogers takes his Passage in the Dolphin Sloop in about a Week, and that we daily expect a fresh Cargo in the Guinea Pacquet, we remain

Your Loving Friends,

RICHARD HULL,
JAMES DAVIS,
JOHN HAMILTON

ON the 12th of *July* in the Evening the Great Shallop, *Geo. Lason* Master, came up hither from *James* Fort By whom I received the following Letter

Mr FRANCIS MOORE

James Fort, July 6, 1733.

Another Letter from James Fort

SIR,

THIS serves to advise you that we have just stopt the Mr —————— from having any thing to do in the Direction here, and that

M

Mr Hugh Hamilton *has resigned the Company's* 1733
Service, and Mr James Conner *is now the Se-*
nior Factor, we have sent for him down, in order
to supply the Vacancy occasion'd by Mr ————
making too free with the Company's Warehouse
here, to our Detriment as well as the Company's.
We have therefore appointed you to succeeed M^r
Conner *at* Yamyamacunda *Factory, and do*
hereby desire you to make all possible Dispatch to
inventory all the Company's Effects now in your
Possession, and deliver the same into the Hands
of Mr James Roots, *whom we have appointed*
to succeed you · And we further advise you, to
give him all the good Advice and Instruction
you can, that he may the better be able to trade,
and conduct himself for his own and the Compa-
ny's Advantage, and then you are to proceed to
Yamyamacunda, *and there likewise to inventory*
all the Company's Effects, and take on you the
Direction of that Factory, where, if you behave
as we wish, in a little time you may expect to be
further promoted ; for we think proper to acquaint
you, that we expect a considerable Addition to be
made to the Chief Factor on the Arrival of the
Guinea *Pacquet, which is now daily expected.*

YOU are to observe those Orders relating to
the two Refugee Captains, that were lately in the
Company's Service We wish you Health and
Success, and are

Your Loving Friends,

RICHARD HULL,
JOHN HAMILTON.

THE next Morning I took an Account of
the Company's Effects, and deliver'd them up

to

1733. to Mr *Roots*, after which I went and hired a
Canoa to carry me up the River, for the
Freſhes were now ſo ſtrong that the Shallop

Author
goes for
Yamama-
cunda

could not proceed, ſo leaving Mr *Roots* as
Chief, and Mr *Barnfather* his Aſſiſtant, I the
next Day ſet out for *Yamyamacunda*, in Company with *Geo. Laſon* the Maſter of the Shallop

Arrives at
Dubcun-
da

On the 15th, about One o' Clock in the
Morning, we arrived at *Dubocunda*, where I
went aſhore to take my Leave of the *Sumi*,
under whoſe Protection *Brucoe* Factory is put,
and alſo to acquaint him of Mr *Roots*'s being
Chief there, and having recommended the
Company's Affairs to his Protection, I embark'd, and proceeded to *Cuttejarr*, where
Meſſ *Leach* and *Cooper* were building a Houſe
in order to ſettle Here we hired Horſes to
go over Land to *Samy*, ordering the Canoa
to make the beſt of her Way to *Fendalacunda*,
about Ten Miles below *Yamyamacunda* That
Evening we reached *Samy*, where we lay at
Mr *Lemaigre*'s The next Morning we deſign'd
to have croſs'd *Samy* River, and ride to *Fendalacunda*, but we were not able to perſuade
the Owners of the Horſes (who went along
with us, to let us ſwim them acroſs the River,

Danger of
Croco-
dles

they being more afraid for their Horſes than
we were for ourſelves, that the Crocodiles
ſhould ſeize them. They are exceeding plenty
in that River, and withal very miſchievous,
for they very often catch Men by the Legs,
and carry them away as they are wading up
to their Knees or Middles in the River to unload Boats or Canoas, which they are at low
Water obliged ſometimes to do Being thus
diſappointed of riding, we croſs'd the River

11

in a Canoa, and set out on Foot for *Fendala-cunda*, where we arrived in about three Hours, being Ten Miles, or thereabouts. We stay'd till the Evening, and then our Canoa arriving we immediately went on Board and proceeded for *Yamyamacunda*, but in a very tiresome Manner, by reason of the Freshes, which were ^{Strong} so strong that we could row against it but very slowly The next Morning we got out of the Canoa, and walked to the Factory, but the Canoa, altho' there were six good Rowers on Board her, could not arrive before the Evening

On the 19th we took an Inventory of the Company's Effects, and about Midnight Mr *Conner* went away in the Canoa which brought me up, by whom I sent the following Letter to the Gentlemen at *James* Fort

Yamyamacunda, July 19 1733.

GENTLEMEN,

THIS comes by *Mr* Conner, *and serves to* ^{Author'} *acknowledge the Receipt of yours of the* ^{Letter} *6th Instant, in pursuance of which, I hired a Canoa, and having deliver'd up the Company's Effects at* Brucoe *into the Possession of Mr* James Roots, *I embark'd for this Place, and after a great deal of Fatigue and Trouble, I am safely arrived here, and have took an Inventory of the Company's Goods, which you will herewith receive, sign'd by Mr* Conner *and myself I must confess I am not a little concern'd at my Removal upwards, and had I not the Company's Interest very much at Heart, I could not comply with your Orders for me to come here, for I am at present*

very

1733   *very ill, and have been so for some Time past, c.*
my Letters have before now made appear to you
I am sorry to tell you, that Mr Dixon *is ..*
at Fatatenda *, and as I believe there will b. son..*
Gentleman sent up there, so I hope you'd pro r
me with an Assistant, for should I when alore ..
any otherwise than well, it might be very preju-
cial to the Company's Affairs Having not ..
aad, I remain,

GENTLEMEN,

Your humble Servant,

FRA MOORE

August   ON the 25th, in the Evening, Mr *Jo .*
Ph'lips came hither from *Fatalenda*, on his
Way down to the Fort, with a very fore Leg,
which had made him lame and feverish The
fame Day a *Mahometan*, who pretends to great
Cures, came to the Factory to fee me I
show'd him Mr *Philips*'s Leg, and he faid he
would make a Cure of it, without the Fatigue
of going Six Hundred Miles in an open Bo ,
which is the Distance between this and *J a*
Fort Mr *Philips* gladly embraced the Prof-
fer, and let him undertake the Cure of his Leg
which he did by fomenting it with Herbs

September   ON the 14th of *September* the Gam .. w
Ga *his*   rose so high, that it began to enter my Cirk,
overflows   which is an Inclosure round the Factory-House,
made with split Cane, ten Foot high, in the
Nature of an Hurdle, supported and well
propp'd up with long Sticks The Water
likewise in the Rice-Grounds and Valleys rose
so high, that it began to come into the Back
                                                    Part

Part of my Cirk, fo that if it continued rifing, it would inevitably have demolifh'd the
Walls of the Factory. The next Morning
finding the Water on both Sides the Houfe
continuing to rife, and that it had undermined
the Walls of it, which began to crack, and
there being already a Communication between
the River and the Rice-Grounds, infomuch
that the Houfe was quite furrounded with
Water, I employ'd all the Servants to build
rea Hutt in the very Middle of the Town
of *Tamyamacunda*, being the higheft Spot of
Ground thereabouts

Occafions the Author to move Houfhold,

T H E next Morning, being the 6th of *September*, the Water having rofe to the very
Walls of the Factory on both Sides of it,
which feem'd ready to fall, the Walls being
built with only a binding Clay, I made all
the Difpatch I could, and removed the Company's Effects to my new Hutt in the Town
And having committed the Slaves to the
Charge of the Head-Man of the Town, I
thought it advifeable to leave the Factory,
there being Frogs, Toads, Snakes and Fifh,
continually coming into it After we had
got every thing out of it, about Midnight
fome of the Walls fell down with a terrible
Noife like Thunder, but the Roof ftill ftood
faft, there was no Body left in it, and no
hurt was done

*and de-
ftroys the
Factory*

F o r thefe ten Days paft, we daily faw vaft
numbers of floating Iflands come down the
River, fome of them very large, being 20
or 25 yards long, with Stumps of Trees, and
fometimes a great many fmall Trees growin,
on

*Floating
Iflands*

on them, with Birds upon them The Roo[..]
being faften with Earth (thick interlace[..]
with one another) made the Iflands float,
which were parcels of Woods torn away bv th[e]
force of the Floods

O n the 18th, early in the Morning Mr
P[.] [.] h[..]ing almoft cured his Leg, went for
[.] [.] [.]over land, in a Canoa, the Road
he[..]e thithe[i] being now fome Feet unde
Wat[.]r

A b o u t two Days afterwards the Water
began to fall apace The Natives told me,
that for thefe eight Years paft, they had not
had fuch an Inundation In the laft, the
Company fuffered a great deal of Damage,
for they had then a Factory at *Cutte[.]a* [.],
which was overflowed, and fcarce any of the
Goods accounted for, which, I thank Go[.],
was not now the Cafe, for I had the pleafure
to find not a bit of Goods loft or damaged,
nor any other Charges accruing to the Com
pany, than the repa ring the Factory Hou e,
wh ch is inconfiderable All the Values he[r]
about w[..]e under Wate[i], the Rice-Ground.
[.]lreft fpo[.]ed w.th lying fo long drowne[d],
Canoas went from place to place over the very
Ro[.]e[.], which in the dry Seafon the Natives
t.[.]vel o [.]foot, and Prov.fions were fo fcarce
t[.] [.] I w[.]s fometimes two Days without a poi-
[.]o [.]ty or getting any, for want of Canoas,
without wh ch I had not been able to go
twen[.]y Yards from my Hutt

O n the 20th, bout Noon came down
Mr P[.] [.], with his Leg in a moft miferable
Co[.]

Condition, he having ftruck it againft the
Stump of a Tree, as he was walking up from
the Canoa to the Factory at *Fatatenda*, it
was fo bad that without fpeedy Relief he muft
inevitably lofe his Life, he therefore defigned
to make the beft of his way down to *James*
Fort, he ftayed all Night, and the next Morning I hired fome People to row him down to
Brucoe

ON the 2d of *October*, the People which
carried Mr *Phillips*, returned with the melancholy Account of his dying about twelve
Miles from *Brucoe*, that they carried him there,
and that Mr *Railton*, the Company's Chief
there, had buried him

ON the 27th having received advice that
there was a Defign to fteal my Slaves from
the Houfe where I had ordered them to be
kept, and finding the Factory-Houfe tolerably
dry, fome part of the Walls, and all the Roof
being left ftanding, I thought it beft to leave
my Hutt, and go live there again, accordingly I removed the Company's Slaves, and other
Effects thither

ON the 3d of *November*, I received the
melancholy News of the Death of Mr *Railton*,
the Company's Chief at *Brucoe*, who had the
Misfortune (as he was chaftifing his Black Boy)
to fall down with his Head againft the Thre-
fhold of his Chamber Door, and fplit his Skull,
and died after lying twelve Hours fpeechlefs

The next Day we had a very fmart Shower
of Rain. Now the Weather began to be very
cold,

1733   cold, Mornings and Evenings, but in the middle of the Day ftill hot.

December   O n the 1ft of *December*, fome of the Natives having got a Net, came and defired I would go along with them to fifh in the Lake overagainft *Yamyamacunda*   We caught a great Number of Fifh, and amongft the reft one fomething like a Gudgeon, but much

Author catches a Torpedo, or Numb Fifh   larger.   None of them cared to touch it, neither would they fuffer me to come near it, telling me that it would kill me   Some of them got long Sticks, and touched the Fifh with it, but as they found the Effect was not fo very ftrong as they imagined, they cut the Sticks fhorter and fhorter, and even at fix Inches Length the Fifh had no Effect, but a laft, when they touched it with their Fingers, they could not bear it the twentieth Part of a Minute.   By this time I underftood it was a Torpedo, or Numb-Fifh, and had the Cu-

It's Quali-ty   riofity of touching it with one of my Fingers, but in a Moment's time my Arm was dead quite up to my Elbow, as foon as I withdrew my Hand, my Arm came to itfelf again I touched it a great many times, and found it have the fame Effect, even after the Fifh was dead   Then I order'd one of the People to skin it, and found that the Quality lay in the Skin only, which, when dried, had no Effect at all

O n the 20th arrived the *Fame* Sloop on her way to *Faictenda*, having brought me Forkillas and other things to rebuild the Factory-Houfe

                                                                    I 4:

THE Factory being so much damaged, it was necessary to be rebuilt, of which I had given an Account to the Chiefs at *James* Fort The best Trees for Forkillas and Ridge-Poles, are Mangroves, which grow below *Joar*; therefore they sent me up Forkillas and other Timbers to rebuild it, and this Day I received them by the *Fame* Sloop, and their Orders for so doing

HAVING pitched upon a rising Ground about 50 Yards distant from the River, I marked a Place for the House 40 Feet Square I first of all got up the Forkillas, (which are the same as Crutches) about 30 Feet long, 4 Feet in the Ground, at 28 Feet distance from each other We laid the Ridge-Pole between the two Forkillas, from each of which we had two Braces, stretched to the Corners of the House, and there rested upon smaller Forkillas, 14 Feet long, 11 Feet above, and 3 under Ground, this made the Square of the House Between the Corner-Forkillas we set a sufficient Number of others, in Lines of an equal size, to support the Plates, from these Plates to the Ridge Pole, we laid the longer Rafters, and from the Plates to the Braces, shorter ones. We used no Iron, but secured the Rafters to the Ridge Pole and Plates by Wyths, of a kind of Wood much tougher and stronger than Willow. The Rafters jetted out about 4 Feet over the Plates, in order that the Eves might secure the Walls.

Manner of erecting a Factory

HAVING thus easily raised the Frame, we next began to build the Walls of Clay, but with the *Negroes* tread with their Feet, and there

N

1-33 thereby temper it so well that it will not crack. We laid the Walls a Foot and half thick, and one Foot high all round the House, and let it stand till it was hard enough to bear the second Layer, and so raised it Foot by Foot, till it was 10 Feet high, leaving one Foot distance between it and the Roof, for Air. As the Wall is of unbaked Clay, if the Plates rested upon it, it would fall, therefore we made the Walls just without the small Forkillas, and if the Wall was exposed to the Weather, it would be wash'd away, which is the reason we made the Rafters to jet out four Feet beyond the Plates, as before mentioned, that the Thatch might cover the Walls. At the same time we raised the Partition-Wall of Clay, of the same Thickness, working the Clay close up to the Doors and Window-Frames. Instead of Trowels they cut and trimmed the Clay very smooth and neat, with Knives made for that purpose.

Porch made.

We next made a Porch, by the Natives called an Alpainter, of the same Materials, only to prevent the Rains soaking in at the joining of the Roofs. we laid hollow split Cabbage Trees for Gutters. The Natives say, they have a right to have an Alpainter or a Porch at every Factory to be without Doors, where they might have Access and Shelter. The Walls and Roof being made, we next tied on Lines upon the Rafters instead of Lathes, upon this we thatched, not as they do in England, by laying the Straw upon the House, but by tying the Straw in Bundles, about the Size of a Man's Wrist, and about 3 Feet long, tying them together upon the Ground into Matts, and then spread on the Rafters,

Row

A PLAN OF
Yamyamacunda Facto...

1	The Alpainn	7	The Kitchen
2	The Hall	8	The Servants Lodge
3	The Stor Rooms	9	The Well
4	The Apartments	10	Two Busheloe Tras...
5	The Corn House	11	The Cerk or Fence
6	The Salt House	12	The Flagg

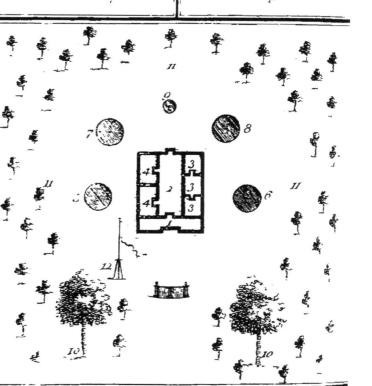

Row above Row, lapping over like Tyles,
and thefe they tie to the Cane Lath. Having covered the Houfe, we floored it with
Clay, hard rammed, we fecured the Store
on the Right-hand fide, from Fire and
Thieves, by fixing a great Number of ftrong ᵀʰᵃᵗᶜʰ-
Iorkillas, 3 Feet in the Ground, upon thefe ⁱⁿᵍ ⁿᵉʷ
we laid Timbers like Joyfts, and crofs'd them
with fplit Ciboa Trees, inftead of Boards,
and upon this we fpread a Coat above a Foot
thick, of the fame tempered Clay with the
Houfe, and worked the fame clofe up to the
Walls, fo that no Wood could appear through
it, and therefore, tho' the Roofs fhould be
burned, the Store-houfe would be out of Danger, it only baking and cracking a little of the
outfide of the Clay, as we have experienced,
when the Factory at *Barroe* was burnt

I have been the longer in the Defcribing
this, becaufe I thought it would be amufing
to the Reader, to fee how eafily the Pooli,
whom we call Barbarous, can procure the Conveniencies of Life Here is a Houfe built, ᴰⁱᵐᵉⁿ-
with a Hall 40 Foot by 13, two Lodging ˢⁱᵒⁿˢ
Rooms 20 Feet by 13, and 3 ftrong Storehoufes, without any Iron-work, Trowels,
Squares, or Carpenters Rules, and with the
fmalleft Expence to the Company, for I did it
with their Servants only, having hired no other
help but the Man who laid and fmoothed
the Clay And the Infide was not only convenient and free from Vermin, but very clean,
and had a cool Look, for the Clay is laid,
clofe, fmooth, and the Walls are alfo very
well

With-

Without the Houſe were two ſhady Biſhelo Trees, and a piece of Ground, of about an Acre, which we incloſed with a Cirk made of ſplit Cane, wove like Hurdles, 10 Feet high. Within this Fence, at proper Diſtances from the Factory, we built four Houſes after the *Mundingo* Faſhion, one for a Kitchen, one for a Salt houſe, another for a Corn-houſe, and the other for the Company's Black Servants to lie in, the Ground between we uſed for a Garden, and ſome Part of it for Fowl, and other Stock.

The Poultry puts me in mind of the *Guinea* Fowls, that are of a dark Colour, with white Spots, and Blue and Red about the Heads, and which are much valued in *England*. Theſe are generally eſteemed to be the tame Fowl of *Africa*, but that is a miſtake, they are wild as Pheaſants in *England*, only much plentier The only tame Fowls of this Country are of the ſame kind of Dunghil Breed, as thoſe in *Europe*, and the Natives have them in vaſt Plenty, but Turkeys, Tame Geeſe or Ducks, they have none among them.

The *Fame* Sloop ſtayed here a Day, and then proceeded up the River, and in about nine Days returned again, having broke up that Factory, and brought all the Company's Goods from thence, and with them, Mr *Thomas Palmer*, the Company's Chief there This Factory is broke on account of the ill Uſage the Company and their Servants have received there, at the Hand of *Hume Badgy* King of *Tenain*, of whom I have before made mention.

FOR

FOR fome time paft I had been very ill
with an Ague and Fever, and wrote feveral *January*
times to the Gentlemen at *James Fort*, to fend
fome body up to relieve me, on the 8th of
January Mr *James Forfyth*, who lately came
from *England*, arrived in the *James* Sloop, in
order to take upon him the Direction of this
Factory, bringing with him a fmall Cargo,
and Mr *Fullwood* for his Writer, with orders
for me to come down to the Fort in cafe my
Illnefs continued; I immediately delivered up Author's
the Company's Effects to Mr *Forfyth*, and on Illnels oc-
the 12th embarked in the *James* Sloop for the cafions
Fort, in order to get cure for my Illnefs, him to go
and to fettle my Accounts. to *James*
Fort

WE ftopt at *Fendalacunda*, and took in
fixty Barrels of Corn for *James* Fort, and
foon after reached *Cuttejarr*, where Mr *Palmer*,
in joint Commiffion with Capt. *Brown*, of the
Fame Sloop, were trading for the Company,
with the Goods brought from *Fatatenda*.

ON the 19th I arrived at *Rumbo's* Port, near
Joar, where the *French* Snow Capt. *Coffin*, a
Separate Trader, was then trading, having
in about a Month purchafed feventy five
prime Slaves, fit for *Cadiz* or *Lisbon*, to one
of which Places he was configned. I ftayed
here one Day, and on the 24th arrived at
James Fort, and was kindly received by Governor *Hull*.

ON the 4th of *February* the Governor, as *February.*
he was riding from *Seaca* to *Gillyfree*, had the The Go-
Misfortune to be thrown off his Horfe, and vernor
breaks his
N 3 break Arm

1734 break his Arm   Soon after arrived the Ship *Phanix*, Capt *Plater Onley*, from *Holland*, who faluted the Fort with nine Guns, and had the fame Number returned , after which he went and anchored at *Gillyfree*

C Coffin,
a Separate
Trader,
des , and
his People
taken by
the Jol-
loiffs.

On the 18th the Company's Sloop *Adventure*, *Harry Johnfon* Mafter, who had been up the River purchafing Corn, came down to the Fort with Advice, that Captain *Coffin* of the *Finch* Snow was dead, and that the Natives had taken his Chief Mate and Surgeon Prifoners, as they were coming on Board from the Shore where they buried him. He was immediately difpatched back again to *Joar* in his Sloop, to give all the Affiftance in his Power to the Snow, and to endeavour to get the beforementioned Perfons releafed from the *Jolloiffs*, for fuch they were that had detained them.

On the 20th came up a *French* Sloop to *Albreda* from *Goree*, with one Monfieur *Benoift*, Chief for that Place, and with him two Affiftants : They faluted our Fort with feven Guns, which returned the fame Number ; after which Monfieur *Benoift* came to the Ifland, to vifit his old Acquaintance Governor *Hull*, they having been in this River together ten Years ago   In the Afternoon the *Finch* Snow arrived from *Joar*, having left the Surgeon and Mate in the Hands of the *Jolloiffs*, and with no more than three White Men on Board that were not ill. She paffed the *Adventure* Sloop laft Night without feeing her , but Mr *Johnfon* hearing that the Snow was come down, made the beft of his Way after her, and arrived here in the

Fyl
Snow
comes to
J Fort

The Go-
vernor
takes care
of her

Even-

Evening. Mr *Hull* fent our Surgeon to look
after the Sick on Board the *Finch*, and alfo put
four *Dutchmen* on Board to look after the Veffel and Slaves.

On the 22d we faw a Veffel coming from
the Sea, which about Noon came to anchor at
Gillyfree, being the *Scipio*, Capt *Gordon*, a Separate Trader, in Twenty five Days from
Briftol. She faluted the Fort with eleven Guns,
which returned the fame Number.

The next Day after the Second Mate and
one Sailor belonging to the *Finch* Snow died.
As there was no Body to take care of the Veffel, or carry any Command aboard, our Governor with fome others and myfelf went on
Board, and had every thing put under Lock
and Key, except the Slaves, of which there
were Sixty fix on Board, and feven Men-Slaves
afhore on the Ifland ; Mr *James Conner* was
order'd to lie on Board the Ship.

The fame Evening the *Adventure* Sloop
was fent up to *Joar*, to get the Surgeon and
Mate of the *Finch* Snow releafed from the *Jol-* *Jolloiffs*
loiffs, who infifted upon being paid 20 Slaves Reafons
in Goods for their Redemption ; and the Rea- for detain-
fon they gave for their detaining them was, *Coffin's*
that the Captain when alive ufed them ill when Mate and
they came to trade with him Doctor.

On the 26th, feeing a Veffel coming from
the Sea, we fired a Shot to bring her to ; upon
which the Captain came up, and acquainted
us fhe was a Separate Trader, the *Thomas* Brigantine, *Henry Smith* Mafter, from *Liverpool*.

1734 At Noon she anchor'd at *Gillyfree*, and saluted the Fort with nine Guns, which return'd
the same Number. The same Day the Boat-
swain of the *Finch* Snow died on Board her.

March   O N the 25th the Governor and myself dined with Capt. *Onley*, and the same Day came
up a Separate Trader, the *Liverpool* Merchant,
Capt *Golding*, from *Liverpool*, and anchor'd
at *Gillyfree*, saluting the Fort with seven Guns,
which return'd the same Number.

The Au-   O N the 27th, being recover'd of my late
thor sent Illness, the Company's Affairs up the River
up the Ri- being ill-managed by some of their Servants,
ver on a   I was sent up on a Trading Voyage in the
Trading   *James* Sloop, *Nap Gray* Master, having first
Voyage   received from the Governor and Chief Merchants the following Instructions, *viz*

James *Fort*, Mar 27, 1734

    S I R,

His Or-   T H E *present Situation of the Company's*
ders.   *Affairs up the River obliges us to send*
you up, in order to enquire into the Conduct of
Messieurs —— *and* ——, *and to remit us*
down a fair and impartial Account thereof, as
likewise you are to report to us the State and Be-
haviour of the Factors and Factories of Tancrowall, Joar, Brucoe *and* Yamyamacunda,
provided that without Loss of Time or Trade you
can call at, or do proceed so high up the River.

    A T *your Arrival at* Joar *you are duly to*
weigh and consider, whether it is better for you
to stay there to oppose *the Shipping at that Fac-*
tory,

tory, *or to try what can be done with them at Cuttejarr , and, if you think proper, to follow them down to* Joar, *and there to make Trade with your Cargo joyn'd to that which you will find at the Factory.*

WHEN *you arrive at* Cuttejarr, *you are immediately to take an Inventory of all the Company's Effects there ashore, or on Board the Company's Sloop* Fame, *wheresoever you shall meet with her*

AS *we are desirous that the small Cargo, on Board with you, be deliver'd with all imaginable Speed to Mr* James Forsyth *at* Yamyamacunda, *so we leave it to you, as you shall judge convenient, whether to proceed to that Port with the* James Sloop, *or to stay on Board the* Fame, *Captain* Brown, *till her Return, and then to dispatch her down with all the Trade, and with such Orders as you shall judge most convenient for to prevent any Disturbance*

AS *the Nature of Affairs you are now sent on requires Caution and Moderation, especially relating to the Differences subsisting between Messieurs* —— *and* ——, *so you are to acquaint the two former, that they are sent for down, that it may be known how truly they have acted, and to enquire as to the Merits of the Accusers and Accused, which Accusations are most scandalous, and tend much to the Hurt and Prejudice of the Company, even if it should prove that such Facts were not committed.*

AS *you have been some Years in the Company's Service here, and have acted consistent with your*
Duty,

Duty; fo we now place fuch Confidence in you, that we do not in the leaft doubt your prudent Management, and conducting of every Concern for the Intereft of the Company. In Confequence thereof, we leave every Affair to be tranfacted, as you fhall think will moft conduce to the Company's Intereft and Advantage. We wifh you Health and Succefs, and are

Your Loving Friends,

RICHARD HULL,
HUGH HAMILTON.

ABOUT Noon I embarked on Board, and having a frefh Gale, I paffed by *Tancrowall* without ftopping, in forty Hours I arrived at *Joar*; and having infpected the Factory, I proceeded on my Way up, and on the 1ft of *April* arrived at *Yammarew*, where Capt. *Henry Smith*, a Separate Trader, was trading in the *Tancrowall* Sloop.

ON the 4th I arrived at *Brucoe*, where I found the Chief without fo much as a Wafte-Book for any Time thefe two Months paft, *April* or any Trade or Expences fet down for that Time. It was not for want of Pens and Paper, but his being fo addicted to Lazinefs, that I am afraid he will die of it in the End. I ftay'd a Day or two at *Brucoe*, and then fet out for *Cuttejarr*, where I arrived on the 7th at Noon, and immediately took Poffeffion of the *Fame* Sloop and her Cargo, and put my own Cargo on Board her alfo; and the next Morning fent the *James* Sloop down to the Fort with Meffieurs *Palmer* and *Brown*.

ON

On the 13th I arrived at *Yamyamacunda*, and the next Day I had a Difpute with thofe People, whofe Charge that Factory is put under, concerning a Horfe belonging to the Company at this Factory, which was feized by the Alcade of *Sutamore* fince my leaving that Place, he alledging that I had not paid him any thing this Twelvemonth paft for keeping him at his Houfe ; which, as he had been fo bafe to fay in my Abfence, induced him to infift upon it to my Face. The Difpute lafted a long while, there being above an hundred People prefent. At laft, having before them all difproved the Lye, I threatned, in cafe they would not deliver me up the Horfe, and bring the Alcade to ask Pardon for telling fuch known Lyes, I would immediately break up the Factory, and carry down the Goods and White Men to *James* Fort, and never fettle amongft them again They were ftartled at my faying this, efpecially when they heard me bind it by fwearing in their own Language, and knowing me to be refolute, they one and all went to the Alcade, and forced him to return me the Horfe, and to beg Pardon in tne moft humble Manner.

On the 5th of *May*, having made up all Animofities here between the Company and the Natives, and having bought fome Slaves, and a pretty good Quantity of Dry Goods, I weigh'd Anchor, and proceeded down towards *Cuttejarr*, in order to make a fair *Oppofition* againft Meffieurs *Cooper* and *Leach*, late Servants of the Company, who were fettled and trading there on their own Accounts.

1734.

Author arrives at *Yamyama-cunda*

Has a Palaver with the Natives

May

Author leaves *Yaryama-cunda*

In

Iɴ two Days I arrived at *Samy* Rɪveɪ's Mouth, where I met the Sloop *Sea Nymph,* with Signior *Valentine Mendez,* a Black *Portuguese,* lately entred into the Company's Service, who was come to settle at *Wallia,* about fifteen Miles up the said River, having a fine Cargo of Goods, and a Parcel of special good Amber. By this Sloop I received the following Letter, *viz.*

Mr Fʀaɴcɪs Mooʀe.

Jaᴍes Fort, Apr. 21 1734.

Sɪʀ,

Wɪ *received yours of the* ɪ*ſt Inſtant, and note what you ſay as to your Conduct at* Joar *Factory, which was rightly done of you. The Boy-Slave you remitted by Capt* Smith *was accepted of by him, and we have credited your Account for the ſame We ſold all Captain* Smith'*s Slaves for four Ounces of Gold each, one with another, and which both Parties are well pleas'd with. We have likewiſe received the Remains of Capt.* Onley'*s Cargo, who ſails for* Maryland *in two or three Days with one hundred and ten Slaves*

NOTWITHSTANDING Mr ——— *had ſuch ſtrict Orders not to entertain, converſe with, correſpond, or have any Dealings with* Leach *and* Cooper, *he has entertain'd the former in an extraordinary Manner, to the no ſmall Diſcredit and Scandal of the Company. This, with our being informed of others of the Company's Servants acting in the ſame ſcandalous Manner, we therefore deſire you to inform Mr* ——— *in particular,*

that

that on his Peril he do not suffer either or both of
the said Persons Leach *and* Cooper *to come into
the Company's Factory, or to converse, correspond,
or have any Dealings with them on any Account
whatsoever.*

WE *impatiently wait the Arrival of the* Fame,
*that we may know the present State of the Company's Affairs with you, and other up-River
Factories. We are*

         Your Loving Friends,

        RICHARD HULL,
        HUGH HAMILTON.

I MADE the best of my Way to *Cuttejarr*, where, as soon as I arrived, I employ'd our Black Servants to make Hutts, in order to live in, and to put the Company's Goods, for the Merchants do not by any means care to trade aboard a Sloop or Ship. The Day after I arrived, I sent a Messenger away to *James* Fort with the following Letter, *viz.* *(Comes down to trade at Cuttejarr.)*

      Cuttejarr Port, *May* 10. 1734.

GENTLEMEN,

THIS *comes by one of my* * Butlers, *and serves
to acquaint you, that my last was of the
8th* ult *by Capt.* Brown, *soon after which I
proceeded up to* Yamyamacunda, *where I had a
great Palaver with the People of* Sutamore
*about the Company's Horse, which I have at
length made the Alcade deliver up to me, but not
without much ado, and even making a Show of
breaking the Factory, since which some of them
have* *(Author's Letter to James Fort.)*

    * Hired Servants

1734. *have been so very insolent as to offer to detain me from going aboard my Sloop, unless I complied with their exorbitant Demands; which I resented very much, and went with Mr* Forsyth *to the Duke of the Country about it, where the Aggressors shewed the utmost Concern for what they had done, and promised to stand by the Company to their utmost, and neither use their Servants ill themselves, nor suffer any others to do it   On which I told them, that if in case they used the Factory ill when I was gone, you would upon the least Notice thereof from Mr* Forsyth *immediately order it to be broke, which they are very sensible will be no small Loss to them, and therefore I am of Opinion that it is now settled on a very good Foundation.*

AS for Mr Forsyth, *he goes on very well, has six Slaves by him, and is very well beloved by the Natives, he tells me that he has lost a great deal of Trade for want of Goods, by which means the Factory has in a great measure lost its Credit, but by its being well supplied for the future, it may be retrieved. And as for Salt, it ought never to be without a large Quantity, by which means the Merchants may be induced to come there, and the Trade of Antonio* Voss's *Canoas lessened, whereas they now carry all before them, by being well supplied with that precious Commodity*

I must now acquaint you, that I have had some Messengers from the King and Great Men of Woolley, *to desire me to let you know, that as* Hume Badgy *is now dead, there is no Body that will in the least molest the Company's Servants or Trade there, and therefore they beg you will send up a Sloop to trade, which*

d-

at Fatatenda *or* Nackway, *where they do affure* 1734.
you they fhall be kindly ufed *They would fain*
have had me gone up thither; *but not having Salt*
enough, nor Orders fufficient, I thought proper to
decline it , but in my Opinion it will be a good
Voyage, and much better than ftaying at Cuttejarr, *fo near to* Valentine Mendez, *who has got*
fo large a Cargo, and fo much better than mine
in every refpeſt. *I have not to add, but that I*
remain,

G E N T L E M E N,

Your Obedient Humble Servant,

FRA MOORE.

ON the 17th of *May,* the *Adventure*
Sloop, *Harry Johnſon* Mafter, arrived with a
Cargo of Salt for me, and another for Mr
Forfyth, Faſtor at *Yamyamacunda*; he ftay'd
here till he had deliver'd mine afhore, and
then proceeded up the River.

ON the 25th, the *Sea Nymph* Sloop arrived Sea-
here on her Way down from *Yamyamacunda* Nymph
and *Wallia,* with Slaves and Dry Goods for Sloop
Account of the Company, He had between robbed by
this Place and *Yamyamacunda* been attacked tives
and robbed by a great Number of the Natives, who had been got up together at the
Perfuafion of a Black Fellow late in the Company's Service at *James* Fort, who told them
that the Governor refufed to pay him his
Wages, and therefore they went and took out
of the faid Sloop one fine Boy-Slave, and feveral other things of Value, fuch as Guns,
Piftols,

1734 Piftols, *&c* Thefe are the Reafons given by
the Mafter of the Sloop; but I find that the
real Caufe of this Robbery is owing to one of
the Sloop's Black Servants being ufed ill when
laft up the River

Natives
Cuftom of
proving
Theft

You muft know, that the Natives do fometimes, to prove Theft, dip their Hands in
boiling Water; if the Perfon is not guilty,
they fay the Water will not fcald him, but
if he is guilty, then it will. Mr —— being
a great Admirer of the Natives and their Cu
ftoms, did one Day, upon his having loft a
Gun out of his Cabbin, challenge his Sloop's
Company, which confifted of three or four
Black Men, and one White Man befides himfelf: Upon denying it, he forced the Black
Fellows to have recourfe to Scalding their
Hands, by which means they all fcalded them
felves much, but one of them, being more
tender-finger'd than the reft, fcalded his Hand
miferably. A Day or two after they came to
underftand that the Captain had found his Gun
(himfelf having miflaid it), upon which one of
the Men quitted the Company's Service, and
went home to *Samy* to his Friends, and com
plained to the Alcade and the reft of his Towns-
People, who one and all joyned in demanding
Satisfaction, and therefore hearing of his be
ing at *Fendalacunda*, took the Opportunity to
fall upon him, and take away the things beforementioned In the Evening I receiv'd
from *James* Fort the following Letter by the
Return of a Meffenger, which I had fent down
from hence the 10th Inftant.

Mr

Mr F R A. M O O R E.

JAMES *Fort, May* 17. 1734.

SIR,

'YOURS by your Land-Meſſenger un- Letter to
'der the 10th we received yeſterday, the Au-
'and obſerve the Contents relating to the Si- thor
'tuation of Affairs at *Yamyamacunda*, and the
'manner you brought about to a good Con-
'cluſion, which is very agreeable to us.   As
'to your Sloop being ſo much out of Repair,
'you may take either of the Sloops up the
'River ; and as to your Opinion as to *Nack-*
'*way* or *Fatatenda*, we can't yet venture the
'Company's Effects till the Country is a little
'better ſettled, and which perhaps may be
'after the Rains, and therefore we the rather
'deſire you to give them Hopes that we ſhall
'again ſettle a Factory at *Fatatenda*, after the
'Rains are over, provided they give us a Spe-
'cimen of their good Will for the Company,
'by their Care of preſerving their Houſe there.
'As you complain of want of Trade where
'you are, we think it more prudent for you
'to go to *Joar*, as your Inſtructions mention,
'than to make a Progreſs higher up, firſt
'taking care to leave your —— at *Brucoe* or
'*Yammarew*, to purchaſe Corn with.

'WE are not a little ſurprized to hear
'from *Yammarew*, that the Shipping are tra-
'ding there for Slaves with the Merchants,
'and that others are gone down to *Cower*, and
'that you ſhould neither adviſe us of their
'paſſing you, or what Number, or even of

O   ' your

' your attempting to trade with them.   This
' is such a Disappointment and Omission, we
' did not in the least expect from Mr *Moore*,
' and is wondred at the more, because you are
' tied up to no Price   The Salt sent up by
' Capt. *Johnson* to yourself and Mr *Forsyth*,
' we hope came timely to hand   On the 15th
' came in here the *Elizabeth*, Capt. *Carter*,
' from *Guernsey*, but last from the *Canaries*,
' but as he is but ill assorted, designs chiefly
' for Dry Goods   We desire you to order
' Messieurs *Forsyth* and *Ellis* to send down their
' Books to the End of *April*, and whereas
' we are inform'd you have given Mr *Ellis*
' Orders not to trade (which is unknown to us,
' if it is so) you are to send Orders to him
' to trade, and buy what comes to the Facto-
' ry. Mr *Oglethorp* is arrived in *England* We
' are, wishing you Health and Success,

Your Loving Friends,

RICH HULL,
H. HAMILTON.

THE next Day, being the 26th of *May*,
by the *Sea Nymph* Sloop I sent the following
Letter to the Gentlemen below.

CUTTEJARR *Port*, May 26. 1734.

Gentlemen,

' YOURS of the 17th came to hand last
'   ' Night ; in answer to which I must
' in the first Place acquaint you, that Mr
' *Gray* has repaired the Sloop in such a man-
' ner that she does not make any Water.

I

' I observe what you fay concerning *Joar*   1734
' Factory, which in my Opinion will be do-
' ing nothing at all, having but an ill Affort-
' ment, and there being fo many Ships at
' *Yammarew* with fine Cargoes I have cer-
' tain Advice, that two Veffels (*viz* a Fri-
' gate and a Sloop) are coming up here from
' *Yammarew*, and am therefore going to vifit
' the King at *Dubocunda*, and Slattee of *Le-*
' *main*; but have firft fent this to acquaint
' you with it, and to know how I fhall pro-
' ceed, and to have your pofitive Orders whe-
' ther to ftay here, proceed higher up, or come
' down to the Fort, I being unwilling to go
' to *Joar* with half a Cargo.

' I observe what you fay concerning my
' not advifing you of the Merchants paffing
' down, in anfwer to which I muft acquaint
' you, that they went on the Back Part of this
' Kingdom, and did not come within two
' Days Journey of this Place, neither did the
' People here know any thing of them till
' they had paffed And therefore, tho' it was
' a Difappointment to you, yet it was no O-
' miffion in me, for I heard nothing of it till
' after my laft Letter was fent away, tho' if I
' had, it would have fignified nothing, for
' they were refolved to go down, and on no
' account to come near *Samy*.

' Since my laft there have feveral fmall
' Coffles of Slaves come to *Samy* with Alcade
' *Donfo*, but moft of them are refolved to pafs
' down, however I have been there, and am
' in hopes of purchafing fome in three or four
' Days, tho' this fame Slattee *Donfo* is a very

‘ odd Sort of a Fellow, and never yet traded
‘ higher than *Joar*

‘ I observe what you fay about the Peo-
‘ ple of *Woolley*, and fhall take care to acquaint
‘ them of it In the mean time fhall order
‘ Meff. *Forfyth* and *Ellis* to fend down their
‘ Books. As to my giving Mr *Ellis* Orders
‘ not to make Trade, it is moft falfe and
‘ fcandalous, nor do I think you can believe
‘ me guilty of fuch a Folly However I have
‘ now wrote to him about it.

‘ I have herewith remitted you Sundries,
‘ amounting to ———, Invoice and Cofts
‘ which are here inclofed

‘ I am forry to find that ——— has met
‘ with fuch ill Ufage from the People of *Si-*
‘ *n*, and muft needs own I do not believe it
‘ can proceed only from the not paying the
‘ Butler, but that fome other Caufe muft be
‘ affigned for it, however, let it be how it
‘ will, they had the Impudence to feize me
‘ and my Horfe, as I was going by the Town
‘ to meet the Merchants, and having demand-
‘ ed their Reafons for it, they told me it was
‘ becaufe I did not come to fee the Slattee,
‘ upon which I excufed myfelf, and then they
‘ let me go, having firft ftole my Cap and
‘ Handkerchief

‘ When I met ——— at *Sany* River’s
‘ Mouth, I gave him two Guns to buy Corn
‘ for me Now as the People of *Sam*, have
‘ forced them away from him, as being the
Com-

' Company's, I defire you'll pleafe to give me   1734
' Credit for the faid Guns

 ' O N E of the Slaves I have now remitted
' has five or fix Teeth wanting, and therefore
' I made them abate the fame Number of Barrs
' in the Price, as you will fee by the Invoice.
' I am furprized to find that Sig *Valentine*
' *Mendez* has not remitted you fo many Slaves
' as I have, and the more, becaufe his Cargo
' is fo much larger and better than mine, you
' having fent him up a Parcel of Amber,
' when I at the fame time daily lofe Trade
' for want of that Commodity   However,
' I can only fay, that I will do my beft En-
' deavours for the Company's Intereft, and
' make what Trade I poffibly can   Having
' not to add, but to wifh you Health, I
' remain,

   Gentlemen,

    Your moft Obedient Servant,

     FRA. MOORE.

 O N the 11th of *June* Captain *Brown* ar-   *June.*
rived here in the *James* Sloop, on his Way
to *Yamyamacunda* with Goods.   He ftayed
here a little while, and then proceeded on
his Way up the River   By him I received
the following Letter from the Gentlemen at
James Fort

    O 3   *Mr*

Mr FRANCIS MOORE.

JAMES *Fort,* June 1. 1734

S I R,

‘ AT Capt. *Brown*’s Return from *Yam-*
‘ *amacunda* we defire you to deliver
‘ him up the *Fame,* and fend down Mr *Gray*
‘ in the *James* Sloop, with Orders to take in
‘ all the Trade and Corn for the Fort that is
‘ at *Brucoe, Tanmareu* and *Joar,* and to make
‘ the beft of his Way down   Give our Ser-
‘ vice to Sig *Valentine,* and defire him to pur
‘ chafe all the Leafas he poffibly can, and
‘ the Bandy-Cloths, and a good Quantity of
‘ Sope, which we are in much want of

‘ WE obferve the Contents of yours of the
‘ 26th *ult* and all we can fay in regard for
‘ your making Trade is, that as you are at fo
‘ great a Diftance, and can by keeping a good
‘ Correfpondence be a better Judge than we
‘ poffibly can, and therefore as you are not
‘ tied up to a Price, and can move for the
‘ Advantage of picking up Trade, you are
‘ the beft Judge how to order your Affairs
‘ And as to your defigned Vifit to *Dubocura*
‘ and *Lemain,* we cannot comply with it, if
‘ defigned to interrupt the Private Traders,
‘ becaufe, as Matters now ftand, they are al-
‘ lowed by the Government to have the fame
‘ Right to trade as the Company

‘ WE are pleafed that what we cenfured
‘ you for want of a due Correfpondence was
‘ no Omiffion, and that the Report of your
‘ Orders

'Orders that Mr *Ellis* fhould not make Trade 1734
'was falfe, and which indeed we could not
'believe was Fact

'As we are affured of Mr ——— Inca-
'pacity; we fhall in about a Month's time
'relieve him; and we wifh, if you can con-
'veniently go down, to take a View of Af-
'fairs there, if the Merchants Trade is not
'expected, and that you leave a little Affort-
'ment with Mr *Gray*, to buy what *Mundingo*
'Trade may offer in the little Time you are
'abfent from the Sloop

'We have agreed with Captain *Nafh* and
'Captain *Ball* for both their Cargoes, and
'for their Sloop to make a fecond Tryal at
'*Portodally*, where, with Mr *Conner*, they
'were difpatched yefterday. As we on that
'and other Accounts want a good many Slaves,
'we defire you to exert yourfelf, and not ftand
'out for a Price. As to *Leach* and *Cooper*,
'we defire you to give them no manner of
'Countenance, by keeping them Company, or
'other ways affifting them. We are

Your Loving Friends,

RICH. HULL,
H. HAMILTON.

On the 1ft of *July* Captain *Brown* came *July*
down hither from *Yamyamacunda*, at which Author
time I put him in Poffeffion of the *Fame* Sloop, fends a
according to my Orders, and then difpatched Sloop to
the *James* Sloop with Mr *Gray* away to *James* *James* Fort with
O 4   Fort, Slaves

1734   Fort, with Slaves and Dry Goods. By the
same Conveyance, Meffieurs *Leach* and *Coote*
not being able to trade againft me, and feeing
their Error in leaving the Company's Service,
they wrote a very handfome fubmiffive Letter
to Mr *Hull* our Governor, to defire he would
take them into the Company's Service again,
which if he would do, they would immediately leave off trading, and break up Houfe-
keeping, and take their Paffage down along
with me to *James* Fort. The Letter I fent
was as follows, *viz*

Cuttejarr *Port*, July 1 1734

Gentlemen,

Author's   ' **THIS** comes by the *James* Sloop, Nat
Letter.   ' *Gray* Mafter, (who, according to
' your Order, has deliver'd up the *Fame* to
' *C. Brown*) and ferves to acquaint you, that
' you will herewith receive twenty Slaves, as
' likewife fome Elephants Teeth and Gold,
' Invoice and Cofts of which are inclofed,
' amounting to ————, by which means I am
' very much difforted, therefore if you think
' proper to continue me here all the Rains,
' I defire you would fend me a Supply, fo
' if I have Goods, I don't doubt making good
' Trade   By reafon of my Trade, I could
' not go down to *Brucoe* as you propofed, but
' the inclofed will let you into the Knowleuge
' of the Situation of that Factory I hear of
' a great Coffle of Slaves now on the Road
' under the Conduct of Slattee *Sanyconta Ma-*
' *debaugh* If it is true that he is coming, I
' fhall heartily wifh for *Valentine Mennez's*
' Cargo, who I am fure will make you ftay

' 3

a long time before he remits you what he   1734.
' is indebted to you for that fine Cargo which
' you have supplied him with, and which he
' intends to keep by him till Slaves are cheap
· I am,

Gentlemen,

Your obedient humble Servant,

FRA MOORE.

ON the 13th, a Messenger brought me an
Answer to the foregoing Letter from the Fort,
wherein they desired me to come down, and
bring with me Messrs *Leach* and *Cooper*, as for
the Remainder of my Cargo, they order'd me
to leave it at *Joar* and *Brucoe*. The next   Author re-
Morning I weigh'd Anchor, and sail'd down,   turns to
having with me Messrs *Leach* and *Cooper*   At *J* Fort.
Night I arrived at *Brucoe*, left some Goods,
and the next Day left that Port, and in two
Days arrived at *Joar*, where lay the *Barrab*
Sloop, Capt. *Nash*, and the *Bumper* Sloop,
Capt *Ball*, trading with some Merchants for
Slaves   The *Bumper* Capt *Nash* had hire l,
to carry Slaves on Freight to the *West Indies*
Here I stay'd a Day or two, and having supp-
ply'd Mr *Brook Gill* at *Joar* Factory with some
Goods, I weighed and proceeded down to
James Fort, where I arrived on the 24th, and
found the Governor gone down to the Mouth
of the River *Gambia*, to visit the Captains of
his Majesty's Ships the *Antelope* and the *Diamond*, where he stay'd four or five Days, and
in his Return back had like to have been lost
in a violent Tornado.

ON

ON the 7th of *August* died Mr *Shuckford*, a Writer, who had been in this Country about eight Months, and was buried in the Evening at *Gillyfree*. About Six o' Clock we saw a Vessel coming up the River, about Midnight she sent up her Boat to tell the Governor that she was the Company's Snow *Dolphin*, Capt *Thomas Freeman*, from *London*

Company's Snow *Dolphin* arrives with Passengers, and *J.B. Solomon* from England

Account of *J. B. Solomon*.

THE next Day about Noon came up the *Dolphin* Snow, which saluted the Fort with nine Guns, and had the same Number returned, after which came on Shore the Captain, four Writers, one Apprentice to the Company, and one Black Man, by Name *Job Ben Solomon*, a *Pholey*, of *Bundo* in *Focta*, who in the Year 1731, as he was travelling in *Jagra*, and crossing the Heads of Cattle across the Country was robbed and carried to *Joar*, where he was sold to Captain *Pyke*, Commander of the Ship *Arabella*, who was then trading there. By him he was carried to *Maryland*, and sold to a Planter, with whom *Job* lived about a Twelvemonth without being once beat by his Master, at the End of which time he had the good Fortune to have a Letter of his own writing in the *Arabic* Tongue convey'd to *England*. This Letter coming to the Hand of Mr *Oglethorpe*, he sent the same to *Oxford* to be translated, which, when done, gave him so much Satisfaction, and so good an Opinion of the Man, that he directly order'd him to be bought from his Master, he soon after setting out for *Georgia* Before he returned from thence, *Job* came to *England*, where being brought to the Acquaintance of the Learned Sir *Hans Sloane*, he was by him found a perfect
Master

Mafter of the *Arabic* Tongue, by tranflating
feveral Manufcripts and Infcriptions upon
Medals   He was by him recommended to his
Grace the Duke of *Montague*, who being pleafed with the Sweetnefs of Humour, and Mildnefs of Temper, as well as Genius and Capacity of the Man, introduced him to Court,
where he was gracioufly received by the Royal
Family, and moft of the Nobility, from whom
he received diftinguifhing Marks of Favour
After he had continued in *England* about fourteen Months, he wanted much to return to
his Native Country, which is *Bundo*, (a Place
about a Week's Travel over Land from the
Royal *African* Company's Factory at *Joar*, on
the River *Gambia*) of which Place his Father
was High-Prieft, and to whom he fent Letters
from *England*.   Upon his fetting out from
England he received a good many noble Prefents from her moft Gracious Majefty Queen
Caroline, his Highnefs the Duke of *Cumber-
land*, his Grace the Duke of *Montague*, the
Earl of *Pembroke*, feveral Ladies of Quality,
Mr *Holden*, and the Royal *African* Company,
who have order'd their Agents to fhow him
the greateft Refpect.

ON the 12th came up a *French* Sloop from
Goree to *Albreda*, who with the Leave of our
Governor proceeded up the River to cut Man-
groves, in order to rebuild fome Part of their
Factory at *Albreda*

ON the 23d I fet out in the *Fame* Sloop with
a pretty good Cargo, to take upon me the
Direction of the Company's chief Factory of
Joar, having firft received the following Orders, *viz*

Author
appointed
Factor at
Joar

Mr

Mr FRA. MOORE.

Sir,

His Orders

THE good Opinion we have of your Integrity and Zeal to serve the Company, induces us to appoint you their Chief Factor at the Company's Settlement at Joar, now under the Direction of Mr Brooke Gill. And as the Commission, Salary, and Allowance of Diet, is much augmented of late by the Company at that Factory, purposely to promote and encourage an honest and reputable Conduct, in regard to the high Trust reposed in you by them, so we promise ourselves that you will so far be a Friend to yourself and your own Reputation, as to do the Company the strictest Justice, agreeable to your most solemn Engagement you have voluntarily obliged yourself to perform. At your Arrival at Joar you are to deliver to Mr Brooke Gill our Orders for him to resign up the Company's Factory and all their Effects into your Custody, which you are immediately to inventory, and give him two proper Discharges for the Particulars and Amount thereof, One of which Mr Gill and you are to send of per first Opportunity.

AS you have been for some Years past conversant in Business at Out-Factories, so we shall now only repeat, that you stick to such Orders as have been formerly given you.

BY this Conveyance comes one Black Man, by Name Job Ben Solomon, whom

are to ufe with the greateft Refpect, and all the   1734.
Civility you poffibly can   We are

Your Loving Friends,

RICH HULL,
H. HAMILTON.

JOB *Ben Solomon* having a Mind to go up *Job goes*
to *Couer* to talk with fome of his Countrymen, *with the*
went along with me.   In the Evening we *Author up*
weighed Anchor, faluting the Fort with five *to Joar*
Guns, which return'd the fame Number.

On the 26th we arrived at the Creek of *Paffages*
Damafenfa, and having fome old Acquain- *on the*
tances at the Town of *Damafenfa, Job* and I *Voyage*
went up in the Yawl , in the Way, going up
a very narrow Place for about half a Mile,
we faw feveral Monkeys of a beautiful Blue
and Red, which the Natives tell me never fet
their Feet on the Ground, but live entirely
amongft the Trees, leaping from one to another at fo great Diftances, as any one, were
they not fo fee it, would think improbable

In the Evening, as my Friend *Job* and I *Job fees*
were fitting under a great Tree at *Damafenfa,* *the Kings*
there came by us fix or feven of the very Peo- *People*
ple who robb'd and made a Slave of *Job,* a- *who made*
bout thirty Miles from hence, about three *of him*
Years ago , *Job,* tho' a very even-temper'd
Man at other times, could not contain himfelf
when he faw them, but fell into a moft ter- *His Beha-*
rible Paffion, and was for killing them with *viour*
his broad Sword and Piftols, which he always *thereupon.*
took

took care to have about him. I had much
ado to diffuade him from falling upon the fix
Men, but at laft, by reprefenting to him the
ill Confequences that would infallibly attend
fuch a rafh Action, and the Impoffibility of
mine or his own efcaping alive, if he fhould
attempt it, I made him lay afide the Thoughts
of it, and perfuaded him to fit down and pre-
terd not to know them, but ask them Queſti-
ons about himſelf, which he accordingly did
and they anfwer'd nothing but the Truth At
laft he ask'd them how the King their Mafter
did; they told him he was dead, and by further Enquiry we found, that amongſt the
Goods for which he fold *Job* to Captain *Py'*
there was a Piftol, which the King ufed com-
Account monly to wear flung about his Neck with a
of the String, and as they never carry Arms with-
King's out being loaded, one Day this accidentally
Death went off, and the Balls lodging in his Throat,
who fold he died prefently At the Clofing of this
Job Story *Job* was fo very much tranfported, that
he immediately fell on his Knees, and return
ed Thanks to *Mahomet* for making this Man
die by the very Goods for which he fold him
into Slavery, and then turning to me, he fuid,
' Mr *Moore*, you fee now God Almighty was
' difpleas'd at this Man's making me a Slave,
' and therefore made him die by the very Pi-
' ftol for which he fold me, yet I ought to
' forgive him, *fays he*, becaufe had I not been
' fold, I fhould neither have known any thing
' of the *Englifh* Tongue, nor have had any of
' the fine, ufeful and valuable Things I now
' carry over, nor have known that in the
' World there is fuch a Place as *England*, nor
' fuch noble, good and generous People as
' Queen

'Queen *Caroline*, Prince *William*, the Duke	1734
'of *Montague*, the Earl of *Pembroke*, Mr	*August.*
'*Holden*, Mr *Oglethorpe*, and the Royal *Afri-*
'*can* Company

ON the 1ft of *September* we arrived at *Joar*,	*September.*
the Frefhes being very ftrong againft us. I	The Au-
immediately took an Inventory of the Com-	thor ar-
pany's Effects, and gave Receipts to Mr	rives at
Gill for the fame. After which we unloaded	*Joar.*
the Sloop, and then I fent her up to *Yamma-*
rew for a Load of Corn for *James* Fort, where
fhe ftayed till the 25th, and then came back
to *Joar*, during which time I made fome
Trade with the Merchants, though at a pretty
high Price.

ON *Job's* firft Arrival here, he defired I	*Job's* Cha-
would fend a Meffenger up to his own Coun-	racter and
try to acquaint his Friends of his Arrival I	Proceed-
fpoke to one of the *Blacks* which we ufually	ings
employ upon thofe Occafions, to procure me
a Meffenger, who brought to me a *Pholey*,
who knew the High Prieft his Father, and
Job himfelf, and exprefs'd great Joy at feeing
him in fafety returned from Slavery, he being
the only Man (except one) that was ever
known to come back to this Country, after
having been once carried a Slave out of it by
White Men *Job* gave him the Meffage himfelf, and defired his Father fhould not come
down to him, for it was too far for him to
travel, and that it was fit for the Young to
go to the Old, and not for the Old to come
to the Young He alfo fent fome Prefents by
him to his Wives, and defired him to bring
his little one, which was his beft beloved,
down

down to him.   After the Meſſenger was gone, *Job* went frequently along with me to *Crwei*, and ſeveral other Places about the Country, he ſpoke always very handſome of the *Engliſh*, and what he ſaid, took away a great deal of the Horror of the *Pholeys* for the State of Slavery amongſt the *Engliſh*, for they before generally imagined, that all who were ſold for Slaves, were generally either eaten or murdered, ſince none ever returned.   His Deſcription of the *Engliſh* gave them alſo a great notion of the Power of *England*, and a Veneration for thoſe who traded amongſt them   He ſold ſome of the Preſents he brought with him from *England* for Trading-Goods, with which he bought a Woman-Slave and two Horſes, which were very uſeful to him there, and which he deſigned to carry with him to *Bundo*, whenever he ſhould ſet out thither. He uſed to give his Country People a good deal of Writing-Paper, which is a very uſeful Commodity amongſt them, and of which the Company had preſented him with ſeveral Reams   He uſed to pray frequently, and behaved himſelf with great Mildneſs and Affability to all, ſo that he was very popular and well-beloved   The Meſſenger not being thought to return ſoon, *Job* deſired to go down to *James* Fort to take care of his Goods, I promiſing to ſend him word when the Meſſenger came back, and alſo to ſend ſome other Meſſengers, tor fear the firſt ſhould miſcarry.

ON the 26th I ſent down the *Fame* Sloop to *James* Fort, and *Job* going along with her,

I gave

I gave the Mafter Orders to fhew him all the Refpect he could.

On the 30th in the Evening *George Lafon* came up to the Factory in his Canoa, having left his Sloop below *Elephants* Ifland, being not able to proceed higher by reafon of the Frefhes, which are fo ftrong that a Canoa can hardly row againft them ; he had brought fome Rum, Silver and Gunpowder

This is the rainy Seafon, in which it is very difficult to fend Goods to upper Factories, no Slaves come down, and therefore it is the time for collecting dry Goods up the River. The increafing the Quantities of dry Goods, the Company have continually been recommending to their Servants. I had always the utmoft Regard to all their Orders, and therefore applied myfelf to enquire after any new kind of Goods that could be had, particularly Gum , this being recommended to me by *Charles Hayes* Efq, (who, fince he has been in the Direction, hath with unwearied Diligence taken all Methods to open new Trades in *Africa*). The fame having been repeated to me by Mr *Hull*, I fent the latter a Sample from *Brucoe* (as I mentioned before) which proved *Gum-Dragon* I ftrove to get more of that Kind, but it being a new thing, the Natives could not be prevailed upon to follow it, fo as to bring in any Quantities, for they would bring in to me all kinds of Gum, ten or twelve Pounds at a time, which I picked and did not find, perhaps, above two Pounds of *Gum-Dragon* in that Quantity , the reft was like *Gum-Senegal*, but not fo good.

P   *Gum-*

1734
September
An Ac-
count of
the *Gum-*
Dragor

Gum-Dragon comes out of a Tree called *Pau de Sangue*, which has a very rough Bark, upon wounding of it, it fweats out in Drops like Blood, which joining together, and being dried by the Sun, congeals into Lumps, I have had fome as large as Pullets Eggs One *Junco Sunco*, a *Jolloiff* of *Yanimarew*, a ftirring Man, having heard that I enquired much after Gum, fent me down a Sample of about a Pound of very fine white Gum, which proved to be *Gum-Arabic* I believe in all, I fent at different times about a Ton of Gum, from the Factories I was at, to *James* Fort I began now to hope, that the Gum-Trade might be enlarged and made confiderable, fince *Joo's* Country, which is called *Foota*, lay on the Edge of the Foreft, and was but four Days Journey from *Fatatenda*, and by his bringing that People into a good Opinion of the *Eng-lifh*, they might be prevailed upon to trade with us, and bring Quantities of that Commodity to *Fatatenda*, from whence it might be carried by Water with fmall Charge to the Fort. And this might not be only the making of the Factors employed in it, but alfo of great fervice to the Royal *African* Company, and to the Nation itfelf, fince there is a great deal of *Gum-Senegal* imported in a Year to *England*, and almoft all of it bought of the *French*, who make a very profitable Trade of it, as appears by Father *Lebat's* new Account of *Africa*, printed in 1728 wherein he fays,

" THAT Country, quite bad as it is, and thofe Roads fo dangerous for Shipping, are neverthelefs eagerly fearch'd out by the *French*, *Englifh*, *Dutch* and *Portuguefe* They all ftrive to fettle there, becaufe they are the only

only Places where a Trade for Gum can be ₁₇₃₄
had, by thofe who are not Mafters of the Advanta-
Senegal River   A Trade that feems a light Gum-
Matter in itfelf, but is, in effect, very confi- Trade
derable, whether we regard the Price the
Moors fell the Gum for, which is very moderate ; or the Price it yields, out of *Africa*,
which is very advantageous ; or, laftly, the
Quantity of *European* Merchandife it takes
off ready wrought, the Vent of which makes
Manufactures, fpread, Money circulate, and
fo finds Work for abundance of Hands, which
is the main End of Commerce.

No wonder, therefore, that the moft ex-
perienc'd of *European* Merchants have ufed all
Endeavours to hit into this Branch of Traffick, becaufe the *French* being fole Mafters
of the * *Niger*, on which thofe other Ports,
where a Trade for Gum may be had, are
fituated, they find themfelves obliged to take
it as it paffes thro' their Hands, fince the Time
there has been no free Trade at *Arguin* or *Portendic*   This is the true Motive that has put
them on fo great Expence to fettle and fecure
a Factory at *Arguin*, and when they were driven from thence, to endeavour an Eftablifh-
ment among the *Moors* at *Portendic*. This was,
in effect, their only Way to come in for Sha-
rers with the *French* in this Commerce, in
purfuit of which they found means at length
to engrofs it wholly to themfelves, by raifing
the Gum to an exceffive Rate, and making
Bargains to their Lofs, in order to engage
the three Nations of the *Moors* to bring their
entire Harvefts to their Market.

P 2   THEY

* *Senegal*

THEY make two yearly Gatherings of the Gum. The firft in the Month of *December*, which is the moft plentiful, and they pretend the Balls are larger, cleaner and dryer, which are all the good Qualities to be wifh'd in Gum The fecond Gathering is in *March*, this is the leaft, and they are convinc'd by long Experience that the Gum of this Gathering is more fqueafy, droffy, and not fo clear.

THEY don't weigh the Gum, but put it in a Cubic Meafure, call'd a *Quantar* or *Quintal*, of a Size agreed upon with the *Moors*, the Capacity of which the *Europeans* take care to augment, when Occafion offers.

THAT which the *Dutch* made ufe of, when they were Mafters of *Arguin*, held 220 Pounds *Paris* Weight.

Price of a
Quintal of
Gum of
220 lb
French
Weight.
IT coft them a fingle Piece of Eight, worth three Livres each.

Or, a Dozen of Padlocks.

Or, two Ounces of Coral.

Or, four Satalas, or Copper Bafons.

Or, half an Ell of fine Woollen Cloth

Or, three quarters of an Ell of ordinary Cloth.

Or, three Bars of flat Iron:

Or, three Ells of Bays.

Or, fix Ells and three quarters of baftas Linnen, *i. e.* blue Cutlin.

Or, fix Ells of Silefias.

Note, The Ells are *Dutch* Meafure, which is about half an Ell *French.* " Thus far *Lebat.*

On

On the 16th we were alarm'd with an
Account of a War breaking out among the
Natives, and that *Joar* was like to be made
the Seat of it. The Boomey of *Cajamore*, a
Country of *Barsally*, about a Day's Journey
from *Joar*, and the Boomey of *Cajawan*, another District in his Neighbourhood, came
to me, out of Friendship to the Company,
being my old Acquaintances, to let me know
that Boomey *Haman Seaca*, Brother to the
King of *Barsally*, who was in Arms against
the said King, was assisted by some of the
People of *Yany* and *Yamina*, and had made
all Preparations for a War, and would certainly invade this Part of *Barsally* very soon.
They therefore inform'd me of it, that I might
acquaint the Governor therewith, in order to
take Measures for the securing the Company's
Effects As soon as they were gone, I wrote
advice of it to the Chiefs at *James* Fort.

1734
October.

THE *Jolloiffs* in general are Men given to
Arms, and have several Customs for keeping
up their natural Fierceness and Hardiness. No
Jolloiff, except the King and his Family, are
allow'd to lye under Tendres (which are Cloths
to keep off Flies and Musquetoes) upon Pain
of Slavery, if the King comes to know of it.
The like Punishment also attends those who
presume to sit upon the same Mat with those
of the Royal Family, unless first ask'd, or
order'd so to do.

Some *Jol-
loiff* Laws
or Severi
ties.

THE Royal Family has a Name, which
is 'N*jay* ∙ They command absolutely, and the
Reverence paid to all that Family is very great,
insomuch that others touch the Ground with

Some Ac-
count of
the Royal
Family

their

1734   their Faces when they come into their Prefence,
yet do they live in great Equality with their
Soldiers   The King gives amongſt his Soldiers
all that he can plunder, taking but juſt what
he wants to himſelf.   This forces him to continual War, for ſo ſoon as he has waſted what
he has got, either by taking an Enemy's Town,
or one of his own, (as I have before mention'd)
he muſt lay out for ſome new Prize to give it
to his Men.   They for want of Spoils ſometimes change their King

An Ac   BOOMEY *Haman Seaca* is one of the Family
count of of the *'Njays*, of a middle Stature, genteel
B *Haman* and ſtrongly made, active, and of a good
Seaca   Countenance, his Teeth white, his Skin the
very blackeſt, his Noſe high, and his Lips
thin, ſo that his Features were like an *Euro-
pean*, as moſt of the *Jolloiffs* are   He was
His Dreſs cloath'd in a white Cotton Veſt with open
Sleeves, and Breeches which came to his Knees,
of the ſame.   His Legs and Arms were bare,
on his Head he had a ſmall white Cotton Cap,
and Gold Rings in his Ears   He rode upon a
Horſe and beautiful Milk-white Horſe, 16 Hands high,
Furniture with a long Mane, and a Tail which ſwept the
Ground.   His Bridle was of a bright Red-
Leather, plated with Silver, after the *Mooriſh*
Manner, his Saddle was of the ſame, with a
high Pommel, and riſing behind.   The Breaſt-
Plate was of Red-Leather plaited with Silver,
but they uſe no Cruppers.   His Stirrups were
ſhort, and as large and as long as his Feet, ſo
as to ſtand firm and eaſy   Upon theſe he
would raiſe himſelf quite upright, ſtand ſteady
at full ſpeed, and ſhoot a Gun or dart a Lance
as well as if upon the Ground.   He always
carried

Fr. Moore delin

carried a Lance or Half-Pike in his Hand a-
bout 12 Foot long, which he held upright,
resting the lower End upon his Stirrup, between
his Toes ; but when he curvetted his Horse,
imitating Action, he brandish'd his Lance high
over his Head. I have seen him do Wonders
upon this Horse, sometimes making him advance 40 or 50 Yards together on his two
hinder Feet, without touching the Ground
with his fore ones, sometimes curvetting round
a Ring, and then straining him so low with his
Belly to the Ground as to carry him under the
Mundingo Penthouses, which are not above
four Foot high Howsoever incredible this
may appear to the Reader, I can appeal to
numbers of Witnesses for its Truth.

T H I S Boomey *Haman Seaca* was King of
Barsally seven Years: For what Reason, or
how he came to lose the Kingdom, I cannot
tell, but a younger Man, of about 25 Years
of Age, who calls him Brother, is the present
King, who visited our Factory at *Joar* twice
in the Year 1731, as I have said before. *Haman
Seaca* was then along with him, also another
Brother younger than him, and a Third younger
than him, call'd *Loyt Eminga* The King has
a Sister who is also absolute, and she and the
Brothers have Soldiers of their own, who obey
their Commands with the greatest Punctuality,
were it even against the King This King's
Sister lives about 20 Miles from *Joar*. She
once sent five Men and six Horses to carry me
to pay her a Visit When I came to her House
she kill'd a Cow for me and my People, and
then made the People set to Dancing and Singing, which continu'd all the Time I stay'd

O N

On the 7th of *November* I received an Answer to the Letter sent 16th *ult* intimating,
that they thought there was nothing in this
Report, for that for several Years past they
never knew one Instance of such Reports com
ing to any thing However, they would have
me send a Present to *Haman Seaca*, in order
to have the Factory protected in case he
should come that Way They further told
me, that Mr *Hugh Hamilton* had, on account
of his ill State of Health, refused to accept of
being Third Chief Merchant and Accomptant,
which the Company had lately conferred up
on him

O n the 19th I received the following Let
ter from the Governor, *viz.*

Mr MOORE.

James *Fort, Nov.* 13, 1734.

S I R,

‘ I Lately received from you a Parcel
‘ of good *Gum-Senegal* sent from *Juico
‘ Sunco* of *Yanimarew* , but as you have given
‘ me no Account, as to where, how far off,
‘ and, what is of the greatest Import, what
‘ Quantities may be yearly produced and
‘ purchased, I desire you, if possible, to go
‘ with Capt *Brown*, or to send up Mr *West-
‘ wood*, and with Capt *Brown* to ask him
‘ about the above Particulars, and to put it
‘ in writing from his and the *Moor's* own
‘ Mouth, and to send it to me by Capt.
‘ *Brown* without the least Delay, which, as
‘ the *Elizabeth* is just ready to go for *England*,
may

‘ may be of great Detriment to the Company,   1734.
‘ if thefe Remarks are not fent home by her.

‘ I DESIRE you would fend me a Line
‘ or two as to what *Fody Cojear* has done
‘ relating to letting *Job*’s Friends know of
‘ his being here, and to defire you to let me
‘ know if he has fent a Meffenger, and when
‘ expected back, in doing which you will ob-
‘ lige *Job*, (who gives his Service to you) and

S I R,

Your humble Servant,

RICHARD HULL.

Being ill with a violent Cold, and fwelled
Throat, I could not go up to *Yanimarew* my
felf, but fent my Writer Mr. *Weftwood* with
Capt *Brown*, having firft given them fuch
Inftructions that they could not avoid receiving fatisfactory Accounts of what they went
about   They fet out at Night, and returned
the next Night, after which I fent the following Letter to the Governor.

JOAR *Factory*, *Nov.* 20, 1734.
S I R,

‘ THIS comes by way of *Damafenfa*, Author's
‘ and acknowledges the Favour of yours Letter
‘ of the 13th Current, in anfwer to which I
‘ muft acquaint you, that not being able (by
‘ reafon of a violent Cold in my Head and
‘ Throat) to go myfelf to *Yammarew*, I fent
‘ Mr. *Weftwood*, who with Capt. *Brown* have
                                ‘ received

' received fatisfactory Anſwers to the Que-
' ſtions which you ordered to be put to *Junco*
' *Sunco*, and the two *Moors*, which are as
' follow, *viz.*

' I As to the Diſtance from *Yanimarew* to
' the *Gum-Trees*, it is no more than five Days
' Journey.

' II. As to the Circumference of the Woods,
' they are ſixteen Days long, and ſix Days
' wide.

' III As to what Quantity might yearly
' be brought to *Yanmarew*, the *Moors* ſay,
' that the Woods are full of very large Trees,
' and that they all produce Gum, ſo that
' there might be vaſt Quantities brought
' from thence in a Year, provided there is a
' good Correſpondence ſettled between the
' People of *Yam*, the People of *Foota* *, and
' the Grand *Jolloiffs*, between which Three
' this Gum Foreſt is equally divided

' IV As to the Name of the Country, it
' has no particular one, but (as I ſaid before)
' equally divided between the People of *Yai*,
' *Foota*, and Grand *Jolloiffs*, which laſt inhaﬁ-
' bit about ſix Days Journey from the Gum-
' Trees

' V As to the Inhabitants, there are none
' at all near the Woods

' VI and VIIth. THERE is no River in
' the Road from *Yanimarew* to the Woods,
                                    ' the

---

* This is *Job*'s Country, being *Pholey*.

' the River *Gambia* being the neareſt to them,   1734.
' and as for the River *Senegal* it is ſeven or
' eight Days Journey from the Gum-Trees.

  ' VIII   T H E Y   are Strangers to all White
' Men, having never traded with any.   But
' *Junco Sunco* ſays, that with a little Trouble
' and Pains the Company might ſettle a good
' Correſpondence, and any Body then may
' travel to the Woods with ſafety.

  ' IX   A s to any other Trade they ſay, they
' are Strangers to it, but that there are vaſt
' Numbers of Elephants thereabouts

  ' T H I S, Sir, is the Subſtance of what I can
' gather from Meſſieurs *Brown* and *Weſtwood,*
' whoſe Notes (as well as an imperfect
' Draught by *Junco Sunco*) I have here in-
' cloſed, not doubting but that ſome of them
' will prove very ſatisfactory both to you
' and the Company.

  ' B E pleas'd to give my Service to Mr.
' *Job*, and to tell him, that his laſt Letters
' went from *Cower* the 9th Inſtant, but what
' Time the Meſſenger will return is moſt un-
' certain   I am,

       S I R,

     Your moſt humble Servant,

       FRA MOORE.

O N the 26th the *Fame* Sloop being at *Da-
maſenſa,* and I having about twelve Slaves
                        by

1734. by me, fent to Capt. *Brown* to come and fetch them down, in order to carry them to *James*

Author goes down to James Fort. Fort, the next Day he accordingly came up, and I having difpofed of all my merchantable Goods at the Factory, I thought it advifable to take this Opportunity of going down to the Fort, where I arrived on the third of December.

December. ON the 9th in the Evening came up the *Dolphin* Scooner, Meffieurs *Norry* and *Rofs*, from *London*, but laft from *Holland*, where they left the Company's Snow *Succefs* juft ready to fail for this Place, with a good Cargo. With this Scooner, came over one Mr *William Cleveland*, Brother-in-Law to our fecond Chief Merchant Mr *Charles Orfeur*, with a full Defign to get a Fortune by trading here againft the Company, having for that purpofe brought over a pretty good Cargo of Goods amounting to 400 l. *Sterling*, intending to fettle and live in Mr *Orfeur*'s Houfe at *Gilfree* However, our Governor Mr *Hull*, being ftrongly rivetted to the Company's Intereft, would not fuffer his Colleague's Brother to fettle and trade againft the Company, upon which Mr *Cleveland* difpofed of his Goods to the Company, for which they paid him in Slaves, after which he went down the Coaft with the faid Scooner.

ON the 12th arrived the Company's Snow *Succefs*, Capt. *Robert Wright*, with a very good Cargo of Goods, and Mr *Thomas Hilton* a Writer.

O ʋ

ON the 26th after I put on board the *Fame* 1734.
Sloop, *John Brown* Mafter, (who was then Author
going a Trading-Voyage up the River, with returns to
Mr *James Conner*, Super-Cargo and Factor) a *Joar*.
fmall fortable Cargo for *Joar*, and in the Afternoon we left *James* Fort, I having Mr
Thomas Hilton as my Affiftant.

ON the 1ft of *January*, whilft we were ly- *January*.
ing alongfide of *Elephants* Ifland for the Tide
of Flood to make, Mr *Conner* and I went a-
fhore to a Town call'd *Neámató*, where I received Advice that Boomey *Haman Seaca* was
up in Arms againft the King of *Barfally*, and
that being advanced within half a Day's Journey of *Joar*, almoft all the People of that
Town had abandon'd it, and, among the reft,
the Perfons with whom I left the Charge of
my Factory. This News furprized me much,
and I immediately hired a fmall Canoa and
three Men to carry me up to *Joar*, where I
arrived the next Day, and found about ten
People in the Town, all in my Houfe, the
Company's Goods fafe, and in the very fame
Condition that I left them.

I WAS not more afraid of their being ftole, Account
than of being fpoiled by a pernicious Vermin of *Bugg-*
called *Buggabuggs*; they are very deftructive *buggs*
wherever they get , their Way of Travelling
is, firft to make an hollow Pipe and Tube of
Dirt, much like an Arch of a Vault, under
which they go without being feen They are
a fort of White Ants, will work very faft, for
in twelve Hours they will make their Tube,
and travel eight or nine Yards to get to a
Cheft, Box or Barrel, wherever they get, they
make

make ftrange Work, efpecially in Woollen Cloths, in fhort, nothing comes amifs to them, for they feed as hearty upon Wood as any thing at all ; and what is moft remarkable is, that they eat the Infide only of a Cheft or Table, fo that when they have entirely deftroy'd it, by eating the Heart and Subftance of the Wood, yet do they appear to the Eye to be ftill found The Sun is their Enemy, for it will kill them for a Time, but I have obfer-ved, that after the Sun is down they will ie-cover their Strength and Vigour Every Bo-dy is obliged to watch thefe Creatures, and to take care they come not to their Chefts, which is done by putting them upon Stands with the Legs of them well tarred, and if they let the Tarr be a Week without new do ing it over, it is ten to one but they will make them a Vifit.

On the 5th Mr *Conner* arrived with the *Fame* Sloop I immediately had my Goods brought up to the Factory, and the next Morning early he proceeded on his Voyage up the River, foon after which I difpatched a Meffenger away to Boomey *Haman Seaca*, with fome Brandy and a Hanger, as a Pre-fent to him from the Company, in order to find good Ufage at the Hands of him and his People, in cafe he fhould take this Road, he being now at a Town call'd *Sanjally*, about half a Day's Journey from *Joar*. The Meffenger return'd the next Day with a handfom friendly Meffage from him, That he valued all White Men, and would therefore never ufe any of them ill, efpecially Me, whom he had known a long time ago, ever fince the time he va

with

with the King of *Barfally*, at the Factory in the Year 1731. and that in cafe the War fhould continue, his People fhould not upon any Account hurt or moleft me

ON the 21ft Mr *Thomas Hilton*, my Affi-ftant, died of a Fever, having been ill about ten Days. I buried him very decently in our Garden under an Orange-Tree The next Day I took an Account of his Things, and found about Forty Pounds Sterling Worth of Goods fit for Trade ; after which I fent down a Meffenger to *James* Fort, with an Account of his Death and Effects, and of the Meffage I receiv'd from Boomey *Haman Seaca*. *Mr Hilton dies*

ON the 29th came up from *Damafenfa* in a Canoa *Job Ben Solomon*, who, I forgot to fay, came up in the *Fame* Sloop along with me from *James* Fort on the 26th of *December* laft, and going on Shore with me at *Elephants* Ifland, and hearing that the People of *Joar* were run away, it made him unwilling to proceed up hither, and therefore he defired *Conner* to put him and his things afhore at a Place call'd *India*, about fix Miles above *Damafenfa*, where he has continued ever fince, but now hearing that there is no farther Danger, he thought he might venture his Body and Goods along with mine and the Company's, and fo came up. *J B Solomon arrives at Joar a fecond time*

ON the 14th a Meffenger, whom I had fent to *Job*'s Country, return'd hither with Letters, and Advice that *Job*'s Father died before he got up thither, but that he had liv'd to receive the Letters fent by *Job* from *England*, which *February A Meffenger returns from Job's Country*

What Ac
counts the
Meſſenger
brought

which brought him the welcome News of his Son's being redeemed out of Slavery, and the Figure he made in *England*. That one of *Job*'s Wives was married to another Man, but that as ſoon as the Huſband heard of *Job*'s Arrival here, he thought it adviſable to abſcond. That ſince *Job*'s Abſence from his Country, there has been ſuch a dreadful War, that there is not ſo much as one Cow left in it, tho' when *Job* was there, it was a very noted Country for numerous Herds of large Cattle With this Meſſenger came a good many of *Job*'s old Acquaintance, whom he was exceeding glad to ſee ; but notwithſtanding the Joy he had to ſee his Friends, he wept grievouſly for his Father's Death, and the Misfortunes of his Country He forgave his Wife, and the Man that had taken her, *For,* ſays he, *Mr Moore, ſhe could not help thinking I was dead, for I was gone to a Land from whence no* Pholey *ever yet returned, therefore ſhe is not to be blamed, nor the Man neither.* For three or four Days he held a Converſation with his Friends without any Interruption, unleſs to ſleep or eat.

March

ON the 8th of *March* the Snow *Dolphin,* Capt *Robert Clarke,* a Separate Trader, came up to *Rumbo*'s Port, in order to trade for Slaves.

Haman
Seaca's
People vi-
ſit the A
with a
falſe Story.

ON the 11th, early in the Morning, arri ved ſixty of Boomey *Haman Seaca*'s People about twenty of them were finely mounted on Horſeback well arm'd, and thoſe on Foot were armed with Bows, Arrows and Piſtols The Head Man who conducted them came into
the

the Factory alone, the others stay'd out at the
Door of my Cirk   He told me, that the
Boomey had fent him to let me know that he
pafs'd by here laft Night, to go to fight the
King at *Cohone* , that he would not bring all
his People here, for fear he fhould not be able
to govern them, and by that means the Factory come to any Damage   I told him to
give my Service to the Boomey, and thank
him for his Care of the Company's Effects,
and having made him a fmall Prefent of a
Piftol and Cutlafs, and fent fome Powder and
Ball by him to the Boomey, he and the reft of
them departed extreamly well fatisfied

On the 16th, in the Evening, arrived Mr Gov *Hull* arrives at *Joar*, on his Way to the Gum Fo-reft
Hull our Governor in the *James* Sloop, who
was going over Land to the Gum Foreft along
with *Job*, in order to open a Trade there   He
brought up with him Mr *Henry Johnfon*, late
Mafter of the *Adventure* Sloop, which is now
broke up   He expected to find Mr *Connet* here,
but being difappointed, and by me defir'd to
take himfelf the Charge of the Company's
Goods, he order'd me to deliver the fame to
the Care and Charge of Mr *Johnfon*, which
I accordingly did   After which he defir'd that
I would joyn with Mr *Johnfon* in the Management of the Factory, and trading with the
Merchants, which I did likewife

Towards the latter End of the Month, B *Haman Benda* vi-fits the Governor.
whilft the Governor was at the Factory, Boo-
mey *Haman Benda*, the King of *Barfally*'s Brother, who ftill ftuck to the King's Part, came
to fee him, with a very great Attendance, I
believe forty Men, moft of them on Horf-
Q   back

back. At Night he return'd to *Cower* to lie, intending the next Day to make him another Visit. *Haman Seaca*, being still at *Sanjally*, hearing of *Haman Benda*'s being now at *Cower*, sent out a Party of about an hundred Men, all well armed, some on Foot and some on Horseback, in order to fight with *Haman Benda*, or take some of his Attendants Prisoners; which he hearing of, immediately fled away into the Heart of *Barsally* as fast as possible, and dispatched a Messenger to acquaint the Governor that he could not wait upon him as he intended, but desired him to send him a Gallon or two of Brandy. Between *Cower* and *Joar* the Messenger was met by *Haman Seaca*'s People; one of whom, without any Ceremony, shot him thro' the Body, and then took his Horse. After which they walked three or four times along the *Savannah*, and finding that *Haman Benda*'s People would not fight them, they came up to the Factory, and drank a Gallon or two of Brandy, and then return'd to *Sanjally*.

ON the 5th the *Fame* Sloop came down with Mr *James Conner*, Factor, from a Trading Voyage up the River, and Mr *Thomas Palmer* and *Thomas Hull*, late Chiefs at *Brucoe*, they having now, by the Governor's Order, broke up that Factory, on account of there being but little Trade about it: Which had they done twenty Months ago (as I advised them) would have saved a good deal of Money to the Company. Mr *Palmer* was design'd for Secretary at *James* Fort, in the room of Mr *Samuel Turner*, who was made Accomptant.

comptant, and Mr *Thomas Hull* was to ſtay 1735.
here as an Aſſiſtant to Mr *Conner*

AND now that I live by myſelf, it may
not, perhaps, be diſagreeable for a Perſon
never out of *England* to hear how I lived in
Africa

I GOT up by Day-break, in order to enjoy
the Cool of the Mornings, and oftentimes took
a Ride of three or four Miles from home, thro'
Woods and Savannahs, the Air being then very pleaſant   As ſoon as I came back I break-
faſted on *Green* or *Bohea* Tea, or for want of
it, a ſort of Tea which grows wild in the
Woods, call'd *Simbong*, Quantities of which
have been ſent to *England*, and ſeveral People
there admired it much   When I wanted Sugar, which was ſeldom, I made uſe of Honey, reckon'd to be very wholſome ; but if
taken too much, is apt to give a Perſon the
Flux   When the Freſhes were ſo ſtrong that
no Veſſels could come up from which I could
get ſome Sugar, and when the Natives had
employ'd all their Honey in making Honey-
Wine, then I was forced to quit my Tea for
Sweet Milk, which is very plenty amongſt
the *Pholeys*   This I eat cold, with Cakes broke
into it, made of Flower of Rice or *Guinea*
Corn, mix'd up with Water, and baked over
a Fire in an Iron Pot   This Country Milk,
whatever is the Reaſon of it, will ſeldom or
never bear boiling without turning , I impu-
ted it to the Sourneſs of the Graſs which the
Cows eat   For Dinner I had frequently Beef,
ſometimes freſh, and ſometimes powder'd, for
it would keep in Salt ſix or ſeven Days toge-

*Account
how the
Author
paſs'd his
Time in
Africa*

Q 2   ther

ther without spoiling: This I either boiled and
eat with Cooscoosh, as the Natives do, or else
I boiled it with Pompkins or Coliloo, like
Spinage, both which are there exceeding plenty. Fowls are so cheap, that you may buy
them for three Charges of Gunpowder ap
and when I wanted either Fish or Game, I
out one of the Company's Servants, who a
a Hunter, allow'd us by the Company to keep
and he seldom fail'd of bringing in either Wild
Hog, Deer, Ducks, Partridges, Wild Geese,
or Crown Birds, all which are plenty in their
different Seasons.

T H E Afternoon was the usual Time for
Trade, but sometimes would last for three
Days together, which being my proper
Business, I never neglected If it ended
soon, I would sometimes take a Trip to
the neighbouring Towns, and return'd home
to Supper, after which I amused myself with
writing, reading, or visiting my Neighbours
till Bed-time, where I commonly was treated
with Palm-Wine, Ciboa-Wine, Honey-Wine,
or else a Fruit call'd Cola, which relishes Water I used frequently to go a Shooting,
which was chiefly Doves and Partridges, they
being found not far from the Factory. Guests
I was used to have sometimes in plenty, some
being Traders, and others Messengers from
Great Men of the neighbouring Kingdoms,
who would frequently send me Presents of
Cows, Cloths, and sometimes a Slave, but
this was not very pleasing to me, because I
was sensible that they expected I should return
them Presents to more than the Worth of
what they sent me. All these Presents were

for the Company's Benefit, and I accordingly
accounted for them.

THE Negroe Women dress'd my Victuals
earthen Ware, sweet and clean, and made
the Natives I had also two Iron Pots from
ues Fort, one of which was for the Use of
Company's Slaves and Servant, and the
her served me on high Days, when I had
Company, or else for an Oven to bake in.
I had a good large Bedchamber, in the rainy
Season I always kept a Fire in it. My Bed
was rais'd from the Ground about two Feet
upon Forks, at the Head and Feet Poles laid
on them, and a Hurdle made of Split Cane
laid above them, which answer'd the Sacking
Bottom of our *English* Bedsteads. I had a
Bed made of coarse Cotton-Cloths, the Produce of the Country, which I got stuff'd with
Silk Cotton, a sort of Down. Besides what I
brought from *England*, the K. of *Barsally*, and
his Sister gave me some Cotton Cloths six
Yards long and three wide, which I used for
Sheets. At the four Corners of my Bedstead
I set up four Poles to support a kind of Pavi-
lion made of thin Cloth, for keeping off the
Musquetoes. In one Corner of my Room I
had a large Jarr of Water raised upon Fork-
killas, to keep it from Vermin Other Furniture, as I had little Occasion for it, I was
not troubled with

ON the 6th, as I was walking about a Author
Quarter of a Mile from *Joar* Factory, I found finds a
the Foot of a Beast, the Carcass having been Wild
devour'd, as I believe, by a Lion, much re- Man's
sembling a Baboon, but as big as that of a
Q 3 Man,

Man ; it was newly kill'd, cover'd with Hair about an Inch long I brought it home, and show'd it Governor *Hull*, and examining some of the Natives, they told us, that it was the Foot of what they call'd a Wild Man , that there are a good many of them in this Country, but they are seldom found , they are as tall as a Man, have Breasts like a Woman, and have a sort of a Language, and walk upon their Feet as Human Creatures.

Author leaves *Joar* On the 8th, having deliver'd up the Company's Effects to Mr *James Conner*, and taken proper Discharges for the same, I embarked on Board the Company s Sloop *James*, to which Mr *Hull* accompanied me, and parted with me in a very friendly manner *Job* His parting with *J B Solomon* likewise came down with me to the Sloop, and parted with me with Tears in his Eyes, at the same time giving me Letters for his Grace the Duke of *Montague*, the Royal *African* Company, Mr *Oglethorpe*, and several other Gentlemen in *England*, telling me to give his Love and Duty to them, and to acquaint them, that as he designs to learn to write the *English* Tongue, he will, when he is Master of it, send them longer Epistles, and full Accounts of what shall happen to him hereafter , desiring me, that as I had lived with him almost ever since he came there, I would let his Grace and the other Gentlemen know what he had done, and that he was the next Day going with Mr *Hull* up to *Yamma- rew*, from whence he would accompany him to the Gum Forest, and make so good an Understanding between the Company and his Country People, that the *English* Nation should

reap

reap the Benefit of the Gum Trade , faying
at laſt, that he would ſpend his Days in endeavouring to do good for the *Engliſh*, by whom
he had been redeemed from Slavery, and from
whom he had received ſuch innumerable Fa-
vours.

IMMEDIATELY after I ſet ſail, and in four
Days arrived at *James* Fort, where the Com-
pany's Snow *Dolphin* lay taking in a Cargo of
Elephants Teeth and Bees-Wax.

ON the 13th of *May*, having ſettled my
Accompts, and got my Accompt Currant ſign'd
by Mr *Charles Orfeur*, I made myſelf ready
to embark for *England* In the Afternoon
Mr *Hamilton*, late C. Merchant, and ſeveral
others beſides myſelf, embarked aboard the
Dolphin Snow, Capt *Thomas Freeman*, for
London. Mr *Orfeur*, and all the other Gentlemen accompanied us down to the Boat, where
we drank a couple of Bottles of Wine; and
then having taken our Leaves of one another,
and put off from Shore, the Fort fired nine
Guns, in complaiſance to Mr *Hugh Hamilton*,
he having been for ſome time Chief Merchant.
We immediately ſet ſail in Company with the
Succeſs, Capt. *Wright*, bound on a Trading
Voyage to *Crutcheo* and *Portodally.* We both
ſaluted the Fort with nine Guns each, and both
had the ſame Number returned.

*May
Author
leaves
Africa,
and ſets
out for
England*

BY reaſon of the freſh Sea-Breezes we were
not able to reach *Banyon* Point in leſs than two
Days, where we ſent our Boat aſhore to purchaſe Fowl, which by the Negligence of the
Sailors was ſtove ; but Capt. *Wright*'s People

Q 4   being

1735   being afhore, were fo good as to bring off our People, and tow the Boat aboard after them The next Day we paffed out of the River *Gambia*, and took our Departure from Cape *Saint Mary*'s, with a pretty frefh Gale going about fix * Knots an Hour.

On the 31ft, about Noon, died one of our Ship-Mates, Mr *James Ellis*, who was ill when we left *Gambia*, but died a Martyr to Rum, for when he was not able to lift a Mug to his Mouth, he made fhift to fuck it thro' a Pipe, and died with a Pipe and a Mug full of Bumbo clofe to his Pillow. He was committed to the Deep, and the Service read over him.

June   On the 28th of *June* we fpoke with a large Ship, Capt. *Shud's* Commander, from the Gum Coaft, but laft from S *Jago*, one of the Cape *Verd* Iflands, bound for *London*, having made a pretty good Voyage.

7'   On the 10th of *July*, in the Morning, we brought to, founded, and found Ground with eighty Fathom of Line, which by the Evening we brought to feventy five Ever fince the 29th of *June* we had hard Gales of Wind, but being directly fair for us, we had not much reafon to complain This Day we fpoke with a Ship for *London* from *Jamaica* in eight Weeks The next Morning we made the *Englifh* Coaft, and foon after we faw the *Edifone* Lighthoufe abreaft of us. The Gale continuing, we went forward right before the Wind at a great Rate At Midnight we were not a little furprized to hear one of our Sailors cry out *Land! right*

* *five Miles,*   *ahead!*

ahead! we judging ourselves at least five Leagues from it. We lowered our Sails, and lay to till Day-light; at which time we perceived the Fellow was under a Mistake, being then out of Sight of Land

ON the 12th we were chased by one of the King's Sloops, who when she came near us fired a Shot, and brought us to, after which one of the Lieutenants belonging to the *Edinborough* Man of War, came on Board us, and after having detain'd us about four Hours, took away three of our best Sailors, and left three others in their Stead   In the Afternoon we made the *Isle of Wight*, and the next Morning at Day light we were got abreast of *Beachy Head*, about nine we came to *Dungenness*, where lay about thirty Sail of outward-bound Ships   Soon after we came to the *Downs*, where lay also a great number of Ships outward-bound, and two or three Men of War. We came to anchor, and waited for a Pilot, at last one came off, with whose Boat I went ashore to *Deal*, having been exactly twoMonths on our Voyage from *James* Fort, in the River *Gambia*   I lay all Night at *Deal*, and refreshed myself; the next Morning I got a Horse and set out towards *Gravesend*, where I arrived in the Afternoon   There I chose to stay all Night, and went up to *London* in a Pair of Oars, from whence by the first Post I sent Letters to acquaint my Friends of my Return from *Africa*, which our *English* People most of them think so unhealthy, that White People cannot live there, by reason of the excessive Heat   The next Return of the Post I received a kind Letter from my Mother, expressing

1735. preffing the Joy and Satisfaction fhe received by hearing of the Return of her Son, whom fhe had for four or five Years paft never expected to fee again; and in the fame Letter fhe fent me the melancholy Account of my Father's Death, as likewife of two Brothers and a Sifter, and feveral other near Relations fince the Year 1730. of which I never before had received the leaft Account.

I WAITED upon the Company, who were very well pleas'd with my Behaviour whilft in their Service; they paid me what Money was due to me, and in the Month of *September* following I fet out for the City of *Worcefter*, where I was kindly received by my old Acquaintance, and returned GOD Thanks, who thro' fo many Dangers had brought me back in Safety to my Friends, Relations, and native Country.

JOURNAL

OF A

VOYAGE up the *Gambia*.

BEING AN

ATTEMPT for making DISCOVERIES, and improving the TRADE of that RIVER, by Meſſ. *Bartholomew Stibbs*, *Edward Drummond*, and *Richard Hull*, in the YEAR 1723.

O N the 7th of *October*, 1723 I arrived at the Mouth of the River *Gambia* with the *African* Company of *England's* Ship *Diſpatch*, having proper Inſtructions for proceeding up the ſaid River with Canoas as far as poſſible, in queſt of the Gold Mines, and making other Diſcoveries in this Country. At Noon I anchor'd at *James Iſland*, ſaluting the Fort with 5 Guns, and then went aſhore, where, to my great Surprize, I found that Mr *Glynn* the Governor had been dead near ſix Months, and was

ſuc-

1723. ſucceeded by Mr *Joſeph Willy*, who was at preſent up at *Joar* with Mr *Orfeur*, Lieut. *Macſwain* and Dr *Caffull*.

I IMMEDIATELY conſulted with Mr *Hull*, who is Secretary and Chief Factor, and with whom the Fort was at preſent entruſted, and who immediately diſpatch'd away a Canoa to Mr *Willy* at *Joar* with the Company's Pacquet I wrote to him myſelf alſo, acquainting him of the Company's having appointed me Chief Conductor of the *Expedition* up this River. Both Mr *Hull* and myſelf deſired he would give ſpeedy Orders for buying up Canoas, and to purchaſe what he could there, for at preſent I found they had none

ON the 16th the Canoa return'd, which carried the Diſpatches to *Joar*, but without any Anſwer to my Letter, and in the Letter to Mr *Hull*, Mr *Willy* ſays there are no Canoas to be bought there, without taking any farther Notice of it, or giving Orders for buying any ; at which we were much concern'd.

ON the 24th two Gromettas (or hired Black Servants) came down from *Joar*, being hired by Mr *Willy* for the Company's Service, but they brought no Letters at all

ON the 26th, late at Night, came down the *Gambia* Sloop, Capt. *Uring*, from *Joar*, with 49 Slaves He brings ſeveral Letters, [which mention nothing of the Expedition] but none for me. From the Captain I underſtood that Mr *Willy* thinks little or nothing of the Affair, that ſome Canoas may be bought there, and that one very good one was offer'd him, but yet was not bought, nor could he ſay that he deſign'd to buy it . That it would be a Fortnight yet, he thought, before Mr

W j

Willy came down , upon which I resolv'd to write again to Mr *Willy,* altho' he has taken no manner of Notice of my former Letter.

ON the 28th the *Gambia* Sloop sail'd for *Joar* again, by whom I sent the following Letter :

To JOSEPH WILLY, *Esq,*

SIR, October 28, 1723.

AFTER *upward of* 20 *Days being arrived here, on an Account which I am very senſible the Royal Company expeᶜts their utmoſt Inteᵣeſt to be employ'd in here, I am very ſorry to find I can neither have the Honour of hearing from you, or ſeeing you ; and, to my further Mortification, to hear that there are no Canoas above, nor ſo much as an Order yet to procure any here below. The Seaſon now advances ſwiftly, and if I cannot be purſuing the Deſign by the beginning of December, it is in vain to think on it afterwards The Ship may ſtay with you, if you think it for the Royal Company's Intereſt But if the Deſign on which I am ſolely and particularly come, thro' any unforeſeen Accidents or Omiſſions, cannot be carried on in the Time abovemention'd, and that you have no Cargo ready by the* Diſpatch, *my Deſign is to return to* England *with Capt.* Rodwell, *unleſs with conſulting with you we can form a ſpeedy Voyage for the Company's Intereſt, which probably it is not difficult to do , but I will ſtay in this River on no account long, (unleſs on the Expedition for which I am ſolely come) but endeavour by a ſpeedy Return to put Matters in ſuch a Poſture, that nothing the next Year may be wanting to purſue an Affair, which I am but too ſenſible the Royal Company have extreamly at heart.*

heart. I beg Leave likewise to assure you, that to go as high as Barracunda, *or somewhat higher, will not at all answer the Royal Company's Intentions, as having long since by many been perform'd, and to go higher after* Christmas *is hardly practicable. Therefore 'twas highly necessary we had gone about it in earnest immediately on my Arrival; for what with* Time *lost in buying the Canoas, and fitting of them, (here being no Carpenter but my own) we had been full late,* † *had the greatest Expedition been us'd at first, but now there is a Month or five Weeks will be elapsed before we can so much as consult or debate upon it. I am heartily sorry for the Royal Company's Charges on this Affair, but more for their Disappointments, and hope next Year we shall pursue it with such Unanimity of Opinions, as may fully make them amends for the Loss of this Season. I am,*

SIR,

Yours, &c

BARTH. STIBBS.

I HOPE the foregoing Letter, with another sent him by Mr *Hull*, will rouse him from his Lethargy, and give him more generous Notions

---

† Mr *Stibbs* himself here mentions his being very sensible, that he set out too late in the Year upon his *Discovery* If he had set out from *Fatatenda* in the beginning of *November*, he might have made his way up much farther by Water. He afterwards seems to think that this "not the *Niger*, because he could not go up high enough whereas he here says, that the reason of his not being able to go up as far as the anonymous Journal mentions, is because it was too late in the Year

Notions of the Expedition than at prefent I learn he has.

On the 29th the *Barrah* Shallop was difpatch'd for *Jenock*, to purchafe Corn and Canoas for the Expedition.

On the 31ft, in the Afternoon, the Company's Pinnace (to our great Surprize) brought down the Corps of Mr *Willy*. It feems he left *Joar* laft *Tuefday* Evening, being then much diforder'd in his Head, and died on Board the Brigantine *Advice*, Capt. *Rodwell*, that fame Night, or rather *Wednefday* Morning, being then off *Elephant's* Ifland. They tell us likewife, that Lieut. *Macfwain* and Dr *Cafful* are fo bad, that their Lives are defpair'd of, and that Mr *Willy* had broke up the Factory at *Joar* before he came away, leaving Mr *Orfeur* (who now is Chief) and Mr *Rogers*, with the *James Ifland* Sloop, to ftay a little longer to fee if the King of *Barfally* would come and make up the Palaver. Mr *Willy* was buried on the North Baftion, where feveral other Governors lie; the Fort firing 16 Guns minutely, and I ten afterwards from my Ship.

On the 1ft of *November*, at Noon, the Fort hoifted the Flag, and fir'd nine Guns to the new Governor's Health (Mr *Orfeur*) it being a Cuftom here, altho' he was at *Joar*, and I fir'd five from my Ship. At Eight at Night came up the *Hamilton's* Boat, Capt. *Kirk*, who has the Miners, &c. on Board for the Expedition, the Ship is without the River.

On the 2d, in the Morning, a Canoa brought down the Body of Dr *Hugh Caffull*, who came out about fix Months ago as chief Surgeon for the Expedition up the River.

He

1723 He died yefterdav Morning on Board the
Brigantine *Aazice*, Capt *Rodwell*, in his Way
down hither from *Joar*. His Body was foon
after fent over to *Grilyfree* to be interr'd, the
Fort firing four Guns   This Gertleman died
univerfally lamented, he having the beft of
Charaĉters, which proves a great Lofs to the
Expedition.

AT Noon the Corps of Lieut. *Matfwain*
was brought down, who died alfo on Board
the Brigantine at Three this Morning   He
was buried in the Evening on the Eaft Baftion,
the Fort firing fix Guns   This young Man
had alfo a very good Charaĉter. In the Evening the *Advice* Brigantine came down from
Joar, and anchor'd between us and the Fort

ON the 4th, in the Afternoon, the *Ham-
tcr.*, Capt *Kirk*, came up, and fent afhore the
Miners and Surgeon in good Health, as
eight Miners, with their Captain, and his
Deputy, and a Smith for them, in all eleven,
and a Surgeon and his Mate, being all for
the Expedition

ON the 5th came down the *Gambia* Sloop
from *Joar*, with Mr *Orfeur* and Mr *Roger*,
the Faĉtory at *Joar* being entirely broke up
At his going on Shore I faluted him with five
Guns, as did the reft, and the Fort with
feven.

ON the 6th I met in Council (being the
firft time) with Mr *Orfeur*, Mr *Rogers*, and
Mr *Hull*, and then open'd my Inftruĉtions
deliver'd me by the Royal Company as Chief
Conduĉtor of the intended Expedition, which
was read , and afterwards open'd the Royal
Company's Inftruĉtions to the Chief and
Council here on the fame Affair ; which

was read alſo, and then adjourn'd to the 8th Inſtant. Meſſieurs *Orfeur* and *Rogers* deſiring to peruſe the Journals, which by the Demiſe of Meſſieurs *Glynn* and *Willy* were fallen into their Hands, and which they had never yet ſeen.

On the 8th we met in Council again, and finding it impoſſible to carry on the ſaid Expedition, thro' Mortality, with the full Number of Hands preſcrib'd in the Royal Company's Inſtructions, 'twas reſolv'd in the mean time, having adjourn'd to the 1ſt of *December*, that the utmoſt Endeavours ſhould be us'd to buy or hire Canoas, as alſo Proviſions (the Company having none here) and then to meet and ſet the Day and Number of Men that ſhould proceed on the ſaid Expedition up the River.

On the 11th, the *James Iſland* Sloop, Capt. *Trevija*, came down from *Joar* with 24 Slaves, ſent thither in a Canoa by Mr *Drummond* at *Cutteyarr*.

On the 15th the *Hamilton* ſail'd for Cape *Coaſt* with 30 Slaves, and the *Gambia* Sloop to *Jenock* for Rice and Corn for the *Advice*, Capt *Rodwell*, for whom 150 Slaves are ready to be carried for *Jamaica*

In the Evening the *Diamond* Man of War's Boat, Capt. *Wyndham*, came up with Lieut. *Percival* in her, the Ship lying at anchor off the Broken Iſlands : The next Morning he went down again.

On the 17th died my Fiſt Mate Mr *John Laughland* In the Evening came up the *William* Sloop, Capt *Elliot*, from *Barbadoes* He informs us, that the Man of War and the
Hamilton

R

1723   *Hamilton* fail'd this Morning from the Broken Iflands.

O N the 23d the *James Ifland* Sloop went up the River for *Cuttejarr*.

O N the 27th the *William* Sloop, Capt *Elliot*, fail'd. Moft of my Men were down with Fevers.

O N the 30th arrived a *French* Sloop from *Goree*, which fame Sloop fail'd the 16th of *Oftober* laft from this Place for *Goree* with 46 Slaves and Goods For thefe laft 20 Days we have had generally very ftrong Eaftwardly Winds, and very cold, beyond Imagination, confidering the Climate.

O N the 1ft of *December* we met in Council, according to our laft Adjournment, and having not enough Canoas yet, tho' daily expected, we adjourn'd to the 7th

T H I S Day came in the *Ruby* Brigantine, Capt *Kidgel*, an Interloper from *London*, belonging to Mr *Godding* a *French* Merchant.

O N the 3d came up the *Gambia* Sloop from *Jenock*, with 190 Barrels of Rice and Corn on Board In the Evening the Slaves were fent on Board the Brigantine, and the next Morning the neceffary Corn, fo that now fhe lies ready for failing.

O N the 5th, underftanding that Monfieur *D'harriet*, the *French* Chief at *Albreda*, was gone to *Tancrowall*, which is contrary to the Agreement between the two Companies of *England* and *France*, which permits them to go no higher in this River than *Vintain* Point, without Leave firft obtain'd from the *Englifh* Governor, in the Evening Meffieurs *Rogers* and *Hull* were difpatch'd in the *Gambia* Sloop to feize him and his Canoa, and to make diligent

ligent Enquiry if he had made any Trade there, particularly with Signior *Antonio Vofs*, or any other *Portuguefe* ; if fo, to bring them down alfo This Step was taken on account of the *French* Chief's declaring before the Governor, myfelf, and the reft of the Council, that he would go up the River as high as he pleas'd, and when he pleas'd, without asking Leave.

On the 9th the *Gambia* Sloop return'd from *Tanci owall* with Mi *Rogers* and Mr *Hull*, who brought with them a large Canoa, which the *French* Chief went up in, but he got away himfelf to *Vintain* over Land. The Canoa being forfeited by thefe Proceedings of the *French*, it was order'd for the Expedition ; and indeed it came in good time, for hitherto we had but four, and now judging thefe fufficient, I immediately order'd my Carpenter to fit them

On the 11th we met in Council, and fettled the Number of Whites and Blacks that were to go on the Expedition, *viz* 19 White Men, including our Linguifter, who is as Black as Coal, thó' here, thro' Cuftom, (being Chriftians) they account themfelves White Men We agreed that the 26th Inftant fhould be the utmoft Limits of our Stay ; but, if poffible, to fit the Canoas fooner, and be gone before.

Mr *Henry Rofe* appointed Mafter of the Boats from *England*, making fome Objections to his going, was order'd to give in his Reafons in Writing on the Morrow To which Time we adjourn'd.

On the 12th we met in Council, and read the Reafons deliver'd in by Mr *Rofe* againft his going on the Expedition, which appear'd

R 2 to

1723. to be very frivolous, and inconfiftent with his Contract, and chiefly intended to the doubling of his Salary Upon which I acquainted the reft of the Council that I would undertake the Charge myfelf, or any other, without any Confideration, rather than the Expedition fhould be impeded either on that or any other Account.

CAME up the *Ruby*, Capt. *Craigue*, an Interloper, belonging to Mr *Wragg* in *London*, who defigns for Slaves to *Carolina*

IN the Evening the *Gambia* Sloop and the *Barrah* Shallop went to *Vintain* to careen

ON the 14th, in the Morning, came down the *James Ifland* Sloop from *Cuttejar*, with Mr *Edward Drummond*, and 40 Slaves, and 9 C. Weight of Elephants Teeth.

ON the 17th, the *Ruby*, Capt. *Craigue*, fail d up the River for *Joar*. The *Gambia* Sloop came down from *Vintain*.

ON the 21ft early, the *Advice* Brigantine, Capt *Rodwell*, fail'd for *Jamaica* with 160 Slaves, with her went the *Gambia* Sloop to fee her fafe out of the River.

ABOUT Noon *Walter Trathern*, Captain of the Miners, was carried to *Gillyfree* to be buried, the Fort fired fix Guns, and myfelf four from the *Difpatch* Ship. He died over Night, after about fix Days illnefs, it was the more furprizing to us, by reafon it did not appear he was in any danger till a few Hours before his Death Ever fince his Arrival he has been always melancholy and difcontented, often wifhing the Expedition was over, that he might return to *England*, not liking this Country at all.

ON

ON the 23d the *Gambia* Sloop came up, having feen the *Advice* Brigantine fafe out of the River the Day before.

ON the 25th the *French* Sloop fail'd from *Albreda* for *Goree*, with 100 Slaves on Board, and other Goods. At Noon we perceiv'd a vaft Swarm of Locufts : They arofe in the Weftward, and by Night came as far as *Gilly-free* At Five in the Afternoon we launch'd the largeft Canoa, which I call'd the *Chandos.* At the fame time we drank his Grace's Health, and the Fort fir'd 11 Guns.

A *VOYAGE* from JAMES Fort up the River GAMBIA, by *Command of the Royal* African *Comp. of* England.

The Difpofitions of the Expedition up this River from James *Fort*

I. *To fet out from* James Ifland *the 26th of De-cember at fartheft*

II. *The* Difpatch *to proceed as high as* Cutte-jarr, *or higher, and to remain there till my Return under the Care of my Mate Mr* Alex-ander Smith.

III. *The* James Ifland *Sloop to proceed as high as* Barracunda, *and there to make Trade, and remain till my Return under the Care and Direction of Capt.* Trevifa.

IV *The five Canoas to proceed to the firft Falls, and there if it be found impracticable to get*

R 3   *the*

*the two great ones above it, to leave them un-
der the Care of* ———, *and to proceed higher with the three smallest.*

V. *And with the three smallest it is our Intention (God willing) to proceed as far as there
is a Possibility, unless we make the Discovery
sooner.*

HERE I think proper to insert the Names
and Number of the White Men, &c. that
went on the Expedition, with the Names and
Number of the Canoas And great pity it is
we were not a Month sooner, for I found it
the general Opinion of all I consulted with there
(that were Natives) that we were too late And
altho' the Royal Company in their Instructions
recommended Privacy and Secrecy in the Affair, yet on my Arrival I found it had long
before been publickly talk'd of, and in the
Mouths of all the Natives, and where ever I
went I found myself generally known, and
pointed at as the Person who was sent out to
bring down the Gold.

Names of the Canoas.	Length		Breadth		Depth		No of Men
	F	In	F	In	F	In	
The *Chandos*	42	6	6	4	4	9	12
Royal *Africa*	37	10	5	4	3	7	12
Gambia	34	0	4	4	3	4	10
Expedition	39	6	3	11	3	2	9
Discovery	33	0	5	3	3	3	10
						Total	51

Sickness and Mortality obliged us to make
some Alterations as to our White Men, and
Mr *Harrison*, Writer, and *John Hodges*, Smith,
on their Petitions were permitted to proceed
with us.

The White Men to proceed on the Ex- 1723.
PEDITION up this RIVER.

Thofe agreed on in Council the 11th of Decemb.

1 *Bartholomew Stibbs,* Conductor.
2 *Edward Drummond,* 1ft Factor.
3 *Richard Hull,* 2d Factor and Metalliſt.
4 *Walter Trathern,* Capt. of the Miners.
5 *John Cummings,* Surgeon.
6 *Matthew Reynolds,* Carpenter.
7 *William Gitthouſe,* Gunner
8 *Walter Reeves,* Writer.
9 *Anthony Penroſe,* Smith.
10 *John Nankiavel,* Dep. Capt. of the Miners.
11 *Baram Fatty,* Linguiſter.
12 *Jacob May,*
13 *Matthew Jacob,*
14 *Richard Collings,*
15 *Zachary Langdon,* } Miners.
16 *Thomas Stoneman,*
17 *Collen Moil,*
18 *Henry Row,*
19 *Henry Petty,*

    Nº of White Men ———— —— 19
    Nº of Gromettas ———— ——— 29
    Nº of Women Slaves for Cooks 3

              Total 51
and three Months Proviſions.

Thoſe that went on the Expedition.

1 *Barth Stibbs,* Conductor. } To com-
2 *Edw. Drummond,* 1ft Factor. } poſe the
3 *Rich Hull,* 2d Fact and Met } Council.
4 *Thomas Harriſon,* Writer and Steward.
        R 4   5 *Walter*

1723.

  5 *Walter Reeves*, Writer
  6 *John Cummings*, Surgeon.
  7 *Matthew Reynolds*, Carpenter.
  8 *William Gitthouse*, Gunner.
  9 *John Hodges*, Smith.
10 *John Nanktavel*, Dep. Capt. of the Miners.
11 *Anthony Penrose*, Smith.
12 *Jacob May*
13 *Henry Petty*.
14 *Cullen Moyle*.
15 *Henry Rowe*
19 Cape Coasters.
11 Gromettas.
  4 Women for Cooks, &c.
  3 Boys.
  1 Linguister.

53 Which go in five Canoas.

There go beside in the *James Island* Sloop, to remain at *Barracunda* to make Trade,
  1 Capt *Trevija*
  5 Gromettas
  2 White Men Sailors
  1 Balaseu, and his Wife and Servant

65 Total to proceed to *Barracunda*

THE 26th of *December* being the Day appointed for proceeding up the River on the Expedition, according to a Resolution of Council of the 11th Instant, I this Morning order'd my Ship *Dispatch* to unmoor, and at Four P. M. weigh'd, and run a League above the Fort, and then anchor'd, the Canoas not being entirely ready.

THE

THE Swarm of Locusts we discover'd 1723. yesterday having devour'd all the Herbage about *Gillyfree*, arose this Afternoon, and took their Flight again, directing their Course to the Eastward, up the River. They spread at least four Miles, darkening the Air as they fly, so that neither the Sky nor the Woods are perceptible thro' them.

ON the 27th, having several high Words with the Governor about the dilatory fitting the Canoas, &c. I went on Board, weigh'd my Anchor, and fell up a League higher, and then anchor'd again. Here I cannot help taking notice, as I have frequently told the Gentlemen here, that it is my Opinion we are too late in the Year, and shall probably find the want of Water above the Falls

ON the 28th, early in the Morning, the Governor and Mr *Rogers* came on Board, bringing with them all the Canoas, and designing to go as far as *Tancrowall* with us I immediately hoisted the Flag at the Maintopmast head and weigh'd, and by Ten turn'd it beyond *Seaca* Point, the Wind at N E. At Four P M. I weigh'd again, and at Midnight anchor'd a League short of *Tancrowall*.

ON the 29th, at Ten in the Morning, I anchor'd at *Tancrowall*, and saluted Sig *Antonio Voss* with five Guns Afterwards the Governor, &c. went ashore, and both dined and supp'd with him. He made us a Present of two fat Bullocks.

ON the 31st, at Eleven in the Morning, we left *Tancrowall* at half Flood, and by Two P M turn'd it as high as *Drum*-Hill, where I anchor'd The Governor, &c. and *Antonio Voss* stay'd on Board and din'd with me. We

drank

1723. drank the Company's Health, Succeſs to the Expedition, *&c.* with firing of Guns. In the Evening the Governor, *&c* went away to *Tancrowall* in the *James Iſland* Sloop, from whence the *Gambia* Sloop carries them to *James* Fort

A t *Tancrowall* it was agreed between us, that (the better to obſerve the Company's Orders and Inſtructions) Capt *Stibbs* do keep the Journal, and take the Bearings and Diſtances of the Points and Reaches of this River, *&c* that Mr *Drummond* keep the Accounts, *&c* and that Mr *Hull* take every Opportunity of going aſhore, in order to make Diſcoveries of Ores, Minerals and Vegetables, *&c* and to collect and keep the ſame.

A t Seven at Night, the Tide ſerving, I weigh'd, as did all the Canoas, and at Three in the Morning anchor'd three Leagues above *Tendebar*

O n the 1ſt of *January*, at Eleven in the Morning, we got under Sail, the Wind being in our Teeth Eaſtwardly, and at Six in the Evening we anchor'd in the *Devil's Reach* Here the River is about a Mile and half broad, with prodigious high, tall, ſtrait Mangroves on both Sides. Here we found the Muſquetoes begin to be very troubleſome in the Night.

O n the 2d, by Sun-ſet, we got up with *Elephants* Iſland, (taking all Opportunities of the Tide both by Day and Night.) We kept in that Channel on the North-ſide of the Iſland, altho' by much the leaſt, it being in ſome Places not above 150 Yards over, but Water enough, and free from Shoals M^r

D *rummond*

Drummond went before in one of the Canoas to *Damasensa*, to get one or two small Canoas, which I am to take there, in order to send into Creeks, where there is but little Water. At Eight at Night I anchor'd at the other End of *Elephants* Island, not quite thro'. This Island, as well as all the River we pass'd, was very full of high Mangroves, and is about six Miles long. Many Fires were in the Country all Night, and the Flies very troublesome.

On the 3d, at Six in the Morning, we got up our Anchor, and at Seven anchor'd again against *Damasensa* River. I immediately went up in my Yawl, and met Mr *Drummond* at Monf *Le Maigre*'s House, who treated us very civilly, and at Noon we return'd on Board, bringing with us one small Canoa only. This Person is a *Frenchman*, and a private Trader, and the only *European* that lives here, nor are there twenty Houses in the Place. It is near five Miles up the River, which at the Entrance may be fifty Yards over, but grows so narrow at last, by reason of the Mangrove Trees, as not to leave room to row. It is full of Alligators, which the *Mundingoes* call *Bumbo*. I saw a great many of them, and Variety of Birds, as Pelicans, Flamingoes, Crabcatchers, Doves, &c. I could not forbear taking notice of a small * Bird, no

bigger

---

* Thefe Birds are in Size and Feather like the Cock Goldfinch, and build their Nefts at the very Extremities of the Boughs of the Trees upon Twigs that hang over the River, which are fo fmall as not to bear much more Weight than the Neft itfelf. Nature having taught them th t this is the means of preferving their Species from the Monkeys, which climb all Trees that can bear them, and who are as fond of Birds Nefts as Children.

1724. bigger than a Chaffinch, which build their
Nests on small Trees, which here and there
hang over the River, and at the very Extremities of the Twigs, in great Numbers Up
this River are no Mangroves for a League
from the *Gambia*, the Land on each Side is
a fine Marsh, free from Trees, and overgrown
with Reeds † and high Grafs. It is in those
Places the Sea-Horses (or more properly River-
Horses) delight and come to feed   I saw their
Beds and Tracts in several Places, but as yet
have not seen the Creature, which when I
have Opportunity will particularly describe

A T Three in the Afternoon we got under
Sail, and at Eight at Night anchor'd on the
West Side of the *Sea-Horse* Island. This Island
is about a Mile and half long, very low, and
full of Mangroves, and navigable only of this
Side, where the River is near a Mile over.
This Evening we pass'd by two considerable
Rivers, *viz* *Sanjally* on the Left, and *India*
on the Right   The Country on both Sides
low, with high Mangroves by the River Sides

O n the 4th, at Eight in the Morning, we
anchor'd at *Joar*, where we found the *Ruby*,
Capt *Craigue*, an Interloper, who saluted me
with five Guns, which I return'd. By this
Gentleman I wrote a Letter to the Royal
Company, directed to Mr *Lynn*, giving an
account of our being here on our Way on the
Expedition.

H E R E we began to see some high Hills
inland, of a reddish Colour, and pretty thin
of

† These Reeds are of the same Kind as those growing
on the *Nile*, of which the *Egyptians* us'd to make the Pa
pyrus, us'd by them to write upon long before the Invention
of Paper and Parchment

of Trees, alfo we faw a great many wild Monkeys, and large Flocks of Crown-Birds, which make a Noife as difagreeable as the Braying of an Afs. At this Place the River is not fo wide as at *Gravefend*, and the Mangroves grow thin and fcrubby.

At Three this Afternoon Mr *Drummond* went before with two Canoas for *Dubocunda*, to purchafe Corn and Rice for the Gromettas againft we came, that no Time might be loft, I intending to follow with the Ship the next Morning. This Evening the *James Ifland* Sloop came up and joyn'd us.

On the 5th, in the Morning, we left *Joar*, having taken in a Linguifter for *Barracunda*, *viz Tagrood Sanea* ; we alfo hir'd a Balafeu (which is a Country Mufician) to chear up the Men, and recreate them in an Evening At Eleven we anchor'd fhort of † *Yarine* River ene Mile. · Weighing again at Five in the Afternoon, at Eleven at Night we anchor'd between *Deer* Iflands. The River here is not above † 200 Yards over The North Channel on the other Side is wider, but not navigable for Ships From *Joar* hither the Country on each Side is fine low Marfhes for four or five Miles, free from Trees

The Ridge of Hills that rifes about *Joar* continues to tend to the Eaftward, at about two or three Leagues diftance from the River, they feem not to be fo high as *Highgate* Hills, are very woody, and inclining to a Red.　　　　　　　　I n

* This River, which he calls *Yarine*, is now known by the Name of *Europina*, there is alfo another River, not by him mention'd, call'd *Nany Jarr*, as appears by the Map.

† He means here but one Channel of the River, it being at this Place divided into many Channels by the Iflands which he mentions

1724

IN thefe Marfhes multitudes of wild Elephants are frequently feen, as well as wild Sea-
Horfes ; tho' as yet I have not feen one of
that Sort.

ON the 6th we weigh'd early in the Morning, and fent the Company's Linguifter, who
belongs to *Cutteyarr*, beforehand to *Caffan* to
buy a Cow. At Noon we anchor'd off *Yammarew*, and underftanding it to be the Anniverfary of his Grace the Duke of *Chandos*,
we this Afternoon drank his Grace's Health,
under a Difcharge of the Guns from my Ship
and the Sloop, alfo Profperity to the Company, and Succefs to the Expedition. Then
I went afhore with Mr *Hull*, &c and paid a
Vifit to the King of *Caffan*, who lives here at
Yammarew, and receiv'd us very civilly. We
gave him a Bottle of Rum, with which he was
well pleas'd. We took our Leave of him,
and Mr *Hull* and the Doctor employ'd themfelves in their Way, and I to my Gun for Diverfion. I prefently kill'd two Brace of *Guinea* Hens, and in the Evening we all return'd
on Board, and got under Sail, and anchor'd
again at Eleven at Night near a low Ifland
lying in the middle of the River, about one
Fourth of a Mile long, it being fo dark we
could not fee our Way. This Ifland is no
laid down in the Map which I had from the
Company, which makes me believe it is fince
made one by what is brought down by the
Frefhes, it lies about a League below *Bir-
Ifland.

Yammarew is the Place defign'd to fix a
Factory at, in cafe the King of *Barfally* doe
not make up the Palaver at *Joar*, 'tis a fine
Country

Country, and the Natives are very defirous the
Company fhould fettle among them.

A t this Port I obferv'd at our Landing three Sticks erected Gallows-ways, with a Calabafh cover'd and feal'd up, hanging on it by a String. On Enquiry I found it to be a *Domine*, *Fetifh*, or Charm to bring all White People afhore who come that Way ; which plainly fhews their Affection for us This Country is fine Champaign Land, and far preferable to *Joar*.

O n the 7th, at Eight this Morning, we got under Sail, paffing on the South Side of *Bird* Ifland, which is about two Miles long, with high Trees, and appears to be a fine Ifland ; 'tis nearest the Northern Shore. Juft beyond it is the Red Mount, bare of Trees, and half a League fhort of *Caffan*.

T h i s Hill is by the Natives call'd *Jerunk*, of which they tell a thoufand idle Stories , as, that once it had abundance of Gold, but that theDevil being angry, carried it all away in one Night It is a fmall round Hill about 20 Fathom high, and is very red and fteep, rifing directly from the River Side, towards which it is perfectly bare, producing nothing. I find by one of the Journals, that this Hill has been already examin'd. So we pafs'd by it and *Caffan* without ftopping (both Wind and Tide ferving) Beyond *Caffan* I obferve there are no Mangroves After I left *James* Ifland the Wind was almoft continually Eaftwardly, and when ever it began to veer from that Quarter it foon after fell calm.

T h e Mufquetoes continu'd very troublefome The Land on each Side of the River for half a Mile or more is generally fpeaking
ing

ing a fine fat Marſh, with very high Graſs and Reeds, in which are innumerable Tracks of River-Horſes, &c. This Creature is by the *Mundingoes* call'd *Malley* ; that Day I ſaw a great many, but all in the Water, in which they ſwim with only their Heads out, ſometimes blowing the Water up thro' their Noſtrils, not unlike a Whale, and often grunting and roaring hideouſly. Above the Marſhes it is a Champaign Riſing Land, with pretty large Trees, and moſtly free from Underwood In the Evening I kill'd a very large Bird, which eat extreamly well, it meaſur'd upwards of ſix Feet from its Toes to the Extremity of the Beak, and by the *Mundingoes* is call'd *Gibbon*, but by the *Portugueſe*, *Goſſreal*

ON the 8th, having a ſtrong Eaſtwardly Wind, and Neap Tides, we got little this Day by turning, but in the Night being calm, we tow'd thro' the South Channel, leaving *Sappo* Iſles on our Larboard Side. We anchor'd near the E. End of them. Theſe Iſlands have a Bar at each End, which choaks up the River almoſt, there not being above two Fathom and two and a quarter Water at the Ends in either Channel.

ON the 9th, the Wind blowing ſtrong and Eaſtwardly, we lay ſtill, not being able to paſs this Barr at the Eaſt End *Sappo* Iſlands till Midnight, and then tow'd thro' it, being very narrow. [*N. B* **Sappo** *Iſlands divide the River here into three or four Chanrels, which I take to be the reaſon of the Shoalneſs of the Water*] We tow'd half a Mile beyond the Iſlands, and then anchor'd, where for half way over the River is Rocks, which we waited for Day-light to paſs. In the Afternoon I
went

went afhore with feveral others with out Guns, and kill'd feveral *Guinea* Hens, Flamingoes, Crabcatchers, Kingfifhers and Doves. We faw abundance of River-Horfes In the Night the Interloper's Longboat (which was at *Joar*) pafs'd us, having been trading a-fhore at *Brucoe.*

On the 10th I weigh'd at Two in the Afternoon with a ftrong Gale at Eaft (right in our Teeth) and turn'd it up as high as *Germi*, anchoring at Six in the Evening We faw 40 or 50 Deer, feveral Crown-Birds, Ducks, Geefe, &c

On the 11th, at One in the Morning, be-ing calm, we weigh'd, and tow'd with the Boat, gaining more than in the Day. I fent the Linguifter before to buy a Cow at *Lemain*, afterwards I fent fome of our People afhore to kill fome Game. In two Hours they re-turn'd with eight *Guinea* Hens and a Partridge, which were then exceeding plentiful. We had very hot Winds in the Day, which poffibly may be caus'd by the multitude of Fires all round us, which makes the Country in the Night appear all in a Flame It being their Cuftom, every Year after the Corn is in, to burn the Stubble, which taking hold of the adjoyning high Grafs (which now is dry) burns into the Woods a great way on every fide, fcorching the Leaves of all the Trees it meets, and fometimes burns the Trees themfelves It is this which gives us the Opportunity of killing the *Guinea* Hens, &c and was it not for the great Cover they have, I believe where we kill one we might kill twenty, they abound in fuch multitudes.

AT

S

1724   A T Two in the Afternoon (Tide ferving) I weigh'd, and took in a Cow under Sail, as I pafs'd *Lemain*, it coft an Iron Barr. At Six in the Evening, being calm, we tow'd thro' *Phole*'s Pafs, anchoring at Seven about half a Mile above *Brucoe*

A T the *Pholey*'s Pafs there is a Ledge of Rocks, which extends from the North Side the River quite over to within 20 or 30 Yards of the other Side, leaving juft room for a Ship to pafs, yet not fo but the Ship brufhes the Trees.

O N the 12th, early in the Morning, I weigh'd, and in four Hours anchor'd at *Du- vocurdi*, to take in Rice and Corn, which having efected by Four in the Afternoon, I got up my Anchor, and tow'd about two Leagues, anchoring again fhort of *Preef*, once a Town, but now broke.

O N the 13th we got but little, the Winds blowing pretty ftrong right down, and the Flood-Tides running very flack We lay part of the Day at the Foot of a fmall Hill, call'd the *Dee's Mount* The River now grows fo narrow, that it is with difficulty we turn with the Ship againft the Wind, often running our Stern into the Bufhes, the Banks of the River being generally fteep too.

O N the 14th, in the Evening, I anchor'd at C——, and faluted the Factory with five Guns, which is fituated clofe to the River on the North Side I order'd my Ship to be moor'd in the middle of the River overagainf the Factory The Banks are fteep too, and three or four Fathom deep all over, it rifes ——t Feet at Spring-Tides, and flows, as at —— Ifard, North and South.

I O B-

I OBSERV'D at the Factory, that this last 1724. Seafon the Freshes rais'd or swell'd the River 14 Foot above the Level of high Water Mark now, by which it is evident a great deal of the Country must be overflow'd, altho' now very firm and good walking. Here in my Walks into the Woods, I found a great deal of that yellow Dying-Wood call'd *Bawtey*, as indeed there is almost every where, but as yet I have not been so successful as to find any other Wood or Simple worth mentioning (if this be). Indeed I never saw a Country yet more destitute of large and good Trees, having not met with any yet, out of which a Plank might be made 12 Feet long and 12 Inches broad * All large Trees hitherto are soft and worthless, such as Cabashiers, Cotton-Trees, &c fit only for Shade, and the Negroes to palaver under and drink Palm-Wine

On the 15th the King of *Catteba* (in whose Dominions *Cuttejarr* lies) visited the Factor on purpose to see the Ship, on Board which he afterwards went I saluted him with five Guns, and afterwards made him a handsome Present

---

* Mr *Stibbs* certainly had not been much on Shore, or else he could not have set down this Mistake, for there are Woods of large Trees in many Places on the River *Gambia*, between *James* Fort and *Cuttejarr*, particularly over-against *Brucoe* And there is hardly a *Mundingoe* Town without some very large Trees, which the Superstition of the People preserves, for they admire and dance under them, and pay Reverence to them They are generally Bisheloes, which is a very hard Wood, and good Timber Some of them are 12 or 14 Feet round, and I remember three at *Joar* that are at least 12 Feet each in Circumference, and near 30 Foot in the Clear before they come to the Boughs, and under those Trees the Chief Men us'd to sit and see the People exercise and dance

1724   Prefent of Coral, Amber, Brandy, &c. it being the firſt time of his coming ſince the Factory was ſettled. He came on Horſeback with two Drums before him, and about 20 Attendants, arm'd with Guns, Swords, Bows, Arrows and Javelins. He left moſt of his Attendants at *Samy*, and made an Excuſe for not bringing them here, becauſe he thought they would be troubleſome , which we were really glad of   He was an old Man, tall, thin, and very black, and left us very well ſatisfied *

Oɴ the 20th we made an End of cleaning our Corn and Rice, and at Night left *Cutte-jarr*, with the *James Iſland* Sloop and five Canoas, having firſt ſent the following Letter to *James* Fort, *viz*

To Meſſ. ORFEUR *and* ROGERS.

Gentlemen,   Cuttejarr, Jan. 20, 1737.

Oɴ Tueſday *laſt*, at Night, *being the* 14th *Inſtant, we arriv'd at the Company's Fac-tory here, all in good Health, excepting Captain* Trevifa, *who had a ſhort Relapſe of his late In-diſpoſition, and two of our Miners, but are now on the mending hand*   We reach'd Joar *the* 4th *Inſtant, where we met with the* Ruby, *Captain* Craigue, *who had then purchas'd but eleven* Saves. *The Captain had ſent his Long-Boat higher up with Mr* Baldwyn *to make Trade* He *went up as high as* Brucoe, *and bought ſix* Mun

dingoe

---

* I believe this was one of the Kings of *Yany*, whom they call *Catteba* , for at preſent there is no King of *Cat-teba*, and *Cuttejarr* lies in Lower *Yany* dingoe *Slaves, at the* † *extravagant Price of* 30 Barrs *per Head. He pass'd us on his Return about Twelve at Night on the 8th Instant, when we lay at anchor between the* Sappo *Isles, and was so civil as not to call on Board us*

We anchor'd on the 6th at the Port of Yani-marew, *and went on Shore there, it is a rising Ground close to the River, and is much preferable to* Joar, *as to its Situation and Healthfulness, for a Company's House to be settled there*

At Dubocunda *we met with an unlucky Disappointment, which not only retarded our Progress on the Expedition for six or seven Days, but has put us to the ill Convenience of loading our Canoas with Corn instead of Rice, which does not please our People so well, and takes up above one third more room in the Stowage, which we can but very ill spare The Slattee* D'foote *has (as we hear) a second time broke* Barracunda, *and has subdu'd all* Woolly, *he is now return'd to his Country for fresh Supplies to make new Conquests in these Parts We are inform'd of Slattee* Sane Conta Madebaugh *being now on the Road with a Coffle of 500 Slaves He has not been here since the Company's last settling in this River, and 'tis said, that he undertakes this Journey to make Tryal of what Encouragement he may expect to trade here for the future There is another Coffle or two on the Road, which we mention, that you may timely supply this Factory with what Goods may be wanted, and that your Instructions as to the Price of Slaves may be suitable to the danger of their falling into the* French

---

† The Price of Slaves augments daily, and what was then call'd an extravagant Price is now very low, for they are now generally sold for 50 or 60 Barrs *per* Head

S 3

1721. French or Interlopers Hands. *We cannot forbear acquainting you, that the want of due Supplies of Goods to this Factory has been no small Hindrance to the Trade thereof, but as that was not your Fault, we don't question but it will be better minded for the future*   Mr Franks *will give you an account of what Trade he has made, and what Goods are wanted for the carrying it on here.*

The Company's Ship Dispatch *will be left here with Captain* Stibbs's *Instructions for his Mate to act by during his Absence*

This Factory is pleasantly situated on a rising Ground, has a fine Prospect, a good Air, and deserves a much better Character than it has met with on the Fort, and is a much better Place of the two   We do not fear convincing the incredulous Part of the World, that the farther up this Country, provided it is high Land, it is still the more wholesome and moderate

We have no more to add, but that, tho' we are so late in the Year, we hope to make such Discoveries as will be very acceptable to the Company, that we shall depart hence this Tide, and to assure you that we are,

GENTLEMEN,

Your most humble Servant,

BARTH STIBBS,
E. DRUMMOND,
RICH HULL.

THE *Dispatch* Ship was left at *Cuttejar*, with sundry Stores, &c for the Settling of a new Factory at *Barracunda*, or above it, if upon Examination we should find it would answer.

anfwer   And on the 21ft, at Four in the Morning, we came to anchor about two Leag beyond *Cuttejarr*, about a Mile beyond *Lefi-Hill*, which in the Journal is call'd the *Maiden's Breaft*   I went up it with Mr *Hull*, and found it, as the Journal fays, compos'd of an Iron Stone (as all the High Lands we have feen are) but we have little reafon to believe that it contains either Gold or Silver, and Time being precious now, we intend to vifit it on our Return   This Hill takes its Name from the obfcene Superftition of the Natives, who never pafs it without fhowing their bare Breeches to it, with dancing, finging and clapping of Hands, believing that if they fhould omit it, they fhould furely die before they return.   Accordingly ours did the fame, which made us laugh heartily, and feeing we White Men omitted it, they perform'd it for us

At Eleven in the Morning, the Tide ferving, we got up our Anchor, and pafs'd by *Samy* River, which at prefent limits the *Portuguefe* Trade, they not daring to go higher at this Time by reafon of Palavers with the Natives.   This is a confiderable River on the North Side, running up as far as a Town call'd *Medina*   The Company had formerly a Factory here, and the Houfe is ftill ftanding.   We bought a Cow here, and procceded on our Voyage at Eleven at Night

On the 22d, at Five in the Morning, we anchor'd half a League fhort of *Crow*, and juft above a Ridge of Land of the ufual reddifh Colour, getting under Sail again at Two P M. and not getting above ten Miles, anchor'd chor'd at Seven this Evening, the Tides running very weak

THE Country continues for the moft part plain, with here and there a Ridge of Hills, which may be 20 Fathom high, and fometimes more, a rich Soil in the Low Land, and the Inhabitants now are moftly *Pho'*, a cleanly, decent, induftrious People, very affable, and far furpaffing the *Murdingoes*

ON the 23d, at Two in the Morning, we weigh'd, towing the Sloop with two Canoas, gaining more in the Night than in the Day, the Wind being right againft us   At this Time the Tides were fo flack, that we gain d little by turning, even the Ebbs are fo weak, that with the leaft Breath of a fair Wind we can go ahead   This makes me dubious there have been no great Rains up in the Country this laft Seafon, for the Current of the River at the beft now runs no fafter than a River in *Eng'and* in the Heighth of Summer, and indeed, were it not for the Sloop (provided there be Water enough) we fhould foon be at the Falls

AT Eight this Morning we anchor'd at *Tammeunda*, below which lie Rocks from the South-Side one third over the River, having not above four Foot Water over them   This Port is on the South Side of the River, but the Town, by reafon of Wars, is remov'd to the other Side.

IT having been a Cuftom to pay a Duty for all Veffels that pafs above this Port to the King of *Tomany*, who lives at *Sutimore*, to which Place this is the Port, and about a League diftant from it, it detain'd us here all Day to adjuft that Affair, we refolving to

pay

pay none, thinking it below the Dignity of the Royal Company to be put on the same Footing with private Traders (such as *Portuguese* and Interlopers.) We therefore came to this Agreement with them, that for the future they never expect or demand any Custom from the Royal Company. In Consideration of this Concession we made the King a Present to the Value of near 20 Barrs, not out of any Obligation, he being utterly unable to oblige it, but to keep up a good Name, which we find very Serviceable, and for the Honour of the Royal Company, whose Fame we find proceeds much faster up into the Country than we can with our Canoas

On the 24th, at Three in the Morning, we left *Tamyamacunda*, and at Night came to *Canuby* This Port is on the South Side, but the Town, for the same Reasons as *Tamyamacunda*, is transported overagainst it on the other Side the River We saw abundance of large Monkeys, which bark just like Dogs. We kill'd two Wild Geese and a Duck. The Geese have Spurs as long as our Cocks, growing out of the middle Joynt of the Wings, with which they'll beat a Dog They are larger than our Wild Geese, and feather'd black and white. The Duck was of a peculiar Kind, and near as big as the Geese, and feather'd like them, with small black Legs, Feet and Bill, and upon its Beak was a black Excrescence of Flesh an Inch and half high. They are fine Fowl, and eat deliciously

In the Evening we left *Canuby*, and having tow'd the Sloop three Leagues, about Eleven at Night came to an Anchor.

On

O n the 25th we got under Sail early, and about Eleven o' Clock anchor'd a little above *Baffy* Port, which is also on the South Side the River In the Evening we weigh'd again, and got up as high as *Nackway*, which Port lies on the North Side of the River, the Town is half a Mile from it, inhabited chiefly by *Mahometans*, half a Mile from the Port on the fame Side the River is a Hill about 30 Fathom high, with a red Snagg hanging over the River.

O n the 26th the Wind blow'd ftrong Eafterly, fo that we proceeded up but flowly At Night we got fix Leagues above *Nackua*, to a Place call'd *Caffancunda*, having in our Way feen many Deers, Monkeys, Crown-Birds, Ducks, Geefe, *Guinea* Hens, Partridges, &c

O n the 28th, at Noon, we anchor'd at *Fatatenda* This Port, like many others, has not a Houfe near it, ferving only for a Landing-Place to fome Town * This is the Port to *Suteco*, about three Leagues from it, but the Town the King of *Woolly* lives in, is 30 Miles from it, call'd *Cuffana*

A s foon as we came to anchor, I caus'd the Sloop to fire five Guns as a Signal to Slattee *Mamadu*, who promis'd to meet us here, and bring us a Man to pilot us as high as the Falls But left he fhould not hear the Guns, we alfo fent our Linguifter to *Suteo* to acquaint him that we were arriv'd at *Fatatenda.* In the Evening Slattee *Mamadu* came

on

* Since the writing this Journal, *viz* in the Year 1732, the Company have fettled a Factory, and had a Houfe built upon the Rock above the Port, by reafon of the Convenience of its Situation for Trade

on Board, but without the Pilot, who was
fick   Here we learn'd that *Barracunda* hath
been lately broke or deftroy'd ; however we
refolv'd to leave the Sloop there to trade   In
all our Enquiries it is evident, that there is
no Body here knows any thing of the River
above *Barracunda.*   Some think it to be the
End of the World, others that it is a large
Wildernefs full of Wild Beafts , others tell
you that there is a Wild Savage People, and
advis'd us to ftay with them, and not to go
higher up   In fhort, no one can give any
juft Account of either Town or Port above
it, ‖ and altho' Slattee *Mamadu* knows, and
has moft of his Relations living there, yet he
knows not how far it is from *Barracunda* by
Water   All confirm that there is nothing to
be bought above it, fo we refolv'd to take
in fome Rice at *Piye*, where it is faid to be
cheap and plentiful   I fhall now defcribe the
Patce Sangue, or Bloodwood, fo call'd from
a Red Gum which iffues from it , it grows
plentifully all up the River, but here at *Fa-
trenda* it is larger than ordinary, and by the
Mundingoes call'd *Cano*, of which they make
the *Balafeu*, a Mufical Inftrument   It is a
very hard Wood, of a beautiful Grain, and
polifhes finely, very proper for Efcrutores, or
Inlaying, and they fay that the *Buggabuggs*
never

‖ The Natives are defirous of trading with White People, and of buying all their Commodities, that they might
fell them up into the Country , therefore it being for the
Advantage of the Black People about *Fatatenda* to prevent
the White Men going farther up the River they gave out
fuch Reports as they thought would incourage them   And
this is very frequent amongft them , for if the Account at
I could hear from difinterefted Natives agree with what *Leo
the African* fays relating to the Countries up the River.

1724. never touch it This Tree does not grow to any great Height or Size, so that it is not easy to find one that will produce a Plank upwards of 14 or 16 Inches broad, when first cut it has an agreeable Smell, it grows generally in a dry Rocky Soil, and against and on the Tops of Hills *

ON the 29th, about One in the Morning, we left *Fatatenda*, and in about five Hours anchor'd at *Prye*, with an Intention to buy Corn and Rice, it being agreed on all Hands that there is no sort of Eatables to be purchas'd above *Barracunda* But there is hardly any Credit to be given to what these People relate, for almost every Port up the River, they to whom it belongs had much rather we should stay and trade amongst them, than go farther up, and in order to induce us to it, they give a dismal Account of the Country above, and of the Barbarity of the People there

THIS Port lies about three Leagues above *Fatatenda*, on the South Side the River, in *Cantore*, having no Town nor House within two or three Miles of it Here is a fine Rivulet, whose Sands we search'd, sending our small Canoa in for that purpose, which by reason of sunken Trees, &c. could not go far In it we caught some small Fish like Smelts, and one large Prawn, but the sunken Trees render'd our Nets useless almost, as they have hitherto the Banks of the River *Gambia*, in which the Fish appear to be very numerous.

Ov

---

* It is this Tree which produces the *Gum Dragon* of which there is more said in the former Journal, and which is capable of being made a very advantageous Branch of Trade.

On the 31ſt, finding (contrary to Expectation) but little Rice or Corn here, having in
all this time purchas'd no more than four
Barrels, we left the Port, and came to anchor about eight Miles above it.

On the 1ſt of *February*, at Two in the *February*.
Morning, we proceeded, towing the Sloop,
and in five Hours anchor'd at *Samatenda*,
which is on the South Side. Here I found
the River to be 134 Yards over, and the
Banks about 20 Feet high. I now find the
River begin to have ſunken Trees almoſt all
over it. Here the Land is low on the South
Side, but on the North Side a riſing Ground,
which a League beyond the Port forms a high
Hill, running near two Miles cloſe to the
River. In the Afternoon we weigh'd from
Samatenda, which is only a Port, where is a
ſmall Canoa to ferry over the River, with
neither Town nor Houſe near it. At Eight
at Night we came to an Anchor eight Miles
beyond it, being entertain'd with the hideous
Noiſes of Elephants, River-Horſes and Allegators, all Night.

On the 2d, at Three in the Morning, we
jogg'd on till Seven, and then anchor'd a little above *Couſſar* Port, which is likewiſe deſtitute of Houſes or Town near the River Here
I firſt obſerv'd, that for want of a Canoa they
ferry over the River on a Bark Logg, or Float
made of Bamboos (Canes), on one of theſe I
ſaw four Men croſs the River at once.

About four Miles before you come to
this Port is a Sand, which extends from the
South Side almoſt acroſs the River, on which
is not above four or five Feet Water.

I 2

I n the Afternoon we proceeded higher, the Flood makes up but very little, altho' by the Shore it flows near two Feet. Soon after we pass'd by another Port on the South Side call'd *Yabutenda*, about a League from *Cuffane* Port, between which two Places it is in a manner one continu'd high Hill, rifing directly from the River. On the North Side it is a large Savannah, in which is a great Lake.

Having gain'd about eight Miles, I anchor'd at Eight at Night in eleven Feet of Water, having juft got over a Shoal, which ftretches from the North Side three quarters over, on which was from four to feven Feet Water. The reft of the River was an Overfall of Rocks (on the South Side) between which in fome Places were ten Feet Water, but on them not above three or four Feet.

On the 3d, at Three in the Morning, we went on our Voyage, and at Eight came to an Anchor in two Fathom and a half Water, about a League fhort of *Barracunda* Port About Four in the Afternoon we weigh'd again, and in an Hour's time anchor'd at *Barracunda* Port, which is on the North Side Here I meafur'd the River, and found it 150 Yards over, Depth of Water between two and three Fathom, and the Banks above 25 Feet high.

Had it not been for our Pilot, 'tis certain we fhould never have guefs'd this Place to have been the Port of *Barracunda*, or that it ever had been a Port or Place of Trade, fo wild is it grown fince the Deftruction of the Town, that at prefent there is not fo much as a Ferry, which is common to all other Ports that we have met with. I went all over

to fee if there were any Veftigia or Remains
of this once famous Trading Town, and to
view the Country.　Immediately on my Landing I found the frefh Footfteps and Excrements
of Elephants (which made me guefs they were
not far off.)　Afcending the Banks the Pilot
fhew'd me where the Town ftood, which at
prefent hath hardly any thing like the Ruins
of Houfes.　On the Tops of the Banks were
vifible feveral Places where Victuals had been
crefs'd, and round about it the Remainder of
their Dainties, *viz* the Skulls and Bones of
River-Horfes, Allegators and Fifh, the two
former of which, as well as Elephants, I obferve the Natives are paffionate Admirers of.
I having my Gun, as ufual, advanc'd a little
way in amongft the high Grafs, which was
12 or 14 Feet high, but as dry as Hay, and
burns (if fet on fire) with great vehemence.
Finding a Tree I mounted it to take a Profpect of the adjacent Country, when I prefently difcover'd a wild Elephant not above
200 Yards from me, flowly walking into the
Country.　It was a very fpacious Plain, with
very few Trees, for above four Miles from
the River, there being nothing like a Hill all
round to be feen　In fhort, it is the largeft
Tract of plain Land that I have yet feen,
tho' it is to be obferv'd it rifes gently inland.

As it was our Defign to leave the *James
Ifland* Sloop there to trade under Capt. *Trevi-
la's* Care, we alfo judg'd it neceffary to ftay
till the Alcade came down to fettle the Palaver, that there might be no Difference or Difpute when we were gone　On our anchoring I caus'd feveral Guns to be fir'd, to give
notice to the Country of our Arrival.　In the
Night-

Night-time we could hardly fleep for the horrible Noifes of the River-Horfes, Allegators, Wolves, and other wild Beafts.

On the 4th, in the Morning, we fent our Linguifter with a Grometta to find out the Alcade, whom as yet we had not feen In the Afternoon he came back, and the Alcade with him, who had not heard our Guns. He told us there were feveral Merchants w th Slaves, Gold and Teeth, at *Jah*, the Town from whence he came, and where he lives, which is about nine Miles off, and where the People of *Barracunda* live fince their Town was broke.

At Noon our Linguifter and hired Servants came in a Body to inform us that they would go no farther, becaufe no Body ever was higher up the River, and that *Barracunda* was look'd upon as the End of the World The moft fenfible of them faid, that if there were a Country beyond, that it was a very barbarous one, and befides that, they underftood that we intended to go afterwards over Land in queft of Gold Mines, and that we would oblige them to go along with us After a bundance of ridiculous Stories, which equally fhew'd their Ignorance and Fear both of the People and Country beyond this Place, we prevail'd with them to go as far by Water as we did, and no farther So the Palaver concluded with a never failing reconciling Bottle of Brandy

On the 5th, in the Afternoon, the Merchants came down, and after a long Difpute we found ourfelves under a Neceffity of contracting with them for ten Slaves, at 23 Barr *per* Head, or elfe they would not fell us their
Gold

Gold and Teeth, which 'twas our Defign only
to buy, till our Return, by reafon we had not
Conveniences for Slaves till then But what
was a further Inducement, on our buying
thefe Slaves, one of the Merchants, named
Gije, had promis'd to go up the River with
us as far as *Tinda*, (where he lives) by which
means we fhould have the Opportunity of knowing the Country on both Sides the River, which
otherwife is impoffible, there being no fuch
thing as a Pilot to be got In the Afternoon
in Council we drew up a Letter, and fent it
to *James* Fort by a Land-Meffenger by way
of *Cuitejari*

ON the 6th, underftanding there was a
Town oppofite to us on the *Cantore* Side, not
bove four Miles diftance, we the Day before
fent to compliment the Alcade of it with a
Bottle of Rum, in return of which he fent us
a Cow, for which we afterwards prefented
him with a Barr of Iron Of the ten Slaves
we the Day before contracted for, we were able
to purchafe but three, chiefly owing to the
Badnefs of our Goods. And by our not purchafing them ten Slaves, we loft the Opportunity of having *Gaje* the Merchant with us,
at which I was very much concern'd, as having no Body that ever was above that Place

OUR Huntfman, whilft we lay here, fhot
a Fallow Deer, by the *Mundingoes* call'd *Ton-
cng*, it had nothing in its Form and Make
uncommon with our *Englifh* ones, but its
Horns and Size were very extraordinary, being as big as a fmall Horfe, and weigh'd (I
believe) 300 Pounds On its Neck it had a
black Lift or Mane four or five Inches long,
which ftood erected. On opening its Head,

T I

I found the Brains full of large Maggots two Inches long, and as thick as my little Finger, altho' it had not been dead above half an Hour, so consequently were there whilst living. The Flesh of it was very sweet and good

OUR Affairs being ended, we left *Barracunda* on the 6th at Night with the five Canoas, leaving the *James Island* Sloop there with Capt. *Trevisa* to trade In three Hours time we anchor'd about two Leagues above it, and the next Morning we weigh'd again, and in half an Hour's time ran aground in the middle of the River. I found near seven Foot Water on the South Side, where I pass'd, and a League farther we came to an Overfall, extending quite over the River, which took me up the greatest part of this Day to get the Canoas over This Overfall is not above three Leagues above *Barracunda* (being the first I have met) and is compos'd of Rocks in the following manner.

FROM the North Side of the River runs a solid Bed of Rocks one third over, having a pretty smooth and equal Superficies, and at this time near 10 Feet above the Water of the River, its Extremity at this time being perpendicular by reason of the Lowness of the Water, is become the North Bank, or Bounds of the River It was close to this Side that I found a Passage, and a very strait one, for our Canoas rubbed the Rocks on both Sides From the South Side, for above one third across the River, was another plain and equal Bed of Rocks. but with this Difference, that this was under Water about ten Inches, over which at Low Water the Current ran with great Force Between these two Beds

o

of Rocks, the reft of the River was choak'd up with large fingle Rocks, interfpers'd in fuch a manner, with not above a Foot of Water upon them (altho' between them was 10, 11, and 12 Foot Water) as render'd a Paffage betwixt them impoffible It was High Water before I could get thro', and altho' it flow'd here not above eight Inches, it gave me great Facility in finding the Paffage , for at High Water it check'd the Force of the Current, fo as to render the Water ftagnant, altho' it was the Neap-Tides: So that with great Eafe we walk'd upon it, and alfo from the adjacent Rocks on the Noith Sde (the Water being very clear) we could very plainly fee where the Paffage lay † This at low Water was impoffible, the Current ran fo violently with fuch Whirlings and Eddies over and amongft the Rocks. At this Overfall I meafur'd the River, and found it 160 Yards over betwixt its proper Banks ; but at prefent the Water runs in the Compafs of 100, and in all probability three Months hence will not take up above 50 Below this Overfall I found three and four Fathom Water, and juft above one Fathom and half, and between in Breadth it was about 20 Yards over. I proceeded up the River at Five in the Evening, and found about half a Mile above the Overfall a large Rock cover'd with Oyfters, very fat, but infipid At Eight at Night we came to a Ford , it was a Quickfand, about two Leagues above the Overfall, not above four Foot deep in the deepeft Part At Nine I anchor'd in eight Foot Water, and

T 2　　　　lay

† It is very remarkab'e, that the Tide flows fo far up the River *Gambia*, there being no other River, that I ever heard of, where the Tide flows up fo far from the Sea

1724.   lay there all Night; the River-Horfes very numerous, fo that it is difficult fleeping for their hideous Noifes; befides, they now grew fo bold, that we fometimes fir'd a Mufquet at them to make them keep farther off, left we fhould receive damage in our Canoas from them, for they are fometimes fo large, that in paffing under the Canoas there may not be room enough, on which they immediately ftrike their Teeth thro' the Bottom, and endanger the prefent finking

On the 8th, at Six in the Morning, we went on, the River growing fo fhoal now, that there's no paffing far by Night Soon after we met with another Flat or Ford It was Sand, and on the deepeft Part had but three Foot and half By Nine, not being come above a League, I came to a Fla, which I found barr'd the River from Side to Side It was a Sand with many dry Patches appearing here and there all over the River After fome time trying ineffectually to pafs, I brought the Canoas to a proper Place. and then afcended the Banks, which here were near 40 Foot high. Upon viewing it, I found the Flat to run up the River for above half a Mile, being Overfalls of Sand Banks, fo intended to fearch diligently for a Paffage betwix them. This Flat is near fix Leagues above *Barracunda*, I found the River here by mea fure 170 Yards over, which great Breadth the Occafion of the Shallows. I now found the Mufquetoes not only very troublefome by Night, but a large Fly, call'd an Liephan Fly, or *Jolloiff* Fly, worfe by Day

On the 9th I try'd again, caufing my Peo ple with Poles in their Hands to walk all over
         the

the River, not omitting any one Channel between the dry Sand-Banks, but higher up we found less Water, *viz* 26 Inches Upon which we resolv'd to proceed up higher with the three smallest Canoas, and leave the two greatest there, with proper Orders.

On the 10th I endeavour'd again, with the *Gambia* Canoa, to find a Passage amongst the Sands, but to no effect, altho' the Canoa drew but 16 Inches Water: For the Sand being quick, runs from under our Feet, so as to render it impossible to hawl with the one tenth of our Strength I afterwards, with Mr *Hull*, &c went ashore with design to try the Hill call'd in the Journal *Matlock Tar*, which is at the upper end of this whole Reach, about a Mile and half off, but before we had got half way, we were drove back in great disorder by a wild Elephant. In the Evening one of the Natives came to us with some Fowls, who told us, that after we pass'd this Place, we could not proceed much farther, however we resolv'd to try, not much minding their idle Reports.

On the 11th we unloaded the *Discovery* Canoa, causing every individual thing to be taken out of her (it being our least Canoa) she then drew but 12 Inches, with which to Morrow early we design to hawl over the Flats, to make some farther Discovery, whilst the other Canoas stay here to wait for the Spring-Tides, and then, if it be possible, to follow.

On the 12th, I being out of Order and Feverish, Mr *Drummond* and Mr *Hull* set out in the Canoa, and by the Assistance of all our

Gro-

T 3

1724 Gromettas they got her over the Flats, and then fent me the following Letter, *viz.*

To Capt B A R T. S T I B B S.

Dear S I R,   Feb 12, 1724

THIS acquaints you, that we are got paſt the Flats   The Carpenter is in purſuit of a wounded Elephant, which paſs'd the River juſt above us, when we were firſt aground   I deſire you to order my Boy to ſend me a Pair of Trowſers, that I may have a Change when I get out to help the Canoa along.   I am

Yours, *&c*

RICH. HULL.

THE ſame Evening I receiv'd the following Letter alſo from them, *viz.*

Dear S I R,   On *Matlock Tar*, Feb 12, 1724.

WE can't forbear adviſing you of our good Proſpect of ſucceeding.   We have not met with leſs than ſix Feet Water ſince we paſs'd the Flats   We ſhall proceed in the Evening   In the mean time we wiſh you better Health, and that you may be able to follow us.   The next Reach promiſes well, and we have had from ſix to eighteen Foot Water, and we gueſs the River ſixty or ſeventy Yards over.   We remain

Yours, *&c*

E DRUMMOND
RICH. HULL.

O

 O n the 13th, at Noon, I receiv'd a Letter
from Capt *Trevisa* at *Barracunda*, dated this
Morning (we being hardly six Leagues above
it) giving me an Account that no manner of
Trade hardly had offer'd since we left him,
nor any Provision, so that he should be necef-
fitated to fall down the River to some other
Place to procure it both for himself and
Slaves

I n the Afternoon I receiv'd another Letter
from Mr *Drummond* and Mr *Hull*, who were
about two Leagues and half higher up, *viz.*

Dear S I R,   Feb 13, Eleven o'Clock, 1734

W E left Matloc Tar *about Four yesterday
afternoon, and about a League up met
with another Flat of Sands, and an Overfall of
Rocks. After some Trial to get over (the Night
coming on) we were oblig'd to put back a little
for deeper Water, and to wait for the next Day
to make a farther Attempt, which was so successful that we row'd thro' without touching either
Sands or Rocks, in four and six Feet Water in
the middle of the River, and met with deep
Water to this Place, where are some Sand-Banks,
one our Rudder just fix'd on, but going towards
the middle we met with three Feet Water. The
Natives here tell us, that there are Rocks in the
next Reach that will hinder our Passage up
higher, but we can't always credit these People
We are resolv'd to proceed in three or four Hours.
We design to get to* Yoik River *before we shall
think of returning, whereby we may judge of the
Possibility of doing any thing this Season We
have found the South Shore steep too for the greatest Part We should have enlarged, but the Elephants are so numerous, and make such a hideous*

T 4   Noye,

Note, that we do not think it safe, for fear of their doing some mischief either to us, our small Stock of Stores, or to our Canoa. Besides, our Stock of Powder and Shot will not allow us to be but on the defensive Part only So say no more, than that we are under a green Shade by the River side drinking your Health, and good Success to the Expedition, about two Leagues below Matlock Tar We are

Your most humble Servants,

E. DRUMMOND,
RICH. HULL

ON the 14th I receiv'd Letters from *Cape Coast*, dated the 11th Instant, which advise me, that no News was arriv'd from *James* Fort since we left that Place, and that my Ship's Crew was very sickly

THE Moon changing yesterday, I found the Tide to rise here six Inches, flowing East and West, but the Flood never ran up, it only became slack Water. By this litting of the Water I am in hopes to get most of the Canoas over At this Flat we have taken up some of the Sands in various Places, in order for Trial at Leisure

ON the 15th, in the Morning, Mr *Drummond* and Mr *Hull* return'd, having been about six Leagues up, and report they found the River, generally speaking, deeper and better On which Encouragement, it being the highest Tides, I resolv'd to unload the *Royal Africa*, and endeavour, if possible, to get her over, and then proceed with that and two more

ON the 16th, finding it impossible to pass the Flats with the Royal *Africa*, I reladed her, and

and got the *Gambia* ready to proceed on the Morrow with the *Discovery*, defigning to go myfelf, being bravely recover'd Our Gromettas and Linguifter abfolutely refufing to go any higher, we refolv'd, as foon as we were gone, that Mr *Drummond* go directly to *Barracunda* with the three Canoas, and there difcharge them.

On the 17th, in the Morning, I took the Opportunity of High Water to fend the Canoas over the Flats. At Ten Mr *Hull* and myfelf went with two White Men, and fet out in the two Canoas *Gambia* and *Difcovery*, mann'd with ten *Cape Coaft* Slaves belonging to the Company, and one Woman and two Boys, intending to proceed as high as poffible, leaving Mr *Drummond* to return to *Barracunda* with the other three Canoas. At Noon we put afhore on the South Side to drefs our Victuals, and to avoid the fcorching Heats of the Sun, having pafs'd not above a League from where we fet out, by reafon of our having pafs'd another Flat of Sand and Rocks in the next Reach beyond *Matlock Tar*, on which was not two Feet Water At this Overfall was a Bark Logg or Sellilefs to pafs over to a Town on the *Cantore* Side, about three Miles off, call'd *Curbambey* · It is behind the Hill which the Journal calls *Matlock Tar*, for what reafon I know not, for on Examination it gives no more Encouragement than others we have tried before We left this Place at Four, and at Nine at Night anchor'd in five Feet Water in the middle of the River, having come ten Miles, and paffing almoft in every Reach fome Flat or Ford from two to three and four Feet, by which means the

River

River is now in a manner fordable all the Way up. Here it may not be improper to hint at the Reasons our *Mundingo* Gromettas broach'd and gave out for going no farther, *viz* That the Natives were combining to cut us off. This fome, that had been fent a little Way into the Country to buy us Fowls and Eggs, faid they overheard as they flept in their Houfes. But I rather believe it of their own forging, from their Fear and Unwillingnefs to proceed any farther ; for we found, where-ever we put afhore, fome or other coming to us with a Fowl or two, *&c* and by their Behaviour feem to be an inoffenfive People, but, however, I always kept myfelf on my Guard for fear of the worft.

On the 18th, at Six in the Morning, we went on our Way, and foon after pafs'd a fteep Hill on the South Side clofe to the River. Mr *Hull* and I went upon it, and had a fine Survey of the Country, and could perceive the Deer feeding all round, and the River-Horfes fporting on the Banks and in the Water in great Numbers. About a Mile beyond this Hill is a Port on the fame Side, call'd *Simmetenda*, with a Bark Logg to pafs over to *Tendecunda*, which is the Town to this Port, and is diftant about two or three Miles from it on the *Cantore* Side. Juft beyond this Port I found the River to run in the narroweft Compafs I have yet met with, *viz* 42 Yards, but it was feven Foot deep all over, altho' it meafur'd 133 Yards from Bank to Bank, but on the North Side at prefent it was all a dry Sand-Bank. At Eleven we faw five large Elephants ford over the River not above half a Mile from us. In paffing this Ford I
found

found in the fhoaleft Place but 16 Inches Water, as foon as we were over we put afhore to refrefh ourfelves and drefs our Victuals, having come two Leagues Afterwards we faw two Negroes ford it over, who brought us Fowls. At Five in the Evening we pafs'd on, and a League farther we came to a Hill on the South Side, fteep to the River, which here takes a fudden fhort Turn to the Eaftward. This Hill I believe was 80 Fathom high I obferved, that in this River is plenty of a kind of Turtle, which in *America* is call'd * *Heccatey* They are very good Food, and peculiar to frefh-water Rivers and Lakes At Nine at Night I anchor'd in 14 Feet Water, having come fince Dinner eight Miles.

ON the 19th, at Six in the Morning, we went on thro' a long, but very fhoaly Reach, on the North Side is a high Hill. I now obferv'd, that the Willow-Tree (the fame which grows by Rivers in *England*) is become very plentiful all along the Banks of the *Gambia* ; alfo abundance of Tobacco, but this is planted by the Natives, not growing wild, as *Vermuyden* in his Journal afferts.

AMONGST thofe Willows, and upon the Water, we found a great many large Ducks; and altho' they fly very well, yet will they not take the Wing till you fire at them, and fometimes not then, for if they are in the Water they moftly chufe to dive Thefe Ducks are both good Food and good Diverfion ; for fometimes 40 or 50 of them will

run

---

* Turtles call'd *Heccatey*, which generally engender in frefh water Lakes, which makes it probable, that there were fome Lakes not far from thence

run along the Sides of the Banks one after another for an Hour together among the Willow-Trees, and so fast as to put us heartily to it to row up with them They are of a peculiar Kind, and take more delight in running along the Banks, than in flying or diving

AT Noon I stopt at a narrow Pass, which I measur'd, and found the Water to run in the Breadth of 58 Yards, and six Feet deep. This is an Overfall, but happen'd to have this clear Channel about the middle, in which at present the Water ran, for on the North Side it is a Ledge of Rocks near half way over, which are now eight or nine Foot above Water, and the South Side is a large dry Sand. We saw vast Companies of very large Baboons. In the Afternoon we pais d on about a League, and meeting fresh Shoals were oblig'd to put back a little for deep Water to anchor in, and wait for Day-light to find a Passage. I chose always to anchor in deep Water, and the middle of the River, if possible, for fear of Accidents.

ON the 20th, by Nine in the Morning, with great Labour and Difficulty I got both Canoas over these Flats and Quicksands, having not more than 12 and 14 Inches Water. About an Hour afterwards I put ashore to refresh ourselves, right against a high Hill, steep to the River on the South Side, having come not above a League from the Shoals. The Natives still follow'd us with Edibles; but as yet neither Tooth nor Slave has been offer'd to us They ford the River after us, be on which Side we will At Four in the Afternoon we went on about a League, and then found more Flats and Sands, which I try'd in vain to pass till 'twas dark, fo went back to deeper Water, and lay all Night   At thefe Flats is a high Hill on the North Side clofe to the River, and on the other Side a large Savannah.

On the 21ft I began early in the Morning to fearch for a Channel all over thofe Flats, and at the fame time fent *John Hodges* with a Cape-Coafter up the River by Land, giving him Orders to go at leaft four Leagues up by the Banks of the River in fearch of *York* River, which the Journalift of *Anno* 1661 mentions to be but 17 Leagues above *Bar-racunda*, altho' I reckon'd myfelf near 20 Leagues above it already   I endeavour'd till Noon with all my People to find a Channel, but in vain, and Experience proves it impracticable to hawl over it, being a Quickfand, which prefently finks from under our Feet with a great Suction, which renders it very difficult to hawl ourfelves out.   The Natives continu'd ftill to vifit us; and all affure us we are too late, tho' we get over here, to get to *Tinda*, inviting us to fettle mongft them, and then they would kill Elephants (which are here very numerous) and bring us Trade, for at prefent I obferv'd they had none.   They all in general affure us, there is no paffing much farther till next Rains, and then if we came again, they would go with us to *Tinda*, which by Land is but a fmall Day's Journey from hence

I WAS in hopes of *John Hodges*'s finding *York* River, from fome imperfect Notions I had from the Natives of a River they call *Cabong*, but on his Return in the Evening, he having been

1724. been between four and five Leagues up, he acquainted me that no Rivers run into this from either Side but what are dry, of which kind I had myself lately met with several. I made another Attempt in the Evening to find a Channel, but to no effect; which makes me now give credit to what the Natives said, which is confirm'd by *Hodges*, who had forded the River that Day a great many times Besides, I find myself the Flats grow more numerous, and have less Water daily, the River being fordable now at every half Mile Here by Measure the River was 160 Yards over, which occasions its Shallowness, the Water expanding and running over the greatest Part of it, excepting here and there a Patch I observ'd the Water here to rise two Inches by the Shore, but the Stream always runs down

THE Country on *Cantore* Side is populous, with small Towns here and there, but none within a League of the River, but on the other Side are no Towns or Inhabitants till you come to *Tinda*.

ON the 22d we tried again very carefully, and after all our Endeavours could find but 10 Inches Water in the deepest Part Finding the Impossibility of proceeding higher this Season, Mr *Hull* and I with Reluctance resolv'd to return ‖ So at Noon we set out, and by Night were got 10 Miles down, and then

♭ Mr *Stibbs* at this Fall gave over his Discovery, and return'd for *James* Fort There were several Reasons to discourage him, for besides the Heat and excessive Labour of rowing up against the Stream, there were the Reports of the Natives, that the River was too shallow to go up to *Tinda* that Year And this was confirm'd by the Tracts made at this Fall.

then anchor'd, being under a Neceſſity of lying ſtill all Night to paſs ſome Flats, which
cannot be done but in the Day time

THOSE Flats and Shoals which ſtopp'd us
lie 59 Miles above *Barracunda*, at the upper
End of a Reach which lies E. N. E. and
where the River turns ſhort at once to South.
On the North Side is a high Hill cloſe to the
River, and on the South is a large Savannah.
Here we tried the Hill and Watergullies, and
took up of the Sands with great Exactneſs,
in order for Trial, as indeed we did at all
Places

THEREABOUTS are great Stocks of diverſe
Sorts of Game, particularly Rock Partridges:
I call them ſo, as being moſtly amongſt Rocks
and Precipices. They are of a dark-ſpeckled
Colour, having a round Snuff-colour'd Spot
on the Breaſt about as big as a Half Crown,
the Legs and Beak are red, as alſo a Circle
about the Eyes, juſt as ſome Pigeons have;
they are not altogether ſo big as Partridges,
but in Shape exactly like them and run as faſt,
only then this erects the Tail, and appears
like a large Chicken. They are exceeding
fine Meat, but difficult to kill.

I OBSERVE too, that the higher up the
River, the more numerous and bold are the
River-Horſes, particularly in ſuch Reaches
where are ſhoal Patches of Sand, and deep
Water between them, into which they plunge
and hide, after you diſturb them napping on
the Sands · I have often ſhot them ſo as to
ſtain the Water with their Blood, yet they
always got away, riſing afterwards at ſome
diſtance, blowing up the Water, grating their
Teeth, and roaring at us with great Anger,
　　　　　　　　　　　　　　　　　　and

and a hideous Noife I hope ftill to have an Opportunity of furveying a dead one, that I might be able to give a juft and exact Defcription of them. *Pomet's* Defcription of them is the beft extant, for *Lemery* is much out when he affirms them to eat Men, Women, *&c.* they living only on Grafs, which is vifible by the Excrements. I have feen one o thefe Creatures (as I take it) preferv'd in th *Dutch* Repofitory at the Cape of *Good Hope*, but I was not fo curious then as to make any Remarks.

I cannot forbear taking notice here, that in the Journal *Anno* 1661, the Author toc notice but of two Hills between *Barraca* and *York* River, and them both on the South Side, when I have found fix, *viz* two on the North Side, and four on the South. No can I fee any reafon for his only mentioning two, and omitting the reft.

On the 23d, at Eight in the Morning, I got over the Flats, and at Five in the Afternoon pafs'd by *Simmetenda*, anchoring a Eight at Night, right againft a fmall reddifh Mount on the North Side, which we intend to examine to-morrow. We have this D come fix Leagues

On the 24th, in the Morning, we pafs on, having firft examin'd the Mount, and brought away a Specimen for Trial This Mount lies eight Leagues above *Barracana* By Noon we got to *Matlock Tar*, and pafs'd the Flats with no fmall Labour and Pains, anchoring at Nine at Night juft above the great Overfall, which lies near three Leagues above *Barracanda*, being oblig'd to wait for Day-light and high Water to pafs it, it roaring

ing almoſt like *London-Bridge* at Low Water
We came that Day ſix Leagues. I kill'd a
Guara five Foot long.

On the 25th, at Day-break, we paſs'd the
Overfall, and at Nine got to *Barracunda,*
where I found Mr *Drummond*, with the *James
Iſland* Sloop, and the reſt of the Canoas, all
well Here we found Letters from Mr *Plunket* the new Governor, who arriv'd at *James
Iſland* the 1ſt Inſtant, and brought ſeveral
Alterations in the Eſtabliſhment, Mr *Drummond* being made Second Chief Merchant,
Mr *Rogers* Third, and Mr *Hull* of the Council, &c. Captain *Treuga* had bought but
five Slaves, and a little Teeth and Gold,
while we were away from him Mr *Plunkett*
writing very preſſingly for the Ship *Diſpatch,*
it was reſolv'd in Council to proceed this E-
vening directly to *James* Fort I ſhall here
inſert his Letter, and Mr *Drummond*s Anſwer, &c

To Capt. BARTH. STIBBS, *Meſſieurs* EDW. DRUMMOND
and RICH. HULL.

Gentlemen, JAMES Fort, Feb. 10, 1724.

I Peruſed yours of the 20th ult. from Cuttejarr to *Meſſieurs* Orfeur *and* Rogers, *and
am* glad to hear you are all in a good State of
Health, and proceeding on your intended Expedition, which I pray God continue, and grant you
Succeſs in the ſame.

The accompanying Letters I brought from
England for the Gentlemen on the Expedition,
which we have order'd Mr Franks to forward
to you with all convenient ſpeed

V Upon

Upon my Departure from England *I expe.. d,
.n cafe you proceeded before my Arrival, to leave
found the Ship* Difpatch *at* James Fort, .
found to the contrary, t at fre had Orders to .
at* Cuttejarr *ti l you return from the Expea on.
What Prudence c as acted in that Man gement,
I leave to your Confideration, and whether .
was not more proper for her to be left here, n
order to purchafe a Cargo for her Return to* England, *or Trading for any Ships that may come
confign'd to us, tlan lie there as an addation l
Charge for the Expedition, without any Proj .
of Advantage We therefore in Council have
thought fit to order you Capt* Bartholomew Stibbs,
Meffieurs Edward Drummond *and* Richard
Hull, *to fend Orders to the prefent M .. .
the faid Sttip, to bring to us of* James Fort .
faid Ship Difpatch, *w th what Trade .. .
made by the Sloop, as alfo what it may be .
Factory at* Cuttejarr, *t at we may keep . . .
f av'd til you Return in trading for t Company's Interet. And incafe you do not think p.o-
per to fend her to us, for fome Reafon . . . .
not cnrt us to us at prefent, then, upon ..
hereof, you are to call a Council, and . . .
your Reafons in writing fign'd by your .
fame.*

Altho' Mr Drummond *is appointed S and
Chief Merchant at* James Fort, *yet being . .
upon the Expedition, and believing his Prefen
to be very receffary there, we are willing to .
penfe w th his coming to us till the Expedit .o.
over, and to undergo the Fatigue here til l . .
rival, that there may be no manner of Excu .
not proceeding on the intended Expedition, and he
himfelf chufes to come and take his Place I.*

H .

We shall endeavour to procure large Quantities of Salt, but shall be very much straitned to get Conveniencies to carry it up the River

The Company in their Letter intimate nothing particular concerning the Expedition, only that they leave it to the Discretion of the Council to make what Alterations they shall judge proper.

If the Sloop has any Number of Slaves, we desire they may forthwith be sent down, being daily in Expectation of a Ship's Arrival, which by Contract is to sail this Month for Carolina. *We wish you Health and Success, and remain,*

Gentlemen,

Your Friends and humble Servants,

ROB PLUNKETT,
ANTH ROGERS.

THE following is Mr *Drummond's* Answer to the foregoing Letter, *viz*

To ROBERT PLUNKETT, *Esq, and*
Mr ANTH. ROGERS.

Gentlemen, Barracunda, Feb 24, 1724.

YOURS under the 10th *Instant* I receiv'd, with the other *Letters from* England, directed to the Council up the *River* Gambia, which Pacquet I broke open. I congratulate you on your late Arrival at Gambia, and wish you Health and Success in your new Government As for your getting the Company's Ship Dispatch to be at James Fort upon your Arrival, I can say nothing to that, as Captain Stibbs gave his Mate his Orders where the Ship should remain till his Return. Capt. Stibbs was here, I would give

U 2

1724. my Opinion for h.. to go down to James For', ;
follow your farther Orders Their being at...
hinders my coming down. I find it proper to ...
here, for fear of any Palaver happening to ..
Gentlemen that are gone up, and the. not having
the Language, nor us'd to the Manners of ...
Country, they might come to some Trouble, ...
they are very villainous People in these Par...
... cannot be too much upon our Guard As ...
as Captain Stibbs returns, which I believe ...
be in a few Days, I will make the best of ...
... down in one of the Canoas Captain Tre
... both to this Date purchased but four S...
... s Goods are very bad, and ill sorted for Trad',
which could not be helped, there being no prop..
Cargoes for these Parts at the Fort when we .. we
up I cannot forward the Letters to Ca...
Stibbs, not knowing where they are, ...
any of the Mundingoes go above this Place, ...
they look upon Barracunda as the World's E..
Wishing you Health and Success, I remain,

     Gentlemen,

       Your most humble Servant,

       EDW. DRUMMOND.

O N the 26th, at Day-light, we weigh'd,
and pass'd on Soon after the Sloop ran ..
ground in the middle of the River After
diligent searching from one Side to the other,
we found there was not Water enough for ..
Sloop to pass till High Water, altho' ..
drew but four Feet and a half: So I lighten'd
her by the Canoas, and at Three P M got
her over, anchoring at Ten at Night about ..
League below *Cussone.*

                   T ..

THIS Flat is near a League above *Tabu-
cunda*, and consists of a Sand from the North
Side three quarters over the River, on which
there were not above four Foot Water. From
thence to the other Side the River lie large
Rocks, scatter'd up and down promiscuously,
so as not to permit a Vessel to pass betwixt,
altho' there is eight and nine Feet Water, but
upon them at low Water were not above two
and three. As we pass'd this Place without
knowing it, going up, it is a Demonstration
that the Water is fell considerably since.

IN the Afternoon we dispatch'd a Messenger to *Cuttejarr* with Letters for *James
Island*, in answer to those we receiv'd at *Barracunda*, and to acquaint them of our coming
down, *viz*

To ROBERT PLUNKETT, *Esq*, *and
Mr* ANTHONY ROGERS.

Gentlemen,   *River Gambia*, 3 Leagues below
Barracunda, Feb 26, 1724

YESterday at Noon we receiv'd yours of the
10th Instant at the Port of Barracunda
We are very glad of your Arrival in this River,
and congratulate you on the Choice the Royal Company has made in your Favour.

The Letters you brought us from England we
receiv'd by the same Messenger. We thank you
for your Care thereof, and for your hearty Wishes
lent us therewith

As we are now on our Passage down, and
making all possible Dispatch to be with you, we
shall defer giving our Reasons concerning the Company's Ship Dispatch being employ'd on the Service of the Expedition till then, not questioning

but that they will be fatisfactory both to you and the Company.

Mr Drummond *informs us, that he has given you an Account of the poor fuccefslefs Trade the Sloop has met with; and as fhe has got fo ill forted a Cargo, and fuch wretched * Money, we have agreed to bring her down with the Ship, and what Trade we can get.*

In our Paffage up Monf Lemaigre *inform'd us of his having cut down a large Quantity of* Bautie Wood; *which we mention, that you might take this Opportunity of having it brought down, if you difpatch Orders to* Damafenfa *for to bring it down to the Water-fide, and that Capt* Stibbs *fhip it on Board; it may be got ready before 'tis poffible for us to get there.*

Capt. Stibbs *and Mr* Hull *return'd yefterday to* Barracunda Port *They went about* 25 *Leag above that Place, but could not difcover* York River, *which Mr* Vermuyden *places about feven or eight Leagues below. We found his Journal remifs likewife as to the moft notable Hills, which promife Metal in abundance; but whether it is impregnated with the nobler Kind, or not, we muft beg your Patience, till we have Conveniency to make Trial thereof. We pafs'd a great many Flats, with no fmall Pains; till at laft we met with one that (notwithftanding our utmoft Efforts to get our damn'd heavy Canoas over) prov'd too hard for us, and oblig'd us much againft our Will*

to

* By Money they mean Trading Goods, for the *Englifh* have in the River *Gambia* much corrupted the *Englifh* Language by Words or Literal Tranflations from the *Portuguefe* or *Mundingoes*, thus they call all Cattle *Cows*, even tho' they are Bulls or Oxen; they alfo call a Difpute *Palaver*, and a Free Servant *a Butler* or *Grometta*, and the ftealing a Man and making him a Slave they call *Panyaring him*.

to return back. We have nothing material to 1724
add, but to assure you that we are,

Gentlemen,

Your Friends and very humble Servants,

BARTH STIBBS,
EDW DRUMMOND,
RICH HULL.

ON the 27th, early in the Morning, we pass'd on. At Eight o' Clock the Sloop ran aground again, on which I resolv'd to leave the Sloop. with one Canoa, to attend her, and proceeded to *Cuttejarr* with the rest, in order to get my Ship in a Readiness as soon as possible, which by the Sickness amongst my Men will take some Time to do. At Noon I pass'd *Zamatenda*, and at Ten at Night anchor'd at *Fatatenda*.

THE next Morning I left *Fatatenda*, and at Ten at Night anchor'd under *Nackway-Hill*, in order to make a Trial of it.

ON the 29th, in the Morning, as I was examining this Hill, I found towards the Top a Lion's Den, and soon after heard the Lion roaring at no great Distance from where we were, which made us make the more haste down. This Den was the only one of that kind I ever met with. It was cunningly chose in a solitary out of the way Place, about three quarters up the Side of the Hill, at the Foot of a Precipice in the Side of the Rock; it was difficult of access, but large and commodious, yet undoubtedly form'd by Nature. The Track to it, with the Footsteps, Excrements, and even some of its Hair, leaves no

U 4 doubt

1724   doubt but that it was the Residence of a Lion, which are pretty plentiful up this River. We frequently hear their Roaring in the Night, but I can't say I have seen one in the Woods, but I have frequently seen large Wolves. At Night we anchor'd about a Mile below *Yamacunda.*

On the 2d of *March*, at Day-break, we got to *Cuttejarr*, and found my Ship in a very weak Condition, most of the Sailors sick, and ore dead. I us'd all the Endeavours I could to rig my Ship and be gone, hoping by Change of Air to save some of my People's Lives.

On the 4th arriv'd the *James Island* Sloop with every Body well on Board. The next Day we sent down three Canoas with 31 Slaves for *James* Fort, under the Care of Mr *Tuon* and *Harrison*; the Reason of our sending them before was on account of Governor *Plunket's* advising us of a Charter'd Ship for *Company* being expected daily at the Fort.

On the 8th, having got my Ship in a tolerable Condition, I left *Cuttejarr*, and at Six at Night we pass'd *Dubocunda*, when falling calm, I towed till Eleven at Night, and then anchor'd a Mile short of *Brucoe.*

On the 9th, at Sun-rising, I went thro' *Pholey's* Pass; the same Day went thro' Six Isles; the next Morning I stopt and took Trial of the *Red Mount* near *Cassan*, and on the 13th, about Noon, came to anchor *Joar*, where were two Interlopers, *viz.* the *Ruby*, Capt *Craigue*, and the *Hope*, Capt *Perry*, the former we left here as we pass'd up the River, it seems his Slaves rose upon him last Week, by which he lost 17 out of 6. About three Leagues before we came to *Joar*

we saw two or three Hundred Elephants in a 1724.
Drove come down to the River to drink,
who rais'd the Dust like the Smoke of a
Glasshouse or Brewhouse Fire.

On the 13th, at Night, we left *Joar*;
and the next Morning saw a large Drove of
Elephants swim across the River, not above
a quarter of a Mile ahead of us. On the 22d,
in the Morning, we came to an Anchor at
James Island, which we saluted with five Guns.
Mr *Orfeur* was gone to settle a Factory at
Purodally. It is to be obferv'd, that we neither buried one Man, nor was there one hardly that were sick, on the contrary, those that
were in a weak Condition on our setting out,
grew afterwards very healthful, fat and strong;
but my Ship which lay at *Cutty*, proved
very sickly and unhealthful. We have been
upon our Voyage from *James* Fort to our Return two Months twenty three Days.

BARTH STIBBS,

EDW DRUMMOND,

RICH. HULL

Observations on the foregoing JOURNAL, *and on the follow-ing Remarks made by Mr* Stibbs *concerning the River* GAMBIA.

THE Author of this JOURNAL having given his Reasons why he thought the antient and modern Geographers Accounts of the River *Gambia* were erroneous, I hope it will not be thought wrong in me to mention some things which might not occur to him, and which justify the Geographers in their Maps of that River, which they call the *Niger*

HE says first, *That the River* Gambia *called by that other* T *Name, and no other*

THE Gentleman must have been led into that Error from want of Conversing with the Natives *Gambia* is not the Name by which the *Mandingoes*, who are the Natives, call the River, for they only call it *Ba'o*, signifying *The River*, by way of Preheminence, as the antient *Ægyptians* did the *Nile*, and which the *Abyssines* do to this Day Whereas the Name of *Gambia*, I believe, took its Rise from the *Portuguese*, and is only used by such Natives as converse with *Europeans*, because they find that the White Men know the River by that Name.

HE likewise says, *That its Original or Head is nothing near so far in the Country, as by the Geographers*

Geographers has been represented, nor does it ⚹ rise from any Lake, or hath it a Communication with any other River.

THE Opposite to this is affirmed by *Leo* the *African*, which I have inserted at length; and his Account is of his own Knowledge, having himself seen the *Niger* at *Tombuto*, where he went with his Uncle, who was sent Ambassador by the King of *Fez* to the King of *Tombuto*. And it is not probable that *Leo* could have invented this Story, since another Author, *viz* the *Nubian* Geographer, gives the same Account of the River *Niger*, which I have also inserted, and the Account they give of the Natives, their Habit, their Manners, Diet, &c. agrees with what we find to be the present Customs on the River *Gambia*. They mention the Salt Pits which are in the *Bail Uhl* or *Joally*, at the Mouth of the River *Gambia*, and of the Fondness the Natives have for Salt up the River. They also mention *Gualata* or *Jualya*, which is the Kingdom of the *Jolloiffs*. They also mention *Ghara* or *Tray*, and our Discoverers have not yet gone further than that and *Woolly*, which may be a Part of what they call *Ghana*. It is not therefore very probable they should be mistaken so as to affirm there was so great a River as the *Niger*, when there was no such River. And the River *Gambia* is so considerable, that the Tide flows up farther than in any River I ever heard of. Mr *Stibbs*'s saying *that this River does not rise so far in the Country as represented by the Geographers*, is giving his Conjecture, which is a negative Weight against the positive Evidence of the two antient Geographers in the Affirmative. But if we are to judge by Conjectures, I shall subjoin the Learned *Ludolphus*'s Opinion upon this Point, which is very curious. I shall also add what *Herodotus* says upon this Subject. Whose Authorities agree in there being a very great River of long Course called the *Nile* or *Niger*, which either divides from the *Nile*, or rises near it, and after having traversed most Part of *Africa*, falls into the *Atlantick* Ocean, as the other *Nile* doth into the *Mediterranean*.

Mr *Stubbs* allows, *that the* Gambia *is a River of the largest Course of any that falls into the* Atlantick Ocean *to the North of the Line, and that it is the* Niger, *if any.* But it seems as if he thought there was no *Niger* at all, for he says, *that the* Gambia *rises so near the Sea as not to agree in any manner with the Account the Antients give of the* Niger.

His Reason for this Conjecture is, *That he never heard the Natives mention any thing of Lakes.* These Natives, very probably, were the Merchants, with whom he spoke, whose Interest it was to conceal from him the Country to which they traded, since they must perceive that his Intention was to go up and trade thither, which if he could do by the River, he would certainly under-trade them, who live by buying the Goods from the *Europeans* near the Sea, and carrying them up and selling them, at great Profit, to the People who live high up the River. The *Joncoes* that I myself have generally spoke to (knowing that I had no Intention to trade up that Way) told me, *That about a Month's Journey from* Joncor *are great Lakes, near which they for*

And that is the general Opinion of the Country, as you'll fee by Governor *Rogers*'s Letter to the Company, which I have alfo added

H I s fecond Reafon is, *That the Natives , the* Gambia *comes from near the Gold Mines, tweve Days Jour ney from* Barracunda *, and that the Fowls walk over it.* This may be true of fome River which falls into the *Gambia* , but the main River of *Niger*, as laid down by the Antients, which agrees with the Courfe of the *Gambia*, comes from South of the Eaft to *Barracunda* , whereas the Gold Mines he fpeaks of, lie more Northerly.

H E fays, *That none of the other Rivers come out of the* Gambia   But he gives no Proof thereof, nor does he mention any one who hath difcover'd the Head of the *Senegal,* or of any of the other Rivers.

H E fays, *That the* French *have not made any Difcoveries of the* Senegal *above* Gallam ; *which is* 5 *or* 600 *Miles up, and being on the Confines of* South B irbary, *partakes of its Sands and Deferts, where it is very fmall*   This is the Defcription *Leo* gives of the Northern Branch of the River *Niger*, and only proves that the *French* have not been higher than *Gallam,* but does not prove that the *Senegal* does not come out of the *Gambia* far above *Gallam*, and it is perhaps the *Senegal* falling out of the *Gambia*, which forms the Ifland 300 Miles in Length, and 150 Miles in Breadth ; which the *Nubian* Geographer mentions in the Kingdom of *Vancara* above *Yary,* and which *Leo* alfo mentions in his 7th Book, defcribing the Kingdom of *Ghinea* , and *Labat,* a Modern *French* Author, in the Second Volume of his Account of *Africa,* fays as follows

‘ I N

‘ I n giving Account of the River *Senega*,
‘ I ſhall indifferently call it by that Name, or
‘ the Name of the *Niger*. In this I follow the
‘ Opinion of all thoſe, both Antients and
‘ Moderns, who have ſpoke with Certainty
‘ of this River They all agree, that the
‘ River which the *Europeans* have for two Ages
‘ call'd *Senegal*, is really the *Niger*, or one of
‘ the moſt conſiderable Branches of it. It is
‘ the Fate of Great Rivers, by the Quantity
‘ of their Waters, to be divided into different
‘ Streams , and by giving different Names to
‘ thoſe Streams, that of the main River from
‘ whence they proceed is forgot The *Rhine*
‘ is a neighbouring Example of this , a little
‘ Brook only, which is loſt amongſt the Sand ,
‘ bears the Name of the *Rhine*, whilſt many
‘ great Branches produced from it fall into
‘ the Sea under other Names.

‘ M a n y things have contributed towards
‘ giving the Name of *Senegal* to that Branch
‘ of the *Niger* The *Europeans* arriving at
‘ the Entry of that River, and not knowing
‘ it, they aſk'd the Name of certain Fiſher-
‘ men that they found there. He of whom
‘ they aſk'd, not underſtanding them, thought
‘ they aſk'd his Name, and anſwer'd them,
‘ * *Zanaga* , which the *Europeans* underſtood
‘ to be the Name of the River, and have ſince
‘ corrupted into *Senegal*, the Name by which
‘ moſt *Europeans* know this River

‘ T h e *Moors* who frequent the Northern
‘ Banks call it in their Language *Huel Nil*,
‘ which ſignifies, if I miſtake not, the *b*
‘ *River*, or *Black or Niger*
　　　　　　　　　　　　　　　　‘ r

* *Zanaga is the Name of one of the Tribes of the M i*

'IF we believe *Sanute*, it was known to
' the Antients under the Name of *Afanaga*,
' not much different from that of *Senegal*,
' which it bears But let the prefent Name
' be what it will, it is certainly the fame
' River The Cuftom of giving new Names
' to Places when they are firft difcover'd or
' poffefs'd, without enquiring into their an-
' tient Names, is not eafy to be prevented ;
' but this doth not change the Situation nor
' the Courfe of the *Niger*.

'THE *Niger*, or *Senegal*, is one of the
' moft confiderable Rivers in *Africa* Without
' fpeaking of what it is beyond the Lake of
' *Bournon*, which is in 42 Degrees of Longi-
' tude, from that Lake to the Sea is 800
' Leagues The antient Geographers fay that
' it is a Branch of the *Nile*, and that thefe
' two Rivers come from the fame Head.
' *Pliny* is of this Opinion, and one of his
' Reafons is, That the Banks produce the
' fame Plants and Animals. If this Argument
' were allow'd, we might by it prove, that
' the River of *Amazons*, and *Janeiro*, and all
' the other Rivers in *America*, came from the
' fame *Nile*, fince they produce *Crocodiles* as
' well as it

'THE moft that we could now learn is
' from the *Negroe* Merchants of the Kingdom
' of *Mundingo* · Their Accounts are not fo
' exact as to be quite pofitive , and we can-
' not but fuppofe that in the Accounts they
' give they will fay nothing that can prejudice
' their Commerce, or excite the *Europeans* to
' break in upon their Trade. What is cer-
' tain, and fo certain that it admits of no doubt,
' is, that the Kingdom of *Gallam*, above the
                                 ' Fort

‘ Fort of St *Joſeph*, abounds in Mines of Gold,
‘ as do the Kingdoms of *Gago* and *Tombuto*,
‘ which lie above that upon the ſame River
    ‘ W E are aſſured, and it is credible enough,
‘ that in the 20th Degree of Longitude the
‘ *Niger* is much larger than it is below, and
‘ it there forms a very conſiderable Lake,
‘ and leaving that Lake, divides itſelf in o
‘ two Branches, the one running due Weſt,
‘ is call’d the *Senegal*, the other running South
‘ Weſt, is call’d the *Gambia* The latter di
‘ vides itſelf again, and the Southern Stream
‘ or it is call’d *St Domingo*, and that again
‘ produces a fourth, call’d *Rio Grande* Theſe
‘ two laſt are divided again, and fall through
‘ ſeveral Channels into the Sea, which form
‘ the Iſlands of *Biſſaux, Biſſagots, Bedam* and
‘ *Buſſ,* and many others
    ‘ T H E *Mandingoes* (who of all the *Negroes*
‘ are thoſe who travel moſt) ſay, that the
‘ *Niger* comes out of a Lake which they call
‘ *Meloa*, but we cannot fix the Situation
‘ of it from their Accounts, becauſe they ca
‘ not obſerve Longitude and Latitude They
‘ ſay, that this River, at a Place call’d *Ba-*
‘ *racot*, divides itſelf into two Branches, and
‘ that that which runs to the Southward ve
‘ call *Gambia*, which after a long Courſe ceaſ
‘ to loſe itſelf in a Lake overgrown with
‘ Cares and Reeds, in ſuch a manner as thro’
‘ their Thickneſs to render the Water unpaſ-
‘ ſable for Boats That having paſs’d this
‘ Lake, it again appears a fine and good
‘ River, as large as where it paſſes by o
‘ cara, to which Place the *Legi* and *Ti-*
‘ *geos*, who reſtded in that River, uſe’d
‘ to trade with the Merchants Little Cara

        ‘   D

can go from *Barracunda* to the Lake of *Canes*, but Barks cannot, not even in the rainy Seafon, becaufe they cannot pafs a Ridge of Rocks which croffes the River; and through which, though there are feveral deep Channels, yet are they fo narrow that nothing ' broader than a Canoa can go through ' them.'

This Account from a Perfon of fome Learning, who had himfelf been in *Senegal*, is very different from Mr. *Stibbs*'s Conjectures; but though I venture to obferve upon his Reafons, yet at the fame Time I fhall not omit mentioning, to his and Mr. *Hull*'s Honour, that they pufhed their Difcoveries very far, even as high as the River was navigable for wide Boats, for he mentions that Ridge of Rocks which *Lebatt* fays ftops the Navigation with large Barks up the *Gambia*. And whofoever knows the Difficulty of Difcoveries in thofe Countries, where Heat, Hunger, Faint-heartednefs of ones Companions, and Ignorance of the Cuftoms and Language of the Natives, equally create numberlefs Oppofitions to the Defign, cannot but praife and commend the Courage and Conftancy of fuch Adventurers as make any Difcoveries at all.

Tranſlations *from* WRITERS,

Concerning the

NIGER-NILE, *or* GAMBIA.

A Tranſlation of ſuch Part of the NUBIAN's Geography, *as relates to the* Niger-Nile, *of which the* Gambia *is ſuppoſed to be one Mouth.*

INTRODUCTION.

THIS Book was written originally in *Arabick,* it was tranſlated by *Gabriel Sionita,* Royal Profeſſor of the *Syriack* and *Arabick* Languages at *Paris,* with the Aſſiſtance of *John Heſronita,* Interpreter of the *Oriental* Tongues to *Lewis* XIII. King of *France* The famous *James Thuanus* Chancellor of *France* encouraging theſe two, as he did all Men of Learning, adviſed them to tranſlate this Book of Geography, which had been printed in *Arabick,* at *Rome,* in the Preſs of the *Mediceys,* into *Latin,* which they accordingly did, and the *Latin* Verſion was printed at *Paris* in the Year 1619, under this Title.

X 2   *GEO-*

GEOGRAPHIA NUBIENSIS, id eſt, Aurauſſima totius Orbis in feptem Climata diviſi Deſcriptı,
continens praſertim exaﬁam univerſæ Aſiæ & Africæ,
rerumque in iis haﬁenus incognitarum explicationem Recens ex Aralico in Latinum verſa   A Gabriele Sionita,
Syriacarum & Arabicarum literarum Profeſſore, atque
Interprete Regis, & Joanne Heſronita, earundem Reg o
Interprete, Maronitis.

IT is a Geography of all that Part of the Wo, ͻ
which was then known to the *Arabiars*, and an
Epitome of a greater Work, called, *The Diver,* ·
of the curious Mind

HE begins with ſhewing that the Earth is a Globe,
and then after a general Treatiſe of Geography, proceeds to divide the Earth into ſeven Climates, the h r?
from the Æquator Northward   The River *Gam* ·
or *Nile*, is in the firſt Climate   He begins at the
Weſtern Ocean, and deſcribes Eaſtward, as far as the
Arabiars knew, all under thoſe Latitudes   Thus he
ſpeaks firſt of that Part of *Africa* which lies on the
Weſtern Ocean, and the Mouths of the *Niger-Nile*,
and proceeds Eaſtward, deſcribing all the Countries
under the ſame Latitude, in which is comprehended
the whole Courſe of the *Niger*, Part of the Courſe of
the other *Nile*, the *Red Sea*, Part of *Arabia*, the Eaſt
Indies, &c   Of theſe we have given only what relates
to the Courſe of what he calls the *Nile*, of which the
Gambia ſeems to be one Mouth

THE Preface of the *Latin* Verſion gives the following Account of the Age in which the Author lived,
and of the Country where he was born, as follows

' AND having given a ſhort Account of the Method
' of this Work, it is proper to ſpeak ſomething of the
' Author's Religion, and the Age and Country he liv'd
' in   Our Author's Name, by Default of the Origina
' Copies, is to us obſcure, but will perhaps appear plain
' to Poſterit , when the Number of Lovers of Arabi
' ſhall be increaſed, and other Impreſſions be thereby oc
' caſioned   He wrote this Book of Geography abou
' four hundred and ſeventy Years ago.   For *Roger*, Kin,
' of S h, whom this *Arabian* Geographer, in the ſe
                                              ' con

' cond Part of his fourth Climate, fays in plain Words,
' reign'd in his Time, died above four hundred and
' fixty-eight years fince, *viz* in the Year eleven hundred
' and fifty one. It is very manifeft from the fame *Ara-*
' *bian* Author, that this ought to be underftood of *Roger*
' the Ift King of both *Sicily's*, and not of *Roger* the
' IId Son of *Tancred*, as *Cafaubonus* will have it Our
' Geographer, in the fecond Part of the third Climate,
' declares that it was that *Roger*, who took *Tripolis*, be-
' longing to the *Barbarians*, and the Ifland *Carcona.*
' Now we find it wrote in the Chronicles, that *Tripolis*,
' the Ifland *Melita*, and other Countries, were conquer'd
' and taken by *Roger* Ift Befides, the City of *Jerufa-*
' *lem* was taken by the *Chriftians* in the Year of our
' Lord one thoufand and ninety nine, and kept till the
' Year eleven hundred and eighty feven, in which Time
' *Saladinus* at laft reduced it under the Power of the
' *Mahometans* And when our Geographer, in the fifth
' Part of the third Climate, affirms that he publifhed this
' Work at the Time when *Jerufalem* was in the *Chrifti-*
' *ans* Power, how can he poffibly mean *Roger* the IId.
' whom we know to have died young, and in his Fa-
' ther's Life Time, in the Year eleven hundred and
' ninety four? Therefore by the certain Concurrence of
' the Times, we muft allow that this Book of Geogra-
' phy was wrote in *Roger* the Ift's Time, and confe-
' quently about four hundred and feventy Years ago

' We cannot guefs at the abovementioned Author's
' Country from any other Place of his Book, but the
' Beginning of the fourth Part of the fecond Climate,
' where fpeaking of the Rife of the Rivers *Nile* and *Ni-*
' *ger*, he has thefe Words, *Nilus Ægypti, qu fecat pa-*
' *triam noftram.* From which Paffage, as it belongs to
' our Purpofe, *Cafaubonus* very groundlefsly thinks that
' this *Arabian* was an *Ægyptian* We however, having
' firft of all carefully confider'd the abovemention'd
' Words, find from them that the Author makes fome
' Difference between *Ægypt*, and the Country which
' he calls *our Country* And then the Map of *Nubia*, (in
' which the fame Geographer teaches us alfo that it is
' watered with the Streams of *Ægyptian Nile*, before
' *Ægypt* itfelf is) being well examin'd, we refolutely af-
' firm he was a *Nubian* by Country. *Erpenius* readily

X 3 ' came

' came into our Opinion, having heard and confider'd
' together with us thefe Reafons whofe Judgment and
' Learning, as it has no fmall Weight with us, fo
' we hope ours will be of more Authority by his Appro-
' bation. And that was the Reafon, learned Reader,
' why we called this the *Nubian's Geography* '

These tranflated Paragraphs of the Preface of the
Paris Edition, were wrote in the Year 1619, which is
119 Years fince, therefore it is 587 Years fince the
Nubian Geographer wrote, and his Book, tho' it is wrote
in a dry Manner and without any Ornaments, muft
be very valuable to the Curious, fince it is an Account
of what the *Arabians* knew of the Countries of the
Negroes fo many Ages ago

This Book hath met with great Applaufe among the
Learned, it was much valued and extolled by the Car-
dinal *Perronius*, the great *Thuanus*, *Scaliger*, *Cafaubon*,
and *Thomas Erpenius*, the famous *Arabick* Profeffor of
Leyden And indeed all the Geographers have made
their Maps of *Africa* from this and *Leo* the *African's*
Account; and though thefe are fo well known in the
learned World, yet they are hardly known by the
Generality of the *Englifh*, and I cannot find that
this *Nubian* Geographer was ever tranflated into our
Language.

He mentions, that from the Ifland *Uhl*, to the City of
Segelmeffa is forty Days Journey, now we know that
Segelmeffa is under the Emperor of *Morocco*, and it is
very probable that that is the Country into which
the *Joncoes* or Merchants go from the River *Gambia*,
where they fay there are Cities and Houfes built with
Stone, and defcribe the Manners of the People to be
like the *Moors* of *Morocco* But the Cities on thefe *Gam-*
bia are either now demolifhed and over-grown with
Wood, or elfe they lie higher up the River than the
Englifh have yet difcover'd, for there are no Store
Buildings in any of the Towns which we know

He alfo mentions *Ghana*, which I take to be *Yam*,
fpoke of in my Journal, then he mentions *Uhl* to be an
Ifland abounding with Salt, a Day's Sail from the Mouth
of the *Nile*. The Salt Pits from whence the Inhabitants
of the River *Gambia* are furnifhed with Salt, are to this
Day in the Iflands called *Joally*, and thofe Salt Pits are
one

one Day's Sail from the Mouth of the *Gambia*, as he says the Salt Pits of *Ulil* are from the *Nile*.

He writes many other Things, which, if the Reader pleases to compare, he will find they agree with my Journal up the *Gambia*, and that of Capt. *Stibb's*, though neither of us had seen the *Nubian's Geography* when we wrote our Journals.

It is proper to advertise the Reader, that, in Translating the *Nubian's Geography*, we have inserted all the Names as he spells them, and the *g* is to be pronounced like *jay* or *j*, and that he uses the Word *Nile* for the River which we call *Gambia*.

THE
Nubian's Geography.

Part I. Climate I.

THIS Climate begins on the *West*, from the *Western* Sea, which is called the *Unknown Sea*, or *Sea of Darkness*, [1] *beyond which what may be, Geographers have no Knowledge of.* There are on that Coast six Islands, call'd the *Fortunate Islands*, from whence *Ptolomy* began his Computation of Longitude and Latitude; and they relate, [2] that in every one of the said Islands is to be seen a Pillar rais'd of Stone,

X 4

of

---

[1] [The *Sea of Darkness*] Is what is now called the *Atlantick* Ocean, the Bounds of which were then unknown, for this Author wrote long before *America* was discovered

[2] And they relate, &c] This is an *Arabian* Tale, and the Author mentions it as such, for he uses in the *Arabick* a Word which is translated *memorant*, but which answers in *English* to The *Tale Teller's Report*, or *their fable, that*

of the Length of a hundred Cubits, each Pillar ſup-
porting a Brazen Image, *with its Hand lifted up and
pointing backwards* Theſe Pillars are Six, and one
of them, as 'tis reported, is the Idol *Cades*, which is
to the *Weſt* of *Andaluzia*, and beyond theſe no one
knows of any Habitations.

In this Part of the Climate are the Cities ' U ,
[2] *Salla*, *Tocrur*, *Dau*, *Beriſſa* and *Muia*, all ſituated
in the *Negroes* Country of *Meczara* But the Iſland
Uhl ſtands not far diſtant from the Continent, and in this
is found theſe famous Salt Pits, the only that we know
in all the Country of the *Negroes*, and 'tis from hence
they are every where ſupply'd with Salt, for M
coming to this Iſland load their Veſſels with S ,
and direct their Courſe to the Mouth of the N ,
which is at the Diſtance of one Day's Sail, along the
Nile they afterwards paſs by [2] *Salla*, *Tocrur*, B
[3] *Ghana*, with the other Provinces of [4] *Vancara* and
Caugha, and all the Country of the *Negroes*, who
the moſt Part inhabit along the *Nile* itſelf, or the
Rivers which fall into it   The reſt of the Countries
lying diſtant from the *Nile*, on each Side, are deſer
Sands and ſolitary Waſtes, altogether uncultivated Theſe
are indeed Wells found in them, but often dry, and
Travellers find no Water for two, four, five, ſix, and
ſometimes twelve Days Journey. Of this Nature re
Road of *Beneſer*, which is upon the Way between S
maſſa and *Ghana*, where for fourteen Days the
no Water, for which Reaſon the Caravans ha e it c
ried with them in all ſuch ways on Camels Backs The
are throughout the Countries of the *Black*, man
of the like Sort, the Soil being moſtly Sand, and
toſt to and fro by the Wind makes it impractical

---

[1] *Uhl* The Iſland U i now called *Joalh*, and t e S
brought from thence is ſold a up the *Gambia*, and the *Jo*
Merchants buy it and carry it over Land as a very va
Commodity

[2] *Salla*] Is what I take to be *Barſall*.

[3] *Ghana*] I believe is *Yani*, which lies next above *Bonda*
tho' the Boundaries are much altered

[4] *Vancara*] Is higher than the *Engliſh* yet know, for
and *Woolly*, which is part of the ancient *Ghana*, is as high a
Engliſh have yet gone

find Water   Thofe Regions are alfo fubject to exceffive
Heat, and the Inhabitants therefore of the firft and
fecond, and of fome Parts of the third Climate, by the
Intenfenefs of the Heat and Burning of the Sun, are of
a Black Colour, and have their Hair curling contrary to
what happens to thofe who live in the fixth and feventh
Climate   From the Ifle of *Uhl* to the City of *Sella* are
¹ fixteen Stations, that City is fituated on the *North* Side
of the *Nile*, it is populous, and abounding with the
beft Merchandizes of the *Negroes*, and the Citizens are
ftout and couragious.   This Place is in the Dominion of
the King of *Tocrur*, who is a mighty Prince, having
many Servants and Soldiers of known Fortitude, Power
and Juftice, with a Country well fecur'd, and expos'd
to no Fears   His chief Seat and Place of Refidence is
the City *Tocrur*, ² ftanding on the *South* Bank of the
Nile, two Day's Journey from *Salla*, as well on the
River as by Land   The City *Tocrur* is larger than that
of *Salla*, and more abounding with Commerce   The
remoter Inhabitants of the *Weftern* Parts bring thither
Shells ³ and Brafs, and carry from thence Gold and
Bracelets for the Legs   Their Diet at *Salla* and *Tocrur*
is a kind of ⁴ large grain'd Millet, Fifh, and Preparation
of Milk, their Cattle are chiefly Camels and Goats,
the common People wear Hair Garments, and Woollen
Caps on their Heads, but the Drefs of the Nobility is
a Cotton Veft and a Mantle   From the aforefaid Cities
to *Segelmaffa* ⁵ is a Journey of forty Days, at the Rate
of the Caravan's Travelling   The neareft Place to this,
within the Limits of the Defart of ⁶ *Lemptuna*, is *Azca*,

at

---

¹ Sixteen Stations] Things muft have changed much fince
this Author's Time, for there is no great City now in *Barfall*
The largeft is *Joar*, as defcrib'd in my Journal, and cannot be
above feven Days from *Uhl*

² This Kingdom of *Tocrur*, which lay on the *South* Side of the
Gambia, muft have been deftroy'd, for *Barfall* is inhibited by
the *Jolloffs*, a *Northern* People, whofe Kings are of the Race
of *Snjay*

³ Cowries are Shells which go as Money

⁴ Is *Indian* Corn

⁵ *Segelmaffa* is fubject to the Emperor of *Morocco*

⁶ *Lemptuna* takes its Name from one of the Tribes of *Moors*,
Vide *Leo* the *African*

at the Diftance of twenty-five Stations; and Travellers carry Water with them for two, four, five and fix Days. In like manner from the Ifle of *Ulil* to *Segelmaffa* are nigh forty Stations, computing by the Caravans Stages *Beriffa* lies *Eaftward* to the *Nile*, at the Diftance of twelve Stations from *Tocrur*; this is a little City, and not wall'd, and feems like a populous Village, but the Citizens here are Merchants, trading to all Parts, and Subjects to the King of *Tocrur*.   To the *Southward* of *Beriffa*, at the Diftance of ten Day's March, lies the Land of *Lamlem*, into which Incurfions are made by the Inhabitants of *Beriffa*, *Salla*, *Tocrur* and *Ghana*, there they take Numbers of Captives, whom they carry [1] away to their own Countries, and difpofe of to the Merchants trading thither; thefe afterwards fell them into all Parts of the World.

In the whole Land of *Lamlem* there are but two fmall Cities, or as it were Villages, and thofe are *Malel* and *Dau*, fituated at the Diftance of four Days Journey from each other. Their Inhabitants, as People of thofe Parts relate, are *Jews*, and indeed moft of them unbelieving and ignorant.   When any of all the Inhabitants of the Kingdom of *Lamlem* comes to have the Ufe of his Reafon, he is burnt in the Face and Temples, this they do for a Token among [2] themfelves.   All their Countries and whole Dominions is near a certain River, flowing into the *Nile*. It is not known that there is any inhabited Place beyond the Kingdom of *Lamlem* to the *South*. That Kingdom joins on the *Weft* to *Meczara*, on the *Eaft* to *Vancara*, on the *North* to *Ghana*, and on the *South* with the Defert, and its People ufe a different Language from thofe of *Meczara* and *Ghana*   Between *Beriffa* abovemention'd and *Ghana*, to the *Eaft*, is a Journey of twelve Days it lies in the Midway which leads to the Cities *Salla* and *Tocrur*.   Likewife from the City *Beriffa* to *Audeghaft* is computed a Diftance of twelve Days Journey, and *Audeghaft* is on the *North* of *Beriffa*

In

---

[1] This fhows that the Slave Trade was begun by the *Mahometan Moors* of *Africa*, and it was from them that the *Portuguefe* learnt it, and the *Englifh* from the *Portuguefe*, upon their fettling in *America*

[2] The *Dachomas*, and the People near *Cape Coaft* are branded in this Manner

In the *Negroes* Countries no foreign Fruit is seen besides Dates, which are brought thither by the People of the Desert of *Vareclan* from the Kingdoms of *Segelmaffa* or *Zab* The *Nile* washes that Country from *Eaft* to *Weft*, and there on the Banks of it *Indian* Canes grow, Ebony Trees and Box, wild Vines and Tamariks, and very large Woods of the like Trees, where their Herds lye down and lodge, and shelter themselves in the Shades from the scorching Heat In these Woods are found Lions, Beafts like Camels and Panthers, Stags, Debuth, Hares, White Weafels and Porcupines. There are also in the *Nile*, various kinds of Fifh, as well small as of a large Size, on which moft of the *Negroes* feed, for they Seafon with Salt and lay up the Fifh they take, which very much excels in fatnefs and largenefs. The Arms of the People of thofe Countries are Bows and Arrows, in which their Force chiefly is; they also make ufe of Clubs, which, by a peculiar Skill and wonderful Art, they make of Ebony, but they make the Bows and Arrows, also the Bow-Strings, of the Reeds of *Sciarac*. The Buildings of this People are of Clay, and wide Beams, for long ones are feldom found among them. Their Ornaments are of Latten or Copper Metal, Grana, and Glafs Necklaces, and counterfeited Jewels Some of the aforefaid Things belonging to the Cuftoms, Victuals, Drink, Cloathing, and Ornaments, are in ufe among the chief Part of the *Negroes*, in all their Country, when it burns with the scorching Heat. Thofe however who live in Cities fow Onions, Gourds, and Pompions, which grow there to a wonderful Bignefs The Plenty of Corn, nor of other forts of Grain, is not fo great among them, as the large grain'd Millet, from which they make their drink Their greateft Dainties are Fifh and dry'd Camels Flefh.

Part II. Climate I.

THE Cities contain'd in this fecond Part of the firft Climate are *Malel* and *Ghana*, *Tirca*, *Marafa*, *Sacmara*, *Ghanara*, *Reghebil*, and *Semegda* From the City *Malel* to the great City *Ghana* are about twelve Stations, through fandy Places and parch'd Plains In
Ghana,

Ghana are two Cities, situated on the two opposite Shores of what they called a fresh Water Sea, and is the largest, most populous, and wealthiest, in all the *Negroes* Coun tries, and thither the rich Merchants resort, not only from all the neighbouring Places, but also from all the remotest Parts of the *West*   Its Inhabitants are *Mussel men*, [1] and the King of it (as it is reported) derives his Pedigree from *Saleh*, the Son of *Abdalla*, the Son of *Hasan*, the Son of *Hosain*, the Son of *Aali*, the Son of *Abi-Taleb*; and the King is absolute, altho' he pays Obedience to *Abbasæus* Emperor of the *Musselmen* [1] He hath a Palace, which is a strong and well fortified Struc ture, on the Bank of the *Nile*   Apartments adorn d with various Engravings, Paintings, and Glass Windows The aforesaid Palace was built in the five hundred and tenth Year of the *Hegeira*   His Kingdom and Dominions is bounded by the Country of *Vancara* abovementioned, very famous for the Plenty and Excellency of their Gold Mines.   And from the confirmed Reports of the People who come from the [2] remote Part of the *West*, it is certain that there is in the Palace of the King, an entire Lump of Gold, not cast, nor wrought by any Instru ments, but perfectly form'd by the divine Providence only, of thirty Pounds Weight, which has been bored through, and fitted for a Seat to the Royal Throne [3] And truly it is a most extraordinary Thing, granted to no other but to him, by which he procures to himself a peculiar Glory, in Comparison of all the *Negro* Kings And that King, as is reported, is the most just of all Men, no other King has so many Captains, who every Morn ing come to his House on Horseback, and one of these carrying a Drum beats it, nor is he silent till the King comes down to the Palace Gate, and when all the Cap tains meet him, he himself gets on Horseback, and going

---

[1] The Empire of the *Caliphs* then subsisted in *Morocco*, and all over *Africa*   The *English* never went so high as the fresh Water Sea or Lakes, and Mr *Stubbs* thinks there are no such Lake

[2] Remote Part of the *West*] He being a *Nubian*, the Inhabi tants within 1000 Miles of the Mouth of the *Gambia* were far *West* from his Country

[3] Seat to the Royal Throne] The *Negroes* chuse very low Seats, and very small withal, not above ten Inches high, and six over, and very often in the Shape of an Hour Glass.

before them he paffes thro' the Streets and Suburbs of the City Then if any be oppref'd or griev'd with any Trouble, he prefents himfelf to the King, nor does he depart from his Prefence till his Caufe be decided. In the Afternoons, when the Heat of the Sun permits, he gets again on Horfeback, and goes out guarded on all fides by his Soldiers Then no Admittance nor Accefs is open to any one Therefore, in a certain and appointed Cuftom, he rides out twice every Day. And fo much is remarkable of his Juftice. He generally wears a Habit of Sattin, or a black Mantle, after the *Arabian* Manner, with Drawers, and leathern Sandals on his Feet He always goes on Horfeback. He has abundance of rich Ornaments, and Horfes, with moft fumptuous Trappings, on folemn Days, led before him He has many Troops who march each with their Colours under his Royal Banner, Elephants, Camels, and various kinds of Animals, which are found in the *Negroes* Countries, precede him In fine, thefe People have in the *Nile* long made Boats, in which they practife Fifhing and Commerce between one City and the other. But the Apparel of the People of *Ghana* are Cloths to cover their Nakednefs and Mantles And the Country of *Ghana* is join'd on the *Weftern* Side with the Kingdom of *Meczara*, on the *Eaft* with that of *Vancara*, on the *North* with the broadeft Defert, lying out between the Countries of the *Blacks* and *Barbary*, on the *South* it joins to the *Infidel* Country, *to wit*, that of *Lamlem*, and other Inhabitants.

From the City of *Ghana* to the Confines of the Country of *Vancara* is a Journey of eight Days, and this of *Vancara* is moft famous for the Excellency and Plenty of Gold. It is an Ifland of three hundred Miles in Length, and one hundred and fifty in Breadth, which the *Nile* furrounds all the Year. But the Month of *Auguft* approaching, and the fcorching Heat increafing, and the *Nile* overflowing, that Ifland, or, at leaft, the greater Part of it, is cover'd over with Water, and remains fo as long as the *Nile* is wont to overflow. But when the Waters decreafe, and the *Nile* begins to gather it felf in its proper Channel, all, who are in the Kingdom of the *Blacks*, living in thofe Iflands, return to their Habitation, and every Day in which the *Nile* decreafes,

creafes, they flightly dig the Earth, and not one of them is difappointed in his Labour, but whofoever he be, by digging, finds more or lefs of Gold, according to the Gift of God   And after that the *Nile* hath entirely betaken itfelf to its former Bounds, they fell what they have fouud, and Merchandize among themfelves, and indeed the greater Part of the Gold is bought by the Merchants of *Vareclan*, and by the remoteft *Weftern* Merchants, and they carrying it into their Countre, ftrike and coin it into Pieces of Money, and by them they are bought, and that every Year

Next to the Cities of the Country of *Vancara* lies the great and populous City *Tirca*, diftant from *Ghara* fix Days Journey, the Road lies along the Banks of the *Nile*   From *Tirca* to the City *Marafa* is reckon'd fix Days   And from this to the Country of *Secmera* is fix Days Journey   From that to the City *Semarda* is eight Days Journey   That is a beautiful and neat City, fituated on the Shore of a frefh Water Sea, and diftant from the City *Reghebil* nine Days   Alfo from the City *Semara* to the City of *Reghebil*, towards the *South* is a Journey of fix Days   The City *Regheb l* lies alfo on the Shore of a frefh Water Sea, and is of a beautiful Form and Bignefs, fituated under a Mountain, which hangs over it on the *South* Side   Between the City *Reghel*, towards the *Weft*, and the City *Ghanara*, there is a Diftance of eleven Days   The City *Ghanara* is on a Bank of the *Nile*, inclos'd with a ftrong Wall, and inhabited by a numerous and robuft People   Alfo from this City to that of *Ghana* is a Journey of eleven Days, where Water is very fcarce.   All thefe Countries a little before mention'd are under the Dominion of the King of *Ghana*

Part III.   Climate I.

THE moft famous Cities which are contain'd in the third Part of the firft Climate, are *Kaugha* and *Kucu, Tanalma, Zaghara, Mathan, Angimi, Nair* and *Tagua*,   The City *Kaugha* is on the *North* Bank the frefh Water, from which its Inhabitants draw to drink   This City is fubject to the Empire of *Van*

nevertheless some of the *Negroes* reckon it under the
Dominion of *Kanem* It is a populous City, without
Walls, famous for Business and useful Arts for the Advantage of its People   The Women of this City are so en-
dued with the Magick Art, that Witchcraft is in a peculiar Manner attributed to them, for they are said to
be very skilful, and their Charms effectual   From
Kaugha to *Semegondam*, towards the *West*, is ten Days
Journey   Also from *Kaugha* to *Ghana* is near a Month
and half's Journey   From *Kaugha* to *Damocla* is
reckon'd a Month's Journey.   Also from that to *Sabia* is
almost a Month   Again, from *Kaugha* to the City
Kucu is twenty Days Journey, towards the *North*, at the
Rate of the Camels travelling   The City *Kucu* is
famous among the *Negroes* for Bigness, it is situated on
the Bank of a River, which flowing from the *North*
Part, washes it, and affords Drink to the Inhabitants;
and altho' many *Negroes* relate that this City *Kucu* is
situated on the Bank of the *Nile*, others place it near a
River flowing into the *Nile*.   It is however, I apprehend
an Opinion, that that River glides along, till it passes for
many Days beyond *Kucu*, and then pours it self out into
the Desert, thro' Sands and Plains, in the same Manner
the River *Euphrates* doth in *Mesopotamia.*

Beside, the King of *Kucu* is absolute, dependant on no
one, he has much Attendance, and the greatest Empire,
Soldiers and Captains, Armour, and beautiful Furniture
These People ride on Horses and Camels, they are of a
martial Disposition, and frequently invade the neighbouring Nations   With respect to the Cloathing of this
Country, the common People cover their Nakedness with
the Skins of Beasts, but the Merchants cloath themselves
with Vests and Tunicks, wear Caps on their Heads, and
adorn themselves with Gold   The Governors and
Nobility are cover'd with Sattin, the Merchants go to,
and are conversant with them, and they change Goods
a way of Truck or Barter   A Wood grows in this
Country, which is called *Serpentine Wood*, and it is said
to be of that Nature, that if it be put to a Serpent's Den,
immediately the Serpent comes out of it   And also, that
he who wears this Wood, can take in his Hand a Serpent
without Fear, but rather, upon touching them, he shall
make them to feel in him some certain Courage   However, the

I uth

Truth of this Thing is only fupported by the Report, of the remote Nations of the *Weft*, and it is probable, that they who hold this Wood, or wear it about their Neck, have not been near any Serpent to try   This Wood is like *Pyrethrum* or *Bartram*, is of a twifted Grain, and of a black Colour

The City *Kucu* is diftant from the City *Guara* a Month and half's Journey, but from the City *Temal u*, towards the *Eaft*, fourteen Days   That is a fmall City, without Walls, frequented by People from the Country of *Kouar*   From *Tamalma* to the City *Mathar*, from the Country of *Kanem*, are twelve Days Journey, This alfo is a fmall City, and none of the ufual Arts are practifid in it, very few Merchandize, and the People have Camels and Goats   From the City *Mathan* to the City *Angim* is reckon'd eight Days Journey, and this alfo belongs to the Province of *Kanem*, it is very fmall, not inhabited by much People, and thefe of a mean Spirit   They are adjoining to *Nuba* on the *Eaft*, and diftant from the *Nile* three Days Journey, and they have no Water but from Wells   From *Angim* to the City *Zagnara* is fix Days Journey   *Zaghara* has many Towns, and populous   And round about it live a certain People, like thofe of *Zaghara*, who hire Camels of the Citizens, and they exercife fome Trade of Merchandize of little Value, and fome Arts among them   Thefe likewife drink Well Water, and eat large grain'd Millet, and dry Flefh of Camels, alfo Fifh mingled with Myrrh, and Milk Meats, with which they greatly abound   They cover themfelves over with Skins, and are the Swifteft in Running of all the *Negroes*   From the City *Zaghara* to *Mathan* is eight Days Journey, and the Emperor and Prince refide there, whofe Soldiers, as they are for the moft Part naked, are Archers   From this City *Mathan* to the City *Tagua* are thirteen Days Journey, and this is the Metropolis of the Kingdom of the Infidels of *Tegua*, obferving no Religion   The Country of thefe is bordering to that of *Nuba*, and to them belongs the little City *Semna*   And fome who have travelled over the Cities of *Kouar* report, that the Chief of *Jalac*, who has his Government from the King of *Nuba*, went into the City *Semna*, burnt and utterly deftroy'd it, and difpers'd its Inhabitants into different Parts,

Paits, and that this was lately ruined From the City *Tagua* to this same are fix Days Journey And from the City *Tagua* to the City *Nuabia*, from whence the Kingdom of *Nubia* its Name, and from thence the *Nubitæ*, are eighteen Days Journey.

Part IV. Climate I.

IN this fourth Part of the firft Climate is contained the Kingdom of *Nubia*, Part of *Æthiopia*, and the reft of the North of *Tagua*, and the inward Put of *Iahat* The moft famous Places and chief Cities of *Nubia*, are *Catla*, *Ghata*, (r) *Dancala*, *Jalac*, and *Sela* But in *Æthiopia*, *Macata* and *Nagiagha* In fine, in the Country of the in *Valat* and upper Part of *Ægypt*, are the Cities *Aguar*, *I..a* and *Redini* ----

In this Part is feen the (s) Separating of the two *Niles*, that of the *Nile* of *Ægypt*, which flowing from South to North, divides our Country, on each Shore of which are fituted the greateft Part of the Cities of *Ægypt*, fome others there are in the Iflands The other Part of the *Nile* flows from the Eaft to the utmoft Bounds of the Weft, and upon that Branch of the *Nile* lie all, or at leaft the moft celebrated Kingdoms of the Negroes

(r) [*Dancala*] Is one of the Kingdoms of *Æthiopia*, fubject to the Negus, and mentioned by *Ludolphus*; fo that the Author has defcribed all the Kingdoms up the *Nile* from the *Atlantick* to the *Abffines*, whofe Empire borders upon the Red Sea

(s) The *Nubian* Geographer in this Place is very clear in his Defcription of the Divifion of the *Nile*, and that one Branch (by Geographers called the *Niger Nile*) flows into the Weftern Ocean, and the other into the *Mediterranean*, and this agrees with what *Herodotus* reports the Priefts of *Ægypt* to have faid of the *Nile*, and it gives more Weight to his Opinion, that it is likely he never faw, nor perhaps heard of *Herodotus*, who wrote in *Greek*, a language very little known to the *Arabians* *Leo the African* alfo fays, that this was the received Opinion of the *Arabian* Geographers

EX-

EXTRACTS

TRANSLATED OUT OF

LEO the AFRICAN.

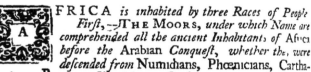

INTRODUCTION.

AFRICA *is inhabited by three Races of People First,* —THE MOORS, *under which Name are comprehended all the ancient Inhabitants of Africa before the Arabian Conquest, whether they were descended from* Numidians, Phœnicians, Carthaginians, Romans, Vandals, *or* Goths *During the* Arabian *Empire under the* Caliphs *all those Nations received the Mahometan Religion.*

By their manner of Living they may be divided into two Kinds, Those who have fixt Habitations, and live in Cities and Villages following Trade or Agriculture And those who live in the Desarts, and change their Habitations after the manner of the Arabs, *supporting themselves by Grazing and Hunting, and whose Profession is Arms.*

These latter seem to be the Descendants of the ancient Numidians. *Of them are five Tribes, who, to avoid the Fury of the* Arabians, *retired Southward into the Desarts of* Libya, *and one of those Tribes, that of* Zanaja, (Leo *says) discovered and conquered those* Negro *Nations which lie on the* Niger

Secondly, — THE ARABIANS, *who under the* Caliphs *Successors of* Mahomet, *after they had conquered Part of* Asia *and all* Ægypt, *passed the* Nile, *and subdued* Africa *Most of these* Arabians *live still in the Desarts upon feeding their Herds, Hunting and War, raising Contributions of the* Moors *who live in Cities, and by Agriculture. Some of their Tribes have rambled Southward as far as the River* Gambia, *and the* Pholeys *seem to be descended from them.*

Thirdly, —THE NEGROES, *who begin to inhabit where the Desart*

Defarts end, along the great River called Gambia *or* Niger, *and from thence Southward as far as the* Cape of Good Hope.

Leo the African *hath given a full Account of all thefe Nations from the* Mediterranean *Sea to the* Gambia, *by him called the* Niger, *and by the* Nubian *Geographer called the* Nile. *I have tranflated fuch Parts of him as fhews the Road from the great Cities of* Morocco *and* Fez, *to the Countries of the Negroes and the River* Gambia, *alfo his Account of the Negroes and the Courfe of the* Niger. *His Book is very curious and methodical, giving an Account of all the* Moorifh *Kingdoms, and exactly defcribing every Town, and the Changes that have happened, particularly the Decay of Arts and Learning which formerly flourifhed in the great City of* Morocco. *He enters into the Conftitution of the Governments, fome of which feem Republican. There were then feveral Kingdoms in* Africa, *and feveral free Towns and Families independent of thofe Kings. About the* 15th *Century, in which he lived, the* Portugueze *had made very great Ravages in* Africa, *for landing upon the Ports on the Ocean, they had pierced even into the Heart of the Kingdom of* Fez *In the Defcription of the different Towns, he gives an Account of thofe Revolutions He divides his Work into* 8 *Parts. I have the fecond Edition of his Book, which was publifhed at* Venice *in the Year* 1554. *In the firft Vol of* Ramufio's *Collection of Navigations and Voyages, the Work is in* Italian, *dedicated to the famous* Hieronimo Fracaftora. *In the Dedication to him the following Account is given of* Leo.

' This Author *(Leo)* was very converfant in all the Courts
' of *Barbary,* and in feveral Expeditions accompanied the
' Kings of that Country, even within our Days.   I fhall
' give a fhort Account of what I have collected concerning
' his Life from a Gentleman of Worth and Honour, who
' knew him at *Rome,* and lived fome Time there with him.
' He was by Race a *Moor,* born in *Granada,* and at the Time
' when the Catholick King *Ferdinand* conquered that King-
' dom from the Infidels, his Family retired into *Barbary,*
' and fettled in the City of *Fez,* where he ftudied the *Arabian*
' Learning, in which Time he compofed feveral Hiftories,
' which hitherto have not been publifhed He alfo wrote an *Ara-*
' *bian* Grammar, which Mafter *James Mantino* has by him Leo
' travelled thro' all *Barbary,* the Kingdoms of the *Negroes,*
' *Arabia* and *Syria,* and kept a Journal of all that he faw
' or heard worthy of Remark In the Pontificate of *Leo*
' the 10th he was taken near the Ifland of *Zerbi,* by Cor-

fairs

' ſairs, conducted to *Rome* and given to the Pope, who
' having ſeen him, and underſtanding he took Delight in
' *Geography*, and that he had with him a Book that he had
' compoſed on that Subject, his Holineſs received him very
' graciouſly, and gave him a handſome Penſion, that he
' might not have any Inclination to leave him.   He became
' a Chriſtian,   the Pope was his Godfather, and gave him
' the Names of *John Leo*.   He lived many Years in *Rome*,
' where he learnt the *Italian* Tongue ſo well, that he him-
' ſelf tranſlated this his Book from *Arabick* into it,
' which Book in his own Hand-writing we have by us, and
' with the utmoſt Diligence we are Maſters of, have cor-
' rected and printed very exactly in the Manner we have now
' laid it before you '

This Account tranſlated from the Dedication of Ramuſio *is
ſo full, that we need add nothing to it concerning the Author,
only that ſince his Time wonderful Changes have happened in
that Country, which he foretold would be the Conſequences of
the arbitrary Power grown up about his Age, which had
brought Government itſelf into ſuch Abhorrence, that he ſays,*
' Pcioche gli huomini di riputatione, & di bonta, no ſi dag-
' nano d'eſſere ammeſſi negli uſici della corte   né ſimiglian-
' temente di dar niunda delle lor figlie à quelli, che ſono
' della caſa del Re.'

*He ſays this bad Government occaſioned univerſal Avarice and
Corruption, and the Contempt of Learning and Education,
extended Ignorance, Immorality and Superſtition, thro' all A-
frica, and would end in Deſtruction   The Event has juſtified
his wiſe Conjectures, for all* Mauritania *is now fallen to the
loweſt State of Barbariſm and Ignorance , ſo that the Poſterity
of thoſe brave and learned* Arabians *and* Moors, *who preſerved
Aſtronomy and Phyſick, invented Alchymy and Decimal Cy-
phers in Arithmetick, who conquered* Africa, Spain, *and Part
of* France, *ſubdued by their own Vices, ſubmitted quietly to*
Muley Iſhmael *for the laſt half Century, and are now ruled by
the Will, or rather by the Whim of an Army of* Blackamoors,
who make or unmake their Emperors

Leo's *Account of* Fez *was too long for to inſert in this Treatiſe, ſo we have only given the Heads of it.   The Road from
thence to* Tombuto, *the Capital Kingdom of the Negroes, lay
thro'* Morocco, Duccala, Hea, Sus, Dara, *and* Segelmeſſe
In this Journey they climb over Mount Atlas, *and* Leo *gives
an Account of a Prince of one of thoſe Mountains, which we*
here

have inferted at large They *also pass thro'* Numidia, *where the Ufe of Dates fupplies Bread, and thence they crofs the dreadful Defarts of* Libya, *of which we have given what* Leo *fays at large, as alfo the Defcription of feveral of the Towns, which, as we think it will give the Curious fome Idea of the Inland Parts of* Africa, *we hope it will not be deemed fwelling this Book with foreign Matter, but rather, that the Labour we have taken in collecting and tranflating many curious Matters for the Information of our Readers, from a Book now almost out if Print, will meet with a kind Reception.*

NOTE *In this, as in the former Geographer, the (g) is always pronounced in the* Arabic *Names like the (j)*

Extracts *from* JOHN LEO

the African's *Geographical History* of Africa

Part I. Sect. III.

O*f the* Division *of* AFRICA.

THE A... Geographers divide *Afri...* ...to ten
C..., R.gions, or P.rts, ...
Bar.ary, Libya, .nd
Numidia, the Land of *Negro*
... Barbary begins at the Mountain of *Meie*, w...
... most Eastern Point of the Mountains of ...
... t araria, being near 300 Miles from t...
On t.e North, the *Mediterranean Sea* bounds it from
Mount *Meies* to the Streights by the *Pillars of H...*
... Westward of those Streights it runs out of the *M...*
... S to the Main Ocean, and exten... to
Western Po... of *Atlas*, which is the Cape re...
the Te.. n of *M...*, .nd it is bounded on the S... b..
Mou.t *A...* ... is the best Region of all *A...*

a Leo begins with a general Description of *Africa*, w.h
w ch the Reader could have no clear Notion where
C... ..s, therefore I have inserted it, since by ..w.th
... .. N.tions and Parts of the World may be con...
... c... .. traded with from the *Gambia*. The *Afri... G...*
g .p.. Manner of dividing the World was into Clim...
con...g.. a certain Number of Degrees, and beginning...
La., ... describe all t.. t Coun.ry Westward till they c...
t... ..rn Sea. Thus Leo begins with *Barbary* near
...y, boun.ed on the No.th by the *Mediterranea Sea* ...
c.. ..o.th b. the Mountains of *Atlas*, and describe .h.t
... rg ...s up the *Niger N.le*, from ..here it empties i...
... ..r Western Ocean, to the Country of the *Al...*

which there are Cities inhabited by civilized People, who make good Laws for the Government of their refpective States, and are of a tawny Colour almoft white.

The fecond Part of *Africa* is by the *Latins* named *Numidia*, but the *Arabians* call it *Biledulgerid* It produces abundance of Dates The Beginning of it Eaftward is at the City of *Eloacat*, 100 Miles from *Egypt*, and it runs to the Weftward as far as the Town of *Nun* upon the Ocean Sea *Atlas* limits it upon the North, do the fandy Defarts of *Libya* on the South It is generally by the *Arabians* called the Land of Dates, this being the Region of *Africa* that bears moft Dates This Region has but one Name, being all of the fame Nature.

The third Part is in the *Latin* Tongue called *Libya*, or by the *Arabians Sarra* (fignifying the Defert) It beginneth Eaftward at that Part of *Nilus* neareft the City of *Eluat*, and runs to the Weft as far as the Ocean Sea. *Numidia* bounds it on the North, the Country of *Negroes* on the South It begins Eaftward at the Kingdom of *Gaga*, and runs Weftward to * *Gualata*, and that *Gualata* borders upon the Sea

The fourth Part of *Africa*, is the Land or Country of *Negroes*, it begins at *Gaoga* Eaftward, and extends Weftward to *Gualata* The Defert of *Libya* inclofes the North Part, and the Ocean the South Part, which is to us unknown (except what we learn'd from the Accounts of the Merchants who come from thence to *Tombute*) In the Country of the Negroes, there is a noble River called *Niger*, which beginneth Eaftward from a Defart, named by the Natives *Seu* Others affirm that the *Niger* fprings out of a Lake, and fo goeth on Weftward till it empties itfelf into the Sea Our Cofmographers fay that it comes out of *Nilus*, and that for fome Space it is hid in the Earth, and afterwards pours forth in fuch a Lake as is before mentioned Some other People think that the Beginning of this River is to the Weftward, and fo running Eaft formeth that great Lake But that is not probable, becaufe they go with the Stream in Boats Weftward from *Tombuto* to *Guinea*, and *Melli*, for thofe Kingdoms are fituated to the Weft of *Tor* - *i* The moft fertile of the Negroe Countries, are thofe which lie upon the Banks of the (b) *Ng*

Y 4 *The*

The DIVISION *of* BARBARY

BARBARY is divided into four Kingdoms. The Ch[...]
of them is Morc[...], which contains seven Prov[...]
[...] Fez, S[...], Guzula, Mec[...], Duccala, Hac[...], and
Tedles. Fez, the next Kingdom of *Barbary*, is also div[...]
[...] seven Provinces, viz. Tor-fic (the Country of Fez)
Azga[...], Er[...]at, Erif, Gur[...]et, and Elcauz. The thi[...]
Kingdom of *Barbary* is called *Telensin*, which compre-
hends three Regions, that is to say, the Mountains, Ta-
nez, and Azaz[...]. The fourth Kingdom of *Barbary* is
Tun[...], containing four Provinces, *Bugia*, *Conflentin*, *Tri-
pol[...] in Barbary*, and *Lezabe*, which is Part of Num[...]

✦✧✦✧✦✧✦✧✦✧✦✧ ✦✧✦✧✦✧✦✧✦✧✦✧

DIVISION *of* NUMIDIA
Which is al/o called the Land of DATES

NUMIDIA is the worst Part of *Africa*, inomuch
that the old *Arabian* Hiftorians will hardly call
[...] Kingdom, because the Natives of it are fo far divided
on one another by the Deferts. For *Teffet*, a Num[...]
[...] City, which contains about 400 Families, is feparated from all Places of Habitation almoft 300 Miles
by the Lib[...]an Defart. But we fhall mention thofe Parts of
Num[...]a which are inhabited, fome of which may be compared with other *African* Regions, viz. *Segelmefs*, a Region of
Num[...]a lying between *Morocco* and the Country of Negroes,
and *Zeb*, fituate againft *Bugia* and *Biledulgerid*, which extends
to the Kingdom of *Tunis*. We fhall referve many Particulars of this Country for another Part of this Hiftory,
and will begin with thofe Places which lie on the W[...]
of Num[...], the Names of which are, *Teffet*, *Gunaen*, [...]
[...], H[...], Dare, Tebelbe't, Todga, Fercale, Sege[...],
B[...], Fighig, Tegua, Tfabu, Tegorarin, Mefab, Tigor[...],
and G[...]ght ------ The Province of *Zeb* hath five Towns
B[...] than the fame Number of Cities. This is
the Divifion of *Numidia*, bounded upon the Weft by the
Ocean, and on the Eaft by the N[...]

DIVISION *of* LIBYA,
or the Deserts which lie between NUMIDIA *and the Land of* NEGROES

THE *Arab* in Geographers have not as yet divided the *Libyan* Deserts, which lie between the Land of *Negroes* and *Numidia*, by any Names, but the *Maritans* who live in them, have divided them into five Parts, and given them Names themselves. The *Moors* who inhabit them are divided into five Tribes, *viz. Zargal, Guenzigi, Terga, Lenta,* and *Berdeva.*

DIVISION *of the Country of* NEGROES *into Kingdoms.*

THE Country of Negroes hath many Kingdoms; and notwithstanding there are many of them, of which we have no Knowledge, yet we will describe those where we have ourselves been, and which are well known to us, also some others, from whence Merchants have travelled to those Towns where I myself have resided, and from them got acquainted with their Countries. I saw (a) 15 Kingdoms of the Negroes myself, but there are several others which I never saw, but the Negroes know them well. Beginning West, and going Eastward and Southward, the following are their

---

(a) The Author had himself been at *Tombuto,* which by his Description must be about the Mid-way between *Ethiopia,* or the Land of the *Abyssines,* and the Mouth of the *Gambia.* *Tombuto* was then the most considerable Part of the Region of the Negroes for Trade, since the Trade was then carried on by Caravans of Camels, who came over-land from *Barbary* to them. And as *Tombuto* lay nearest to the River *Dara,* which was the Place where the Deserts were narrowest, and Water easiest to be had, that Conveniency settled the Trade then there, for Trade follows Conveniency of Carriage, which is the Reason that the Negroe Merchants now come down to the River *Gambia,* because the Things they want are easily brought thither by Water from *Europe.*

t__ N_mes, __ (^) G__ _t_, (n) Gl_n_a, M_t, T_m__
G__, C__, _g_u_, Cano, Cufina, Zegzeg, Zenfu
(_i_g_u, Bu_no, (c) G_g__, (d) N_be Thefe 15 K__
_oms __ meftly _tu__ __on the N_g_, _hro' ___ __
_M_ h__ go from G__ua to the City of _d_, __
(_) _g_t. The Journcy is not dangerous, but ver_ l__

T_

( ) G_la_,] is what I take to be t_e Kingdom of the
J_u__Ts, or *Jualafas*

_n_ [Gh_nea,] I take to be the upper Part of w_a_ _ called
Ja_, and a_l *W_olly* The other Towns are at pre_c_ un
known to u_, the *F_gl_fh* have never gone up nigher in th
Ri_e_ than *H__u*, Whether the other Kingdoms do n_w _oo
_ft or n__, is a g_eat Do_bt Th_y were founded b_ _ne
M_o_rs or *Nu__d_iars* who came from *L_b_a,* introducing t_e __a
_om_tan Rel_gion with their Arms and Governme_t They
were _up__ed w_th Clothe_, _rm_, Iron-Wor_, and the o_her
_h_ngs they wanted, from the Kingdoms of *Barbar_,* from
_he_ce _hey fir_t c_me, and where the Manufacturer_ were
w_o m__e _hofe Goods

_c_ [G_nza,] I_is Region _s defcribed by *Ludolph_,* being
on_ of the kingdom_ of the *Ab_ffine* Empire above *Æthiop_a*

__ [N_b_,] _s _ell known, being what was antiently called
Æ___ lying South of _Eg_pt _his was the *Nub_an*
Geographe_'s Na_ive Countr_, in which he fays the *N_g_r*
__ de_ _rom the *N_le* The Inhab_tants were formerl_ Chr_f_i
__s of the _*lex__d_in* Church, but are _ow Mahometans

__ [Æ_pt,] in _hat _ime w_ich was before any Goods were
c_r_ ed b_ _he Sh_pping from *Engl_nd* to the Mouths of the *Gam*
_a _he _race _as carried on from *Gualata,* or the Land of
_he *J_l__s* to *Ak_n* in *Æg_t* the whole Breadth of *A_r_a*
__ ca__e_ Sa_t made at *J_ct_,* or *L_l,* and in their W_y
_nch_r_e_ _t for Go_d, and w_h it in *_Eg_pt,* the_ boug_t
Pr_d__ C_u_fl__, K__e_, Iron, D_gger_ and other Th_ng_, w_h
__ch th_y furn__h_d the Countr_e_ on their Return But the
Co_rle of _rade is now qu__e changed, and thofe N_t_on_
_h__ l_e n_a_c_t the *G_rb_* are no _le_t fupplied with Goods,
_or th_f_ upon the R__e_ *C_mb_a* b_ng able to buy Goods
_rom the *Engl_f_,* not onl_ furn_fh them with their Gold a_d
Sl__e_ but the Bl'ack Merch__t_, or *J_r_oe_,* go up into the
Co__tr_e_ to b_y Go_d and S_a_e_, and bring them d_wn to
_h_f_ _ the _o_e__ C_unt_r_, _here to fell to the Sh_p_g
_h_s l_ng March f_om G__ to *Æg_p_* feems almoft in_re
__ble f_n_e _ne ca_ __rc_ conce_ve ho_ any Goods cou'd bear
_he _c___ __ r_o _o _onn a L_nd Carr_age, but _ho' th__ car
n__ _e _ou__ b_ r_co___led, _he N__ure of that Count_r_
w_ll

The Kingdoms join upon one another, ten of them are separated by the *Niger* or Sandy Deserts Formerly they had all distinct Kings, but now they are governed by three only. The King of *Tombuto*, who has the greatest Part, the King of *Borno*, who has the least, and the Residue subject to the King of *Gaoga* There are several other Kingdoms bordering upon the Southern Parts of them, viz *Bito*, *Jemian*, (f) *Dauma*, *Medra* and *Goclam*, whereof the Natives and Governours are rich and industrious, and live by Rules of Equity and Justice, but some of them lead a brutish kind of Life The *Arabian* Historians say that in former Times no Part of *Africa* was inhabited, but that which is now named the Country of *Negroes* or *Blacks* And it is past Contradiction, that *Barbary* and *Numidia* were for several Ages destitute of Inhabitants The tawny People were named (g) *Barbar* from *Barbara*, to murmur, because the Tongue of the *Africans* is esteemed by the *Arabians*, as that of Beasts, without Accents ----------

Of

will make it less surprizing, since the Carriage costs little The Slaves carry each their Burden, and some Corn, which is very cheap, and the Main of their Nourishment is, Locusts, wild Honey, Roots, Ostriches, and other Game which they find in the Woods and Deserts, and when once they come to Roads passable for Camels, it is a Question if the Carriage upon those Beasts is not equally cheap to Carriage by Sea, considering that 250 Camels, with a few Men to attend them, carry equal to a Ship of 100 Tons, that they live upon what they find in the Fields, with a very small additional Allowance of Balls made up with Flower and Molasses, whereas a Ship requires a great Out-set, Men, Provisions, Wear and Tear, &c

(f) [*Dauma*,] by the Name and Situation of it, to the Southward of the *Gambia*, seems to have an Affinity with the *Dau Lamau*, a very formidable Nation lying far within Land, Part of whom have made a great Figure, by lately invading the Kingdoms of *Whidah* and *Ardah* near the *Gold Coast* But the *Arabians* knew very little of what was South of the *Gambia*, so that these are dark Guesses

g [*Barbar*,] the Derivation of *Barbary* may be from the *Latin* Word *Barbarus*, for the old Inhabitants of *Africa* keep the Tongue they had before the *Roman* Time, which by their Conquest was something mixt with the *Latin*.

Of the Original of the Moors of Africa

THE *Arabian* Historians are not agreed about the Original of the *Moors*, or Tawny Inhabitants of *Africa*. Some of they are descended from the Inhabitants of (*a*) *Palestine*, whom the *Jews* drove out of their own Country, and at last came to *Africa*, where the Pleasantness and Fruitfulness of the Soil induced them to make it their Place of Habitation. Others say that their Original was from a People of *Arabia Felix*, called the (*b*) *Sabeans*, and that ever before the *Ethiopians* drove them out of that Country. Others say that they originally came from a certain People of *Asia*, who, chased thence by Wars, fled into *Greece*, which at that Time was not at all inhabited, but the Enemy pursued them, and forced them to cross the Sea of *Africa*, or *Mediterranean*, they arriving in *Africa*, settled there, but their Enemies stayed in *Greece*. These Things are to be understood of the Origin of the *Moors*, the *Barbarians* and *Numidians*, for the *Negroes* are all descended from (*d*) *Chus*, the Son of *Chan*, who was the Son of *Noah*. Notwithstanding the Difference between the *Moors* and *Negroes*, they had all one Beginning, being descended from the *Philistines*, and they from *Mizraim*, the Son of *Chus*. But the *Moors* are descended from the *Sabeans*, for *Saba* was begotten of *Rama*, the eldest Son of *Chus*. There are more Opinions concerning the *Africans* Original, but we shall omit them as unnecessary.

O,

(*a*) [*Palestine*] This may be meant of the famous Republick of *Carthage*, which was founded by the *Tyrians*, who were of *Palestine*.

(*b*) It is very probable the Original of the *Numidians* was from the *Sabeans*, for their Customs, when the *Romans* came first acquainted with them, were very like those of the *Arabians*.

( ) It seems as if this was a mistaken Account of *Cyrene* and other Colonies settled by the *Grecians* in *Africa*.

(*d*) This Account being also of Matters which happened before the Time of *Mahomet*, the Reader will receive it without thanks it, but I thought it would be a Matter of Curiosity, to shew what was the *Arabic* Opinion of the Original of the *Moors*.

Of the Tribes of the Moors of Africa.

THE (a) *Moors* or *Numidians* are divided into 5 Tribes, *Sanhagia, Mufmuda, Zeneta, Haoara* and *Gumera* The Tribe of *Mufmuda* inhabits the South Part of the Mountain of *Atlas*, and all the Inland Plains of that Region ----- The two Tribes of *Mufmuda* and *Gamera* live by themselves, but the other three are difperfed ll over *Africa* ----- Some of the *Zeneta* govern all *Africa*, having formerly o ercame the Family called *Idris*, from whom it is id, the true and natural Generals of *Fez* derive their Pedigree, who were the Founders of the fame City, and their Succeffors were called *Meenafa* Another Family of the *Zeneta*, called *Magrasa*, came out of *Numidia* of ervands, who chafed the Family of *Meenafa*, with their Chefs, out of their Territories It was not long after that, before the Tribe of *Magrasa* was chafed out in the fame Manner by fome of the *Sanhaga* Race, called *Luntuna*, who came from the Defart of *Numidia* This Family wafted and utterly deftroyed the Country of *Temefne*, and flew all the Inhabitants, except fuch who were either of their Tribe or Kindred, and to them they gave the Country of *Dueula* to live in, who built the City of *Morocco* Since that or *Elmahdi*, the Head of the *Mahometan* Preachers thereabouts, conipiring with thofe of the *Mufmuda* Family, called *Hargu*, drove out ll the *Luntuna*, and governed the Kingdom himfelf When he died, one of the *Sanhaga*, called *Habdul Mumen*, a Barganogel, fucceeded nim, and that Family poffefled the Kingdom 120 Years, to which moft Parts of *Africa* were it ert ----

Of the Language of the Africans

THE foregoing five Families were multiplied into Hundreds of Families, and tho' there are innumerble Nations, yet they ufe ll one Language, by them named

(a) He is fpeaking of the *Moors*, whom he diftinguiftes from the *Italians*

Apel

... *Aquil Amarg*, the Noble Tongue The *Africa* ...
call it a barbarous Tongue, but it is the general La ...
of *Africa*, quite different from other Tongues, yet ...
great many *Arabian* Words in it, which occasions t ...
trun ?, that by lineal Descent the *Africans* are de ... tr ...
the *Saracens*, a People of *Arabia Fælix* Others thin ...
Language was in Being before the *Arabians* came int *A* ...
but their Authors were so negligent, that the ... W ...
times either to prove or disprove it   They who ... ...
and trade with the *Arabian*, do mostly speak ... L ...
guage ---- The *Negroes* have a good man ... lang ...
mongst them, of which one named (*b*) *Sunga* is ... ...
a great many of their Kingdoms, *viz.* *Gu... , Gu...*
Tombuto, *Melli* and *Gego*   They have nother call'd *G...*
which is used by the Inhabitants of *C... ?, C... ?, P...*
greg and *Guangra*   *Borno* hath a Language of ... ...
like that used in *Gaga*   The Tongue used in *N...*
Mixture of the *Chaldean*, *Ægypt* and *Arabian* L ... ...
but all the Towns near the Sea, from the Mou... ...
Atlas to the Mediterranean Sea, speak broken *Arab... , e...*
cept *Morocco* and the *Numidians* Inland bordering upon *F...*
Tremzen and *Morocco*, who speak the Langu... ...
Barbarian.   Those over-against *Tunis* and *Tr... ...*
bad *Arab...*

Of the Arabians *who inhabit the City of* Cairoan

OTMAN, the third Califf, sent an Army ou... ...
subdued many Regions, and at length 80,000 o... ...
came into *Africa*, the Commander of whom ... ...
himself there, whose Name was *Hucha Huru Nat...* ...
built the great City of *Cairoan*, because he was ... ...
the Inhabitants of *Tunis* would betray him by ge... ...
cours from *Sicily*, and therefore took all his Treas... ...
Defart about 120 Miles from *Carthage*, and there b... ...

(*a*) *Leo* certainly gives to these Languages the *Arab...* Nam...
which are quite different from the Names given by the People of the
Country, for the Language spoke by the *Jolloiffs* is call'd *Jo-*
loiff, and that spoke by the *Negroes* is called *Mandi go*
(*b*) [*Sungai*] That is at this Time the Name of ... ...
mi's of *Berial.*

nd *Car oan* He ordered his People alw ns to defend th m-
felves in the Def rts, nd not to depend upon the S eng h
of Fortifications or Rocks, nor to dwell ne r them, nd
tus the *Arabians* remained fafe, conquered ll *A*, .., and
mixt with the Natives. -----

※※※※※※※※※※※※※※※※※※※※※※※※※

The Customs and Manner of Life of those Africans who inhabit the Defarts of Libya.

THE five Tribes of *Sarhagia*, &c are by the *Latins*
called *Numidæ* They live in the following Manner
They have no Rule, nor least Form of Government their
Dress is a Piece of coarfe Cloth, which covers but a little of
their Body, upon their Heads they wear a fmall Turbant
of black Cloth, their principal Men, to distinguish themfelves, wear a short Gown of blue Cotton, which comes to
their Knees, with wide Sleeves, which they buy from the
Merchants that come from the *Negrees*, they ride only upon
Dromedaries or Camels, between the two Belfes, or the
between the Bofs and the Neck, they use no Stirrups, and
prick the Beaft on with a Goad inftead of Spurs Thofe
Dromedaries that are broke for riding, have the Grifle of
their Nofes bored, as the Buffloes have in *Italy*, thro' which
they run a Leather-Strap, which they use for a Bridle Inftead of Beds they use Matts, very finely made of Reeds and
Canes, their Tents are of Cloth made of Camels Hair, or
of the Fibres of the Date-Trees, as for their Food, thofe
who have not feen would not believe with what Patience
they fupport Hunger and Thirft, from their Infancy they
are brought up to live without Bread, or any kind of Grain,
but they are nourished with Camels Milk, and they in the
Morning generally drink a large Draught of it, which ferves
them till Supper, when they eat fuch Flefh as they can get
boiled in Milk or Butter, when it is dreft they take the
Pieces out with their Hands and eat it, as we would a Cruft
of Bread, without Plates or Knives, when the Broth is almoft cool, they take it up with the Hollow of their Han
inftead of Spoons, if they have it, they even drink a Cup of
Milk, which is the End of their Supper Whilft they have
Milk they do not want Water, and during the Spring when
they have Plenty of it, they are so wicked as to g ve no

W e

Weeks without Wafhing(*a*), and their Camels alfo require no Water whilft they have green Grafs to feed on　They fpend their whole Lives in Hunting, or in plundering their Enemies ; they ftay but a few Days in one Place, becaufe their Camels in that Time have eat up the neighbouring Grafs. Though, as I faid above, they have no Rule or legal Form of Government, yet each Party has a Chief, whom they honour and obey as their King , they are not only ignorant of Letters, but of all Arts, Sciences and Virtue (*b*), for amongft this People it is very difficult to find a fingle Judge who underftands the Law , fo that fhould there fuch a Thing happen as a Law-fuit, it would be neceffary for the Plaintiff to ride at leaft fix Days Journey to find a Judge learned in the Law, for very few of the Profeffion care to live amongft fuch poor Wretches, or can bear with their Cuftoms or manner of Life. ---- Their Women are plump, well-featured, and finely limbed, but of dark-coloured Skins　They are very civil, and will permit you to touch their Hands, and kifs them, but he who goes farther, does it at the Rifque of his Life, for in cafe of Adultery a *Moor* would, without Mercy, put both the offending Parties to Death　Thefe People are very generous and courteous to Strangers, and when any Travellers pafs thro' their Defarts, they will not go to their Tents to afk any thing of them, nor will they go on the great Road to beg or defire any thing, but every Caravan that comes thro' their Defart pays to the Prince thro' whofe Territories it paffes, a coarfe Cloth worth a Ducat for every Camel　I paffed with a Caravan thro' the Defart of *Araon*, where a Prince of the Race of *Zenaga* ruled , we went to him, and found him accompanied with 50 Men mounted upon Dromedaries, we paid him the ordinary Tribute, and he invited us to go to his Camp, and repofe ourfelves two or three Days , but that as it was out of our Road, and that our Camels were tired, the Merchants excufed themfelves, and gave him great Thanks, on which he told them their Camels and Baggage might go forward, and that thofe who were on Horfeback might go along with him, and eafily after-

wards

(*a*) The not wafhing is a high Crime among the *Mahometa.s*
· (*b*) *Leo* being bred a *Mahometan* Lawyer, will not allow any Man to be virtuous that does not underftand their Commentators, who pretty near anfwer our *Coke* upon *Littleton*

wards overtake their Camels.   He carried all us and the Merchants with him, and entertained us with great Abundance, according to the Nature of the Place.   We were no fooner arrived but he ordered Camels, and Camel-Calves, and other Cattle, to be killed ; and Oftriches, and other Kind of Game, which he had taken by the Way, to be dreft for our Provifion.   We defired him not to kill fo many Camels for us, for that they were very valuable, and that we feldom eat of their Flefh but when all other Food failed us.   He anfwered, That he fhould be afhamed to entertain Strangers with killing only the fmaller Cattle, and that he would treat us with the beft he had, and with his largeft Camels.   Our Feaft was compofed of Flefh boiled and roafted , the Oftriches were roafted, and ferved up in Bafkets made of Cane   They were ftuffed with fweet Herbs and Pepper, which they have from the Country of the *Negroes*.   They gave us alfo Cakes made of Millet and Manfaroke (*a*), which were extremely good and well tafted. The Defert was Dates in vaft Abundance, and huge Veffels filled with Milk   The Prince honoured us with his Prefence, and that of his neareft Relations ; but they eat by themfelves, and had fome religious Men with them, none of them touched any Cakes, or Bread, or Dates, but only eat Flefh or Milk.   The Prince perceiving that we were furprifed at this, told us, with a fmiling Countenance, that they were born in that Country, where no Corn grew, and that it was proper they fhould live upon the Produce of their Native Land   *That Corn was a foreign Luxury*, and that they kept it only for to oblige Strangers with.   It is true, they eat Bread upon the higheft Feftival Days ; but that was little, and only by way of Sacrifice.   We ftaid two Days with him, and the Quantity of Food dreft in that Time was furprifing , as alfo the Courtefy and Joy with which he treated us.   The third Day he gave us Leave to depart, himfelf accompanying us till we joined the Caravans   And certainly the Beafts which he killed during the Time we were there, were in Value ten Times the Tribute we paid.   The other four Tribes of *Numidia* have the fame Cuftoms, and live in the fame Manner.----

(*a*) *Vid* Journal, p 31

Z   *Of*

Of the Religion of the Moors, and other an-cient Africans.

THE old *Africans* were much given to Idolatry, some Persons fill Life, some of them worshipping the ~~~ I ~~~ and some the Sun ~~~ And they had, in *Tingis*, noble Temples built to the Honour of both the Sun and Fire, in which they kept continual Fires, as the vestal Virgins did at *Rome* ---- Those *Africans* of *Libia* and *Numidia* worshipped each a particular Planet, to which they offered Prayers and Sacrifices ~~~ Others of the Land of *Negroes* worship the *Guighinuge*, *i. e.* The Lord of Heaven ~~~ Which their Religion was not given them by any Prophet, but they were inspired with it by God himself ~~~ The *Jewish* Law prevailed amongst them ~~~ to wards of many Years ~~~ and that they profeſſed Chriſtianity, till the 268th Year of the *Hegira*, at which Time some of *Mahomet*'s Diſciples deceived them, so that they followed their Opinion, and all the Kingdoms of the *Negroes* adjoining to *Libia*, turned *Mahometans*, and ſlew all that were not of that Faith; ſo that even till now there are no Chriſtians at all among the *Negroes*, but thoſe near the Sea are great Idolaters, with whom the *Portuguize* do ſtill keep, and have for a long Time kept up a great Traffick.

Of the Letters and Characters of the Africans.

THE ancient *African* Hiſtorians think that the *Africans* uſed the *Latin* Characters only, and that ſcruple not to alter, that when the *Arabians* invaded *Africa*, no Characters were found amongſt them but the *Latin*. They allow that the *Africans* have a peculiar Language, but ſay that they uſe the *Latin* Letters ~~~ With Accounts the *Africans* have of the ancient *African* Hiſtory, as tranſlated from the *Latin* Books, ſome of which were very ancient, and ſome wrote in the Time of *the African* ~~~ L ~~~ the Titles of them have ſlipt my Memory, tho it is probable their Works were very voluminous, for I remember an *Arabian* Author, who quotes a Paſſage out of the 70th Book of one of thoſe (a) Hiſtories ~~~ They did not in the Tranſla-

cor

(a) It is reported that *Titus Livius* is the Book here meant.

conform to the Method of the *Latin* Authors, but took the History of one particular Monarch, and mix'd his Exploits with other Kings of the same Times But the *Mahometan* Princes commanded all the *African* Books to be burnt, imagining that the *Africans* would contemn the Doctrine of *Mahomet*, as long as they were acquainted with natural Philosophy and other Sciences On the other Side, the *Africans* had (as some Historians affirm) peculiar Characters to themselves, which were utterly destroyed from the Time the *Romans* subdued those Regions of *Africa* It is not improbable that a vanquished People should use the Letters and Customs of those who overcome them For the same Thing happened to the *Persians* at the Time the *Arabian* Empire flourished, all their Books were burnt by the Order of the *Mahometan* Prelates, for fear they should be induced by those Books to despise *Mahomet's* Doctrine ---- Whenever any of the People of the Cities of *Barbary* are desirous of recording any Verses to Posterity, they make use of the *Latin* Letters All these Things put together, makes me think that formerly the *Africans* had Letters proper and peculiar to themselves, in which they described all great Actions It is probable that the *Romans* (as Conquerors generally do) as soon as they had overcome those Provinces, destroyed their Letters and Memory, and used their own instead of them, that the *Roman* Honour and Fame might be only continued there Every one knows that the *Goths* did the same to the *Roman* Edifices, and the *Arabians* to the Monuments of the *Persians* The *Turks* in the time, or when they take any Town from the Christians, they immediately destroy the Images of their Saints ---- No Wonder that after so long a Time, and so many Alterations, the *Africans* are destitute of Letters, considering the *Arabians* had been Masters nine Hundred Years, therefore, whoever doubts that the *Africans* had any peculiar Kind of Writing, may as well doubt their having any Language ----

Description *of the* Lands *in* AFRICA.

AFRICA being divided into four Parts, the Face of the Country is not every where the same That which lies along the *Mediterranean* Shore, as from the

Stieights of *Gibral r* to the Frontiers of *Ægypt*, abour a
in fome Places with Mountains To the Southward they
reach anout 100 Miles, from the Ridge of thofe Mountains
to Mount *Atlas* is a very large Plain and many fmall
Hills In this Part, there are a great many Fountains which
meet together, and form Lakes, from whence fpring crystal
Streams and pleafant Rivers This Plain is bounded on
the South by Mount *Atlas*, beginning Weftward at the
Ocean, and extending Eaftward to the Borders of *Æg*
Beyond *Atlas* lie the Plains of *Numidia*, which produce
plenty of *Dates*, the Soil thereabouts is moftly Sand Between the Land of *Negroes* and *Numidia*, lies the fandy Defart of *Libya*, in which it is true there are fome Mountains, but the Merchants chufe not to go that Way,
becaufe Thieves make it dangerous Beyond the De-
of *Libia* lies the Land of *Negros*, which is chiefly a level
fandy Soil, excepting thofe Parts upon the River N
or near fome River or running Stream, which are very
fruitful

Of the wild and fnowy Mountains of Africa.

THE Mountains of *Batary* are more fubject to
Cold then Heat For feldom comes a Gale of Wind
without Snow The Mountains produce plentier of Fruit
then of Corn Barley Bread is the chief Subfiftence of
the Natives, from the Mountains iffue forth Rivers and
Springs Thefe Mountains are full of fine Trees and
wild Beafts But the Valleys and fmall Hills which
lie between thefe Mountains and Mount *Atlas*, abound
in Corn, being watered with the Rivers which fpring
out of *Atlas*, and run towards the *Mediterranean* Sea
Nor ditending thefe Plains and Valleys produce fo
many Woods, yet they are fruitful, as is evident in the
Regions of *Morocco*, *Dukkala*, *Tedla*, *Temefna*, *Affa*,
and that Country near *Gibraltar* Streights

The Top of the Mountains of *Atlas* are very barren
and cold, the Sides are cover'd with high thick Woods
produce little Corn, but almoft all the Rivers of Af
are formed from *Atlas* The Fountains are fo cold even
in the middle of Summer, that if a Man puts his Hand

ſ them for any confiderable Time, he endangers the loſing it. But all the Parts of theſe Mountains are not equally cold, for ſome are ſo temperate that they ſwarm with Inhabitants. The Places not inhabited are either extremely cold, or elſe very unpleaſant, notwithſtanding which they feed their Cattle there in the Summer, but cannot in the Winter, by reaſon of the Northerly Wind, which blows ſo hard, and brings ſuch abundance of Snow, that the Cattle then there, and a great many of the People are ſtarved, ſo that whoever wants to travel that Way in the Winter, chuſes to go between Numidia and Mauritania. The Merchants who bring Dates to other Nations out of Numidia, and cannot ſet out before the End of October, are ſometimes overtaken by a ſudden Shower of Snow, ſo that perhaps all of them periſh in it; for when it begins to ſnow in the Evening, and continues all Night, the Carriages and Men are covered and ſtifled under it, ſo that their dead Carcaſſes are not found till the Sun melt-en the Snow. I myſelf, by God's Providence, twice narrowly eſcaped being loſt in the Snow ---- Beyond At-las there are ſome Places very hot and dry, watered with very few Rivers but what flow from *Atlas* itſelf, ſome of which run into the Deſarts of *Libya*, where they are dried up with the Sands; but there are others which form Lakes. Notwithſtanding theſe Places bring forth Dates in Plenty, yet do they produce but little Corn. Some other Trees there are which bear Fruit, but not ſo as to be of any Profit, or indeed to anſwer the Trouble of tending. In that Part of *Numidia* near *Libya*, are ſome barren Hills, with no Trees upon them, but only a few Shrubs. There are no Springs or Rivers amongſt theſe Hills, nor any Wa-ter but what is in Pits, which few of the Inhabitants know any thing of, neither have they for ſix or ſeven Days Journey any Water but what the Merchants carry with them upon Camels Backs, eſpecially upon the Road from *F* to *Tombuto*, or from *Them* to *Arad*. Were it not for a very large Lake in the Road, that Journey which the Merchants have lately found out over the Deſarts of *Libya*, from *Fez* to *Alcair*, would be exceeding dangerous. But in the Way from *Fez* to *Tombuto* are ſome Pits ſurrounded and piled in, either with Camels Bones or Hides. In Sum-mer Time the Merchants run very great Hazards of their

Li-

Lives ın paſſing that Way, for often ıt happens, that by the South Wınd all thoſe Pıts are filled wıth the Sand, and when that happens, they muſt ınevıtably perıſh, and theır Carcaſſes are often found lyıng about, drıed up wıth the Sun. To remedy theır not findıng the Water Pıts, and to prevent theır dyıng wıth Thırſt, they kıll one of theır Camels, ın whoſe (*a*) Stomach they find a good Quantıty of Water, whıch they drınk, and carry about wıth them, tıll ıt ıs all gone, and they die wıth Thırſt, or tıll they find ſome more Water. ---- I dıd intend to wrıte more fully of what happened to myſelf and my Companıons on our Journey thro' the Deſerts of *Libya* to *Gualata* Sometımes when we were athırſt, we could not find any Water by loſing the rıght Path, at other Tımes our Enemıes ſtopt up the Pıts whereın Water ıs uſed to be So that we took very ſparıngly, for what would hardly ſerve us for fıve Days, we were ſometımes oblıged to make ıt hold out for ten Days ---- The Land of *Negroes* ıs very hot, but ıs moıſtened by the Rıver *Niger* runnıng thro' the Mıddle of ıt, and abounds wıth Cattle and Corn. I ſaw no Trees, but ſome great ones, whıch bear a bıtter Fruıt, lıke a Cheſnut, called by them (*b*) *Coran* There are alſo Onıons. Cucumbers, Cocoas, and ſuch lıke Fruıts and Herbs There are no Mountaıns ın the Land of *Negroes*, or ın *Libya*, but a great many Lakes and Fens, whıch (ſome People ſay) the *Niger* left behınd when ıt overflowed. The Woods ın theſe Countrıes abound ın Elephants, and other wıld Beaſts

Of the Climate and Aır of Africa.

COLD and ſtormy Weather generally begıns ın *Barbary* about *October*, but ıt ıs ſomewhat colder ın *December* and *January*. --- In *February* the Cold begıns to abate,

(*a*) [*Stomach*] Sır *H Sloane* diſſected a Camel, and found ın ıts Stomach certaın Veſſels compoſed of lıttle Cells, whıch preſerved the Water that he drank, and could contaın ıt many Days, tıll by Degrees the Stomach preſſes ıt out And thıs contaınıng the Water, makes the Camels able to travel ſo many Days wıth out drınkıng

(*b*) [*Coran*] Thıs Fruıt ıs called by the Natıves *Cola*, and ıs eaten by them as a great Delıcacy for to relıſh Water. *Vıde* p. 132 ın my Journal

bate, and the Weather changes often   The northerly and westerly Winds generally blow in *March*, at which Time the Trees bloſſom   The Cherries are ripe commonly at the End of *April* and the Beginning of *May*.   They gather their Figs about the Middle of *May*, and their Grapes are ripe in ſome Places about *June*, and in that Month and *July*, their Pears, Quinces and Damſons, are commonly ripe.   Their Figs are (a) again ripe in *Auguſt*, but not ſo plentiful as in *September* --- In *Auguſt* they uſually dry their Grapes and make Raiſins, and if they cannot fiſh in *September*, they then make Wine of what Grapes are not gathered   In *October* they gather the Pomegranates and Quinces, and take in their Honey   In *November* they gather their Olives, by climbing up the Trees and beating them off with long Poles, notwithſtanding they know it is prejudicial to the Trees.   There are alſo large Olive Trees, the Fruit of which not being fit for Oil, is eat by the Natives   They have always three Months Spring in a Year, beginning the 15th of *February*, and ending the Middle of *May*, during which Time it is ſerene and temperate Weather   If between the 25th of *April* and the 5th of *May* they have no Rain, they reckon it unlucky , and what falls during that Time is called by them *Naiſan*, i e bleſſed of God   Some keep it by them as a holy Relique   Their Summer is to the 16th of *Auguſt*, with clear and hot Weather, except ſometimes Showers in *July* and *Auguſt*, which are ſo infectious, that it brings Fevers upon thoſe who are wet with it, ſo very violent, that few who have it recover   The Autumn is from the 17th of *Auguſt* to the 16th of *November* , but in *Auguſt* and *September* it is not ſo hot as before   From the 15th of *Auguſt* to the 15 of *September* is called the Furnace of the Year, and in that Seaſon it is, that the Quinces, Figs, and ſuch kind of Fruits are ripe, and in their Luſtre   Their Winter is from the 15th of *November* to the 15th of *February.*   As ſoon as it begins they till their plain Ground , but in *October* they plow that on the Mountains   The *Africans* are firmly of Opinion, that there are 40 exceeding hot Days following

(a) [Again ripe in *Auguſt*] In hot Countries the Figs produce twice a Year , for the little green Figs which with us dry and wither upon the Trees, would, if there were ſufficient Heat and Moiſture, grow to Perfection in Autumn

the

the 12th of *June*, and the fame Number of very cold D

immediately fucceeding the 12th of *December* Their

quinoctia are the 16th of *March* and the 16th of *Sep*

ter Their Solftitia they reckon the 16th of *June* and

16th of *December* They are curious Obfervers in

Things, as they are alfo in Husbandry, Navigation and

my, which they teach their Children when very

There are a great many People in *Africa*, who, tho

cannot read, yet will difcourfe of Aftrology in a

Manner, and bring good Reafons for what they

Whatever Knowledge they have in Aftrology, they

originally from the *L*, and call their Men by

fame Names as, *a*, they do They have a large Book in

Volumes, called *the Treatife of Hufbandry* When

was Lord of *Granada*, this Book was tranflated from

Latin into their Language, in which is every thing

to Husbandry, fuch as Change of Weather, Manu

fowing, and abundance of other Things, which I

believe are now to be found in the *Latin* Tongue,

ftanding this was at firft tranflated from it   In regard

their Law or Religion, they compute by the Courfe

Moon Their Year is 354 Days, for to fix Month

give but 30 Days each, and to the other fix but 29

which the Reafon of its being eleven Days lefs th

Year of the *Latin* Some Part of Autumn, all W

and the Spring, they have bluftering Winds, with

der, Lightning and Hail, and in fome Parts of *B*

great deal of Snow The Eaft, South, and South

Winds, which blow in *May* or *June*, do a great

Hurt, by fpoiling the Corn and preventing the

the Fruits The Snow likewife hurts their Corn

Mountains of *Atlas* they divide the Year into no

two Parts The Winter continues from *October* to *A*

and from *April* to *October*, Summer, but the Tops

the Mountains are covered with Snow all the Year rou

In *Numidia* they gather their Corn in *May*, and their D

in *October*, from *September* to *January* is Winter

if *September* is rainy, they have a bad Crop of Date

the *Numidian* Fields are watered by the Rivers, but

Mountains have no Rain fall upon them, then the R

(a) [*Treatife of Hufbandry*] *Varro* tranflated it into *Arabic*
the Reign of *Mar/or* King of *Granada*

grow div, and the Fields want watering If *October* brings
no Rain, there is no Hopes of a good Crop, neither is
.... if it does not rain in *April*, tho' the Dates grow bet-
.. without Rain, which, in *Numidia*, are more plenty
.. Corn, for which they barter Dates with the *Arabians*
I the Weather changes in *October* and *December*, and *January*
..some Part of *February* prove rainy, it is surprifing to
fee what Abundance of Grafs it produces in the *Libyan* De-
... Then there are Fens and Lakes to be found every
where, which makes it the propereft Time for the Merchants of *Barbary* to travel to the Country of the *Negroes*
If moderate Showers happen to come in *July*, it ripens the
Fruit much But in the Land of the *Negroes* the Rain
..e neither Good nor Hurt For the River *Niger*, with
..e Water which falls from some Mountains, moiftens the
Ground fo much, that no Places can be more fruitful,
..r *Niger* to the Land of *Negroes*, is the fame as *Nilus* to
..e Land of *Egypt*, and the River *Niger* (*i*) increases like
..to *Nilus* for 40 Days after the 15 th of *June*, and de-
creases after that for the fame Number And whilft
..increafes, one may go in Canoes all over the Land of
Negroes. -----

BOOK II.

IHAVE before given an Account of the Towns, and
Divifions, and other memorable Things of *Africa*, now
I will defcribe the Provinces We fhall begin at the
Weft Part of *Africa*, and go on Eaftward to the Borders
of *Egypt* ------

Of the Region of HEA, *lying on the Weft of*
AFRICA

HEA is one of the Provinces ..., be..led on
the Weft and North by the main Ocean, Southward
.. the Mountains of *Atlas*, and Eaftward with the River
...., which fprings out of the faid Mountains, runs
into

(*i*) This might be true at *Tombuto*, but the Time of the Rifing and
..ing of the River below *Tataterda* is not certain It rifes fome-
..es in *July*, and fometimes not till *Auguft* and fometimes begins
.. to fall till *October* *Vid* my Journal, p 1-4

into the River *Tenſiſt*, and divides *Hea* from another Province.

The Soil of this Country of *Hea* is rough and uneven, full of ſtony Hills, Woods thick with Trees, and Rivers all over it, and is very rich, and well inhabited. They have amongſt them great Numbers of Goats and Aſſes, but not ſo many Oxen, Horſes and Sheep.

Of the INHABITANTS *of the Beginning oſ* Mount ATLAS.

THE moſt Part of the Inhabitants of *Hea* live upon Hills, ſome are called *Ideuaeal* Such are they who live upon that Part of *Atlas*, which extends as far as *Igilin gigil* Eaſtward from the Sea, and which parts *Hea* from *Sus* I my ſelf was three Days croſſing this Mountain from *Te ſethne* to *Meſſa*. Every one that knows this Country, is ſenſible how full it is of Towns and People. They live upon Goats Fleſh, Barley and Honey They wear no Shirts nor any Garments ſewed together, becauſe none of them know how to ſew with a Needle Their Garment is a Mantle, which they tie with a Knot over their Shoulders Their Women wear ſilver Rings in their Ears. They ſometimes faſten their Apparel upon their Shoulders with ſilver *(a)* Buttons, ſome of them ſo large that they weigh an Ounce. The richer Sort of People wear Rings of Silver upon their Legs and Fingers, but thoſe who cannot afford Silver, wear Copper or Iron Rings There are ſome Horſes in this Country wonderful ſmall, and very ſwift. They have plenty of Hares, Deer, and wild Goats but the People care little for hunting They have likewiſe a good many Springs and Trees, eſpecially Walnut-Trees They change their Places of Living often, as the *Arabian* do. They uſe a ſort of a Dagger crooked like a Wood Knife, and Swords as thick as Scythes. They are very ignorant of Learning, and have no Prieſts, Judges nor Moſques They are *(b)* lewd and vile, and give themſelves up to all kind

c

(a) [*Buttons*] This was the Manner of the ancient *Roman* faſtening their Garments, the Button was called *Bulla*, or *Fibula* and theſe People being ſafe in unacceſſible Mountains, may have preſerved many of the *Roman* Cuſtoms

(b) [*lewd and vile*] *Leo*, an *Arabian* Lawyer, and half a Prieſt deteſted thoſe who conformed not to the Craft, againſt which the Remains of the *Roman* Colonies preſerved their Freedom

of Wickedneſs This Mountain, I heard ſay, could raiſe upon Occaſion 20,000 Soldiers.

Of the REGION *of* SUS.

IT lies beyond *Atlas* overagainſt the Territory of *Hea,* in the extream Part of *Africa* It begins Weſtward from the Sea, and Southward from the Sandy Deſerts ; the fartheſt Town of *Hea* bounds it on the North, and the great River *Sus* on the Eaſt In this Region are the Cities and Towns following, *viz Meſſa, Terjeut, Tarodant, Tedſi* and *Tagauoſt,* a Caſtle called *Gartgueſſem,* and the Mountains *Hanchiſa* and *Ilalem*

Tedſi is a large Town, built a great many Years ſince by the *Africans,* in a very pleaſant and plentiful Place, in it are above 4000 Families, it is 30 Miles Eaſtward of *Taro-dint,* 60 from the Sea, and 20 from *Atlas.* Here is plenty of Corn and Sugar A great many Merchants come hither from the Land of Negroes to trade The Citizens live in Peace with their Neighbours, and Amity with each others ; and the Commonwealth is very flouriſhing It is governed by Six Magiſtrates, who are choſen by Lots ; the Governor is choſen every 16 Months The River *Sus* is 3 Miles from it There were many *Jews,* who were Goldſmiths, Carpenters, and of other Trades There was a very fine Moſque, with a great many Prieſts, who were maintained at the publick Charge Their Market was on a *Monday,* to which came a great many *Arabians,* both of the Mountains and the Plains In the 920th Year of the *Hegera,* the People of his City ſurrendred themſelves to the Seriffo ; at which time the Common-Council was there erected.

Tagouſt is the nobleſt City of all *Sus,* it contains above 8000 Families, the Walls are built of rough Stones It is about 60 Miles from the Sea, the Inhabitants are divided into 3 Factions, a good many Tradeſmen and Shops among them. They are at civil War one with another, the *Arabians* favouring that Party which pay them beſt Their Wool is coarſe, and they have abundance of Cattel and Corn They make Garments in this City, which are carried by the Merchants every Year to *Tombuto* and *Gualata,* and other Parts of the Land of Negroes. They have a Market twice a Week, they are decent in their Dreſs, the Women are handſome, but the Men ſwarthy and tawny, thoſe who

have

h've moſt Riches have moſt Authority. I myſelf w .. h..
in the 919th Year of the *Hegera, Anno Dom* 1510

The RECION *of* MOROCCO.

IT beg... Weſtw.rd from the Mountain of \.f.., .nd
exte.ds .o .he Mountain of *H..ⁱ*er Eaſtw...,
Northw..e .o .hat Place where the Rivers *To*, &
Af.. r.co, .. upon the Eaſtern Border of *H*
is, in . m.nⁿer, Triangular, . very pleaſant Country,
.bounds with C.ttel, it is very fertile, and p.o.uces
thing th.t .el.ghts the Senſes of Sight and Smell,
pl.ⁿ C..ⁿry like to *L.* .. .., the Mount.ns which
round .. a e barren and co.d, and produce noth.ng
B.rl.y

Cf the G.eat CITY *of* MOROCCO

MO.. . was .mongſt the l.rgeſt Cities of .he W..
.... *Afr..*, it was built by *J ..*
to *T* ... K. g. .he Mooriſh Tribe of *Lantuⁿ* ...I ..
r.. .. .re A.vice of excel.ent Artiſts, and ..os ..
g... Circu.t of Ground, .nd in the Reign o *H*, S.o
K.. *J* p., it conſiſted of 100,000 *Hartis*, .nd w..
.. ..th ſtrong W.lls and Towers beautifully ba.. o
F .eS..ⁿs the R.ⁱer *T.rⁱſt* ran within 6 M.les of .. h
this C.. were great Numbers of Moſques, and Coll..
L.. ..e Hiſtory, .. wh.ch they purſued their Studie.
A .. Meⁱhod The Moſque of *H.l B.. Joſⁱph* .. ..
t'.rm.ſt o. the C.. a moſt magnificent Edifice. Tⁱ.
was .ⁿother Moſque that ſtood near the C.ſſ.s, w..
Mu.. er.cⁱed by c.rrⁱing round it on all Sides . P..
ſo C.ⁱs w.de, adorⁿed with Pillars, which he h.. ..
to .e brought from *St..* .. Underneath he made C.. .
es l.r.es the Moſque itſelf, which being cover'd with .. .
the Ra.n th.. fell on the Top ſupplies the Ciſt .. .
nea .. He added .lſo a Tower built of he.n Stⁱ.., ..
Stones .s l.r.e, and put together in the ſ.me m... ..
thoſe of *Veſp.f..n*'s Amphitheatre at *Rome* Th.s l.. ..
.. .s 100 *Turr.* Ells in Circumference, and higher th.n ..
Tower of *A.u.t. Bel.g.a*. Upon the Top o.
To.er ſtood a Sp.re ſh.ped like an Obel.ſk, wh.ch ..

bout 36 Foot in Height.   Upon the Top of the Obelisk was a Balcony of excellent Workmanship, and it was finished with 3 Balls of Silver one above the other, the lowest much the largest   From the Balcony the Height was so great, that one could not look down without Giddiness; you could see from hence all the Plains of *Morocco* lying under you, and the Mountain of *Azafi*, 130 Miles distant This was the largest Mosque in the World, and not inferior in Workmanship to any Church that I have seen in *Italy* It is now but little frequented, the City of *Morocco* being much decay'd, the Streets round the Temple are all in Ruin, and the Houses fallen in them, in such a manner, that it is difficult climbing over them In the Portico round the Mosque Booksellers Shops used to be kept, and tho' there were formerly in this Place only an hundred of them, here is but one now left in all *Morocco*, and that meanly furnished and the poor City has lost above two Thirds of its Inhabitants, the Places where Streets stood within the Walls, are now planted within Palm-Trees and other Fruits

There was a Castle equal in Bigness to a little City, the Walls were strong and high, the Gates were lofty, and built of Marble   In the midst of the Castle was a magnificent Mosque, with a beautiful Tower, upon the Top of which there were three Balls of Gold, one under another, fastened with an Iron Bar run thro' them, they were reckoned together to weigh 130,000 Ducats, and the superstitious People believe them to be preserved by Magick, or some supernatural Power, which had taken so deep Root, that in our Time the King of *Morocco*, intending to make use of that Gold for his Defence against the *Portuguese*, was by the Superstition of the People prevented In the Castle was a College, in which were three long Chambers, where great Numbers of Scholars used to lodge, and in the Court was a noble Hall, where Lectures were formerly read to them. When this City flourished, all these Scholars had Food and Raiment, and the Professors Pensions from the King proportionable to their Learning The Apartments were adorned with *Mosaic* Work, and *Dutch* Tiles In the middle of the Square of the Castle was a beautiful Fountain of white Marble Of all the Students there are now but five, and one Professor, and he illiterate

There was also a Granary for Wheat, the Roof of which was flat, the Stairs or Ascent was made so easy, that load-

ed

ed Horses went up to the top, where there was a Hole, into
which they shooted the Corn so as to fall down into the
Magazine, and they had Entrances below, which they open'd
and let the Corn run out at   There were also in the said
Castle twelve Courts, finely built by King *Munser* In the
first there were formerly about 500 *Christians*, who carried
Crossbows before the King   Near that was the Lord-Chan-
cellor's Apartment, as also that of the King's Privy-Council, which was call'd the *House of Affairs*, another
call'd the *Court of I ..y*, because in it was kept the Am-
munition and Arms of the City   Another of the Courts
belonged to the Great Master of the King's Horse   The
Stables join'd to that, each of which held 200 Horses
There were also two other Stables, one for Mules, and the
other for 100 of the King's Horses only   Next to the
Stables were two Magazines, one for Straw, the other for
Barley   There was also an Hill, which served for a School
for the Kings and Noblemens Sons   Near this was a large
Four-square Building, which contained a great many Gal-
leries with Glass-Windows, many Histories were finely paint-
ed in the Galleries, and the gilt and bright Armour was
there to be seen   Next to this was another Building, in
which some of the King's Guard lay next to that was the
Place where State Matters were disputed, and adjoining to
it was the Place for Ambassadors to confer with the King's
Privy-Council, there was also a proper Apartment for the
King's Concubines and other Ladies, and next to it the King's
Sons lodged   On that Side next the Fields, not far from
the Wall of the Castle, was a large pleasant Garden, in
which was a Collection of almost all kinds of Trees there
was also a magnificent Portico built of fine square Marble,
in the middle of which was a Lion of Marble, out of whose
Mouth a Stream of Water ran as clear as Crystal, which ran
into a Cistern within the Portico, and at each Corner of the
Portico there stood a Leopard of white Marble, curiously
spotted with Black, this sort of Marble was found no where
but in Mount *Atlas*, about 150 Miles from *Morocco* Near
the Garden was a Park walled round, in which were kept all
kinds of wild Beasts, as Lions, Elephants, Stags, &c.
&c. and at this time that Place is called the Lion's Den
Tho' there are now but few Monuments of Antiquity in
Morocco yet those that are, do sufficiently show, that it
was a noble City in the Time of *Munser*.   The Courts and
A 2

Apartments before-mentioned, do now lie defolate, unlefs
to one in which the King's Grooms who look after
the Horfes and Mules do ftill lie   The reft is left to the
Fowls of the Air to build Nefts in   That Garden,
which might well have been called a Paradife, ferves
now to receive the Dung and Naftinefs of the City ----
The Manfor, which we have fo fpoken of, was certainly a great and mighty Prince , for his Dominion
reached from the Town of Meffa to the Kingdom of Tri-
pan Barbary, which is the beft Region in all Africa,
and fo large, that the Length of it is 70 Days Travel
by Mar, and the Breadth at leaft 15   This Manfor
was alfo King of Granada , nay, his Territories in Spain
reached from Tariffa to Arragon, and over Part of Portugal and Caftile   His Grandfather, his Father, himfelf,
and his Son Mahumet Enafir, poffeffed all the aforefaid
Dominions , but the latter being overcome in the Kingdom of Valencia, with the Lofs of 60,000 Horfe and
Foot, with much ado efcaped to Morocco   This Conqueft fo encouraged the Chriftians, that they purfued
their Victories, and in thirty Years Time were got in
Poffeffion of the following Towns, viz Valencia, Denia,
Alzira, Murcia, Cartagena, Cordova, Sivillia, Jaen, and
Lorca   After this the Decay of Morocco began   Mahumet Enafir died, leaving ten Sons, all grown up , they
contending for the Kingdom, the Marine Tribe took
the Opportunity of it, and ufurped the Government.
The People called Hadical, took Poffeffion of Tremi-
fen, turned out the King of Tunis, and appointed another in his room   Now I have given you an Account
to the End of Manfor and his Succeffors , after which
time Jacob, the Son of Halalalad, was the firft King of
the Marine Family   Laftly, the noble City of Morocco
fell to Ruins, by Reafon of the Outrages which the A-
rabs continually made   This fhews the Uncertainty
of all worldly Things   What we have here mentioned
of Morocco, we faw Part of it happen in our Time,
and Part we read in the Hiftory of one Ibnu Abdul
Malad, an exact Hiftoriographer of what concerned Morocco, and other Parts we took from that Book concerning the Mahometan Law which we ourfelves wrote

The Region of GUZZULA.

THIS Region is very populous, on the West a n[...] to P[...], Mou[...] of *Sus*, on the North to [...] nd extends Eastward to the Region of *Ha* The I ha[...] b tun[...] ve plen s of Cattel, but little Money, and [...] a e fierce and savage --- They have no Governor or K [...] and are at War continually with one another

DUCCALA REGION.

THIS Region begins Westward from the River *T* [...] the Ocean bounds it on the North, the River *H*[...] on the South, and the River *Omuabth* on the E ſt [...] two Days Journey broad, and about three Days lon [...] is very populous, the Inhabitants are rude and [...] It hath but a few walled Cities, viz *Azaph*., C [...] *Elm dira*, *Centum*, *Pure*, *Sale t*, *Tamerace*,[...] *Te* [...], B [...] *lannan*, *Azan e*, and *M,ame*, and the Moun[...] *Ben.mgler*, and that called the Green Mountain ---- But [...] ſtands upon the Side of *Omrulin* River, [...] ſiſting of about 500 Families   There was a noble Hoſp [...] tal, conta n ng a great Number of Apartments, in wh [...] all Strange s reſl[...] that Way were elegantly ente [...] d at the common Expence of the Town   The People [...] abundance of Corn and Cattle, ſome of them reap[...] or 3000 Meaſures of Corn in a Year   In the 919 h Ye[...] of the *H g r*, the Brother of the King of *Fes* w [...] can Governer of *D* [...] Region, who comi g to [...] Town, was acquainted that the *Portugueze* Cap[...] General was coming there with a great Force to [...] the Town and make Priſoners of the People   He [...] upon ſent Seo A cers and 2000 Horſemen to det [...] but unfort[...] happened, that at the very I [...] were entering the Town, there arrived a g[...] Nu[...] *Port gueſe* Sol [...], accompanied by 2000 h[...] be ng more in Numb[...] than the others, the [...] them, as d[...] cre [...] o on the A che, exce [...] twelve, who [...] m ch by flying [...] Horſemen [...] Alce[...]   I myſelf was p[...] his Fi[...], mar[...] on a [...] Horſe about a M

...rt from the Town ; being then travelling from *Fez* to
Morocco, with a Meffage from one King to the other

Azamur was built by the old *Africans* upon the Sea, near
the Mouth of the River *Ommirabih*, about 30 Miles from
Elmadina It is large, and well peopled, containing about
5000 Families. A good many *Portugueze* Merchants inhabit this Place. The Inhabitants are very civil, and drefs
themfelves decently They are divided into two Parties,
notwithftanding which, they live peaceably Their Orchards produce nothing but Figs, but they have great Plenty of Corn and Pulfe Their Fifhing is worth 6 or 7000
Ducats a Year to them, it lafts from *October* to *April*
The *Portugueze* ufed to trade here for Fifh every Year,
the Gain of which induced them often to attempt the furprifing and taking of this Town The firft Fleet they
fent, was, by the Indifcretion of the General, difperfed
at Sea, and a great Part loft Afterwards they fent fuch
a Fleet, that at the very Sight of it the Citizens fled,
and that fo precipitately, that there were 80 Perfons killed
by thronging out at the Gates, and a Prince, who came
to help them, was obliged to be let down by a Rope o-
ver the back Walls of the City It was a piteous Sight
to fee how the poor old Men, the tender weak Women
rather Children, fled away barefooted Before ever
the *Portugueze* attacked the Town, the *Jews*, who lived
there, opened the Gates to let them in, on Condition
that no Injury fhould be done unto them. The Inhabitants after they were drove out, difperfed themfelves fome
about, and fome to *Fez* The People of this Town
are abominably given over to the deteftable Sin of So-
domy, and I believe, for that Reafon, it was that God
fuffered this Affliction to happen to them — —

The Green MOUNTAIN.

Is very high, and divides *Duccula* from Part of *Tia-*
It begins Eaftward from *Ommrabih* River, and
runs Weftward to the Hills called *Hafara* It is rough,
and very woody, produces Pine Apples and Acorns
and dried Fruit, which the *Lords* call *Afro*
about this Mountain there are good many Hermits,
and there are the Wells Fled there are two

A 7 are

some Fou..., as also old Houses and Prayer-P...
There is a Lake at the Foot of this Mountain which resembles that of Bojara in ...; In it are vast Numbers of Eels, Pickrel, and other Fish   Once I was
with Mahomet, King of Fez, when he was marching this
Way to Morocco, and encamped a Week upon the Lake-
Side   Some of his Company fished in it, a good many
of whom I saw take their Coats and Shirts off, and only
sewing up the Cellars and Sleeves, they put Hoops in
them, and used them for Nets, in which they caught
many Thousands of Fish; though not near so many ... the
... had Nets indeed   The Reason of their catching
such great Numbers was this The King being accompanied with 14,000 Arabian Horsemen, who brought ...
many Camels, and his Brother having 5000 Horsemen
under his Command, and a vast Army of Foot, he ordered them all at once to enter the Lake, which ...
contained Water enough to satisfy the Cattle   Trees
grew upon the Sides of this Lake, in which there are ...
Numbers of Turtle-Doves, that the People the ...
make a great Commodity of them   Eight Days ...
Mahomet stayed to refresh himself by this Lake ...
Time cheese, he went to see the Green Moun... , ...
a great many Attendants I also went with him ...
he had viewed the Mountain, he went a hundred ...
hawking, whereby we caught plenty of wild Geese, Tu-
tle-Doves, and Duck ---- The next Day he we...
broad with his Hounds, Eagles, and Faulcons, and ...
a great many Hares, Porcupines, Roe-Bucks, W...
Quails and Deers, no wonder we had such ... Sp...
when there had not been any Hunting here for a Hun-
ared Years before   After some Stay here, the King, ...
his Army, marched to Elmadin, a Town of Dua...
I was sent with a good Number of Soldiers ...
Embassy to Morocco.

The REGION of HASCORA.

IT is bounded, on the West, with a River runn...
the Foot of the Mountain of Hadimmes, on the N...
with a Range of Hills belonging to Ducala, Eastward by ...
...ed River, which is ... from Hascora. ...

ple of this Region are more civil than those of *Duccala*
It produces plenty of Oil, *Morocco* Skins, and Goats, of
the Hair of which they make Saddles and Cloths The
neighbouring Countries bring hither their Goat-Skins, of
which the *Morocco* Leather is made The *Portugueze*
trade with them pretty largely, giving them Cloth in
barter for their Saddles and Leather. This Country supplies some of the *Arabians* with Oil and other Necessaries In this Region are the Towns of *Elmadin*, *Aleman*, *Tagodast*, *Elgiumuha* and *Bzo* , and the Mountains
Tineues, *Tenfita*, *Gogideme* and *Tefeuon*

Elmadin is built upon the Side of *Atlas*, and contains
above 2000 Families , it lies about 90 Miles Eastward
from *Morocco*, and 60 from *Duccala*. ----

Aleman stands four Miles to the West of *Elmadin*, in
a Valley between four Hills ---

Tagodast is built upon a high Hill, with four others
round about it Between the Town and those Hills
are fine Gardens, which produce abundance of Fruit
They have plenty of Vines, which make natural Walks
and Bowers, the Grapes are red, and so large, that in
their Language they call them Hens Eggs They have
a great deal of Oyl and Honey , the latter both white
and yellow Here are a great many Fountains, which ar-
rise, and supply several Water Mills near the Town The
People are civil, and their Women handsome, and finely
cloathed

Elgiumuha stands within five Miles of *Tagodast*, built
on the Top of a high Hill, containing about 500 Families ----

Bzo is an ancient Town, about twenty Miles to the
Westward of *Elgiumula* The River (Guadelfed) runs
within three Miles of it ----

The Mountains of *Tineues* lie over-against *Hafeora*,
upon that Part of *Atlas* which runneth Southwardly
Here are a great many brave Men, and a great many
Horses of low Stature It produces a good deal of Bar-
ley and Wood, but has no other Grain but Barley
Here is Snow to be seen at all Times of the Year
The Nobility, which are numerous, are subject to a Prince
to whom they pay an annual Tribute to maintain his
State, he being continually at War with the People of
Tedla The Prince hath always about him 1000 Horse

Horfemen, and the Noblemen of this Mountain keep about the fame Number at their own Charge. To attend his Perfon he has about 100 Bowmen and Harquebufiers Once I went to fee this Mountain, where I happened to meet that Prince, who, I believe, had no Equal for Courtefy and Civility. He loved the *Arabian* Tongue, tho' he did not underftand it well, and was proud of hearing any thing conftrued to him which was wrote in Praife of himfelf. *When my (a) Uncle was fent to* Tombuto *as Ambaffador from the King of* Fez, *I went along with him.* As foon as we were got into the Region of *Dara*, a hundred Miles from this Prince's Dominions, he hearing of the Fame of my Uncle, as a very good Orator, and excellent Poet, fent to the Prince of *Dara*, to defire he would perfuade my Uncle to pafs by *Teneues* on his Way to *Tombuto*, that he might have the Satisfaction of feeing and converfing with him My Uncle fent Word that he could not delay his Mafter's Bufinefs to go out of the Way to vifit any Prince, but to fatisfy his Curiofity in fome meafure, he fent me to him to compliment him I took Prefents to him, which confifted of a fine Pair of Stirrups double gilt, and wrought after the *Moorifh* Fafhion, which coft 25 Ducats; a rich Pair of Spurs of 15 Ducats, two Girdles of Silk intermixt with Gold, one tawny, the other blue He fent likewife a fine Book of the Lives of fome famous Men of *Africa*, and fome Verfes in Praife of the Prince himfelf On the Road I made a Copy of Verfes in Commendation of the Prince, and carried two Horfemen to bear me Company. When we arrived there, the Prince and his Attendants were gone a hunting. As foon as he knew I was come, he fent for me, and I prefented him my Uncle's Prefents, and when I gave him my Uncle' Verfes he immediately ordered one of his Secretaries to read them; the Prince, while they were expounding feemed wonderfully delighted with them. After he had done with the Verfes, he fat down to Supper, and ordered me to fit next to him --- Supper ended, we went to Bed The next Morning I breakfafted with him, after which he gave me a hundred Ducats for a Prefent to my Uncle and for myfelf 50 Ducats and a good Horfe, and to each of my Servants he gave ten Ducats He told me, that the hundred Ducats to my Uncle, was not in Return for

h

(a) Lee's Uncle, *Ambaffador to* Tombuto.

his Prefents, but for his Copy of Verfes   He ordered one of his Secretaries to fhew us the Way, and fo I returned to my Uncle. ----

The Region of *Tedles* begins Weftward at the River *Guadelhabid*, and extends to that Part of the large River *Ommirabih* where *Guadelhabid* begins.   To the South it borders upon *Atlas*, and ftretches northward to that Place where *Guadelhabid* falls into *Ommirabih*.   This Region is three-fquare, for *Ommirabih* River and *Guadelhabid* fpring both out of *Atlas*, and run northward, till by degrees they meet all in one

In this Region is the Town of *Tefza*, which is the chief, built by the *Africans* on the Side of Mount *Atlas*, the Walls of which are of fine Marble, by them called *Tefza*, from whence the Town is named   A great many rich Merchants live in this Town, and about 200 Families of *Jews*.

Efza ftands two Miles from *Tefza*, upon a little Hill at the Bottom of Mount *Atlas*, containing about 600 Families, moftly Tradefmen and Hufbandmen, who are fubject to the Governor of *Tefza* ----

Citherib lies upon a lofty Hill, ten Miles from *Efza*, well inhabited by rich People.   This was built by the *Africans*, the Fields near it are full of Vineyards and Gardens, producing a great deal of Fruit ---

Eithiad is about twelve Miles from *Citherib*, built upon a fmall Hill of *Atlas*, by the *Africans*   Towards the Mountain there is a Wall, but towards the Plain it is naturally fortified by Rocks   It contains about 300 Families ----

The Mountain of *Seggheme* begins Weftward from that of *Tefauon*, it reaches Eaftward to Mount *Magron*, out of which the River *Ommirabih* takes its Beginning   Southward it borders upon Mount *Dedes*.   The Inhabitants are originally defcended from the People of *Zanaga*, they are warlike and comely ----

The Mountain of *Magran* begins to the Weftward of *Seggheme*, bordering to the South upon the Region of *Fniila*, near the Defert of *Libya*, and extends Eaftward to the Mount of *Dedes*.   I myfelf was in this Mountain, as I travelled from *Dara* to *Fez*.

Dedes is a cold high Mountain, containing a great many Woods and Springs.   It is about eighty Miles long   It begins Weftward at *Magran*, Southward it borders upon

Todga Plains, and reaches almost to the Mountain of *Adesan.*
Formerly there was a City built upon the very Top of
this Mountain, of which a few Ruins are still to be seen
Some think it was built by the *Romans*, but I never found
any thing of it mentioned by any *African* Author, only
Seriffo Essacalli, in one of his Stories, says that *Tedsi* is
near *Dara* and *Segelmesse*, but does not say whether or no it
is built upon Mount *Dedes* ---- The Inhabitants dwell
under Ground in Caves, whose Food is Elhasid and
Barley.   Goats and Asses they have in great Plenty
The Caves where they put their Cattle abound in Salt
Petre ; which, if it were near *Italy*, would, I believe, be
worth 25,000 Ducats a Year ; but these People have no
Way of using it. -----

BOOK III.

The Kingdom of FEZ.

BEgins Westward at the River *Ommirabih*, and reaches
Eastward to the River *Mulvia* ; it is bounded on the
North, partly by the Ocean and partly by the Mediterranean Sea   It is divided into seven Provinces, *viz Temes-
ra, Fez, Azgar, Ethabet, Eirif, Garet* and *Elchauz*, e-
very one of which had formerly a separate Governor

Temesna, a Province of *Fez*, begins at *Ommirabih* West-
ward, and reaches to *Buragrag* River Eastward   The
South Part lies upon *Atlas*, and the North upon the Ocean
It is all a plain Country, about 80 Miles from West to
East, and about 60 from North to South.   This is the
principal Province of all the seven, and contains 300 Ca-
stles and 40 great Towns ; all peopled by *Barbarian
Africans*

Anfa, a Town of *Temesna*, was built upon the Sea
Shore, by the *Romans*, 60 Miles Northward of *Atlas*   Its
Situation is more pleasant than any other Town in all
Africa.

Nuchaiia is a little Town almost in the Middle of *Temesna* ; formerly it was well inhabited, and produced such Plenty of Corn, that they gave a Camel Load for a Pair of
Shoes

Adendum

Adendum was formerly a Town of *Temesna*, about fifteen Miles from *Atlas*, and twenty-five from *Nuchaila* , but there is now to be seen only some of the Ruins

Tegeget lies upon the Side of *Ommirabih* River, close to the Road from *Tedles* to *Fez*.

Hain Elchallu is a little Town standing on a Plain not a great Way from *Mansora*, built, I believe, by the *Romans*.

Rebat is a noble large Town, built by *Mansor* the King and Patriarch of *Morocco*, upon the Sea-Shore. It is built upon a Rock ; on one Side of it is the Sea, and on the other the River *Buragrag*. This Town resembles *Morocco*, only it is much less

Sella lies a Mile from *Rebat*, built by the *Romans* upon the River *Buragrag*, two Miles from the Sea, the Way to which from *Sella* lies thro' *Rebat*

Mader Azuam is a Town built in my Time upon the Side of *Buragrag*. It is said to be built only for the Sake of the Iron Mines which are near it. It was afterwards utterly destroyed by the *Marine* Family : Some of the Steeples and Walls are still to be seen.

Thagia is a small Town, built upon some Hills of *Atlas* by the *Africans* : The Soil about it is barren, and the Air is very cold They have scarcity of Corn, but plenty of Honey and Goats

Zarfa was a Town built by the *Africans* upon a large Plain, abounding with Rivers and Fountains. It is now destroyed, and Corn grows where the Town stood.

The Territory of *Fez* begins at the River *Buragrag* Westward, and extends Eastward to the River *Inaren* about a hundred Miles , the River *Subu* bounds it on the North, and to the Southward it borders upon the Foot of *Atlas*. The Soil is excellent for Fruits, Corn and Cattle ; there are a great Number of Villages, worthy to be called Towns.

Of the Great CITY *of* FEZ, *being the* CAPITAL *of* MAURITANIA.

THE City of *Fez* was built by a *Mahometan* Heretick, or Rebel against the Eastern Caliphs, who call themselves the Orthodox Church of *Mahomet*, under the Reign of the Caliph *Aron*, in the Year 185 of the *Hegeira* It

was

was called *Fez,* becaufe they found Gold as they dug to lay the Foundation of the City, and the Word *Fez* in *Arabic* fignifieth *Gold.*

DESCRIPTION *of* FEZ.

FEZ is a very Great City, furrounded with high and beautiful Walls, it is almoft all Hills and Valleys, fo that only in the midft of the City there is any flat Ground A River, which is divided into two Streams, runs thro' the City; from this River little Channels are drawn into every Part of the Town; fo that all the Mofques, the Colleges the King's Palaces, and the Houfes of the Great Men, are furnifhed with Water. They generally have in the middle of the Court fquare Bafons of Marble, and the Water coming thro' marble Pipes, which are in the Wall, and falling down with a pleafant Murmur, fills them, and they being full what runs over wafhes the Streets, and falls again into the River; they are generally three Cubits deep, four broad, and twelve long. The Houfes are either of Brick, or of Stone very well built, the greateft part of thofe of Stone are finely ornamented with Mofaick Work, thofe of Brick alfo are adorned with Glazing and Colours like *Dutch* Tiles, and the Wood-work and Cielings are carved, painted and gilt, the Roofs are flat, for they fleep on the Tops of the Houfes in Summer, and for that purpofe fpread Carpets on them, moft of the Houfes are of two Stories, and many of three, they are built round a Court, and on the infide generally have Porticoes and open Galleries, confifting of as many Stone as the Houfe doth, fo that in each Story you may go under Cover from one Apartment to another (*a*), and thefe they adorn very much with Gilding and gay Colours. All their Porticoes are fupported either with Pillars of Brick, faced on the Outfide with glazed Tiles of various Colours, or elfe with Pillars of Marble, and the Arches which extend from one Pillar to another are all adorned with Mofaick Work and the Timbers and Joifts that fupport the Floors are carved in Scroll-work and Flowers, painted with various bright Colours, moft large Houfes have great Cifterns of Water, from whence they fupply fome little Fountains in their

(*a*) The *Chateau de Madrid* in the *Boys de Boulogn* near *Paris* is built after this *Moorifh* Tafte.

their lower Apartments ; fo that they have large Vafes of Marble in each Room, which are continually full of clear running Water, there being wafte Pipes properly placed to prevent its running over, and carry it off unfeen, they have Baths within their Houfes for to cool themfelves in the Summer-time , the Rich build above their Houfes a Tower, confifting of feveral Stories , thefe Rooms are their chief Delight, and they fpare no Expence to furnifh them beautifully, it is there that the Ladies divert themfelves after they have done Embroidering, and other Works, for from thence they can fee moft part of the City of *Fez.*

There are near 700 Mofques great and little, 50 of thefe are very confiderable, and are adorned with Pillars of Marble, and other Ornaments , they have Fountains of Marble, and their Arches are beautified with Mofaick Work, Painting and Carving , their Pillars are made in the fame manner as thofe in *Italy*, the Pavement is covered with the fineft Mats, fo are the Walls as high as a Man, every Mofque has a Tower, round which there is a Gallery, where a Man ftands and calls the People to Prayer at proper Hours, as in *Europe* they ring Bells ; the principal Mofque is called *Carruven*, it is near an *Italian* Mile and half in Circumference, and hath thirty one lofty Gates , the middle Building of the Mofque is 150 *Tufcan* Yards in length, and 80 wide, the Tower is proportionably high , round the whole Building, towards the Eaft, towards the Weft, and towards the North, there are great Colonades 30 Yards wide, and 40 long , there are 900 Lamps lighted every Night, for there is at leaft one Lamp under each Arch, but in the Centre of the Mofque there are great Brazen Candlefticks, one of which can hold 500 Lamps, thefe were made of Bells taken from the *Chriftians*, along the Sides of the Walls there are feven Pulpits, from whence the Doctors of the Law teach the People, it is only Men of Learning that are allowed to preach, for the Prieft of the Mofque, his Bufinefs is only to read Prayers, and to give the Alms to the People, for this Mofque hath great Revenues which they give out in Alms, the Revenues arife from the Rent of Shops and Houfes, and alfo from Farms, where they employ Labourers, and they divide the Produce among the Poor In our Days the King borrowed from this Mofque a great Sum of Money, which he never hath paid Befides the Mofques, there are two Colleges for Students, finely built after the *Moorifh* Manner, and adorned

with

with Marble and Paintings. One of thefe Colleges hath
an hundred Rooms, they were built by the Kings of th
Marin Race; the Beauty and Magnificence of the Hall, which
was built by the King *Abu Henon*, is furprizing In th
middle of the Hall is a great Vafe of Marble which holds
Tun of Water, the Sides are adorned with Pillars of various
coloured Marble, finely polifhed; the Capitals are gilt, and
the Roof fhines with Gold, Azure and Purple, on the Wall
are wrote in large Characters feveral *Arabic* Verfes in Praife
of the Founder King *Abu Henon*; the Gates are of carved
Brafs, and there is a Roftrum for reading Lectures inlaid with
Ebony and Ivory; the Whole is a moft wonderful Piece of
Work, and univerfally admired by all that have feen it, the
Treafurer of the King who built it (in order to diffwade
him) urged to him the vaft Expence, to which *Abu Henon*
anfwered him in two *Arabick* Verfes; ' *That which is perfectly*
' *beautiful, becaufe it deferves its Price, is not dear, and no*
' *Price is too great for to fatisfy the virtuous Defires of th*
' *Heart.*' There are feveral other Colleges in *Fez* built in Imi
tation, but none near fo large or fo beautiful, they had al
Lecturers and Scholars, who were maintained at the Expence
of the Founders both in Food and Raiment, but in the War
of *Sahid* their Endowments were either deftroyed or taken
away, fo that this Univerfity, as well as that of *Morocco*, is
now gone to ruine, and this Neglect of Learning is one of
the Reafons, that not only the People of *Fez*, but thofe of
all the neighbouring Regions are degenerated from their an
tient Virtue

There are many Hofpitals in *Fez*, fome of which are not
much inferior in Building to the Colleges. Formerly all
the Strangers which came into the City, and defired it, were
entertained there three Days gratis, the Endowments which
enabled them to make thefe Expences were then very great,
but in *Sahid*'s War, the King, ftanding in need of Money
fold the Eftates belonging to the Hofpitals, fo that there are
now no Endowments, yet there are ftill fome Hofpitals,
where the Sick have Food, but not Medicines Formerly
there were great Numbers of all neceffary Officers to thefe
Hofpitals, and when I was a young Man, I my felf was
Notary to one of them for two Years

In the City are above an hundred Baths, many of them
very ftately Buildings, each of them have befides the Stove

five Halls with Galleries ; there are Baths for the Women as well as for the Men, and they are the Places of Aſſembly where all the News of the Town is told , there are above two hundred Inns or Taverns in this City, and four hundred Corn-Mills All Arts and Trades in this City are ſeparated from each other, thoſe of the ſame Profeſſion live in the ſame Street or Quarter ; the moſt genteel Trades have their Quarter near the Great Moſque, firſt the Notaries, next the Bookſellers, then thoſe who ſell Boots and Shoes of *Morocco* Leather. Over-againſt the principal Gate of the Moſque ſtands the Fruit-Market, abounding in all kinds of Fruits, and in the Herb-Market there are Bowers made of the green Boughs of Orange, Lemon, and other Trees, with the Fruit on, which they change every Day, under the Shade of which is mighty pleaſant ſitting there is a Milk-Market, and there ſcarce paſſes a Day in which there is not twenty Tuns of Milk ſold there ; there are infinite Numbers of other Trades, each of which hath a different Station Beſides this, there is an Exchange as big as a ſmall City, ſtrongly walled round with Towers and ſtrong Gates , there are Shops here ſtored with the richeſt Silks, and fineſt Carpets, Linen, Woollen, and other Goods , even in times of Wars and Inſurrections this Place hath hitherto never been plundered The Town, which is divided from the other only by the River, contains a great Number of Moſques, Palaces and Colleges , there are alſo ſeveral Caves dug in the marble Rocks, which they uſe as Storehouſes for their Corn ; the South-ſide of the City within the Walls is all Gardens and Villas belonging to the Great Men ; they are planted with the fineſt and choiceſt Fruit-trees, Lemons, Oranges, Citrons, Pomegranates, &c. Theſe Gardens are exceeding beautiful, being full of all kinds of odoriferous and flowering Shrubs, which thrive wonderfully, ſuch as Myrtle, Roſes and Jeſſamines, of which they make covered Arbours, which are paved with white Tiles, and thro' which they bring little Streams of Water, which give a delightful Coolneſs in the hotteſt Weather , the Air all round this Quarter is perfumed by the Flowers, and the Eye not leſs amuſed with the various Dies, than the Ear is with the Falling of Water, and the Singing of the Birds , ſo that the *Arabians* ſay, this Part of the Town is a terreſtrial Paradiſe.

The

The People of *Fez* are cloathed in Winter in Tunicks an
Vefts, and a large loofe Robe or Mantle , they wear a fmal
Turbant on their Heads, and Slippers of coloured *Morocc*
Leather, but the common People are not fo well cloathed
the Ladies drefs very expenfively, yet in the Heat of th
Weather they wear nothing but a Shift, and tie their Fore
heads with a Scarf, their Hair being braided with Strings o
Pearl, and other Jewels.   In Winter they wear Robes o
Damask, with vaft large Sleeves, when they go abroad the
wear Veils, which cover them quite over, fo that nothing
but their Eyes are feen, and they wear Bracelets of Gold o
their Arms and the fmall of their Legs , their Tables ar
well ferved with all kinds of Foods, as well Butchers Meat
as Game, Fifh, and Fruit, fuch as Melons, Grapes, Pome
granates, &c. they have one Difh called *(a)* Cuscusu peculia
to the *Moors*, which is made of a Lump of Dough, which the
fqueeze thro' a Plate full of Holes, and roll it into fmal
Pieces of the Size of *Coriander*-Seed, then they cover th
Veffel that is boiling with that Plate or Cullender on which
they lay the Dough, and fo ftew it over the Steam , this
which is a kind of artificial Rice, they eat with the Broth
and Meat.   The People of the beft Fafhion take grea
Delight in playing at Chefs, and in Poetry ; and whilft th
Marin Family flourifhed, there were feveral excellent Poem
wrote both in the *Arabick* and *Moorifh* Tongues, which ar
ftill in being.   Learning being neglected, Ignorance and Su
perftition have encreafed, and the People do now univerfally
believe in *Fortune-Tellers, Inchanters, Conjurers, Jugglers*
and *Monks*, and are fo deluded, that Thoufands of thof
Wretches fubfift on the Fat of the Land   Northward from
the City, upon a high Hill, ftands a Palace, in which ar
the Monuments of feveral of the *Marin* Race ; thefe Tomb
are of Marble, beautifully carved, with proper Epitaphs en
graved upon them   Eaft and South of the City are grea
Numbers of Gardens, full of Fruit-Trees, and watered b
Canals drawn from the River; their Fruits are delicious, an
in the Seafon 500 Cart-Loads of Fruit are daily carried t
the Markets of *Fez*, without reckoning the Grapes   To
tne Eaft of *Fez* is a Plain 15 Miles broad and 30 long, which
o a marfhy Soil, watered by a Number of Springs and Ri
                                                    vulets

(a) This feems to be the fame which is called *Coo'coo* by th
Negroes   Vide my Journal p 108.

rulets; this did belong to the Great Mosque, and was let out to Gardeners, who raised Hemp, Melons, Turnips, Radish, and all kinds of Roots and Pot-Herbs, so that the Great City of *Fez* was furnished from hence with all kinds of Herbage

By the Conquest of the *Caliphs*, the Law of *Mahomet* was established in *Africa* By that Law no Person can be created a King or Prince, either by the Election of the People, or by any Human Authority whatsoever; for the true *Musulmen* believe Dominion to be founded in Grace, and that none can justly and legally bear Rule over others but the *Caliph*, who is inspired, and whom they call *Holy*, and who ought to be the Legitimate Successor of *Mahomet*, and who is *Emperor* and *High-Priest*. This Doctrine was maintained whilst the *Saracen* Empire continued, but upon the Decline of it, the wild People, such as the *Turks*, the *Curdes* and *Tartars*, revolted in *Asia*; and in the West of *Africa*, the Tribes of *Zeneta* and *Luntuna* threw off the Ecclesiastical Government, and the Kings of the Families of *Luntuna* and *Marin*, being Laymen, reigned with great Glory for a Time; but afterwards Tyranny began to be established, nor is there now any regular Hereditary Succession among them. They name their Successors in their Lives, either their Sons, Nephews, Brothers, or whom they love best, and get the Great Men to take an Oath of Fidelity to them, who often, on the Death of the King, fail in their Oaths, and fall into Wars and Confusion, for the Superstition of the People is generally such, that they believe them all to be Usurpers, and that no Oaths are binding against the Right which is in *Holy Men*, being of the Posterity of *Mahomet*. As soon as a King of *Fez* is acknowledged, to strengthen his Interest, he generally chuses one of the most powerful Men to be his chief Minister, to whom of course one third Part of the Revenue belongs, he then appoints a *Secretary*, and a *General of the Horse*, also *a Governor over each City*, to whom he gives all the Revenues of it, on condition to maintain a certain Number of Horse for the King's Service, when called upon to joyn the Army, then he names *Commissaries*, or *Legates*, to the Nations who inhabit the Mountains, and the *Arabians* who acknowledge his Authority These are Men of the Law, who administer Justice according to the Customs of those People, and collect the King's Revenue amongst them He gives Fees to
Knights.

Knights; every one of which confifts of a Caftle, or two or three Villages, fufficient to maintain a Knight in fuch manner as to be able to follow the King to the Wars, when fummon'd. Befides which, the King hath a Body of mercenary Horfe in the Nature of a Guard, whom he pays in Money in Time of War; in Time of Peace he cloath and feeds them, but pays them little Money. He allows them *Chriftian* Slaves to look to their Horfes. He hath *Commiffary*, who hath Charge of all the Camels, and takes care that there are Beafts of Burden enough, not only for to carry the Tents and Baggage, but alfo the Provifions for the Army. There is a *Stud-Mafter General*, who takes care of breeding and maintaining a fufficient Number of Horfes for all his Servants.

The King hath fifty Horfemen, who are near Attendants on his Perfon in the Nature of Meflengers, whofe Bufinefs is to obey his Commands, by making Prifoners, or putting to Death fuch Perfons as he fhall order. He has a Troop of Standard-bearers, Men thoroughly acquainted with all the Paffes of the Country, he appoints him who knows the Province they march through beft, to carry a Standard before them, and guide the Army. Their Horfe have Drums of a vaft Size, much larger than thofe of *Italy*, which make a horrible loud Noife. A Horfe can carry but one of them. They have alfo great Numbers of Trumpets and other mufical Inftruments. His legitimate Queen is always of the *Moorifh* or *Arabian* Race, but his Women Slaves and Concubines are often Black-moors, and fome are *Portugal* or *Spanifh* Women. Tho' the King of *Fez* hath large Dominions, yet they being affign'd to Governors for maintaining Troops, or to Knights as Fees for Services, his Revenues in Money paid to himfelf are but fmall, yet the People are wonderfully preffed with the Tribute. In fome Parts the Subjects pay a Ducat and a Quarter a Year, for as much Ground as a Team of Oxen can plow in a Day. In others they pay Hearth-Money; they alfo pay a Poll-Tax of a Ducat for every Male above fixteen Years old, and raife other Taxes upon the People, which are very heavy upon the Peafants, but more fo upon the great Towns. And this is the more grievous to them, becaufe, by the Law of *Mahomet*, no King is to take more Tribute than what is limited by it, *viz.* A Perfon who has a hundred Ducats is to pay two and a Half per

Annum, and no more ; and the Peafant is to pay the Tythes of the Fruits of the Earth, and no more ; and this is to be paid to the Caliph or High Prieft, and not to any Layman ; and he is not to confume them in Pleafures for his own Gratification, but they are to be expended by the Caliph for the Service of the State, and with them he is to fupport the Poor, the Sick, the Widows, and the Orphans, and to maintain the Wars againft Enemies But fince there have been no more Caliphs, and the Lords abovementioned have ufurped a tyrannical Power, calling themfelves Kings, they have not only feized upon thefe Revenues, but robbed the Poor, the Hofpitals, and the Churches of their Endowments, and raifed a great many oler Taxes, and fquandered them away to gratify their own Lufts, Follies and Paffions ; and they have added Taxes upon Taxes, in fuch a manner, that thro' all *Africa* the common People can hardly afford wherewithal to cloath themfelves, and they are become fo hateful by thefe Extortions, that no honeft nor learned Man will fo much as eat or fit down with any of the King's Officers or Courtiers, much lefs will they take any Gifts or Penfions from him, becaufe they know that all he hath is plundered from the Publick and the Poor, and they look upon it as fo much ftolen Goods, and that the taking any Allowance from him is fharing with the Thief We faid before that the King of *Fez* keeps a Body of Horfe in conftant Pay, they are in Number 6000, befides which he has 500 Crofs Bows, and 500 Harquebufiers But befides hefe in Time of War he can form a very great Army, by calling out the Forces of the Governors of the *Arabian* Tributaries, and of the Knights Fees

The prefent King defpifes all Ceremony and Appearances of Magnincence, and even in the moft folemn Proceffions he wears only a plain Habit, and is known from his Attendants by his not being fo fine as they are, and he never wears a Crown, for the Law of *Mahomet* forbids it, it being againft the Humility which *Mufulmen* ought to hew in all their Actions

When the King takes the Field, they firft pitch his Tent in the Centre of the Camp, it is in a fquare Form like a Caftle, 50 Yards on each Side, it is furrounded with Cotton Cloths, like a Wall with Battlements, at the Corner are Towers made of the fame
Cloth

Cloth with Battlements; all which are fupported with Poles and Cords, as Tents are, the Tops of the Towers end in Spires, with Gilt Balls; to this Linen Wall are four Gates, each guarded by Eunuchs. In the Square within it are many Tents, that which contains the King's Bedchamber is very magnificent, and yet is eafily ftruck and moved. Next to the King's are the Tents of the principal Officers of the Court, and between him and the Linen Wall are the Tents of the Guard, which are fmall and of Camel's Hair. Within this Incloiure alfo is the King's Kitchen, and neceffary Offices, round the Linen Wall on the Outfide is an Efplanade, and round the Efplanade the King's 6000 Horfe are encamped, they have Tents for her Horfes, which are very caretully tended. In the Rear of the Horfe is the Baggage, where there are Shops which fell all Neceffaries, and an open Market kept, beyond which, to the Right, and Left, and the Rear, and in the Front of the King's Quarters, the *Arabians*, and the Forces of the Governors and Mountaineers are encamped. The whole Camp makes a kind of City, of which the King's Quarters is the Caftle in the Centre, fo that no Enemy by Surprize can come to it. And in the Efplanade round the King's Quarters there are Patroles all Night, befides the Guard belonging to the Army. Yet the *Arabians* are fo dexterous at Surprizes, that there have been Attempt, and People taken in the very Midft of the King's Quarters, who were got fo far in order to kill him. In the prefent declining State of their Government the King is forced to keep the Field moft Part of the Year, as well to to awe the *Arabians*, and his other Subjects, as to make Head again the *Portuguefe*. He is alfo very fond of Hunting, and for the Conveniency of the Sport often encamps in the Mountains.

✿✿✿✿✿✿✿✿✿✿✿ ✿ ✿✿✿✿✿✿✿✿✿✿✿✿✿✿

BOOK VI.
Of NUMIDIA.

*D*ARA is a Province, which begins at Mount A, and ftretcheth Southward towards the Defarts of L. This Province is very narrow, for the fruitful Land along the Side of a River of the fame Name,

which extends from the North to the South   Upon the
Sides of the River are great Numbers of Villages, and
some Castles walled with Stone,   and all the Land within
six Miles of the River on each Side is planted with Palm-
Trees   They bear the most excellent Dates, which may
be preserved, if kept in a good Magazine, for six or seven
Years   They have a more ordinary Kind of Date, with
which they feed their Horses and Camels   The Palm-
Trees are Male and Female , the Female produces Fruit,
but the Male nothing but Flowers   If they do not grow
near each other, the Dates are not good   The Food of
the Inhabitants of all this Province is Dates   They rarely
eat Bread , when they do, it is a Feast   All the People of
Wealth in this Country deal in Gold, and there are a great
many Goldsmiths and *Jews* who work up the Metal, it
being the great Road between *Fez* in *Mauritania* and *Tom-*
buto   This Trade inriches the Province, so that there are
four great Towns in it, in which there is a great Resort
of foreign Merchants, and great Numbers of Snops well
furnished with all Kinds of Goods   The principal Town
is called *Bensaby*   Here is Plenty of Indigoe, which they
sell to the Merchants of *Fez*

Segenesse is a Province which takes its Name from the
principal City,   which lies upon the River *Ziz* , it is inhabited by many Races of the ancient *Africans*, of the Tribes
of *Zeneta, Zanhagia* and *Haora*   It extends along the River *Ziz* 120 Miles , in it are 350 Villages , the principal
Place in it is *Tregent*, containing about a Thousand Families   *Tebuhasait*, in which there are a great many foreign Merchants, Artizans and *Jews* , they coin Money
here, both Silver and Gold , they trade down to the Country of the *Negroes* with Goods which they buy from *Dar-*
bar), in Exchange for which they purchse Slaves and Gold
Some are of Opinion that the Town of *Segenesse* was built
by a *Roman* General,   who, having conquered all *Numi-*
dia, built this Town upon the Borders of *Mesic*, which he
called (a) the Seal of *Mesia*   It was formerly built in a
goodly Manner,   the Ruins of which still remain   The
Town was exceeding rich, by reason of the Commerce
with the *Negroes*   There were in it many magnificent
Mosques and Colleges, but the Town was destroyed of late

Civil Wars, and nothing now remains but the Ruins, yet is the neighbouring Country ſtill very populous.

Of TEBELBELT.

THIs is a little Town in the *Numidian* Deſart, 200 Miles South of *Atlas*, and 100 South of *Segelmeſſe* There are Plantations of Palm-Trees round it Water is ſcarce, and Fleſh ſtill more ſcarce, They eat *Oſtriches* They trade to the Land of *Negroes*, and are ſubject to the *Arabians*.

Of BENIGUMI.

THIs is a Habitation upon the River *Ghir*, and there are abundance of Palm-Trees near it, their Trade chiefly lies in buying Horſes in the Kingdom of *Fez*, and ſelling them to the Merchants who trade to the *Negroe* Country I is about 150 Miles S. E from *Segelmeſſe*. It contains 8 Caſtle, and 15 Villages

After what we have ſaid of *Numidia*, the Second Diviſion of *Africa*, we ſhall proceed to the Deſarts of *Libya*, which, as I ſaid before, is divided into Five Parts We ſhall begin with that of *Zanaga*, which is a dry and ſandy Deſart, reaching from the Ocean Sea on the Weſt, as far as the Salt Pits of *Tegaza* Eaſtward Northward it is bounded by *Su*, *Haca* and *Dara*, which are Parts of *Numidia*, and Southward it ſtretcheth to the Country of the *Negroes*, and is bounded by the Kingdoms of *Gualata* and *Tombuto* In this Deſart no Water is found, unleſs it be here and there at 100 Miles diſtance, and even what is, is ſalt, and bitter, and drawn out of very deep Pits, particularly upon the Road between *Segelmeſſe* and *Tombuto* This Deſart abounds with ſtrange Creatures and Serpents In the Deſart there is one Part of it ſtill more dreadful than the reſt, which is called *Azoad*, in which there is no Inhabitant, and nothing but Sands for 200 Miles, viz from the Well of *Azoad* to the Well of *Aroan*, the latter of which is 150 Miles diſtant from *Tombuto* In this Deſart, by exceſſive Heat, and want of Water, it often happens that both Men and Beaſts who travel croſs it periſh

From the ſame Salt-Pits of *Tegaza*, where the Deſart of *Zanaga* ends, we reckon the Deſart of *Zuenziga* begins It reaches Eaſtward to the Deſart of *Hair*, where the Trade

T. g.

Targa inhabits; Northward it is bounded by *Segelmeffe, Tebel-hilt* and *Benigumi*, in *Numidia*, and Southward it reaches to the Defart of *Ghir*, and the Kingdom of *Guba* It is a moft barren and comfortlefs Place, even more terrible than the former, yet over this the Merchants pafs from *Telenfi* to *Tombuto*

In the Region of *Tegaza* they dig great Quantities of Salt, which is exceeding white At the Entrance of the Pits from whence they dig the Salt, are the Cottages in which live the Workmen, who fell the Salt to fome Merchants, who carry it upon Camels Backs to *Tombuto* Thefe People who dig the Salt have no Provifions but what the Merchants bring them, for they are almoft 20 Days Journey from any Habitations, fo that they often die by the Merchants not bringing them Provifions in due time I my felf lived 3 Days here, during which time I was obliged to drink Water drawn out of Wells, which was very brackifh

✧✧✧✧✧✧✧✧✧✧✧✧ ✧✧✧✧✧✧✧✧✧ ✧✧✧✧✧✧✧✧✧

B O O K VII.

Of the Land of NEGROES, *and of the Confines of* ÆGYPT.

OUR Antient *African* Geographers, *viz* Bichi and *Mefhudi*, were ignorant of all the Land of *Negroes*, except the Countries *Guechet* and *Cano*, all other Places of the Land of *Negroes* being in their Time undifcover'd But in the Year of the *Hegeira* 380 it was difcover'd by the following Means The Family or *Luntuna*, and all the Tribes of *Libya*, were by a famous Preacher drawn to receive the *Mahometan* Religion He then came up to live in *Barbary*, and ftrove to inform himfelf, and did acquire a Knowledge of the Countries of the Negroes All that Country was then inhabited by Men who lived in the manner of Beafts, without King, without Lords, without Senates, without Government or Taxes They hardly fowed Corn, they had no Cloathing but the Skins of Beafts, nor no Property in their Wives They fpent the Day either in tending their Herds, or in labouring of the Ground, and at Night they met in little Companies of ten or twelve Men and

Women, and passed the Night together in Bowers covered
with Boughs of Trees, each Man and Woman consorting
as Love directed   The Ground itself, covered with the
Hides of Cattle dried with the Hair on, served for Beds
They never made War, nor travelled into other Countries,
but they contentedly lived all their Days in their native
Country, and never set their Feet out of it   Some of them
adored the *Sun* with Songs, as soon as he appeared above the
Earth, others worshipped the *Fire*, as did the People of
Guelra, and those who inhabited the Kingdom of *Gaoga* in
the East, were true *Christians*, which Doctrine they had
received from *Egypt*   *Joseph* of the Family of *Luntuna*,
Founder and King of the City of *Morocco*, and of the Five
Libyan Tribes, conquer'd all these *Negroe* Nations, and
taught them the *Mahometan* Religion, and the Arts of Life,
and then great Numbers of the Merchants of *Barbary*, travelled into that Country to sell them Goods, and learnt their
Language   The Five Tribes of *Libia* divided the whole
Country into Fifteen Parts, or Kingdoms, and Three of
those Parts were granted to each Tribe, who sent out some
of the Nobility of their Families, who each conquer'd their
Part, and erected them into Kingdoms   It is true, that the
present King of *Tombuto* is not a *Libyan*, but a *Negroe*   He
was General to *Seni Hali*, King of *Tombuto* and *Gabo*, of the
Family of the *Libyan* Tribes   After the Death of his Master, he rebelled against his Master's Son, whom he put to
death, and shaking off the *Libyan* Yoke, the *Negroes* then
were governed by a *Negroe*   Having reigned Fifteen Year,
and in that Time conquer'd many Kingdoms, and having
settled all Things in profound Peace and Quiet, he went on
a Pilgrimage to *Mecca*, in which he spent all his Wealth,
and became in Debt 150,000 Ducats.   All these Fifteen
Kingdoms of *Negroes*, which are known unto us, extend
along the *Niger*, and the Rivers that run into it from the
Sea to the Heads of that River   And all the Land of *Negroes* is situate between two vast Desarts, for on the one
side is the main Desart between *Nun aia* and it, which is
extended unto this very Country, and to the South-side of
it is another Desart, which reacheth to the main Ocean in
the West, beyond which Desart many Nations inhabit,
with whom we are not acquainted, for none of our People
have travelled thither, by reason of the Length of the Journey, and the vast Distance, and also the Diversity of L -

guages and Religions   They have no Dealings with us; but we have heard, that they traffick with the Inhabitants near the *Ocean Sea*

A Description of the Kingdom of GUALATA.

IF this Kingdom be compared to the others, it is small; containing only three large (a) Towns, besides Villages, and Plantations of Palm-Trees.   These Towns are distant from *Nun* Southward about 300, from *Tombuto* North-west 500, and from the Sea about 200 Miles   The People of *Lbya*, whilst the Country of *Negroes* was subject to them, held their Royal Seat in this Region, unto which great Numbers of *Barbary* Merchants resorted at that Time But afterward, in the Reign of *Hel*, King of *Tombuto*, who was a very Great Prince, those Merchants left *Gualata*, and began to frequent *Tombuto* and *Gago*, by which means the King of *Gualata* became extremely poor   These People speak the Language called (b) *Sungai*, the Inhabitants are black, and receive Strangers with great Hospitality   This Region being in my Time subdued by the King of *Tombuto*, the Prince thereof fled into the Desarts, to those *Lbyan* Tribes from whence his Family came, whereof the King of *Tombuto* having Information, and being apprehensive of the Prince's Return with all the People of the Desarts, granted him Peace on condition that he should pay a great Yearly Tribute to him, and so the Prince hath continued Tributary to the King of *Tombuto* until now   The Manners and Fashions of the People differ not all from those of the Inhabitants of the next Desart   It produces some Quantity of *Indian* Corn, and great Plenty of a (c) little round white

(a) These three Towns of *Gualata* seem by the Situation to be what is now called the Kingdom of the Grand *Jolloffs*   The *Jolloff* Race, who are now Kings of *Barsalh*, seem descended from them, their Name being *Njai*, here called *Senga*, and in other Places *Sanagoi*, and their Language different from that of the *Mandingoes*, or *Negroes*   The little Religion they have is *Mahometan*, and in their Love of Milk and Horses they resemble the People of the Desart

(b) The Names of the present Kings of the *Jolloffs*   Vide P 214 of my Journal

(c) The small *Guinea* Corn   Vide p 31 of my Journal

white Grain, the like whereof I never saw in *Europe*, but there is great Scarcity of Flesh among them. The Heads both of Men and Women are so covered, that all their Countenance is almost concealed. They have no Form of a Commonwealth, neither are there any *Lawyers* or *Judges* among them, but they lead a most miserable Life

A Description of the Kingdom of GHINEA.

THis Kingdom, which the Merchants of our Nation call *Ghineca*, the Natives themselves call *Germi*, and the *Portuguese*, and other People of *Europe*, (a) *Ghinea* It joins to the aforementioned, but between them there is a Desart 50 Miles over, so that *Gualata* lies on the North, *Tombut* on the East, and the Kingdom of *Melli* on the South of it It is almost 500 Miles in Length, and extends 250 Mile along the River *Nger*, and bordereth upon the Ocean in the same Place where *Nger* falleth into it It is very fruitful in Rice, Cattle, Fish, and Cotton Their Cotton they exchange with the Merchants of *Barbary* for *European* Cloth, brazen Vessels, Armour, and other such Commodities Their Money is uncoined Gold, they use Barrs of Iron for Money in Matters of small Value, some Pieces of which are a Pound, some half a Pound, and some a quarter of a Pound-weight Throughout the whole Kingdom there is no Foreign Fruits but Dates, and they are brought from *Gualata* or *Numidia* There is neither Town nor Castle, but one great Village, which is inhabited by the Prince of *Ghinea*, together with his Priests, Doctors, Merchants, and all the principal Men of the Region Their Houses are built in the Shape of Bells pointed on Top, the Walls of Clay, and the Roofs they cover with Reeds The Apparel of the Inhabitants is black or blue Cotton, with which they cover their Heads also, but the Priests and Doctors of the Law wear white Cotton The Overflowings of the *Nger* yearly surround this Region in manner of an Island, during the three Months of *July*, *August*, and *September*, in which time the Merchant of

Ten

(a) If the G is pronounced soft like the *J*, the Difference is not great between ṭ and *Yar*, It seems by the Situation to be the same now call'd so, only that which is now *Barjah* seems to be part of the antient *Ghinea* conquer'd by the *Jolloffs*, if so, the present king doms of *Parrot*, *Bariselli*, *Yar*, and *Woolley*, lie in the same Country, which in the Time of *Leo* was call'd *Ghinea*.

Tombuto bring their Wares hither in Canoes or narrow Boatt made of one Tree, which they row all Day, but at Night they faften them to the Shore, and encamp upon the Land. This Kingdom, as well as the others, was formerly governed by a King defcended from the *Libyan* Tribes, which Family became tributary unto King *Soni Heli*, but the Family of *Soni Heli* being deftroyed by *Izchia* his Succeffor, *Izchia* invaded the Country, and taking Prifoner the laft King of the *Libyan* Race, held him Prifoner in *Gaoga* till the Time of his Death, and govern'd this Kingdom by a Deputy.

Of the Kingdom of MEILI.

THis Region is extended almoft 300 Miles along the Bank of a River which runneth into *Niger*, and bordereth Northward upon *Ghinea*, Southward upon certain Defarts and dry Mountains, Weftward upon large Woods and Forefts reaching to the Sea-fhore, and Eaftward upon the Kingdom of *Gago*. This Kingdom contains a Town of 6000 Families, called *Melli*, from whence the whole Kingdom is fo call'd, here the King hath his Refidence. In this Region is abundance of Corn, Flefh and Cotton. Here are great Numbers of Artificers and Merchants, and yet all Strangers are honourably entertain'd by the King. The Inhabitants are rich, and have plenty of Wares. Here are many Mofques, Priefts and Profeffors, but Lectures are read by the Profeffors in the Mofques only, there being no Colleges at all. The People of this Region are in Wit, Civility and Induftry, fuperior to all other *Negroes*, and were the firft that embraced the Law of *Mahomet*. They were firft conquer'd and govern'd by a Prince of one of the nobleft Families of the Tribes of *Libia*, he was Uncle to *Jofeph* King of *Morocco*, and his Pofterity continued to govern till the Reign of *Izchia*, who made him his Tributary in fuch a manner as to deftroy entirely his State and Power; fo that he and his Family were forced to live in the fame manner as the reft of his Subjects

Of the Kingdom of TOMBUTO.

THE Name of this Kingdom is modern · It was fo call'd (as fome think) from the Name of a certain Town which (they fay) was built by King *Menfa Sulmen*,

in the Year of the *Hegira* 610, fituate within twelve Miles
of a Branch of the *Nger* The Houfes here are built in
the Shape of Bells, the Walls are Stakes or Hurdles,
plaifter'd over with Clay, and the Houfes cover'd with Reeds,
yet there is one ftately Mofque, the Walls of which are
made of Stone and Lime The Royal Palace is alfo built
of Stone by an excellent Artift from *Granada*, as alfo many
Shops of Artificers and Merchants There are great Numbers of Weavers of Cotton-Cloth Hither the Cloth of
Europe is brought by the *Barbary* Merchants It is cufto-
mary here for all the Women to go with their Faces cover'd,
except the Maid Servants, who fell Food The Inhabitants,
and efpecially the Strangers that refide there, are very rich,
infomuch that the prefent King gave both his Daughters in
Marriage to two rich Merchants Here are many Wells,
the Water of which is excellent, and as often as the *Nger*
overfloweth, its Water is convey'd into the Town by certain Sluces There is great Plenty of Corn, Cattle, Milk
and Butter, in this Region, but Scarcity of Salt, which is
brought hither by Land from *Tegaza*, 500 Miles abfent
When I myfelf was here, I faw one Camel's Load of Salt
fold for 80 Ducats The rich King of *Tombuto* hath in his
Poffeffion many golden Plates and Scepters, fome whereof
are 1300 Ounces in Weight, and he keeps a fplendid and
well-furnifhed Court In travelling he rideth himfelf upon
a Camel, and one of his greateft Officers leads his Horfe after
him He alfo in War rideth a Camel, but all his Soldiers
ride on Horfes Whofoever will fpeak to the King, muft
proftrate himfelf at his Feet, and then taking up Duft, muft
fprinkle it upon his own Head and Shoulders (a), which
Cuftom is obferved by them that never faluted the King before, or come as Embaffadors from other Princes His
Attendance confifts of 3000 Horfemen, and a great Number of Footmen, who ufe poifon'd Arrows They have
frequent Skirmifhes with thofe that refufe to pay Tribute,
and their Captives they fell to the Merchants of *Tesset*
There are too many Horfes bred here, and the Mercurs,
and Courters have certain the Nags to ride upon, for
their beft Horfes come from *Barbary* When the King is
informed of a Merchant's coming to Town with Horfes, he
orders a certain Number to be brought to him, and chufing
th

the beft, he payeth a great Price for him   He hath fuch an inveterate Hatred againft all *Jews*, that they are not allowed Admittance into his City , and whatfoever *Barbary* Merchants he finds to traffick with them, he immediately commandeth their Goods to be confifcated   The King at his own Expence liberally maintaineth here great Numbers of Doctors, Judges, Priefts, and other learned Men.   There are Manufcripts, or written Books, brought hither out of *Barbary*, which are fold for more Money than any other Merchandize   Inftead of Money, they ufe Barrs of Gold. They have likewife certain Shells, which are brought hither from the Kingdom of *Perfia*, and thofe they ufe in Matters of fmall Value, 400 of which Shells are worth a Ducat ; and fix Pieces of their golden Coin, with two third Parts, weigh an Ounce   The Inhabitants are of a mild and gentle Difpofition, and are wont to fpend great part of the Night in Singing and Dancing   They have many Men and Women Slaves, and their Town is very apt to be fet on fire ; when I was there the fecond time almoft half the Town was burnt down in the fpace of five Hours , without the Suburbs they have neither Gardens nor Orchards.

Of the Town of CABRA.

THis large Town is built in manner of a Village without Walls, and is fituate upon the River *Niger*, about twelve Miles from *Tombuto*   From hence the Merchants that travel unto the Kingdoms of *Ghinea* and *Melli*, go by Water   The People and Buildings of this Town are not inferior to thofe of *Tombuto* , and this Place is frequented by great Numbers of *Negroes* that come hither by Water   In this Town a Judge is appointed by the King of *Tombuto* to decide all Controverfies , for it were tedious to go thither on every Occafion.

Abu Baer, firnamed *Pargama*, the King's Brother, is an intimate Acquaintance of mine, who is black in Colour, but moft beautiful in Mind and Difpofition   In this Town are many Difeafes, which carry off a great many People, and which proceed from the unnatural Mixture of their Meats ; for they mix Fifh, Milk, Butter and Flefh, all together ; which Food is alfo commonly ufed in *Tombuto*.

Of the Town and Kingdom of GAGO.

THE Great Town of *Gago* is without Walls also, and is distant Southward of *Tombuto* almost 400 Miles, inclining somewhat to the South-East. Its Houses are very mean, except those in which the King and his Courtiers live. Here are very rich Merchants, and it is much frequented by *Negroes*, who buy Cloth brought hither from *Barbary* and *Europe.* In this Town there is great Plenty of Corn and Flesh, but Scarcity of Wine, Trees and Fruits. It aboundeth likewise with Melons, Citrons and Rice. Here are many Wells also, in which is sweet and wholesom Water. Here is a Place where Slaves are to be sold on those Days when the Merchants assemble, where a young Slave is sold for six Ducats, they likewise sell their Children. The King of this Region maintaineth a great Number of Concubines and Slaves in a private Palace, which are kept by Eunuchs, and his Body-Guard consists of a sufficient Troop of Horsemen and Footmen. The King himself decideth all his Subjects Controversies in a Place walled round about, between the first Gate of the Palace and the inner Part thereof, and altho' he dischargeth his Office with great Diligence, yet hath he his Counsellors, and other Officers, namely, Secretaries, Treasurers, Factors and Auditors. The Plenty of Merchandize that is brought hither daily, and the Sumptuousness of every thing, is surprising to all People. Horses bought in *Europe* for 10 Ducats, are sold here for 40 or 50 Ducats a-piece. The coarsest Cloth of *Europe* is here sold for 4 Ducats an Ell, if it be at all fine, for 15, and for an Ell of *Venice* or *Turkey*-Cloth, they will give 30 Ducats. The Value of a Sword is 3 or 4 Crowns. Spurs, Bridles, and such like Commodities, as also Spices, are sold at a great Rate, but Salt is the dearest here of all Commodities. Here are nought but Villages throughout the whole Kingdom, which are inhabited by Husbandmen and Shepherds, who in Winter wear Beasts-Skins, and in Summer go entirely naked, except their Privities, and sometimes they wear Shoes made of Camels Leather. They are very ignorant, for one learned Man is not to be found in the Space of 100 Miles. Grievous Taxes are continually imposed upon them, so that they are scarce able to maintain them-selves.

Of *the* KINGDOM *of* GUBER.

THIS Kingdom is situate almost three Hundred Miles Eastward of *Gago* , between them is a vast Desart, which is in great Want of Water, being about forty Miles distant from the *Niger* This Kingdom of *Guber* is surrounded with high Mountains, and its Villages, which are many, are inhabited by Shepherds and other Herdsmen · Here is great Store of Cattle both large and small , here is also abundance of Artificers and Linen-Weavers, and they make such Sandals here as the ancient *Romans* used to wear, which for the most part are carried to *Tombuto* and *Gago* It aboundeth likewise with Rice, and other Grain and Pulse, such as I never saw in *Italy*, but some Places of *Spain* I think produce the like All the Fields of this Region are overflowed at the Inundation of the *Niger*, at which Time the Inhabitants cast their Seed into the Water only Here is a Town consisting of almost six Thousand Families, among whom are many Merchants *Izchia*, the King of *Tombuto*, in my Time slew the King of this Country, made Eunuchs of his Sons, and kept his Court for some Time here , afterwards he sent Governors rither, who tyrannized over the People, and impoverished those that were before rich , most Part of the Inhabitants they made Captives, whom *Izchia* kept for Slaves

Of *the* CITY *and* KINGDOM *of* AGADEZ

THIS City bordereth on the Confines of *Libya*, and not long ago was walled round Its Inhabitants are whiter than other *Negroes*, and their Houses are stately, built in the Fashion of *Barbary* The Citizens are for the most part foreign Merchants, the rest are either Artificers or Stipendaries to the King Every Merchant is attended by a great Number of Servants and Slaves in their Journey from *Caro* to *Bornu* , that Road being so infested by Thieves called *Zingani*, that they dare not travel without Arms for their Defence, which in my Time were Cross-Bows At their Arrival in any Town they immediately set their Slaves to some Business , that they may not live in Idleness,

only

only about a Dozen they keep to attend upon themselves,
and their Wares. The King of this City hath const.. ..
in his Retinue a Guard, and resides for the most part at a
Palace in the Midst of the City. His Subjects that habit the Deserts and Fields are most regarded by him, for
they will sometimes expell their King, and chuse another,
so that whoever is most in their Favour, is sure to be
King of *Agadez*. The remaining Part of this Kingdom
lieth Southward, and is inhabited by Shepherds and Herdsmen, whose Cottages are made of Boughs, and carried a-
bout from Place to Place on the Backs of Oxen. Their
Cottages are always built on the same Spot of Ground
which they intend to feed their Cattle on, which is likewise the Custom of the *Arwaez*. Large Duty is laid on
Merchandize brought from other Places, and this Kingdom
pays yearly almost an Hundred and Fifty Ducats to the
King of *Tombuto* for Tribute.

Of the PROVINCE of CANO.

THE great Province of *Cano* is situate to the East of
the *Niger*, almost five Hundred Miles. The Inhabitants are some of them Herdsmen, and others Husbandmen, and live in Villages. It produces abundance of
Corn, Rice and Cotton. Here are many Deserts like..
and woody Mountains, in which are many Springs of
Water. In these Woods there is great Store of wild Citrons and Lemons, the Taste of which is not unlike the
best Sort. There in the Midst of this Province is found
called by the same Name, the Walls and Houses whereof
are made of a kind of Clay; the Inhabitants are rich
Merchants, and very civil. Their King formerly was a
Man of much Power, and had mighty Troops of Horsemen at his Command, but he has since been brought in
to the Kings of *Zegzeg* and *Cosena*, who were either more
treacherous... of... *Izta*, King of *Tombuto*, pretend..
to... their Favour. He then waged War with the King
of *Cano*, whom, after a long Siege, he took, and obliged
him to marry one of his Daughters, replacing him on the
Throne on these Conditions, that he should pay him the
... a Part of all his Tribute, for the Receipt of which

some of the King of *Tombuto*'s Courtiers perpetually reside at *Cano*.

Of the KINGDOM of CASENA.

CASENA bordereth Eastward upon the Kingdom last
described, and is full of Mountains and dry Fields,
which yield great Plenty of Mill-Seed. The Inhabitants
are of an exceeding black Complexion, with great Noses,
and broad Lips. Their Habitation is in poor forlorn Cottages, none of their Villages containing above three Hundred Families, and beside their poor Condition, they are
mightily oppressed with Famine. They had formerly a
King, who was slain by *Ischia*, King of *Tombuto*, since
whose Death they have been tributary to him.

Of the KINGDOM of ZEGZEG.

THE South-East Part of this Kingdom bordereth on
the Confines of *Cano*, and is almost 150 Miles
distant from *Casena*. The Inhabitants are rich, and
deal much with other Nations. This Kingdom is partly
plain and partly mountainous, but the Mountains are extremely cold, and the Plains intolerably hot. The Sharp-
ness of the Weather in the Mountains is scarce to be endured, they therefore kindle great Fires in the Midst of
their Houses, having the Coals under their Bedsteads, and
so go to sleep. Their Fields abound with Water, and
are exceeding fruitful, and they build their Houses after
the Manner of those of *Casena*. They in Times past were
governed by a King of their own, who being slain by
Ischia, they have ever since been subject unto him.

Of the REGION of ZANFARA.

THIS Region bordereth Eastward upon *Zegzeg*, and is
inhabited by poor and rustical People. Their Fields
produce great Plenty of Rice, Mill, and Cotton. The
Inhabitants are of a tall Stature, and are of a Complexion, having broad Villages, and most savage and sh

D 3

Difpofitions Their King likewife was flain by *Izchia*, and themfelves made his Tributaries.

Of the Town *and* Kingdom *of* GUANGARA.

THE South-Eaft Part of this Kingdom bordereth upon *Zanfara*, it is very populous, and governed by a King, who maintaineth a Garrifon of feven Thoufand Archers, and five Hundred Horfemen, and receiveth yearly great Tributes. It contains none but poor fmall Villages, except one, which is fuperior to the reft, both in Largenefs and fine Buildings, the Inhabitants are very rich, and have continual Dealings with the adjoining Nations. To the South of it there is a Region abounding with Gold, but their Traffick is now cut off with foreign Nations, for they are environed on both Sides with moft cruel Enemies, having on the Weft *Izchia*, and on the Eaft the King of *Borno*, who, when I was there, having raifed a great Army, defign'd to expel the Prince of *Guaga* out of his Kingdom, only he was prevented by H---, the Prince of *Gaoga*, who began to attack his Kingdom, wherefore the King of *Borno* returning with his Forces into his own Country, was forced to give over the Conqueft of *Guangara* When the Merchants travel unto the Region abounding with Gold, they carry their Wares on Slaves Backs, (for the Roads, on account of their Roughnes, are unpaffable for Camels) who being laden with great Burdens, generally go ten or twelve Miles a Day, and fome of them make two Journeys in one Day It is furprifing to fee what great Loads they carry, for befides their Merchandize they carry Provifion for their Mafters, and likewife for the Soldiers that guard them

Of the Kingdom *of* BORNO.

THIS large Province bordereth Weftward upon *Guangara*, and from thence extendeth itfelf E the way five Hundred Miles It is diftant almoft a Hundred and Fifty Miles from the Fountain of the *Nger*, the Sout...

Part adjoins to the Defart of *Set*, and the North Part to that Defart that lies towards *Barca*. It's of an uneven Situation, Part of it being mountainous, and Part plain, the latter of which contains feveral Villages, which are inhabited by rich Merchants, and produce great Plenty of Corn The King and his Courtiers dwell in a large Village, the Mountains bring forth Mill, and other Grain to us unknown, and are inhabited by Shepherds and Herdfmen The Natives in Summer go naked, fave their Privities, which are covered with a Piece of Leather, but in Winter they wear Skins, which they ufe for Beds alfo. They embrace no Religion, neither *Chriftian*, *Mahometan*, nor *Jewifh*, but live after a Brutifh Manner, and have Wives and Children in common, and (as a Merchant told me that was with them a long Time) ufe no proper Names, but each Man receiveth a Name according to his Length, Fatnefs, or fome other Quality. They are governed by a powerful King, who is lineally defcended from the *Libyan* People, called *Bardoa*. His Guard confifts of Horfemen to the Number of three Thoufand, who are in continual Readinefs, and likewife a great Number of Footmen · All his Subjects pay him great Obedience, and at his Command will immediately arm themfelves, and follow him They pay him no Tribute, but the Tythes of their Corn, neither hath he any Revenues, but the Spoils taken from his Neighbours in War He is at perpetual Enmity with a People dwelling beyond the Defart of *Sea*, who formerly marching over the Defart with a large Army, laid wafte a great Part of this Kingdom, the King immediately fent for the *Barbary* Merchants, and ordered them to bring him a great many Horfes, for one of which fometimes he gives fifteen or twenty Slaves. They brought the Horfes, and were forced to ftay for their Slaves till the King returned Home in Triumph with a great Number of Captives, and then he fatisfhed his Creditors Sometimes the Merchants ftay three Months before the King's Return from War but they are maintained all that while at the King's Expence Sometimes he doth not bring home Slaves enough, and at other Times they are conftrained to wait a whole Year together, for the King maketh Invafions but once a Year, and that at one particular Time I myfelf faw fome Merchants, who defpairing of the King's Payment, becaufe they had

trufted

truſted him a Year, reſolved never to ſerve him again
with Horſes   The King, to all Appearance, is very rich,
for his Spurs, Bridles, Platters, Diſhes, Pots, and other
Veſſels, are all of ſolid Gold   The very Chains of his
Dogs are Gold alſo , neverthelefs he is extremely cove-
tous, and chuſes rather to pay his Debts in Slaves than in
Gold   This Kingdom contains great Multitudes of Negroes, and other People, whoſe Names I could not learn,
becauſe I ſtaid here but one Month.

Of the KINGDOM *of* GAOGA.

THE Weſtward Boundary of it is the Kingdom
of *Borno*, it extendeth Eaſtward to the Confines
of *Nubia*   Southward it adjoineth to a Deſart ſituate upon
a crooked and winding Part of the *Nile*, and is encloſed
Northward with the Frontiers of *Ægypt*   It is in Length
five Hundred Miles from Eaſt to Weſt, and as many in
Breadth.   The Inhabitants know neither Humanity nor
Learning, but are of a brutiſh and ſavage Nature, eſpecially thoſe that dwell in the Mountains, who go naked all
but their privy Parts   Their Houſes are made of Boughs
and Rafts, on which Account they are ſubject to Burning.   They have great Store of Cattle, which they
watch with exceeding Diligence   Theſe People were free
for many Years, till they were deprived of it by a Negro
Slave of the ſame Country , who, one Night travelling
with his Maſter, a wealthy Merchant, and conſidering he
was not far from his own Country, killed him, took Poſſeſſion of his Goods, and returned home   Then buying
ſome Horſes, he began to attack the neighbouring People,
and commonly came off Conqueror , for he led a valiant
Troop of Horſemen againſt his Enemies, who could make
but a poor Defence   By this Means he took many Captives, and exchanged them for Horſes that were brought
from *Ægypt* ; ſo that at laſt he was eſteemed by all the
ſovereign King of *Gaoga*   He was ſucceeded by his Son,
by no means inferior to him in Courage and Valour, and
he reigned forty Years   After his Death his Brother *Mo-
ſes* came to the Throne, whom his Nephew *Homara* ſucceeded, who now beareth Sway   This *Homara* hath very
much increaſed his Dominions, and hath made a League

with the Soldan of *Cairo*, who frequently makes him magnificent Presents, which he moſt bountifully returns He is alſo preſented with precious and rare Things by the Merchants of *Ægypt*, and the Inhabitants of *Cairo*, who highly commend his Liberality. This Prince hath a great Value for all Men of Learning, and particularly ſuch as are deſcended from *Mahomet*.

Of the Kingdom of NUBIA.

THE Kingdom of *Nubia* bordereth Weſtward upon *Gaoga*, from thence it ſtretcheth itſelf to the *Nile*, Southwardly it is encloſed by the Deſart of *Goran*, and on the North-ſide by the Confines of *Ægypt*, yet they cannot paſs by Water from hence into *Ægypt*, for in ſome Places a Men may wade over the *Nile* on Foot. The principal Town call'd *Dangala* is very populous, and containeth 10,000 Families. They build the Walls of their Houſes with a kind of Clay, and cover the Roofs with Straw. They are civil, and very rich, having great Dealings with the Merchants of *Cairo* and *Ægypt*. All the other Parts of it are inhabited by Huſbandmen, who live in Villages ſituate upon the *Nile*. This Kingdom produceth great plenty of Corn and Sugar, the Uſe of which is entirely unknown to them. In the City of *Dangala* there is ſtore of Civet and Sandal-Wood. There is much Ivory here likewiſe, becauſe they kill many Elephants.

The King is at continual War, partly with the People of *Goran*, who are deſcended from the *Zingi*, and inhabit the Deſarts, ſpeaking a Language unknown to all other Nations, and partly with other People living in the Deſart, that lieth Eaſtward of the *Nile*, and ſtretcheth itſelf towards the *Red*-Sea, being not far from the Borders of *Suachea*. Their Language (in my Opinion) is mix'd, reſembling very much the *Chaldean* Tongue, the Language of *Suachea*, and that of *Æthiopia* the higher, where *Peter Gante* is ſaid to rule. The People are call'd *Bugiha*, and are vile and miſerable, living only upon Milk, Camels Fleſh, and thoſe Beaſts they take in the Deſarts.

And thus much concerning the Land of *Negroes*. The Fifteen Kingdoms whereof agreeing much in Rites and Cuſtoms, are ſubject to Four Princes only.

Extract of Ludolphus's *History of* ÆTHIOPIA

*N*ILUS, owing to *Habassia* for its Source, for plenty of Water, for Sweetnefs, Wholefomnefs, and Fertility of the fame, excels all other Rivers of the World In S W r by reafon of its Excellency, it is fometime R _ abfolutely, and particularly *Siachin*, from its black Colour, and by the *Greeks*, for the fame Reafon, *M* , becaufe it runs with a black muddy Water Some of the Antients tell us, that it was then by the *Æthi* an call'd *Aflapus* , and that the left Channel of it about er was named *Aftesia*, which others have underftood concerning other Rivers that flow into *Nile*. But this we let pafs as obfcure and doubtful, whether meant of *Nilus* and our *Æthiopian* , or no, for the *Abyffines*, in their vulgar Language, have no other Name for *Nile* than that of *Abawi* , and that as fome think, from the Word *Ab*, which fignifies *a Parent* as if *Nilus* were the Parent of all other Rivers But this Derivation neither fuits with Grammar, nor does *Ab* fignify *a Parent*, neither, if you rightly confider it, is it agreeable to Senfe , for *Nilus* does not fend forth from his own Bowels, but receives the Tribute of all other Rivers So that he may be rather faid to be their Captain and Prince, than the Father of them. And therefore the *Ægyptians*, out of a vain Superftition, call'd him their *Preferver*, their *Sun*, and their *God*, and fometimes, Poetically, *Parent* In our *Æthiop k*, or the Language of the Books, this River is call'd *Geion*, or *Gewon*, by an antient Miftake from the *Greek* Word *Geon*, and that from the *Hebrew* Word *Gihon*, becaufe it feem'd to agree with the Defcription, *Gen* i 13 *which encompaffes the Land of* Æthiopia whereas it only encircles *Goiam*, but glides and paffes by all the other Kingdoms of *Æthiopia*

If you object, that *Gihon* had its Source in the Terreftrial Paradife, it is twenty to one but that they extol their own Country for Paradife For you muft underftand, that many of the Fathers of the Church were of the fame Opinion, which, that they might defend, they brought the River *Nile* under Ground, and under the Sea, into *Ægypt*, well knowing that no Body would follow them thither, leaving their Readers to find out the Way.

Con-

Certainly the Antients never enquired so curiously into the Nature or Source of any River, as they did into that of *Nile*, neither were they ever so deceived For it was a thing altogether unusual for any other River in the World to overflow in the most sultry Season of the Year, an Inundation so wholsom and profitable to *Ægypt* So that the Ignorance of the Cause of it filled the Minds of the Antients with so much Admiration, that both Princes and private Persons desired nothing more than to know the Head of that River, which was the Original of their Happiness, insomuch that there were some Emperors and Kings who sent great Armies in quest of the Satisfaction of their Curiosity, tho' with ill Success. Most of the antient Geographers, by meer Conjecture, placed the Fountains of the River beyond the Equinoctial Line, in I know not what *Mountains of the Moon*, to the end they might deduce the Cause of its Swelling from the Winter Rains of those Regions For they could not perswade themselves, that the Sun being in the Northern Signs, so much Winter or Rain could be so near to cause so great an Increase of the Flood, tho' there were some who made it out plainly enough, but that Credit would not be given to them But by the Travels of the *Portugueze* into *Abyssinia*, and the Sedulity of the Fathers, those Fountains and Spring-Heads have been since discover'd, so long and unsuccessfully sought for by the Antients. *Athanasius Kircher* has described them from the Relation of *Peter Pays*, who viewed them himself " In the Kingdom of *Gojam*, says he, and in the Western Part thereof, in the Province of *Sabala*, which the *Agawi* inhabit, are to be seen two round Spring-Heads, very deep, in a Place somewhat raised, the Ground about it being quaggy and marshy, nevertheless the Water does not spring forth there, but issues from the Foot of the Mountains. About a Musquet-Shot from thence, towards the East, the River begins to flow, then winding to the North about the 4th part of a League, it receives another River, a little farther, two more, flowing from the East, fall into it, and soon after, it enlarges itself with the Addition of several other Streams About a Day's Journey farther, by the Relation of the same *Peter*, it swallows up the River *Jema*, then winding Westward some 20 Leagues, it turns again to the East, and plunges itself in to a vast Lake "
  This Relation differs not from what *Gregory* has discoursed to me, only he particularized the Names of the Countries,

that

that perhaps were the more special Denominations of the Place, of which *Sait* was the more general Name. For he related to me, the Spring-Head of *Nile* is in a certain Lake call'd *Sait*, upon the Top of *Dengla*, which perhaps is the Name of a Mountain. He also affirmed, that it had five Spring-Heads, reckoning in the Heads of other Rivers, which have no particular Name, and are therefore taken for the *Nile*. But it passes thro' the Lake *Tzanicum*, preserving the Colour of its own Waters, like the *Rhosne* running thro' the Lake *Leman*, and the *Rhine* thro' *Acronius*, or the Lake *De Zell*. Then winding to the South, it washes on the left Hand the principal Kingdoms of *Abyssinia*, *Begemsa*, *Atbera*, *Waku*, *Sewa*, *Damota*, and takes along the Rivers of those Countries *Basilo*, *Tzohha*, *Kecem*, *Jema*, *Roma* and *Waret*. Then on the right Hand embracing *Goam*, its native Country, almost like a Circle, and swell'd with the Rivers of that Region, *Maga*, *Abaja*, *Afua*, *Tinci*, *Gult* and *Tzu'*, it turns again to the West, as were bidding farewel to its Fountains, and with a prodigious Mass of ramass'd Rivers, leaving *Abyssinia* upon the right Hand, rolls to the North thro' several thirsty Nations and hardy Desarts, to enrich *Ægypt* with its Inundations, and there makes its way thro' several Mouths into the Sea. For the more certain Demonstration of the Truth, it will be of particular Moment to insert the Relation of *Gregory* himself, perhaps the first that was ever made publick by an *Æthiop*.

" The Course of *Nile* is like a Circle, it encompasses *Goam*, but for that it river returns back to its Head, making a certain Space, and therefore *Goam* lies always upon the right Hand of *Nile*, but all the other Kingdoms of *Æthiopia*, well though but the near as those at a Distance, remain upon the left. As it flows along, it takes in all the Rivers great and small, with several Torrents, as well Foreign as *Abyssinian*, which by that general Tribute acknowledge him for their King, who having thus muster'd together all the Waters of *Ægypt*, jocundly takes his Leave, and proceeds on his Journey, like a Hero, according to the Command of his Creator, to drench the Fields of thirsty *Ægypt*, reduced to the Drought of Thousands.

The Spring-Head of this Famous River first shews itself in a Region called *Secut*, upon the Top of *Degla*, in the *Goam*, West of *Begemsa*, *Dara*, the Lake of *Tzana* and *Bada*   Rifing thus, it haftens with a direct Courfe Eaftward, and fo enters the Lake of *Dara* and *Bed*, as it were fwimming over it   Paffing from thence, it flows between *Gojam* and *Eugenia*, but leaving them upon the right and left, fpeeds directly towards *Abda*   Having touched the Confines of *Abda*, he turns his Face towards the Weft, and girdles *Gojam* like a Circle, but fo that *Gojam* lies always upon the right Hand of it   Having pafs'd the Limits of *Hunara*, it wafhes the Corner of *Waluka*, and fo on to the extream Bound of *Nega* and *Sleua*. Then it flides between *Bgama* and *Gega*, and defcends into the Country of the *Shankelites*, he proceeds onwards to the right Hand, and leaves by degrees the Weftern Clime upon the left Hand, to vifit the Kingdom of *Sennar*   But before he gets thither, he meet with two great Rivers, that plunge themfelves into his Stream, coming from the Eaft, of which one is call'd *Tacaze*, that falls out of *Tigra*, and the other *Gumgue*, that defcends from *Damlea*   After he has taken a View of the Kingdom of *Sennar*, away he travels to the Country of *Dengula*, and fo comes to the Kingdom of *Nubia*, and thence turns to the right Hand, in order to his intended Voyage for *Alexandria*, and comes to a certain Country which is call'd *Abrim*, where the Stream is unnavigable by reafon of the Cliffs and Rocks, after which he enters *Ægypt*   *Sennar* and *Nubia* are feated upon the Shore of *Nile*, toward the Weft, fo that they may drink of his Waters, befides that, he guards their Eaftern Limits, as for he approaches near them.   But our People and Travellers from *Sennar*, after they have crofled *Nubia*, quit the River *Nile*, leaving it upon the right Hand toward the Eaft, and ride thro' a Defart of 15 Days Journey upon Camels, where neither Tree nor Water, but only Sand, is to be feen, but then they meet with it again in the Country of *Rilfe*, which is the upper *Ægypt*, where they either take Boat, or travel a-foot in Company with the Stream "

But as to what he wrote concerning the Flowing of great and fmall Rivers into Nile, *he explains himfelf in thefe Words*

' All greater Rivers and fmaller Torrents flow into *Nile*, excepting only two, the one is call'd *Hanago*, which rifes in *Hangota*, and the other *Hauafh*, which runs near *Dawara* and *Fatagara* "

But as if this had not been enough, he goes on with a farther Explanation in another Epiftle, as follows

" But

" But whereas I told you, in a Defcription of *Nile*, that all the Rivers of *Æthiopia* flow'd into it, except two, I am not to be underftood as if I fpoke of all *Æthiopia* For thofe Rivers that are upon the Borders of the Circuit of *Æthiopia*, which are near the Ocean, they fall into the Sea, every one in their diftinct Regions Now the Countries adjoyning to the Ocean are thefe, *Cantat, Guaraghe, Enurta, Zandera, Wel, Wat, Ca*, and fome others "

The native Country of *Nile* being thus difcover'd, the Caufe of his Inundation is manifeft For moft of the Countries under the Torrid Zone, when the Sun returns into the Winter Signs, are wafh'd, as we have faid, with immoderate Showers So that the prodigious Mafs of Waters, that rendezvoufes from all Parts, cannot be contained within its Channel, and therefore, when it comes into the Levels of *Ægypt*, it prefently difburthens itfelf. Thofe Northern Winds, from their anniverfary Breezes call'd *Etefiæ*, add little to the Increafe Tho' fome have written, that their forcing the Sea againft the Mouths of the River, drives back the Waters of *Nile*, and augments the Caufe of the Deluge A thing not likely, in regard they are the moft temperate of all the Winds, and blow only in the Day-time Thus far indeed they may prevail, as they blow flacker or ftronger, to render the Increafe fomewhat the more unequal, and that is all. Vainly therefore did many believe, that the Snow that melted from the *Æthiop* Mountains, deluged into the River *Nilus*, for them, that profound Tracer of Nature, *Seneca*, has folidly refuted, which makes it a Wonder that *Paulus Jovius* fhould report the fame, as what he had gather'd from the certain Conjectures of the *Abyffines*, who at another time fpeaks of the very fame thing, as a great Secret of Nature, which no Man had ever dived into, nay, he reproves it for Weaknefs, with an oftentatious Wit to be over-diligently curious in the Search of fuch Matters.

Yet tho' the Fountains of *Nile* are known, the Courfe of it is not fo well difcover'd to the *Abyffines* themfelves after it has left them But the antient and conftant Report is, that it does not fall entire into *Ægypt*, but that it is divided into two Channels, and that the right Channel runs to the North, as is well known, but that the left runs Weftward, and keeping a long Courfe divides the Country of the *Nigrites*, till it falls into the Ocean This the antient *Ægyptian* Priefts were not ignorant of, for *Herodotus*, the

foremoft in Hiftory, after he had difcourfed concerning the
Springs of *Nile*, learnedly reports, That he had heard from
an Auditor of the Money facred to *Minerva*, that half of
the Water of *Nile* flow'd Northward into *Ægypt*, the other
half Southward toward *Æthiopia*, which none of our Geographers either obferved or minded. *But the* Nubian *Geographer puts me quite out of doubt, when he writes,*

" And in this Part of *Æthiopa* are the two *Niles* parted ;
that is, *Nilus* which waters our Country, or *Nubia*, directs
his Courfe from South to North, and moft of the Cities of
Ægypt are feated on each Side of his Banks, and in his I-
flands. The other Part of *Nile* flows from the Eaft toward
the Weft, and upon this Part of *Nile* lies the whole Country of the *Nigrites*, or at leaft the greater Part of it.

A little after he adds, concerning a certain Mountain And
near to that, one of the Arms of *Nile* turns off, and flows
to the Weft And this is the *Nile* that belongs to the Country of the *Nigrites*, many of their Provinces lying upon it "
But near the Eaftern Side of the Mountain, the other Arm
turns off, waters the Country of *Nubia*, and the Land of
Ægypt, and is divided in the lower *Ægypt* into Four Parts, of
which Three fall into the *Syrian* Sea, and the other empties
itfelf into a Salt Lake, which is near to *Alexandria* The Words
are every way moft clear, and very probable it is, *That the
Separation of the two* Niles *might be caufed by the Refiftance of
fome rocky Mountain, that conftrained the two Streams to part,
fince they could not undermine it* To which the Words of
Leo Africanus relate, *The Region of the* Nigrites, *thro' which*
Nilus *is faid to flow* , which feem to intimate, that he had
heard fomething by Report concerning this fame left Channel Nor am I a little confirm'd by the Judgment of *Gregory*, which he expreffed to me by Writing in thefe Words :

But as to what is reported, that Nile *does not flow altogether and entirely into the Land of* Ægypt, *but that it is
divided another Way.* " This, all thofe Perfons of whom I
have enquired, aver to me to be Truth. This I alfo in-
cline to believe For fhould it defcend entirely thither in
the Winter-time, the *Ægyptians* could never be fafe in their
Houfes " But as to what concerns its Separation, they fay,
That Parting happens after the River has paffed by Sennar *in
the Country of* Dangula, *before it arrives in* Nubia . However
they fay, *That the greateft Mifs of Water flows into* Ægypt,
and that the feparated Part runs directly to the Weftern Ocean,

yet

yet ſo, that it comes not into Barbary, *but deſcends toward the Country of* Elwah, *and ſo throws itſelf into the Weſtern Ocean*

Now, that the River *Niger* ſhould be the left Channel of *Nile,* is moſt probable from hence ; for that, as *Pliny* writes, and Experience confirms, it partakes of the ſame Conditions with it, agrees in Colour and Taſte of the Water, it produces the ſame ſort of Reed, the ſame ſort of Papyr, and the ſame ſort of Animals, and laſtly, encreaſes and over-flows at the ſame Seaſons Neither does the Name itſelf contradict the Conjecture ; in regard, that, as we have ſaid *Nilus* itſelf is by the *Hebrews* and *Greeks* call'd *Niger* But as to what the *Ægyptian* related to *Herodotus, That the left Channel flowed toward the South* ; that, perhaps, might be for ſuch a Diſtance of Land ; not but that afterwards it might vary its Courſe, and wind towards the Weſt Which Opinion, after I had communicated to the moſt famous *Bochart,* ſo highly ſkilled both in the antient and modern Geography, and the beſt Judge of theſe Matters, he wrote me in anſwer · *Il eſt tres vray, que le* Niger *eſt une Partie du* Nile : *Moſt certain it is, that* Niger *is a Part of* Nile

Extract from HERODOTUS, *Lib.* 2d.

NONE of the *Ægyptians,* or *Africans,* or *Grecians,* with whom I had any Diſcourſe, would own to me their Knowledge of the Fountains of the *Nile,* except only a Scribe of the Sacred Treaſury of *Minerva* in the City *Saïs* in *Ægypt.* He, indeed, chearfully told me, That he certainly was acquainted with them. But this was the Account he gave : That there were two Mountains with peaked Tops, ſituate between *Syene* a City of *Thebaïs,* and *Elephantina,* the Name of one of which was *Krophi,* of the other *Mophi, (a) That from the midſt of theſe two Mountains aroſe the bottomleſs Fountains of the* Nile *; one part of its Stream ran towards* Ægypt *and the North, the other part towards* Æthiopia *and the South* But that the Fountains were bottomleſs, he ſaid that *Pſammeticus,* a King of *Ægypt,* had made the Experiment , after having tied together Ropes of great Length, and let them down into the Fountains, he could not reach the Bottom.

(a) Τὰς ὦν δὴ πηγὰς τῦ Νείλου ἐούσας ἀβύσσους, ἐκ τῦ μέσου τῶ ουρέων τουτέων ῥέειν Καὶ τὸ μὲν ἥμισυ τῦ ὕδατος ἐπʹ Αἰγυπτου ῥέειν, τὸ πρὸς βορέην ἄνεμο. τὸ δὲ ἕτερον ἥμισυ ἐπʹ ᾽Αιθιοπίης τι καὶ νότου.

A LIST of WORDS,
English and *Mundingo*.

THE Sun, *Tillo.*
The Moon, *Corro.*
Fire, *Dimbau.*
Rain, *Sanju,*
Thunder, *Corram-Alla.*
Wind, *Funnio.*
Whirlwind, *Sau.*
Water, *Gee.*
Heat, *Candeea.*
Smoak, *Sizee*
A Star, *Lolo*
The Earth, *Banco.*
A Hill, *Coanco.*
A Rock, *Barry.*
A Sand, *Kenne kenne,*
The Sea, *Bdto bau.*
A River, *Bato.*
An Island, *Jouroe*
The East, *Tillo woolita.*
The West, *Tillo busta*
A Year, (or one Rain)
Sanju killin.

God, *Alla.*
The Devil, *Buaw.*
Hell, *Jebonama.*
A Grandfather, *Kea bau*
A Grandmother, *Mos-*
fa bau
A Father, *Fau.*
A Mother, *Bau*
A Brother, *Barin-kea.*
A Sister, *Barrin-moosa.*
A Wife, *Moosa.*
A Servant, *Buitlau.*
A Stranger, *Leuntong.*
A Man, *Kea.*
A Woman, *Moosa.*
A White Man, *Tobar-bor.*
A Factor, *Mercadore.*
A Singing-Man, *Jelly-*
kea.
A King, *Mansa.*
A Thief, *Sunear*
A Fool, *Toorala.*

a   A

A Drunkard, *Serrata.*
A Whore, *Jelly moosa.*
A Slave, *Jong*
A Witch, *Buaw , i e*
Devil.

A Lion, *Jatta*
A Seahorse, *Molly*
An Elephant, *Samma.*
Elephants Tooth, *Sam-*
ma-ning
A Wolf, *Stllo.*
A Wild Hog, *Seo.*
A Camel, *Comaniong.*
A Horse, *Sooboe.*
A Mare, *Sooboe moosa.*
A Cow, *Neesa moosa.*
A Bull, *Neesa kea.*
A Calf, *Neesa nding.*
A Sheep, *Cornell.*
A Deer, *Toncong.*
A Dog, *Woolloe.*
A Great Dog, *Woolloe*
vau.
A Cat, *Nearcom.*
A Crocodile, or Alle-
gator, *Bumbo.*
A Cameleon, *Minnue.*
A Goat, *Baw*
A Baboon, *Come.*
A Snake, *Su*
A Fowl, *Scosee.*
A Cock, *Doontoung, or*
Soo,ee kea
A Hen, *Soosee moosa.*
A Guinea Hen, *Commee.*
An Owl, *Buaw; i. e.*
Devil.

A Duck, *Brue.*
An Oyster, *Oystres*
A Fish, *Heo.*
A Louse, *Crankee*
An Egg, *Soosey killy.*
Honey, *Lee*
Sugar, *Tobaubo Lee.*
Bees-Wax, *Leconno.*
Palm-Wine, *Tangee*
Ciboa-Wine, *Bangee*
Nuts, *Teab.*
Salt, *Coe.*
Butter, *Toolon.*
Milk, *Nunno.*
Bread, *Mungo.*
Paper, *Coito.*
Corn, *Neo*
Amber, *Lamlre.*
Crystal, *Crystall*
Silver, *Cody.*
Brass, *Tasso.*
Red Cloth, *Murfee.*
Beads, *Connum.*
Pewter, *Tasso qui.*
A Canoa, *Caloon*
A Ship, *Tobaubo Caloon.*
A Gun, *Kiddo*
Gunpowder , *Kiddo*
mungo.
A Bullet, *Kiddo cass,*
A Bow, *Culla.*
An Arrow, *Bennia.*
A Knife, *Moroo*
A Fork, *Garfa.*
A Cutlass or Sword,
Fong.
A Spoon, *Coolear.*

A

English *and* Mundingo.

A Cloth, *Fauno*
A Bed, *Larong.*
A Chest, *Conneo.*
A Chair, *Serong*
A Table, *Meso*
A Barrel, *Ancoret.*
A Candle, *Candea.*
A Pipe, *Da.*
A Calabash *Merong.*
A Plate, *Prata*
A Medicine, *Boiru.*
War, *Killy*
Friendship, *Barrialem.*
A Town, *Cunda.*
A House, *Soo.*
A Room, *Boong.*
A Door, *Dau*
A Window, *Jenell.*
The Head, *Coong.*
The Mouth, *Dau.*
The Tooth, *Ning.*
The Leg, *Sing*
The Hand, *Bulla*
Right Hand , *Bulla bau.*
Left Hand, *Bulla rding*
Left Leg, *Sing rding*
Right Leg, *Sing bau.*
White, *Que*
Black, *Iin*
Red, *Woollima*
Handsome, *Neemau.*
Dirty, *Nota.*
Great, *Bau*
Little, *N'dug*
Sick, *Mun coiue*
Well, *Candee*

Dead, *Sata.*
Good, *Abetty.*
Bad, *Munbetty.*
True, *Atoniala.*
False, *Funniala.*
Lazy, *Narita.*
Fearful, *I, aunee.*
Hot, *Candeea.*
Cold, *Ninny.*
Dry, *Mindo.*
Heavy, *Cooleata.*
Hard, *Acoleata.*
Sweet, *Timeata.*
Sour, *Acommota*
Stinking, *Acooneata.*
Drink, *verb, Amee.*
Hear, *Amoi.*
Touch, *Ametta.*
Feel, *Mamaung.*
See, *Ajubee.*

One, *Killin.*
Two, *Foolla.*
Three, *Sabba.*
Four, *Nani.*
Five, *Looloo*
Six, *Oro.*
Seven, *Oronglo.*
Eight, *Sye.*
Nine, *Corrnti*
Ten, *Tong*
Eleven, *Tong ning killin.*
Twelve, *Tong ning foolla*
Thirteen, *Tong ning sabba.*

a 2   Four

Fourteen, *Tong ning nani.*

Fifteen, *Tong ning looloo.*

Sixteen, *Tong ning oro*

Seventeen, *Tong ning o-ronglo.*

Eighteen, *Tong ning sye.*

Nineteen, *Tong ning co-nunti*

Twenty, *Mwau*

Thirty, *Mwau ning torg.*

Forty, *Mwau foolla*

Fifty, *Mwau foolla ning torg.*

Sixty, *Mwau sabba*

Seventy, *Mwau sabba ning tong*

Eighty, *Mwau nani.*

Ninety, *Mwau nani ning tong.*

A Hundred, *Kemmy*

A Thousand, *Woolly.*

I, *Inta,*

You, *Ita.*

This, *Ning*

That, *Olim.*

Sit down, *See dooma.*

Rise up, *Woolly.*

Go, *Ta*

Come, *Na.*

Come here, *Na va ni*

I know, *Alo*

I don't know, *Malo*

How do you do? *A-nimbctti monta?*

Swearing by Mumbo Jumbo, *Tye n ma-ma-man*

I will give, *M'f d*

Take, *Amoota.*

Sell, *Sawn.*

Buy, ditto.

What do you want? *Laffeta muni am.*

Nothing at all, *Feng o' feng.*

A P.

APPENDIX. No. I.

Contract of the Author with the African Company.

THIS INDENTURE, made the Twenty-third Day of July, in the Year of our Lord One Thousand Seven Hundred and Thirty, and in the Fourth Year of the Reign of our Sovereign Lord GEORGE the second, by the Grace of God, King of Great-Britain, &c Defender of the Faith, &c Between the Royal African Company of England of the one Part, and Francis Moore of London, Writer, of the other Part Whereas the said Company upon the good Testimony, and Character, they have received of the said Francis Moore, have entertained him the said Francis Moore into their Service in the Quality of a Writer at James Fort on James Island, in the River Gambia, or elsewhere, as the Company, or their Governors or chief Merchants for the Time being, in any of their Settlements in Africa, within the Limits of their Charter shall direct and appoint, for the Term of three Years certain, to commence from the time of his Arrival at James Fort, on James Island aforesaid, and for as long time more as he shall be by the said Royal African Company continued in the Place or Factories hereafter mentioned, to be employed in all or any of their Traffick, Merchandizes, Business or Affairs in any Place or Places whatsoever in Africa, wherein they or by them authorized shall think fit to use or employ him. Now this Indenture Witnesseth, that the said Francis Moore himself, his Executors and Administrators, doth covenant, promise and agree to and with the said Company and their Suc-

a 3   cessors

ceſſors by theſe Preſents, that he the ſaid *Francis Moore* ſhall
and will from henceforth during the ſaid Term of three Years
and every part of the ſame, and for ſo long Time after as he ſhall be
uſed or employed in the ſaid Service of the ſaid Company or their
Succeſſors well, duly and honeſtly ſerve the ſaid Company and
their Succeſſors in all and every ſuch Place and Places, and all and
every ſuch Affair and Buſineſs whatſoever, wherein they or ſuch
as ſhall be authorized ſhall employ or intruſt him   And ſhall alſo
from time to time, and at all times obſerve, keep, and purſue all
and every the Orders, Directions or Inſtructions, which from time
to time he ſhall receive from the ſaid Company, or any other Perſon or Perſons thereto authorized, or appointed by them, and to
the utmoſt of his Power and Skill reſiſt, and withſtand all and every
ſuch Perſon or Perſons as ſhall break, or endeavour to break the
ſaid Orders, Directions and Inſtructions, or any of them, or ſhall
attempt or practiſe any Matter or Thing whatſoever, to the hindrance or Damage of the ſaid Company or their Succeſſors, or of
their Goods, Merchandizes, Trade or any of them, or any Part
thereof   And as much as in him lies alſo prevent and defeat all
and every ſuch Practice, Attempt and Actions whatſoever, which
ſhall or may tend to the Damage, defrauding or Prejudice of the
ſaid Company, or their Succeſſor, or of their Goods or Traffic
or any Part thereof in any wiſe, and that he ſhall and will from
time to time, and at all times from henceforth conceal and not
diſcloſing to any Perſon or Perſons whatſoever, all ſuch Matters as
be delivered unto him as Secrets by any of the Agents, Factors,
or any other Officers of the ſaid Company, or their Succeſſors,
that may any ways concern the ſaid Company, or their Succeſſors
to have the ſame concealed   *And further*, that he the ſaid *Francis*
Moore ſhall and will from time to time, and at all Times from
henceforth, give true Notice and Intelligence, with all convenient
Speed unto the ſaid Company or their Succeſſors for the time being, or to ſuch as ſhall be by them authorized in that behalf, or
ſome of them, of all and every intended Deceits, Wrongs,
buſes, Breach of Orders, Inconvenience, and Hindrance as
the ſaid *Francis Moore* ſhall know, or underſtand, or credibly
to be contrived, done, practiſed, offered or intended to be done
againſt the ſaid Company or their Succeſſors, or their Goods or
Trade, or any of them, or any Perſon or Perſons by them em-
ed, or in their Service in any Place or Places, together with the
Names of thoſe Perſons by whom the ſame ſhall be ſo contrived
offered, practiſed, or intended   *And alſo*, that he the ſaid *Francis*
Moore ſhall and will from time to time, and at all times
henceforth, during his ſaid Employment, keep a true and particular Journal of all his Proceedings relating to the Affairs of

said Company, and also Books of Accompts, wherein he shall day,
duly, and truly enter the Accompt of all and every particular
Buying, Selling, Receipts, Payments, and all other Transactions relating to his Trust in the said Employment, and shall not charge,
place, or put to the Accompt of the said Company for any
Goods, Merchandizes, Negroe Servants, or Gold, which he shall
buy, any more or greater Sums, or other Things than he shall
really and *bona fide* pay, deliver or exchange for the same. And
also shall bring to Account in the said Books, the full Rates and
Prices of all such Goods and Commodities as he shall sell, barter, or pay in Exchange for any Negroe Servants, Gold, Elephants
Teeth, Beeswax, or other Commodities, which he shall be allow'd
to purchase for the Accompts of the Company. Which said
Books shall be produced and delivered to the said Company, or
any other by them appointed to receive the same, whensoever the
same shall be demanded or sent for. And shall also on Demand
well and truly deliver and pay unto the said Company, or their
Successors, all and every such Monies, Goods, Negroe Servants,
Gold, or Merchandize whatsoever, as by the Foot of the same Accompt or otherwise shall appear to be due to him, or to remain in
his Hands or Possession, or for which he ought to be chargeable or
answerable in any Manner whatsoever. *And moreover*, the said
Francis Moore doth for himself, his Heirs, Executors, and Admi-
nistrator, covenant and promise to and with the Company and
their Successors by these Presents, that he the said *Francis Moore*
shall not, nor will at any Time from henceforth during the time
of his said Service, directly, or indirectly, by himself or any
other, deal in, use or practise any buying, selling, taking, bartering or merchandizing in any Gold, Negro Servant, Animuni-
tion, Goods, or Commodities of any Sort or Kind whatsoever.
And shall not engage or employ either the Books of the said
Company, or any Part thereof, or make use of the Credit of the
said Company in trading for any Commodities, either for himself or any others whatsoever, that in case he the said *Francis
Moore* shall at any Time hereafter, during the time of his Im-
ployment in the Affairs of the said Company or before he shall
be discharged out of their Service, directly or indirectly by himself or any other, with his own Money or Merchandize, or with
his own Credit, or with the Monies, Merchandize, or Credit of
any other, deal in, use or practise any Buying, Selling, taking
or merchandizing for himself, or for any other Person or Persons
whatsoever but only to and for the proper Use, Benefit, and Accompt of the said Company, or their Successor. That then he
shall lose and forfeit to the said Company his growing Wages, or
Salary, hereafter mentioned, and the Arrears thereof. And also
a certain Commission Money that shall then be or become due to

h m f om the faid Company Neverthelefs all and every o her
the Covenant, Claufes, Contracts and Agreements in the e Pre
fen.s con a ned, fhall ftand and be in full Force and Virtue. And
moreover, the faid *Francis Moore* doth for himfelf, his Heir,
Executor, and Adminiftrators covenant and grant to and with the
faid Compan and their Succeffors, that in cafe he the faid Fr-
c . . r or any o her in Truft for him, or by his Order and Dire
tior f an contrary to thefe Prefents, buy, barter, fell, trade, or
me cr u e in or with any of the Goods, Negroe Se vant, Gold
and merchandize above-mentioned, or in any other Good or
Merchandizes whatfoever, that then he the faid Fr c M ,
his Executor and Adminiftrators upon Demand after every fuch
buying, felling trading, or merchandizing in any of the Com
modities prohibited aforefaid, or in any Merchandize wh at
ever, fhall and pay un o the faid Company or their Succeffors
according un r all Sorts of Merchandize, as a Damage already agree
en and d afer, after the Rate or Price of three hundred Pounds
Sterling per Tun, and fo for a grea er or lefier Quantity than a
Tun And alo fr Gold four Pounds Sterling *per* Ounce, and
for Negro o very Pounds Sterling for each Negroe And ,
tra he he faid Fr y M re fhall from Time to Time, and at fit
Time from henceorth, with all convenient Speed give Intelli
gence and Notice o the faid Company, or their Succeflors for the
Time er affel of all and every fuch Perfon or Perfons who
now are, or at a time hereafter fhall be employed in the Se
vice or Affairs of the faid Company, as fhall ufe, exercife, or
practice any, Trading, Buying, Selling, or merchandizing in any
Place or Places in any the Commodities, Negroe Servants, Gold
or Merchandizes above-mentioned, or in any other Merchandize
to a cever o her to, from, or on the Coaft of *Africa* aforefaid,
or in any Place within the Limits of their Charter, other than for
the proper Account and Benefit of the faid Company, and their
Succeffors As alfo of every Particular of the fame trading and
dealing according to his beft Knowledge and Underftanding
And alfo, that he the faid *Francis Moore* fhall and will f om Time
to Time, when and as often as he fhall be thereunto required by
Letters, Order, or Authorities from the faid Company, or
me to any of their Factories where they fhall fo direct, require
or appoint him And alfo fhall come and return for *England*,
when he fhall be by the Order and Direction of the faid Com
pany thereun o required And in cafe the faid *Francis Moore*
fhall refufe or reglect to remove or to return into *England* when
he fhall be thereunto required as aforefaid, that then it fhall
and may be lawful to and for any Perfon or Perfons, thereunto
authorized by he faid Company, to feize upon the Perfon of him

the said *Francis Moore*, and send or bring him the said *Francis
Moore* to and for *England* as aforesaid. And also to seize upon,
secure, and inventory all and every the Goods, Merchandizes,
Negroe Servants Gold, and all other the Chattels of him the said
Francis Moore in the Parts and Places of *Africa* within the Limits
of the Charters of the said Company, and the same to transmit
and send over into *England* to the said Company, there to rest in
the Possession of the said Company, until the said *Francis Moore*
shall clear his Accompt, and make good what he shall owe or
stand indebted to the said Company. And lastly, the said *Francis
Moore* doth covenant and agree to and with the said Company,
that he shall and will at all Times, and in all Things during the
Time of his Service as aforesaid, faithfully and diligently use,
behave, and demean himself as a good and faithful Servant towards the said Company and their Successor and those by them
authorised. And the said Royal *African* Company in Consideration of the Covenants and Agreements in these Present contained, to be done and performed by him the said *Francis Moore*,
and provided that the said Covenants and Agreements be severally
and respectively done, performed, fulfilled, and executed by him
the said *Francis Moore*, and not otherwise, do for themselves and
their Successors covenant and agree to and with the said *Francis
Moore*, that they shall and will pay and allow unto him the said
Francis Moore the Wages and Salary of thirty Pounds Sterling *per
Annum* (and Diet according to the Company's present Establishment) in Manner following, (that is to say) two third Parts thereof
early and every Year, and the other third Part to remain in the
Hands of the said Company, until the End or Expiration of
the Time agreed upon for him the said *Francis Moore* to serve the
said Company, and then, and upon his the said *Francis Moore*'s clear-
ing and evening all Accompts which shall be between him and
the said Company, the same shall be paid and delivered unto him
the said *Francis Moore*, his Executors, Administrators or Assigns. *In
Witness whereof* the said Royal *African* Company of *England*
hath to one Part of these Indentures caused their common Seal
to be affixed, and the said *Francis Moore* to the other Part of these
Indentures has set his Hand and Seal, the Day and Year first
above written.

James

APPENDIX. No. II.

Inftructions *to be obferved by* Meffrs William Roberts *and* Francis Moore, *Factors, at* Joar.

Meffrs *William Roberts,*
  and
Francis Moor,

James Fort, 22 J
  1731-2

OUR laft to you, Mr *Roberts,* was of the 15th Inft. which acknowledged the Receipt of your Letter of health with your Books of Accompt, all which we have per... but have not as yet had Time to give you our Obfervations thereon.

This now goes by the *Fame Sloop,* Capt *John B..,* and we is to cover Invoices of fundry Goods and Merchandize, amount... 1674 Bars, 4 s. o d. which we hope will come fafe to Har..., and prove to Content, they being in all Refpects agreable to our own Indent.

We are in the firft Place to acquaint you, Mr *William R...,* that whereas the Company in their Letter to us, have fignified their Pleafure concerning *Joar* Factory, that it being a Place of grea Truft, ought not to be left under the Direction of one Factor. You are hereby required to admit Mr *Francis M...,* be your Colleague, and from the Receipt hereof to be with jointly concerned in the Management of the Company's Aff..., and for the better carrying on the fame, you are to obferve... nothing be tranfacted but what fhall firft meet with the Approbation of the other, for as you are equally concerned and accoun... to it is but reafonable that each Perfon fhould have it in Power to prevent any thing being done that to him fhall feem to be to the Prejudice of the Company. You are therefore on Receipt hereof (if you, Mr *Moore,* are not fatisfied that the Remains in Store do correfpond with Mr *Roberts*'s Books from 1ft Inftant) to take an Inventory of all the Company's Effects in the Factory firft and which if it fhould be thought neceffary done, you are hereby required and directed, that Capt *B...* there prefent, in order to enable him to fign and teftify to us the same is an exact and just Inventory of all the Company's Effects there

The Company has highly reflected and resented our Conduct for suffering and passing by without showing due Resentment, (by discharging all such Factors and others in the Service, and sending them home with such Characters as they deserve, in order that they recover the Damages of their Bondmen) to all those who have squandered away and have been lavish of their Capital Goods, even in Trade, and other ways appropriated them to their own Uses, to such who have run themselves in Debt, particularly those who have left Powers of Attorney behind them, and to those in particular who are at Out Factories, such as formerly made good Remittances of dry Goods, and of late none, they, in particular, the Company absolutely commands us to use with no show of Compassion, nor admit of any Excuse or Pretence, but forthwith to send them home as aforesaid, they being but too well assured, that the Reason proceeds from the Factors applying them to their own Uses. They also complain very much of those that give their Money without shewing good Reason for so doing, and they require for the future, that all such be placed to the Factor's Accompts, and in Default of which, they will place the same to ours. These strict Injunctions of the Company, and the Reproaches we have received, carrying with it a show of Justice, as you, Mr *Robert*, cannot but allow, Witness your own Books lately come down, to say nothing of time at *Ginga*, where above 120 Bars were deficient more than you cared to on, and for which you gave Mr *Pinzant* the inclosed Note. We say those Reproaches, &c. oblige us to acquaint you that no Excuse will avail with us for the future, in case you relapse into any of those Proceedings before mentioned, and that there shall be no room left to plead an Excuse, we repeat to you the following Orders, which you, Mr *M——y*, must also observe for your future Government, *viz*.

1*st* 'You are to observe, that the keeping of your Books do commence immediately after you have taken an Inventory, 'and at the latter End of *March* next to send down an 'Abstract or Ballance Sheet of your Accompts to the same and 'at the latter End of *June*, two Setts of your Book, (*viz.* Journal and Ledger, and such other Books as are used by us to be kept ballanced and signed by your selves, one of which to be 'sent to the Company, the other to remain here on the Fort

2*dly*, You are on no Account to omit sending us an exact 'Journal of the real Goods as well as Price you pay for what ever 'Slaves, Teeth, Wax, or Gold you remit to the Fort from time to 'time, whereby we may see in what manner you are and

and

‘ and to give you Credit for the same in our Books, conforma-
‘ ble to the Company’s Inſtructions

3d, ‘ You are to take a particular Care that you charge no
‘ Goods upon Trade, but what you really and *bona fide* pay for the
‘ ſame, and as it has formerly been a Cuſtom to enter Goods given
‘ in Preſents on account of Trade, as paid for the Trade you af-
‘ terwards made, you are now to charge all ſuch Preſents in
‘ Trade, &c in diſtinct Accompts by itſelf, that the prime Coſt
‘ of all Trade may appear in your Books without any additional
‘ Charges, by which Means it will be a Guide for new Comers
‘ hereafter to go by

4th, ‘ You are to be very frugal in your Expences, and on
‘ no account to make unneceſſary Preſents, and for ſuch as you
‘ find neceſſary to make, you are to be very particular, in enter-
‘ ing the ſame in your Books, aſſigning your Reaſons for ſo do-
‘ ing, and for what Account, without which it is the Company’s
‘ expreſs Order you to charge all ſuch Expences, &c to your
‘ reſpective Accompts

5th, ‘ You are to be very careful and circumſpect in your
‘ Choice of Slaves, that you on no account purchaſe any but ſuch
‘ as ſhall be merchantable, free from Sickneſs, Diſtempers, Rup-
‘ tures, and loſs of Limbs, all ſuch as you ſhall purchaſe that appear
‘ to have any of the above Ails, or are otherways unmerchant-
‘ able, are (if the Company direct in ſuch Caſe) to be placed to
‘ your Account, charging you for each Slave 50 Barrs, without a
‘ Power to diſpoſe of the ſame again unleſs you firſt obtain Li-
‘ berty from the Governor and Council for ſo doing

6th, ‘ In caſe of Mortality of any Negroe, you are to enter
‘ the ſame in your Books, and charge no more than the prime
‘ Coſt of the Slave that die, drawing out two Certificates, ſpeci-
‘ fying the Manner of his dying, with the Diſtemper as near as you
‘ can gueſs, which Certificates muſt be atteſted by whatever White
‘ Men are at the Factory, and ſend the ſame to the Fort, one of
‘ which to be ſent to the Company

7th, ‘ You are on no Opportunity of adviſing us of the
‘ State of our Affairs, whereby we may be able to ſend you
‘ what Supplies you may have Occaſion for from time to time,
‘ and if no Opportunity happens in 15 Days, to ſend a Meſ-
‘ ſenger

8th, ‘ You muſt take particular Care, that the Company’s
‘ Goods ſuffer no Damage, either by the Bugabugs, or any other
‘ Accident, the Company’s Orders being that all ſuch Goods
‘ are damaged by your Neglect, are to be charged to your Ac-
‘ compts

9th, ‘ You are on no Account to abſent your ſelves from the
‘ Factory, unleſs Leave be firſt granted you from the Gover-

' and then for no more than one, to prevent Losses in the mean
' time

10*thly*, ' You are on no Account whatever to lend any of the
' Company's Servants or Natives any Money, except those that
' reside with you, except you receive particular Orders for so
' doing from the Governor or chief Merchants

11*thly*, ' Whereas the Company has of late received great
' Abuses by their Servants, appropriating to their own Use a
' great deal of dry Good, as Teeth, Wax, Gold, and of en-
' times Slaves, and it being one and the chief Reason, we have
' recalled Mr *Saxby* from *York*, and rendered him unfit to serve
' the Company You are hereby to observe and take due Notice,
' that you are not on any Pretence whatsoever, to use on your
' Account, dispose of, sell, barter, or deliver to any Person or Per-
' sons, any Slaves, Teeth, or Wax, on any Account, neither
' are you to buy any of the said Commodities, nor any other
' Person or Persons for you (for any other Use, Intent, or Purpose,
' or Account, than the Royal *African* Company of *England*)
' And for the better preventing such gross Abuses for the future,
' you are hereby to observe, that for every Pound of Teeth, or
' Wax, which you shall sell, barter, deliver, or make use of, with
' out our previous Knowledge and Consent thereto, you shall be
' mulcted 100 Barrs, (such Wax except as shall be judged ne-
' cessary to expend for the use of the Factory) for every Slave
' 200 Barrs, and for every Ben, or Sixteenth Part of an Ounce
' of Gold 100 Barrs, and be rendered incapable to serve the
' Company hereafter

Having inserted the above Orders, you are further to observe,
that as we have no immediate Call or Demand for Slaves, you are
not to exceed 50 Barr a Head, or above for Slave Trade, and
Customs all Charges and Customs included, especially Slaves, of
which we have but very little, and no further to answer the
Demands that the Trade for any Goods require We therefore
think it a Matter of the greatest Consequence to endeavour to
reduce it to three Barrs a Head in that Commodity, provided in
lieu thereof you advance in Brass and Alanges to 5 or 6 Bars
a Head, the only Reason we have not to give you Orders perem-
torily, to give no more than three, because we would willingly
prevent the Merchants from going down Our other Consideration
only we would have you give for, the Prevention of
which would perhaps strengthen a Proposal the Company have
given us Orders to make them that they are content so to supply
them with Slaves on certain Conditions, upon which they
would come into the town, it is not therefore in our Power
to prevent the Trade from coming down in the Factory

We

We having said what we thought proper on the Slave Trade, come next to that of Gold, Elephants Teeth, and Beeswax, Commodities that the Company strenuously recommend us to encourage, and as such we also in the most pressing Manner repeat to you, and as you have a Competitor (Capt. *Clark*) with you, you are at Liberty to out-bid him, rather than any should fall into his Hand. And now we have given you this Liberty, we shall think it your Neglect intirel and ill Management, if any fall to his share, especially as you have a far better Assortment of Goods than he possibly can have.

As for Cotton, you are to buy none but what's cleaned from the Seed, except you can get it cleaned by the Natives before you rend it down, and this we strenuously recommend, if it is possible, even if you could get but 25 Pounds for an Iron Bar, or any other of the best Goods.

The Company expects that by this Time you've procured a great Quantity of the Allum Salt, and that it is refined according to the Receipt left you. We don't find that they will accept of any Excuse whatever. You are therefore to apply yourselves with all Care and Vigilance, and in particular to send us the Reasons to the contrary, that we may remit them to the Company, they being not satisfied but that it is our Neglect only.

They also recommend us to give Orders to all our Out Factor, and especially to do all we can and which we now repeat to you, that we endeavour to procure what Quantities you can of the following Commodities, and to give Encouragement to the Natives to procure the same, viz. Indigo, Hides, a sort of Spice or Pepper, which grows in Jessu, Goatskins, Deers, and Buffaloe, Horn, *Palm Oil*, Seed, Gums, and three Sorts of Wood, called Lon Wood, Bar, and *Fustick Sangree*, which are to be cut as large as can be so as to bear for Embarkation.

And as the Company will admit of no Excuses from us, and plainly tells us our Non-performances proceed from our Negligence and not commanding our Factors to pursue the same, and to give due Encouragement. We shall expect without fail your Answers to show that the Company may at least be satisfied with our Endeavour, we mean in Regard to our giving the necessary Order. We therefore expect that you'll exert yourselves, and give due Encouragement, and as to the Prices we must leave it to your own Prudence to agree with the Natives in the best Manner you can or obtain it, what Reasons you can have to urge to the contrary.

We are also by our own Persons good Informations, that the King of Jalou has laid a foundation of forming a bad Design against our Crew and Factory or their Affair, on account of your having some Slaves or Theft, to prevent which, and of two Evils, the leaft is to be chofen, we have releafed him, not being proper by any Means for the fake of gaining one to run fo great a Rifque, as the fhipping him off would ll Probability create, fo that all we can fay on that Head, is recommend more prudent Meafures for the future, and not to Wolves to watch your Sheep

You are to acquaint old *Serin Donfo* with our Orders concerning Trade, and that Mr *Rogers* can't poffibly come up, but t Mr *Harrifon* will in his way up the River call there about a Fortnight's Time, in the mean Time acquaint him we expect the Performance of his Promifes to us when down , in every Refpect

You are not to detain the Sloop longer than while you are loading her, and than you have finifhed the Survey as afore- provided it is thought meet We have not to add but main

Your Friends and Servants,

Anth. Rogers.
Tho. Harrifon.

APPENDIX. No. III.

TRANSCRIPT of a PAPER dif covering a Quantity of Gold up the River GAMBIA.

It is fuppofed to have been written by one that fought great Riches in King Charles the Second's Time in his Progrefs up that River. His Defcriptions of the Ot...s... Turnings of the Gambia, the Inlets of other R...s... it, the adjacent Mountains, &c. may be a good G... Undertaker, how to find out the Place where on... t'or met with Gold, even to Sa...e's. Who he a... force le hurein, he having contiued his Fren...... gre...n Series, being (as fuppofed) afraid to b... or taked of, h he fhould le commanded away by... ...e Government, upon another Expedition from... ...only in...ny Retirement he enjoyed, after... g...ion of fufficient Wealth.

YOUR Importunity, together with my Gra......... for your moft curious Informations and Instruct... the Mechanicks without which, I confefs, my L... been n'ar' has extorted th... om me, which, I confe... to't on I had a re... reer to the contrary, in... ng n... divulge either for Love, or Force, to which End I... cording to your faithful and folemn Vows of Secret the Bufine... ea, and likewife of which I would not... fro n to t e King for 10000 being content with what P... tion it hath pleafed God to affign me, as well as with the... Rever... Nor fhall I witholk, or tel y, difcover the v... tr tion of God I difcovered there, being o much, ro... o communicated o Paper, a ro kro ig to whofe L... tho th w ot He as h... ome I fhould o...e...
t is more doubled o leave is Vhu late to firm my I... tlan o oring do n i I go, and I a content, that i... te ... es upon this Dec...g, and fol m le Directions...
til a a ant ur Purpose, you... ur all will be of... ror, for a ... t... If a... ... W...' p...

if he lose his Soul So I say, What will the Riches of both the *Indies* advantage, if thereby you forfeit your Security, Life and Freedom ? And how will you be affured of any of thefe, if thefe Things fhould come to the Knowledge of fuch as have Power of you, and to command you in what they pleafe ? That I do truly tell you, did I not value my own Peace and Quiet at fo high a Rate as I do, I fhould come willingly, and manifeft it to his Sacred Majefty, tho' I am not fatisfied in that neither, as not knowing whether the Information may prove good or bad to the Publick ; however I conjure you a-new, that, whatever you attempt, you conceal me, fo that directly or indirectly I be not difcover'd

If you go on the Bufinefs, let your Boat be flat-bottom'd, for mine, being fome feven Tons, or thereabout, and made after the common Fafhion, was extremely troublefome, both at Fords and at Falls, where we were forced to unlade her, and, having un- laded her, to heave her, or launch her over Land You ought alfo to have a little Boat for common Ufe, which you will find extreme ufeful You advifed me to take 20 Pounds of Quick- filver for Trials, if you go, take at leaft 100 Pounds, for fome in working will be loft, as you know better than myfelf Your Advice alfo for 50 Pounds of Lead is too little, take 150 Pounds, much more you cannot well carry, for the peftering of your Boat

The *Sal Armoniack* I ufed little of, for it I can give you no Advice The *Borax* I ufed all, wifhed for more, if you go, carry 50 Pounds. My Sand ever did me great Service, I ufed it all, better have 10 Pounds too much than too little, therefore take 40 Pounds I am confident, if I had carried the Philofopher's Bel- lows, I had done very well, I was fo troubled with fitting the other, tho' I confefs them better when a-new placed *Antimonia Horn* did me little Service, I believe it rather from my Ignorance, or wanting the perfect Ufe and Inftruction you gave me Ingots I would take two, I carried but one, I wanted another for Expe- dition Wedges 12, with a Sledge or two, or Beetle, for about 12 *Englifh* Miles from the firft Fall, or fomewhat more to the Southward, in the Side of a barren Rock, looking Weft ard, there is a Cliff in the Rock, rather   moft rich between the Stones, almoft half a Handful thick in fome Places Our Pickaxes did here ftand us in no great ftead, but having with us fome Iron Tools, that we could hardly fpare, with much ado made a fcurvey Iron Wedge, and prefently we found the Ben ie of that for fome 12 or 14 Days, till improvidently one of us cra- ving the Wedge up to the Head, and not having another to re lieve it, we were forced to leave it behind, to our great Lofs and Grief Wooden Bowls from E.. . . wrought, a . . v neceffary, and will do better than Go.., . .1 was forced to make ufe of; you may take Store of them as no I in

For the Crucibles I muſt inform, that four large melting Pots, in our large Work, will ſtead you much, and make better Diſpatch than 6 Neſts of Crucibles, tho' you cannot well ſpare thoſe. I was forced to make uſe of a broken Earthen Pot, that I carried along with me, I made uſe of it till it broke, had I had Crucibles and Pots enough, I had brought ſo much Gold in Sard or T ber.

For the ſeparating and diſſolving Waters, I uſed but little, becauſe their Uſe was troubleſome, neither had I Conveniencies to erect a Still aſhore, but for the *Aqua Regis* I us'd it all, and could have done more, if I had had it, yet, in my Opinion, the Trials of Quickſilver are better, had I had it But I carry Coals to *Newcaſtle*, you know better the Operation than myſelf Let your Mortar be of Iron, and large, I wiſh I had follow d your Directions in that, for my Braſs one put me to a double Trouble, and I was entorced to leave the Refining of much, till I came into *England*, for the *Mercury* got a *Spurea* from thence, which is communicated to my Gold, which no Art, I underſtand, could free it from, in this Particular you left me lame, or m Memory much failed.

There is a Tree much like our Corners in *England*, but very large, which we fel'ed, and made a Shift to make Charcoal of, which we did thus, we cut off the Boughs, for we wanted a Saw, and therefore could not meddle with the Body of the Tree, and cut them into ſhort Pieces, then we digged a good large Pit, or Hole, in the Ground, about a Yard wide, and ſo deep, or deeper, in the Bottom we kindled a Fire, and filled it with Wood, and when it was well burnt, threv Earth upon it, and damped it, and wren it was cold, we took out the Coals You will eaſily find the Place, if you obſerve but the Cautions You will come to a broad Gathering together of Waters, not much inferior to *Ronnaird Meer*, in the Edge of *Lancaſhire*. Here we ſpent a Week in ſearching many Creeks and In-falls of Rivers, but we followed that which points South Eaſt and by Eaſt My miſerable Ignorance, in the Mathematicks, cannot direct you, neither for Long tude nor Latitude Up the buffing Stream, with ſad Labour, we wrought, and ſometimes cou'd not go above two Miles in a Day You may paſs the firſt Fall, yet there my Exceed of Gold va 47 Grains from 10 Pounds of Sand When we or you come to the upper Fall, you will be much troubled, I believe, as well as I, to get your Boat over Land, but being up, proceed till you come to the In fall of a ſmall Stream to the South, directly thence liſten, and you ſhall hear a Fall of Waters, you cannot get your Boat turther, by reaſon of the ſmallneſs of the Brook, you will there find our Reliques on the ſide of the Rock, with many of our Name, I mean Letters of our Names, cut with our Knives Here, tho the Sand, by the Waſh, yield plentifully, yet do you aſcend the Top of the Rock, and, pointing your Face directly, Weſt,

Weft, you will obferve a Snug of Rocks fomewhat to the Left Hand of you, and under that, if the Rains and Force of Weather have not wafhed away the Earth and Stones, you will difcover (they being unmoved) the Mouth of the Mine itfelf, where, being provided with Materials fit for that Work, you will not defire to proceed any further, or with a richer Vein.

Take this, all along, for a conftant Rule, which I, in my Search, obferved up the River, That in the low, and woody, and fertile Country, I could never find either Metal or rich Mine, but always among barren Rocks and mountainous Countries, and commonly accompanied with a reddifh kind of Earth   Other Inftructions I fhall not give you, being (as I conceive) a thing needlefs to you, unlefs I fhould return you your own Princpal, this being but only the Intereft of what is due, befides that Obligation which tieth me unalterably to remain, &c

I began my Voyage up the River, December the 4th, about two Hours before the Sun fet, in my Company no more than feven Men, befides myfelf, all Englifh, and four Blacks, whereof one was a Maribuck, who, being acquainted with the Portugal Language, I intended for an Interpreter, if I fhould ftand in need; but the main was, to help us in our Labour againft the Stream My Provifions were chiefly of two forts   For my Voyage and for Accommodation, three Barrels of Beef, ten Gammons of Bacon, two Barrels of white Salt, befides Bay-Salt for Trade, alfo two Hogfheads of Bifket, befides Rice, half a Barrel of Gunpowder, and Shot proportionable, Strong-Water, Vinegar, Paper, Beads, Looking-Glaffes, Knives 18 d per Dozen, fome Iron, little Brafs-Chains, Pewter-Rings, and a deal of fuch-like Stuff, as Occafion permitted   The other fort of Provifions were, a Pair of Goldfmiths Bellows, Crucibles four Nefts, Scarnelles two Nefts, Quickfilver, Borax, Sal-Armoniac, Aqua-Regis, Aqua Fortis, a Mortar and Peftle, and Leather Skins to ftrain, Barfs Scoops and Ladles with long Handles, to take up Sand, and other Implements for my private Defign   All which had laden my Boat far deeper than I defir'd, for thereby I drew much Water, which, I was jealous, might hinder our Progrefs over the Flats, if we fhould meet with any

December the 7th, we arrived near Settico, being 14 or 15 Leagues above where our Men ftay'd, but paffed one half League further up, where we anchored, the River there being broad, we always chufing the Middle, as being freeft from Difturbance, tho' it oft fell out otherwife, for our ugly Neighbours, I mean the Sea Horfes and Crocodiles, (it feems) ill pleafed or unacquainted with any Co-Partners in thefe watery Regions, did often difturb us in the Night, not only with their ugly Noifes, but their Vicinity to our very Boat, which caufed us to keep Watch

De

D_____ _____ the 23d, we were much troubled that Day with getting over a Flat, under the Wash of a steep and high Mountain bearing South. Here I first put in Practice my Design, and took up some Sand at the first Trial of the Ford, and out of five Pounds Weight of that Sand, got three or four Grains of Gold. I tried also in another Place or the same Ford, but did get less. I saw neither Town, nor House_, nor People, since we left *Barra* ____

J___ __ __ 14th __ a Ford between two high Mountains, I ___ __ ___, and out of 10 Pounds Weight of Sand, I wa_ _d ___ ___ __ Gold. I mad_ a Trial likewise with Mercury, and _____ __ __ 5 Pou_d 47 Grains. Here my Hopes increased, __ ___ __ ___ to try higher

J__ __ the 27th, __ were much troubled with great Trees, that la_ in the Water upon the _i_e of a Rock, on a craggy, barren Mou___ __ adjoining. I a'cend_d, with three Men with me, to make Discovery, _rd carrying a Pick-axe with me, as _e __ were digging up a Piece of Ore, as I conce'v'd, we were a___ _____ with an incredible Numb_r of monstrous great Baboons, whom no O___ but our Guns could persuade to let us retrea_ to ___ D___, for having k__led two or three of them, so incens'd the re__, that had not the Report of our Guns terrified them, I verily believe they would have torn us to pieces. Having attained our B_at I fell to try m_ Ore, which proved but a Sparre

Febr_ar the 6th I made a Trial of a certain glittering Sand, which I took up from the __de of a Rock, the River here incli_ng So__ ward, with a sudden Turning lik_ an Elbow. The Wash of th__ afforded 41 Grains from 10 Pounds Weight of Sand __ other T__al_, from 5 Pounds Weight of Sand, 57 Grains. He_e I though_ to make a Stand, yet, upon more serious Advice, had re__ _olved to proceed

February the 15th, at Night, a Sea-Horse struck our Boat thro' w__ one of his Teeth, which troubled us __re, being all bad Carpenters, which caused us to unload her on a small Pinnacle to mend her, and, to prevent the like Mischief for the future, I invented th__ Device. To hang a Lanthorn at our Stern, and thereby we were freed from all after-Troubles of that Nature, they not daring to come w_thin three or four Boats length of Light shining in _he Water

February the 24th, I _ried the Use of *Virga Div_na* upon a high, barren and rocky Mountain. But, whether it afforded no Metal, or whether my Rod, being cut in *England*, and being dried and carried far by Sea, had lost its Virtue, or whether it hath no such Quality (which I rather believe) I am not certain. However my Companions laugh_d me out of the Conceit

March the 16th, Between two mountainous Rocks issued a Creek, and putting up therein, discover'd a Fall of Waters from the South __ __ River. Here, making Trial by the Way, I found _

Gra_i

Grains of Gold from 5 Pounds Weight of Sand   Other Trials, more exact, afforded very large Proportions, fo that here we fpent 20 Days, and, plying hard our Work, in that Iime had gotten 12 Pounds, 5 Ounces, 2 Pennyweights, 15 Grains, of good Gold.

March the 31ft, Our Materials wafting apace, I was wil'ing to try further, here beginning our greateft Toil, for often in a Day we were conftrained to ftrip ourfelves, and leap into the Water, with main Strength to force our Boats over the Flats   Nor was this our greateft Affliction, for the River-Water fmelt fo f eet and musky, that we could not drink of it, nor drefs our Meat with it, and, as we conceive, by reafon of the Abundance of Crocodiles, which have the fame Scent

April the 7th, We perceived the In-fall of a fmall River South, the Current quick, the Land all rocky and mountainous, and, in the Silence of the Night, could hear the Noife perfectly of a great Fall of Waters, and before the Mouth of it anchor'd that Night.

In the Morning into that we put, and came as near the Fall as we well could   Our Water failed, but our indefatigable Induftry overcame all Difficulties, for, what I could not by Water, I did attempt by Land   Where arriving, I found the long expected End of our moft toilfome and long Voyage, for I believe never any Boat, nor any Chriftians, have been fo high in that River, as we   Here, upon the firft Trial I made, the Exceed of Gold was fo much, that I was furprized with Joy and Admiration   However, here I was refolved to fet down my Staff, and to that End, the firft thing I did, was to go   the Boat, and about a League and half thence I found Wood   Here we practifed to turn Colliers, and laded our fmall Boat with as much as fhe could well carry back, we went and fell to Work, for which I hope (to G o d alone be Praife) none of the Company hath Caufe to repent, for the great Pains and Labour he took, tho' we chofe the worft Time of the Year almoft, the Waters being then at the very loweft, but had we gone immediately after the Rains, which is *June*, *July* and *Auguft*, or before the Waters were fallen fo low, we had been free from much of that Trouble, at Fords and Falls, by having Water enough to carry us over.

A P P E N D I X. No. IV.

Extracts of Letters from the Chief Merchants at GAMBIA, *to the Royal* AFRICAN *Company, relating to the* Gum-Trade.

James *Fort,* Sept. 23, 1733.

Parag 6. WE have proceeded to make Discoveries up *Vin a n* River, which falls on the South into the *Gamba* about 3 Leagues above the Fort, which River hitherto was not known above *Geregia* by the Company's Servants here. For this end Mr *John Hall,* Factor at *Geregia,* was sent in a Long Boat, and he found at four Tides beyond *Geregia* a very fruitful Country, and the People very civil, and much more industrious, *as he says,* than they are in these Parts, and very solicitous to have the Company settle among them. The People, as their Country is rather more fruitful, so are their Towns more thick and numerous than here abouts, and their Cattle and Fowls are of a larger Breed, and, I believe, that a large Quantity of Cotton, Indigo, and some Hides may be procured from thence. I have a Sample of Gum by me, that they promise Quantities of, and by the Description of the Tree and Leaves, seems to be the same I find mentioned in the History of Drugs, that the Gum *Arabic* or *Senegal* comes from. I have made Trial of it, and I find it to be of a different Nature from all I have hitherto met with in these Parts, which dissolves into a Mucilage, but this is of a stiff and glewy Nature, as Gum *Arabic* and Gum *Senegal,* and therefore, I am sure, if we can depend on the Natives, as to the Quantity promised, it will be a valuable Commodity. I intend about *November* next to pay a Visit to these Parts, in order to make further Observations, and to do what is necessary to promote the Trade there, and, if please God to give me Health, I shall afterwards proceed to *Joar,* to try what can be done as to the Allom Earth there, and that we procure what Quantity we can to send to *England,* we have likewise dispatched a few Hands to cut some *Byœelo* Wood at *Geregia.*

R. HULL.

James *Fort*, Dec. 5, 1734.

Parag 5 I Have now fucceeded in my Attempt for the Difcovery of Gum *Senegal*, or rather Gum *Gambia*, and for bringing the Whole of that Trade into the Company's Hands only. Among the reft of the Samples, you have a fmall Parcel of this Gum, fuch as never before came from *Gambia*, which was fent me by *Jonco Sonco* of *Jantmarow*, to whom, when here about 12 Months fince, I gave Encouragement for to fend two *Moors* of his Arquaintance, named *Malacai Con* and *Malacai See*, inland on the North of that Port, which they purfued, and fome Months fince they returned with Succefs, and fent me a Sample by a Canoa that was up the River before the Frefhes came on, fince which, as foon as the Frefhes would give me leave, I fent up Capt *Brown* to that Port with Inftructions, in order to get the beft Informations as to the Country, Diftances, &c a Copy of which, and the Anfwer you have herewith inclofed, and likewife my Remarks thereon, by all which I do not doubt but to procure this Trade with great Advantage to the Company   The Gum is very fine, and a great part may well be called Gum *Arabic*, and will ferve the Purpofes both Gums are ufed for, as well as either will do for the purpofe commonly ufed for, and is a very wholefome and nourifhing Food, when the Body is in Health, as well as a pleafant and moft effectual Remedy in many Diftempers.

R H u l l.

James *Fort*, June 19, 1735

Parag 7 MR *Hull* arrived here from up the River about three Weeks fince, after having travelled to the inland King of *Yany*, and fettled Affairs relating to the Gum-Foreft with him and all the Great Men, Commanders of all the ftrong Trowns, and other Great Men, who give ftrong Affurances, that the Company only fhall be allowed to have the Produce of that part of the Foreft belonging to them, he had likewife fome Affurances from the Grand *Jolloifs*, with a Sample of Gum from that Part of the Foreft, which was fent home by the *Dolphin*; but the King being killed in Battle juft at that time, and the Country unfettled, nothing further could be done on that Side; from the King of *Tuta*, a Return of a Meffenger is daily expected, Mr *Hull* cou'd not proceed to the Foreft, it being the latter End of the dry Times, and for want of a Conveniency of carrying Water, which at that time Provifion muft have been made for going and returning for about feven Days, fo he refolved to go as foon as a good Shower of Rain or two had fell, and accordingly had again been on the Road for that end, if the *French* had not offered fome Propofals, and attempted to difpute the Rights of th s

River,

River, which will hinder him from settling the neceſſary Correſpondence until *October* next; however we hope to ſend you a Tothat we expect will be procured by ſome Perſons employ'd to go into the Grand *Jolloiffs'* Country, to acquaint them that the Company have ſettled a Factory at *Yanimarew*, and engaged that the Road will be free and open from any Moleſtation or Seizure, as hitherto have been uſual

HULL *and* ORFEUR

James *Fort*, July 21, 1735

Parag 12 THE Perſon, Mr *Hull*, ſent from *Yanimarew* into the Country of the Grand *Jolloiffs*, to purchaſe Camels, is returned with four· The ſame Meſſenger was order'd to come by the way of the Gum-Foreſt, and to bring with them their Loading of Gum , but he was hindred by there being ſo univerſal a Scarcity of Corn, that a Famine was cauſed in thoſe Parts, and which reaches even to *Yanimareu,*, and Places adjacent on the North of this River, it's with theſe Camels that Mr *Hull* is in *November* next to ſettle an inland Factory, as our laſt informs your Honours, to border on the Gum Foreſt, and which we conceive to be the beſt Means of ſecuring the Gum, and other valuable Trade to the Company only

HULL *and* ORFEUR

APPENDIX. No. V.

The Royal African *Company's Establishment at* James *Fort, in the River* Gambia, 1730.

A Nthony *Rogers*, First Chief Merchant and Governor

Bartholomew Stibbs, Second Ditto and Warehouse Keeper.

Thomas Harrison, Third Ditto and Accomptant

James Davis, Secretary

> *Thomas Saxby,*
> *William Roberts,*
> *James Conner,*
> *Robert Downham,*
> *Younger Nelme,*
> *Charles Houghton,*
> *John Hamilton,*
> *John Nurd*
> } 8 Factors.

> *Robert Forbes,*
> *William Russling,*
> *Robert Bank,*
> *John Brown,*
> *Hugh Hamilton,*
> *Percival Serjeant,*
> *James Payzant,*
> *Thomas Palmer,*
> *John Harrison,*
> *Francis Moore,*
> *Philip Gould,*
> *Thomas Burse,*
> *Samuel Turner*
> } 13 Writers

c

Joseph

Joseph Bick, Wax-Refiner
Richard Castell, Tanner
Benjamin Ives, Surgeon
James Ross,
Edward Riddon,   } Surgeon's
Joseph Vanderplace,   } Mates
David Wilson, Surveyor
Edward Redwood, Gardiner
Domingo Vos,   } Masons
Emanuel Lopez,   }
Charles Du Costa, Linguister

Henry Johnson, Steward
James Collins, Armourer
Charles Boastin, Bombay
John Cooley and   } Cooper.
Jeremiah Thomas,   }
Nicholas Todd, Joiner
John Pyre, Carpenter
Dioge Rodriguez, Purveyor
Tobias Cluseman, Gunner
John Creed, Gardiner

William Kerr,   CAPTAIN
John Jackson,   SERJEANT
James Breese,   DRUMMER

Jeremiah Cordo,
Andrew Cordo,
John Scott,
Ely Thornton,
Robert Evans,
William Walgrave,
Rouland Edwards,
Tho. Manwaring,
William Copland,
Charles Osmond,
Frederick Presso,
Charles Macclay,
Thomas Skyes,
Francis Allen,
Felix Castell,
John Westwood,
John Hall,   } 33 SOLDIERS
John Skinner,
Richard Buerton,
Thomas Guller,
William Child,
Naphtali Gray,
William Abraham,
John Sral,
Owen Morgan,
Thomas Smith,
William Wheeler,
Daniel Defaure,
Roger Comber,
Elias Boulter,
Robert Butler,
James Hodgkin,
Aaron Groves

Thirty two C A S T L E - S L A V E S

Besides this Establishment, there were

$$
\left.\begin{array}{l}
\text{Sloops,} \\
\text{Shallops,} \\
\text{Canoas,} \\
\text{Boats}
\end{array}\right\} \text{With their Crews}
$$

And, during the Time of my Abode there, 8 OUT-FACTORIES, with Black-Servants belonging to them, besides the WHITE-FACTORS, WRITERS and LINGUISTERS

F I N I S.

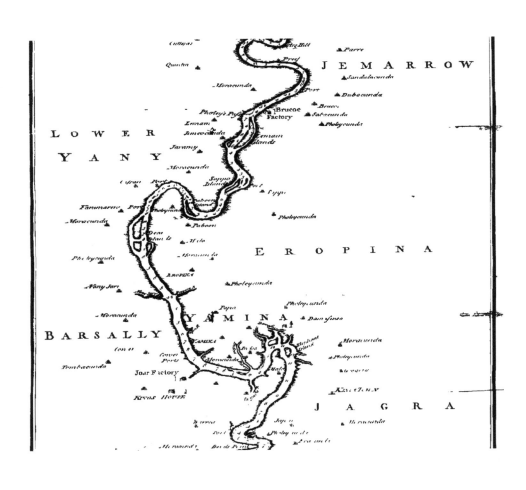

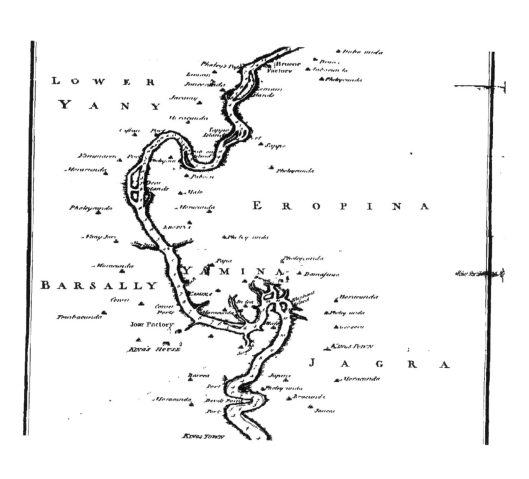